RE-IMAGINING OFFSHORE FINANCE

# Re-Imagining Offshore Finance

MARKET-DOMINANT SMALL JURISDICTIONS
IN A GLOBALIZING FINANCIAL WORLD

Christopher M. Bruner

# OXFORD
UNIVERSITY PRESS

Oxford University Press is a department of the University of Oxford. It furthers the University's objective of excellence in research, scholarship, and education by publishing worldwide. Oxford is a registered trademark of Oxford University Press in the UK and certain other countries.

Published in the United States of America by Oxford University Press
198 Madison Avenue, New York, NY 10016, United States of America.

Library of Congress Cataloging-in-Publication Data

Names: Bruner, Christopher M, 1972- author.
Title: Re-imagining offshore finance : market-dominant small jurisdictions in
  a globalizing financial world / Christopher M. Bruner.
Description: New York : Oxford University Press, 2016. | Includes bibliographical
  references and index.
Identifiers: LCCN 2016003368 | ISBN 9780190466879 ((hardback) : alk. paper)
Subjects: LCSH: International business enterprises—Law and legislation. |
  Financial institutions, International—Law and legislation.
Classification: LCC K1322 .B78 2016 | DDC 346.09—dc23 LC record available at
https://lccn.loc.gov/2016003368

**Note to Readers**
This publication is designed to provide accurate and authoritative information in regard to the subject matter covered. It is based upon sources believed to be accurate and reliable and is intended to be current as of the time it was written. It is sold with the understanding that the publisher is not engaged in rendering legal, accounting, or other professional services. If legal advice or other expert assistance is required, the services of a competent professional person should be sought. Also, to confirm that the information has not been affected or changed by recent developments, traditional legal research techniques should be used, including checking primary sources where appropriate.

*(Based on the Declaration of Principles jointly adopted by a Committee of the American Bar Association and a Committee of Publishers and Associations.)*

**You may order this or any other Oxford University Press publication by visiting the Oxford University Press website at www.oup.com.**

*For my parents, Richard and Sharon Bruner*

# Contents

# List of Figures

# Preface

THE SUBJECT MATTER of this book spans the globe, and numerous fields of law and finance. Accordingly, so do my debts of gratitude.

For their very helpful comments, suggestions, and conversations regarding various aspects of this project at various stages of its development, many thanks to Michael Anderson, Douglas Arner, Godfrey Baldacchino, Richard Bruner, John Carroll, Andrew Campbell, Abdelaziz Chazi, Weitseng Chen, John Cioffi, Robert Danforth, Nigel Davis, Steven Dean, Tyler Dickovick, Michelle Drumbl, Jonathan Eastwood, Ian Fox, Bryant Garth, Michael Hatfield, Syren Johnstone, Cally Jordan, Jeffrey Kahn, Edward Kleinbard, Jayanth Krishnan, Karen Lai, Lin Lin, Luh Luh Lan, Maximo Langer, LaiYee Leong, Clark Lombardi, Gerard McCormack, Bryane Michael, Andrew Morriss, Dora Neo, Erin O'Hara O'Connor, Maisie Ooi, Duncan Osborne, Mark Osborne, Adam Rosenzweig, Jacqueline Ross, Mark Rush, Gerhard Schnyder, James Shipton, D. Daniel Sokol, Aylwin Tai, Hans Tjio, Robert Vandersluis, Rolf Weber, Chenggang Xu, and George Zhou. Thanks also to workshop participants at the American Society of Comparative Law 2014 Comparative Law Work-in-Progress Workshop, the Law and Society Association 2014 Annual Meeting, the Society for the Advancement of Socio-Economics 2014 Annual Conference, the National University of Singapore, the University of Hong Kong, and the University of Washington. I am also grateful for the constructive and thoughtful comments received from anonymous reviewers, and to Alex Flach and Elinor Shields of Oxford University Press for support and encouragement.

In pursuing this project I have benefited enormously from the opportunity to conduct comparative research as a visitor to some extraordinary research centers and universities. I am deeply grateful to the Centre for Banking & Finance Law at the National University of Singapore (NUS), where I was a Visiting Scholar in the spring of 2015, and particularly to Dora Neo and Hans Tjio of the NUS Faculty of Law; the Asian Institute of International Financial Law at the University of Hong Kong (HKU), where I was a Visiting Fellow in the summer of 2015, and particularly to Douglas Arner of the HKU Faculty of Law; and the Centre for Business Law and Practice at the University of Leeds, where I was a Liberty Fellow in the fall of 2015, and particularly to Andrew Keay, Joan Loughrey, Gerard McCormack, and Jingchen Zhao of the Leeds School of Law.

Throughout the writing of this book I have been a faculty member at the Washington and Lee University School of Law, and I deeply appreciate the professional and financial support of W&L Law and the Frances Lewis Law Center. For support and encouragement I am particularly grateful to Mark Drumbl, Russell Miller, Dean Brant Hellwig, and Associate Dean Sam Calhoun. Many thanks also to Tyler Cragg and Amanda Lyons-Archambault for able research assistance; to Linda Newell and Bonnie Gates of the W&L Law Library, who located numerous (and often obscure) sources; and to Wendy Rice for superb administrative assistance throughout.

As always, I remain most grateful to my family, without whom nothing of consequence that I have done could have happened. My wife, Lia Pierson Bruner, and our kids, Cullen and Claire, are daily sources of joy and optimism. I dedicate this book to my parents, Richard and Sharon Bruner—thank you for everything.

Before turning to the book itself, some housekeeping items should be addressed. First, I refer to monetary values in various currencies throughout the book. Dollar values refer to U.S. dollars, unless the text or context indicate otherwise. Second, I refer to Internet sources throughout the book. All such website references are believed to be current as of this writing, but whether they will remain stable is unknowable. Third, I refer throughout—principally in footnotes—to material appearing elsewhere in the book. Cross references to material appearing in other chapters refer to the relevant chapters, parts, and sections as applicable (e.g., "*supra* Chapter 2.B.iii"), whereas cross references to sources or material appearing elsewhere in the same chapter generally refer to the relevant footnotes (e.g., "*supra* note 8" or "*supra* note 32 and accompanying text"). I adopt these differing conventions because, for the reader's convenience, I have independently and consecutively footnoted each chapter. Finally, although my debts of gratitude to those named above are substantial, they do not necessarily share all viewpoints expressed in the book, and any errors or omissions are of course mine.

*Lexington, Virginia*
*April 2016*

# I Small Jurisdictions in Cross-Border Finance

# 1 Introduction and Overview

OVER THE LAST century—and particularly over recent decades—small jurisdictions have become big players in cross-border financial services. Although comprehensive data remain elusive,[1] it is widely believed that trillions of dollars are held in so-called "offshore financial centers" (OFCs)—sometimes referred to more pejoratively as "tax havens," a moniker reflecting estimates that governments around the world have lost billions of dollars in tax revenue through the use of opaque foreign accounts in such jurisdictions.[2] *The Economist* cites estimates ranging from $8 trillion

---

[1] *See, e.g.,* RONEN PALAN, RICHARD MURPHY & CHRISTIAN CHAVAGNEUX, TAX HAVENS: HOW GLOBALIZATION REALLY WORKS 46–50 (2010); GABRIEL ZUCMAN, THE HIDDEN WEALTH OF NATIONS: THE SCOURGE OF TAX HAVENS 3, 39–40 (Teresa Lavender Fagan trans., 2015); Philip R. Lane & Gian Maria Milesi-Ferretti, *Cross-Border Investment in Small International Financial Centers* 3–4 (IMF Working Paper No. WP/10/38, 2010); International Monetary Fund, Monetary and Exchange Affairs Department, *Offshore Financial Centers,* at pt. II.A (IMF Background Paper, June 23, 2000), https://www.imf.org/external/np/mae/oshorc/2000/eng/back.htm; Salim M. Darbar, R. Barry Johnston & Mary G. Zephirin, *Assessing Offshore: Filling a Gap in Global Surveillance,* FIN. & DEV., Sept. 2003, at 32, 33; *Storm Survivors,* ECONOMIST, Feb. 16, 2013, http://www.economist.com/news/special-report/21571549-offshore-financial-centres-have-taken-battering-recently-they-have-shown-remarkable.

[2] JAMES S. HENRY, THE PRICE OF OFFSHORE REVISITED: NEW ESTIMATES FOR "MISSING" GLOBAL PRIVATE WEALTH, INCOME, INEQUALITY, AND LOST TAXES 41–43 (July 2012) (report for the Tax Justice Network); PALAN ET AL., *supra* note 1, at 61–64. *See also* ECONOMIST, *supra* note 1 (observing the difficulty of estimating tax losses resulting from offshore holdings).

to $21 trillion in offshore deposits globally (with over 30 percent of global foreign direct investment thought to occur through offshore jurisdictions),[3] whereas others put the number as high as $32 trillion.[4] Such figures remain disputed, although the more dependable estimates tend toward the lower end of that range.[5] In any event, there is widespread agreement that substantial sums of money have departed the United States, Europe, and other major economic powers, often finding their way to a discrete set of remarkably small places.[6]

Although competition for capital is nothing new,[7] major-market efforts to staunch the flow of funds have taken on considerably greater urgency since the 2000s—ostensibly due to concerns regarding money laundering and terrorism financing following the 9/11 attacks in 2001, and the heightened political salience of tax receipts prompted by budget austerity following the onset of the financial crisis in 2007.[8] Public resentment in the United States and other major markets substantially grew, however, following a 2013 data leak of 2.5 million files regarding over 120,000 offshore companies and trusts obtained by the International Consortium of Investigative Journalists. These files vividly illustrate the extent of offshore holdings and the convoluted legal structures sometimes employed to obscure the identities of the account-holders, revealed to include a number of high-profile individuals from around the world and approximately 4,000 Americans.[9] More impactful yet

---

[3] ECONOMIST, supra note 1. See also HENRY, supra note 2, at 16–20; Gabriel Zucman, Taxing across Borders: Tracking Personal Wealth and Corporate Profits, 28 J. ECON. PERSP. 121, 138–42 (2014).

[4] See HENRY, supra note 2, at 5. See also Scott A. Schumacher, Magnifying Deterrence by Prosecuting Professionals 51 (Univ. of Wash. Sch. of Law Legal Studies Research Paper No. 2013-17, 2013), http://ssrn.com/abstract=2243093.

[5] See ZUCMAN, supra note 1, at 3–4, 36–45 (concluding that "the total amount of private offshore wealth reaches $7.6 trillion," equaling "a total of 8% of the global financial wealth of households," and critiquing higher estimates). See also Richard Gordon & Andrew P. Morriss, Moving Money: International Financial Flows, Taxes, and Money Laundering, 37 HASTINGS INT'L & COMP. L. REV. 1, 93–110 (2014).

[6] See, e.g., Lane & Milesi-Ferretti, supra note 1, at 3, 8–9, 25.

[7] See, e.g., PALAN ET AL., supra note 1, at 108–22.

[8] See, e.g., id. at 208–12, 225; ROBERT S. MCINTYRE ET AL., OFFSHORE SHELL GAMES 2015: THE USE OF OFFSHORE TAX HAVENS BY FORTUNE 500 COMPANIES 18 (2015) (U.S. PIRG Education Fund and Citizens for Tax Justice report); ZUCMAN, supra note 1, at 52–55; Jefferson P. Vanderwolk, The Role of Hong Kong's Tax Policies, in DAVID C. DONALD, A FINANCIAL CENTRE FOR TWO EMPIRES: HONG KONG'S CORPORATE, SECURITIES AND TAX LAWS IN ITS TRANSITION FROM BRITAIN TO CHINA 171, 177, 181 (2014); Andrew Higgins, Data Leak Shakes Notion of Secret Offshore Havens and, Possibly, Nerves, N.Y. TIMES, Apr. 4, 2013, http://www.nytimes.com/2013/04/05/world/europe/vast-hidden-wealth-revealed-in-leaked-records.html; Tax Havens: The Missing $20 Trillion, ECONOMIST, Feb. 14, 2013, http://www.economist.com/news/leaders/21571873-how-stop-companies-and-people-dodging-tax-delaware-well-grand-cayman-missing-20.

[9] See Gerard Ryle et al., Secrecy for Sale: Inside the Global Offshore Money Maze (International Consortium of Investigative Journalists report, Apr. 3, 2013), http://www.icij.org/offshore/secret-files-expose-offshores-global-impact; Higgins, supra note 8; Scott Higham, Michael Hudson & Marina Walker Guevara, Piercing the Secrecy of Offshore Tax Havens, WASH. POST, Apr. 6, 2013, http://articles.washingtonpost.com/2013-04-06/news/38326013_1_raj-rajaratnam-trusts-accounts.

was the 2016 release of the so-called "Panama Papers"—11.5 million files covering a 40-year time frame, leaked from Panama law firm Mossack Fonseca, that "unveil the offshore holdings of 140 politicians and officials, including 12 current and former presidents, monarchs and prime ministers," and involving "at least 33 people and companies blacklisted by the United States for allegedly doing business with rogue states, terrorists or drug barons."[10] Further fanning the flames, meanwhile, are recurrent news accounts of the lengths to which U.S.-based businesses have gone to reduce their tax liabilities—including (but not limited to) Apple's use of Irish subsidiaries to ensure that profits derived from foreign sales remain untaxed.[11] As

---

[10] *The Lessons of the Panama Papers,* ECONOMIST, Apr. 9, 2016, at 14–16. *See also* Ian Bremmer, *These 5 Facts Explain the Massive Political Fallout from the Panama Papers,* TIME, Apr. 6, 2016, http://time. com/4283587/these-5-facts-explain-the-massive-political-fallout-from-the-panama-papers/; *The Panama Papers: A Torrential Leak,* ECONOMIST, Apr. 9, 2016, at 59–61; Steven Erlanger et al., *Iceland's Prime Minister Steps Down amid Panama Papers Scandal,* N.Y. TIMES, Apr. 5, 2016, http://www.nytimes. com/2016/04/06/world/europe/panama-papers-iceland.html; Aamer Madhani, *American Executives' Names Surface in Panama Papers,* USA TODAY, Apr. 7, 2016, http://www.usatoday.com/story/news/ 2016/04/06/panama-papers-americans-with-past-financial-crimes/82704788/; Jethro Mullen, *The Panama Papers: 7 Things to Know,* CNN.COM, Apr. 6, 2016, http://www.cnn.com/2016/04/04/world/ panama-papers-explainer/. As of this writing, the Panama Papers had forced Iceland's Prime Minister Sigmundur David Gunnlaugsson from office (following public outrage at an apparent conflict of interest arising from his family's undisclosed offshore interest in failed Icelandic banks at a time when he was involved in negotiating a deal for claimants) and created substantial negative publicity for British Prime Minister David Cameron (who profited from an offshore investment fund established by his father). In neither case was there any immediate indication of illegality. For additional background see Bremmer, *supra*; Steven Erlanger, *David Cameron Releases Tax Data after Panama Papers Uproar,* N.Y. TIMES, Apr. 10, 2016, http://www.nytimes.com/2016/04/11/world/europe/david-cameron-panama-papers-tax-return.html?_r=1; Erlanger et al., *supra*; Brooke Harrington, *Panama Papers: The Real Scandal Is What's Legal,* ATLANTIC, Apr. 6, 2016, http://www.theatlantic.com/business/archive/2016/04/panama-papers-crimes/477156/; Elizabeth Piper, *Offshore Trust Admission Deepens British PM's Problems,* REUTERS, Apr. 8, 2016, http://uk.reuters.com/article/uk-panama-tax-britain-cameron-idUKKCN0X42KN; *PM's Anger over "Untrue" Tax Claims about Dad,* SKY NEWS, Apr. 12, 2016, http://news.sky.com/story/ 1676597/pms-anger-over-untrue-tax-claims-about-dad.

As of this writing, Mossack Fonseca denies wrongdoing. *See* Mossack Fonseca, *Media News: Resources,* http://mossfonmedia.com/ (last visited Apr. 2016); Press Release, Mossack Fonseca, Statement Regarding Recent Media Coverage, Apr. 1, 2016, http://mossfonmedia.com/wp-content/uploads/2016/04/ Statement-Regarding-Recent-Media-Coverage_4-1-2016.pdf. Obviously, however, such an extraordinary disclosure of confidential client matters would create an existential crisis for any law firm. *See* Emily Taylor, *Cyber-Security—Kryptonite for Lawyers,* SC MAG. UK, Apr. 15, 2016, http://www.scmagazineuk.com/ cyber-security---kryptonite-for-lawyers/printarticle/489116/.

[11] *See Apple's Tax Arrangements: Biting Criticism,* ECONOMIST, May 21, 2013, http://www.economist.com/ blogs/schumpeter/2013/05/apples-tax-arrangements; Jesse Drucker, *Man Making Ireland Tax Avoidance Hub Proves Local Hero,* BLOOMBERG, Oct. 27, 2013, http://www.bloomberg.com/news/2013-10-28/man-making-ireland-tax-avoidance-hub-globally-proves-local-hero.html; Lee Sheppard, *How Does Apple Avoid Taxes?,* FORBES, May 28, 2013, http://www.forbes.com/sites/leesheppard/2013/05/28/how-does-apple-avoid-taxes/. Lee Sheppard explains that "Irish law asks where a company is managed and controlled to determine its tax residence," whereas "U.S. law asks where the company was organized," permitting Apple's Irish subsidiaries to "claim tax residence nowhere." Sheppard, *supra*. Numerous other major companies have been similarly criticized. *See generally* MCINTYRE ET AL., *supra* note 8. *See also* ZUCMAN, *supra*

of February 2013, *The Economist* reported that "American companies are thought to hold $1.6 trillion offshore, which most are reluctant to repatriate unless offered a tax break."[12] Others place the number higher.[13]

Notwithstanding such bad press, however, the legitimacy of "offshore" finance remains hotly contested.[14] Critics emphasize the secrecy and opacity associated with these jurisdictions, which are widely thought to facilitate money laundering, fraudulent financial schemes, and tax evasion.[15] With respect to the latter, critics further argue that "diversion of capital offshore erodes the tax bases of onshore jurisdictions," permits the affluent to enjoy public goods at others' expense, undermines tax progressivity, and more broadly due to generalized anger at the foregoing reduces tax compliance.[16] Others respond that a full cost-benefit analysis must also weigh potential upsides, said to include financial and regulatory innovations developed in these jurisdictions, as well as efficiency gains through enhanced competition—arguments familiar to scholars of U.S. federalism.[17] Minimally, they argue, acknowledging that the cost-benefit analysis remains incomplete would "help keep the welfare-enhancing baby from being thrown out with the money-laundering bathwater" as major economic powers formulate responses to heightened cross-border financial competition.[18]

---

note 1, at 102–04; *The Price Isn't Right: Corporate Profit-Shifting Has Become Big Business*, ECONOMIST, Feb. 14, 2013, http://www.economist.com/news/special-report/21571557-corporate-profit-shifting-has-become-big-business-price-isnt-right; Zucman, *supra* note 3, at 124–26; James R. Hines, Jr., *Lessons from Behavioral Responses to International Taxation*, 52 NAT'L TAX J. 305, 313–18 (1999) (describing evidence indicating that "tax considerations strongly influence" cross-border transaction structure).

[12] *The Price Isn't Right*, ECONOMIST, *supra* note 11.

[13] *See* MCINTYRE ET AL., *supra* note 8, at 1 ("Fortune 500 companies are holding more than $2.1 trillion in accumulated profits offshore for tax purposes.").

[14] *See* PALAN ET AL., *supra* note 1, at 154–58.

[15] *See* Anna Manasco Dionne & Jonathan R. Macey, *Offshore Finance and Onshore Markets: Racing to the Bottom, or Moving toward Efficient?*, *in* OFFSHORE FINANCIAL CENTERS AND REGULATORY COMPETITION 8, 10–11 (Andrew P. Morriss ed., 2010) (summarizing these concerns).

[16] Craig M. Boise, *Regulating Tax Competition in Offshore Financial Centers*, *in* OFFSHORE FINANCIAL CENTERS AND REGULATORY COMPETITION, *supra* note 15, at 50, 59–61 (summarizing these arguments). *See also* J.C. SHARMAN, HAVENS IN A STORM: THE STRUGGLE FOR GLOBAL TAX REGULATION 43–44 (2006) (same).

[17] *See* Andrew P. Morriss, *The Role of Offshore Financial Centers in Regulatory Competition*, *in* OFFSHORE FINANCIAL CENTERS AND REGULATORY COMPETITION, *supra* note 15, at 102, 107, 115, 136–38. *See also The Good, the Bad and the Ugland: Havens Serve Clean as Well as Dirty Money*, ECONOMIST, Feb. 14, 2013, http://www.economist.com/news/special-report/21571551-havens-serve-clean-well-dirty-money-good-bad-and-ugland.

[18] Andrew P. Morriss, *Introduction*, *in* OFFSHORE FINANCIAL CENTERS AND REGULATORY COMPETITION, *supra* note 15, at 1, 7. *See also* Andrew P. Morriss & Clifford C. Henson, *Regulatory Effectiveness in Onshore & Offshore Financial Centers* 8 (Univ. of Ala. Sch. of Law Working Paper, 2012) http://ssrn.com/abstract=2016310.

The nature, legal status, and market roles of small jurisdictions that actively pursue various forms of cross-border corporate and financial services (for the sake of brevity, referred to below as "cross-border financial services"[19]) remain under-theorized—and the resulting lack of conceptual clarity hampers the analysis. Lacking a sufficiently nuanced theoretical framework to describe the functions that such jurisdictions perform in cross-border finance—and the peculiar strengths of the small jurisdictions that have achieved global dominance in the cross-border financial marketplace[20]—we find ourselves unable to evaluate their impact and significance in a comprehensive manner.

This book advances a new conceptual framework with the dual aim of refining the analysis and directing it toward more productive inquiries, and the remainder of Chapter 1 provides a brief overview of the work. Chapter 2 canvasses extant theoretical frameworks used to describe and evaluate the roles of small jurisdictions in cross-border finance. These include literatures exploring globalization and the development impact of English legal origins, as well as others variously characterizing small jurisdictions active in cross-border finance as "tax havens," "offshore financial centers," "microstates," and "global cities." Finding each of the extant conceptual paradigms incapable of accounting for the range of small jurisdictions achieving global dominance, Chapter 2 concludes with a historical account of the rise of capital mobility in the late nineteenth and early twentieth centuries and the resulting competition among jurisdictions around the world to attract increasingly mobile capital through legal and financial innovations. This discussion includes not only the commonalities between domestic and international forms of regulatory competition, but also the degree to which U.S. states and foreign jurisdictions compete directly with one another to attract cross-border financial business.

The book then proposes a new concept that I argue better captures the salient characteristics, competitive strategies, and market roles of small jurisdictions achieving substantial dominance in cross-border finance—the "market-dominant

---

[19] Professional firms routinely refer to "corporate and financial services" as a field encompassing general corporate and transactional services, as well as more specialized services relating to capital markets, various forms of private and institutional investment, structured finance, and insurance. *See, e.g.,* Willkie Farr & Gallagher LLP, *Corporate and Financial Services,* http://www.willkie.com/services/practices/corporate-financial-services (last visited Apr. 2016). Likewise, professional firms routinely tout a suite of "corporate and financial services expertise" in various cross-border and regional contexts. *See, e.g.,* Goodwin Procter LLP, *Asia,* http://www.goodwinprocter.com/Practices/Asia.aspx (last visited Apr. 2016) (citing the "tradition of corporate and financial services expertise" among their "skilled team of Hong Kong-based lawyers" as evidence of their "outstanding Asia advisory capacity"). I employ the more succinct "cross-border financial services" solely to render more concise the numerous references to such a suite of services throughout the book.

[20] *See* ECONOMIST, *supra* note 1 (observing that relatively few have achieved such success).

small jurisdiction" (MDSJ). Chapter 3 sets out an "ideal type" of MDSJ, identifying the central, consequential features giving rise to their competitive strengths and fueling their dominance in cross-border finance. Some of these features reflect the historical, cultural, and geographic circumstances in which the given jurisdiction finds itself, while others reflect development strategies consciously pursued in light of those circumstances.[21] Specifically, MDSJs:

- are small and poorly endowed with natural resources, limiting their economic development options;
- possess legislative autonomy (though not always complete sovereignty);
- are culturally proximate to multiple economic powers, and favorably situated geographically vis-à-vis those powers;
- heavily invest in human capital, professional networks, and related institutional structures; and
- consciously endeavor to strike a delicate balance between close collaboration with, and robust oversight of, the financial professional community, seeking at once to convey flexibility, stability, and credibility—the aim being to satisfy both mobile capital and foreign regulatory counterparts.

These features—reflecting a range of geographic, cultural, social, political, and economic features that condition their development options and strategic opportunities—go a long way toward illuminating how and why certain small jurisdictions have achieved extraordinary successes in cross-border finance.

Given the causal dimension of this argument, Chapter 3 concludes with a brief methodological discussion of the comparative approach employed throughout the remainder of the book. As discussed below, the book primarily focuses on a small number of jurisdictions exemplifying the MDSJ paradigm (Chapters 4 through 9). Limiting the analysis exclusively to jurisdictions that are both "small" and "market-dominant" in the pertinent respects, however, would amount to selecting on the dependent variable, precluding strong causal claims.[22] Accordingly, the book concludes with a broader mode of comparative analysis, building upon the identification of MDSJ commonalities through comparison of this category of jurisdictions with others that are not "small" and/or not "market-dominant" (Chapter 10). The

---

[21] *See* Darryl S.L. Jarvis, *Race for the Money: International Financial Centres in Asia,* 14 J. INT'L REL. & DEV. 60, 82–83 (2011) (characterizing favorable geography as necessary but not sufficient in the absence of "a policy framework that encourages cross-border financial transactions").

[22] *See* Barbara Geddes, *How the Cases You Choose Affect the Answers You Get: Selection Bias in Comparative Politics,* 2 POL. ANALYSIS 131, 132–34, 140 (1990).

principal aim is to establish more compellingly that the characteristics and strategies that I identify with MDSJs in fact contributed to their successes—by showing that the absence of such characteristics and strategies contributed to other jurisdictions' failures.

The ideal type described above provides a conceptual benchmark against which to evaluate jurisdictions that are not merely successful, but literally globally dominant in specialized areas of cross-border finance. Although a number of jurisdictions might have been selected for such a study, I have settled upon six in order to contain the comparative analysis to a manageable undertaking[23] while canvassing the diversity and commonalities exhibited by the category of jurisdictions identified. The jurisdictions selected present different types of legal jurisdiction, exhibit substantial specialization in cross-border finance, rose to prominence over different time frames, are situated in different geographies, exhibit different cultural affinities, and vary in the magnitude of their domestic economies. Notwithstanding the very real idiosyncrasies and divergences among them, however, distinct and illuminating patterns do emerge across these six jurisdictions, permitting generalizations to be offered regarding the role and strengths of small jurisdictions in cross-border finance, and conclusions to be drawn regarding how they managed to achieve and sustain their successes.

Six chapters examine, in turn, the competitive characteristics and strategies of:

- Bermuda, well established among the world's preeminent insurance markets (Chapter 4);
- Dubai, an increasingly dominant center in the emerging field of Islamic finance (Chapter 5);
- Singapore, a rising power in wealth management (Chapter 6);
- Hong Kong, a critical gateway to and from China's enormous domestic market and production capabilities (Chapter 7);
- Switzerland, long dominant in cross-border banking (Chapter 8); and
- Delaware, the predominant jurisdiction of incorporation for U.S. public companies and a global competitor in the organization of various forms of business entities (Chapter 9).

The aim of Chapters 4 through 9 is not to provide a comprehensive account of these jurisdictions, their market structures, and/or their regulatory frameworks—although

---

[23] *See* CHRISTOPHER M. BRUNER, CORPORATE GOVERNANCE IN THE COMMON-LAW WORLD: THE POLITICAL FOUNDATIONS OF SHAREHOLDER POWER 24 & n.45 (2013) (observing the "geometric growth in complexity" of comparative analysis as the number of jurisdictions grows).

they do vary in their depth of treatment, reflecting my assumption that an English-speaking and predominantly Western audience will require additional background to be able to engage meaningfully with certain jurisdictions.[24] The goal of this part of the book is to establish that these disparate jurisdictions can usefully and coherently be described as a "type" of jurisdiction previously unrecognized by extant literature, and in so doing to generate hypotheses and conclusions regarding how they achieved their successes historically, and how they sustain their successes today. To this end, I have consciously chosen six jurisdictions that differ substantially in their respective geographic locations, cultural affinities, social and political dynamics, economic spheres, financial services strengths, regulatory postures, and legal traditions.

Examination of the foregoing jurisdictions is effectively bookended by Switzerland and Delaware, which are briefly introduced in Chapter 2, due to their historical significance in the rise of two very important forms of regulatory competition over the course of the late nineteenth and early twentieth centuries—tax competition in the case of Switzerland, and corporate charter competition in the case of Delaware. Part II then proceeds to evaluate various jurisdictions with that history in mind, beginning with Bermuda, a straightforward and compelling illustration of the MDSJ ideal type; proceeding then to Dubai, a less obvious but I believe equally compelling exemplar of the suite of characteristics and development strategies associated with the MDSJ concept; and then turning to Singapore and Hong Kong, grouped together not only because they represent the most competitive financial centers beyond New York and London, but also due to the competition between them for dominance in East Asia (a dynamic touched upon in each of these chapters, but developed more fully in the latter chapter on Hong Kong); and finally returning to Switzerland and Delaware for fuller re-evaluation in light of the common MDSJ characteristics and development strategies explored throughout Part II. In the case of Switzerland, this facilitates a more contextualized discussion of their current prospects in light of the substantial competitive pressures they now face from more recent entrants, and also allows discussion of the diplomatic pressures recently directed toward them by major economic powers to contribute more directly to the discussion of larger jurisdictions and international organizations presented in Part III. In the case of Delaware—a jurisdiction that many readers will have previously encountered solely through U.S. corporate law scholarship—re-evaluation

---

[24] Notably, the discussion of Dubai's role in Islamic financial markets includes additional background on the Middle East and Islamic financial structures. *See infra* Chapter 5. Similarly, the discussion of Singapore's rise as a wealth management center and Hong Kong's role as a gateway to China provide additional historical background. *See infra* Chapters 6–7.

by reference to other jurisdictions with similar characteristics and strategies will further illuminate the rationale for my categorization of this small U.S. state as an MDSJ, and further contribute directly to the discussion of U.S. policy, and the U.S. role in "offshore" finance, that follows in the final part of the book.

As noted above, Chapter 10 tests the MDSJ concept's explanatory power through broader comparative analysis. Specifically, Chapter 10 further emphasizes commonalities across the six exemplars of the MDSJ concept by contrasting these jurisdictions with two other categories of jurisdictions—small jurisdictions that have endeavored to create vibrant financial centers yet failed, and substantially larger jurisdictions that are active in cross-border financial services.

The first category of comparisons presented in Chapter 10 tends to bolster the explanatory power of the MDSJ concept to the extent that such failed efforts reflect deviations from the ideal type described in Chapter 3. Although a number of jurisdictions might have been selected, once again, I have focused on two particularly vivid examples. The first is the South Pacific island of Nauru, which lacks favorable geography, and failed to invest meaningfully in human capital, professional networks, and related institutional structures to develop real value-added financial services capacity, relying almost exclusively on low taxes and financial secrecy.[25] The second is the former Caribbean island group of the Netherlands Antilles, which relied heavily upon a single favorable provision in a tax treaty with the United States (exempting Antillean residents from the withholding tax that otherwise applied to interest payments from U.S. borrowers received by foreign persons), rendering their financial services sector highly vulnerable upon revocation of that singular treaty-based tax advantage.[26]

Such comparisons also illustrate further how the MDSJ concept relates to alternative explanatory paradigms. For example, although I argue that Bermuda, Dubai, Singapore, Hong Kong, Switzerland, and Delaware are more aptly described as MDSJs than tax havens, the reverse would appear to be the case with Nauru and the Netherlands Antilles, acknowledging that the term "tax haven" must minimally include those jurisdictions relying heavily or exclusively on low taxes and financial secrecy, with little else to offer.

Chapter 10 also explores the degree to which the characteristics and strategies that I associate with MDSJs are in fact peculiar to such jurisdictions. Critical

---

[25] *See, e.g.,* J.C. Sharman, *Canaries in the Coal Mine: Tax Havens, the Decline of the West and the Rise of the Rest,* 17 NEW POL. ECON. 493, 508–09 (2012); J.C. Sharman, *South Pacific Tax Havens: From Leaders in the Race to the Bottom to Laggards in the Race to the Top?,* 29 ACCT. F. 311, 311–15, 318 (2005).

[26] *See generally* Craig M. Boise & Andrew P. Morriss, *Change, Dependency, and Regime Plasticity in Offshore Financial Intermediation: The Saga of the Netherlands Antilles,* 45 TEX. INT'L L.J. 377 (2009).

comparisons in this regard include the world's two most significant capital markets, "Wall Street" in New York and "the City" (sometimes referred to as "the Square Mile") in London. These major global financial centers exhibit certain traits akin to the MDSJs studied—notably their geographic and cultural concentration—while differing starkly from them in other respects—notably their locations, historically positioning them as gateways to major domestic economies, their lower degrees of regulatory autonomy, and their greater breadth of financial services offerings, underwritten by the greater credibility that each derives from the support of a large sovereign.[27] These comparisons also help illuminate the particular types of specialized roles that MDSJs play in cross-border finance, relative to the world's largest and most diversified financial centers.

Chapter 11 concludes, suggesting that notwithstanding MDSJs' apparent vulnerability to exertions of economic and diplomatic pressure by major markets, their significance will likely continue to grow—as will the need for a more effective means of theorizing the roles they play in cross-border finance, and the global dynamics their ascendance reveals. Accordingly, I argue that we should not remain content with incomplete conceptual categories and vocabularies that lack sufficient nuance, all too often facilitating one-sided critiques of their impacts. Just as charged labels such as "tax haven" or "offshore financial center" tend to obscure the value provided by such jurisdictions, such labels conversely tend to obscure the degree to which major economic powers themselves engage in the very practices for which they criticize their smaller competitors. At the same time, the sorts of advantages associated with the MDSJs identified and analyzed in this book strongly suggest that these jurisdictions will survive such developments and continue to flourish.

As the analyses provided in Chapters 10 and 11 suggest, the United Kingdom (through the City) and the United States (through the combined efforts of Wall Street and Delaware) now represent substantial "offshore" financial services markets that themselves function as "tax havens" vis-à-vis other jurisdictions around the world. The aim of this discussion is certainly not to suggest that these major markets can justly be portrayed in singularly negative terms, or that their negatives outweigh their positives. Rather, the more modest point is that their financial services functions in fact reflect both positives and negatives, much like the MDSJs studied in this book—a recognition that tends to undermine the black-and-white, "us"/"them" dichotomies often drawn in the prevailing literature and political discourse.

---

[27] Large metropolitan areas are the principal focus of the "global cities" literature. *See* Saskia Sassen, *The Specialised Differences of Cities Matter in Today's Global Economy*, in REFORMING THE CITY: RESPONSES TO THE GLOBAL FINANCIAL CRISIS 209, 209–10 (Sam Whimster ed., 2009). *See also* SASKIA SASSEN, CITIES IN A WORLD ECONOMY 83–84, 112–15, 126 (4th ed. 2012).

As discussed below, I am prepared to assume that greater transparency regarding both tax information and beneficial ownership of legal entities will eventually be achieved, and that this will be a good thing—if applied in an even-handed manner to both small and large jurisdictions alike.

The ascendance of MDSJs has much to tell us about the future of financial globalization, territorial sovereignty, and territorial financial regulation in the twenty-first century. The sooner we begin to take them seriously, the better.

# 2 Conceptualizing the Role of Small Jurisdictions

A NUMBER OF literatures have addressed the role of small jurisdictions in cross-border finance, or at least have spoken generally to the legal and market terrain they inhabit. This chapter discusses a number of relevant theoretical frameworks, evaluating their capacity to account for the range of small jurisdictions that have achieved positions of market dominance in cross-border finance.

I begin with the globalization literature and then turn to a number of specific characterizations applied to small jurisdictions, including "tax havens," "offshore financial centers," "microstates," and "global cities." Finally, I assess the English legal origins of many such jurisdictions, which do appear to arise with some regularity from remnants of the British Empire. Ultimately I conclude that none of these theoretical frameworks can accommodate the range of salient features exhibited by those small jurisdictions that have achieved global dominance in cross-border finance. Each, however, offers important insights contributing to the alternative framework developed in this book.

For the reader's convenience, the theories and the principal shortcomings discussed below are summarized in Figure 2.1.

| Theory | Shortcomings |
|---|---|
| *globalization* | • production centrifugal, but finance centripetal |
| *tax havens* | • cannot replicate successes through tax policy<br>• tax competition not unique to small jurisdictions |
| *offshore financial centers* | • unclear who/what is "offshore" |
| *microstates* | • some not "micro," some not "states" |
| *global cities* | • non-municipal governments<br>• legislative autonomy the key competitive resource |
| *English legal origins* | • successful civil-law competitors<br>• cannot explain stability/change over time |

FIGURE 2.1 Small Jurisdictions in Cross-Border Finance: Extant Theories.

## A. Whither Globalization?

The principal thrust of the globalization literature is that the significance of geography—and with it, territorial sovereignty—is attenuating over time, slowly giving way to a single global marketplace posing a deep challenge to nationally defined regulatory structures.[1] The international legal domain effectively represents a "horizontal" system in which legal personality is monopolized by sovereigns nominally treated as equals[2]—a conceptual structure reflected in the word "international" itself.[3] Accordingly, economic activity has historically been conceptualized in terms of national markets coextensive with national regulatory spaces.[4] Indeed, as Stephen Kobrin has observed, "national markets were created by political authorities in part to *territorialize* economic activity."[5] The globalization literature, however, teaches that growing cross-border trade and investment—and particularly growing capital mobility in an age of electronic communication and trading technology—is undermining nationally defined markets and regulatory autonomy due both to growth in effective market size and the strange metaphysics of

---

[1] *See* Christopher M. Bruner, *States, Markets, and Gatekeepers: Public-Private Regulatory Regimes in an Era of Economic Globalization*, 30 MICH. J. INT'L L. 125, 125–28 (2008).

[2] PETER MALANCZUK, AKEHURST'S MODERN INTRODUCTION TO INTERNATIONAL LAW 2–3 (7th rev. ed. 1997). *See also* IAN BROWNLIE, PRINCIPLES OF PUBLIC INTERNATIONAL LAW 291 (7th ed. 2008). The U.N. Charter itself lists as the first of its organizing "Principles" that "[t]he Organization is based on the principle of the sovereign equality of all its Members." U.N. Charter art. 2, para. 1.

[3] *See* Stephen J. Kobrin, *Economic Governance in an Electronically Networked Global Economy, in* THE EMERGENCE OF PRIVATE AUTHORITY IN GLOBAL GOVERNANCE 43, 45, 56 (Rodney Bruce Hall & Thomas J. Biersteker eds., 2002).

[4] *Id.* at 43.

[5] *Id.* at 60.

multi-jurisdictional transactions, which defy straightforward association with any particular geographic location.[6]

To regulate effectively, governments must increasingly work cooperatively through cross-border networks and rely on private-sector entities to undertake functions historically performed through centralized governmental agencies.[7] Such trends have led some to suggest that "place no longer matters"[8] and that "[g]eographic space is losing meaning as the basis for the organization of markets,"[9] rendering the underlying framework of territorial sovereignty "more and more antiquated."[10] To be sure, careful commentators acknowledge that globalization does not necessarily spell the demise of territorial sovereignty or territorially defined states—indeed, as Kobrin rightly observes, "[s]tate autonomy has never been absolute, and decision-making power has always been constrained by international economic transactions; the tradeoff between the efficiency gains from crossborder economic activity and autonomy is far from new."[11] Nevertheless, the "international financial system" is identified as "the best current example" of a non-spatial, transcendent marketplace "which is no longer nationally centered," the ease of electronic transfers prompting the claim that financial globalization represents "the end of geography."[12]

In a sense, the rise of small, finance-oriented jurisdictions such as those studied here would seem to confirm such claims, given their dependence upon frictionless transfers of money facilitated by the very technological advancements that preoccupy the globalization literature. The resilience of such jurisdictions, however, suggests that reports of the death of geography and territorial sovereignty are exaggerated.[13] Indeed, the persistence and extraordinary financial successes of certain small jurisdictions stand in tension with core predictions of the globalization literature in a critical respect. Dependent though they may be upon a global network of electronic money transfers, their ability to attract those transfers is itself dependent

---

[6] *See* Bruner, *supra* note 1, at 128; Kobrin, *supra* note 3, at 43–44, 47–52, 61.

[7] *See* Bruner, *supra* note 1, at 128–33.

[8] SASKIA SASSEN, CITIES IN A WORLD ECONOMY 11–12 (4th ed. 2012) (ascribing this claim to the "dominant account" of globalization).

[9] Kobrin, *supra* note 3, at 46.

[10] *See* MALANCZUK, *supra* note 2, at 7.

[11] Kobrin, *supra* note 3, at 56–58, 66.

[12] *Id.* at 61.

[13] *See Sunshine and Shadows: Offshore Financial Centres Will Always Be Controversial, But They Will Stay in Business,* ECONOMIST, Feb. 14, 2013, http://www.economist.com/news/special-report/21571559-offshore-financial-centres-will-always-be-controversial-they-will-stay. *See also* WILLIAM BRITTAIN-CATLIN, OFFSHORE: THE DARK SIDE OF THE GLOBAL ECONOMY 37 (2005); SASSEN, *supra* note 8, at 11–12. I paraphrase Twain, who wrote in 1897 that the press' "report of my death was an exaggeration." *Misquotation: "Reports of My Death Have Been Greatly Exaggerated,"* OXFORD ACADEMIC, Apr. 18, 2013, http://oupacademic.tumblr.com/post/48310773463/misquotation-reports-of-my-death-have-been-greatly.

upon their capacity to enact attractive financial regulations. Accordingly, these jurisdictions are profoundly dependent upon territorially defined financial regulatory authority—legislative autonomy ultimately rooted in their own territorial sovereignty or that of a larger jurisdiction to which they remain linked. In this light, their successes reflect the continuing vibrancy of territorial sovereignty, in turn suggesting that these jurisdictions—as well as the myriad businesses and financial institutions constituting their customer base—have every incentive to maintain the stability of this territorially defined regulatory framework.[14]

## B. Theorizing Small Jurisdictions

A brief introduction to the MDSJs examined in Chapters 4–9 will facilitate the discussion of potentially useful theoretical frameworks that follows. Accordingly, Figure 2.2 provides a preliminary summary of certain basic characteristics of these jurisdictions.

Bermuda, an Overseas Territory of the United Kingdom located in the north Atlantic Ocean, has become one of the most important global players in insurance—particularly in so-called "reinsurance" (effectively insurance for insurers) and "captive insurance" (a sophisticated form of self-insurance). Dubai, one of the seven emirates comprising the United Arab Emirates in the lower Arabian (Persian) Gulf, has become recognized as one of the most prominent markets in the world for Sharia-compliant Islamic financial services. Singapore, a former British colony with full sovereignty

| | Jurisdiction | Population | Land Area | Geography | Specialization | Timeframe |
|---|---|---|---|---|---|---|
| *Bermuda* | British Overseas Territory | 70,196 | 54 sq km | Mid-Atlantic islands | (re)insurance, captives | 1960s |
| *Dubai* | UAE emirate | 2.4 million | 3,885 sq km | Lower Arabian (Persian) Gulf | Islamic finance | 1970s |
| *Singapore* | sovereign | 5.7 million | 697 sq km | Southeast Asia | wealth management | 1960s |
| *Hong Kong* | PRC Special Admin. Region | 7.1 million | 1,100 sq km | Southern China | Mainland finance | 1950s |
| *Switzerland* | sovereign | 8.1 million | 41,277 sq km | Central Europe | cross-border banking | late 19th C. |
| *Delaware* | U.S. state | 935,614 | 5,133 sq km | Eastern U.S. | business entities | early 20th C. |

FIGURE 2.2 Case Studies: Market-Dominant Small Jurisdictions.*
*See Chapters 4–9 and sources cited therein.

---

[14] See BRITTAIN-CATLIN, *supra* note 13, at 22–24, 37, 114–15.

since 1965, has established itself as a critical Asian financial center with growing dominance in wealth management. Hong Kong, a British colony (later, a "Dependent Territory") for over 150 years before becoming one of two "Special Administrative Regions" of the People's Republic of China, has long served as a critical gateway to and from China's enormous domestic market and production capabilities. Switzerland, a long-time sovereign confederation of linguistically and culturally diverse "cantons" in the heart of Europe, has been firmly established since the early twentieth century as a leading jurisdiction for cross-border banking. Delaware, then, a small U.S. state located on the Eastern Seaboard, has achieved substantial dominance in the organization of corporations and other business entities over roughly the same time frame.[15]

Far more remains to be said of each jurisdiction. As a threshold matter, however, this section assesses whether any of the extant theoretical frameworks provide a promising means of describing the salient commonalities among such a diverse range of jurisdictions.

## I. TAX HAVENS

Notwithstanding the attention so-called "tax haven" jurisdictions have received over the last decade, the concept remains somewhat imprecise. Although there is no broadly accepted definition, the concept typically connotes "countries and territories that offer favourable tax regimes for foreign investors."[16] The related concept of "tax flight" refers to circumstances where "an individual or entity opens accounts or creates entities that, putting aside tax considerations, would not exist."[17]

It bears emphasizing that the most problematic practice is illegal "evasion" of tax owed—as opposed to legally ordering one's affairs to "avoid" a tax one might otherwise have owed.[18] The distinction, however, is notoriously indeterminate because

---

[15] *See infra* Chapters 4–9.

[16] Dhammika Dharmapala, *What Problems and Opportunities Are Created by Tax Havens?*, 24 OXFORD REV. ECON. POL'Y 661, 662 (2008). *See also* Reuven S. Avi-Yonah, *The OECD Harmful Tax Competition Report: A Retrospective after a Decade*, 34 BROOK. J. INT'L L. 783, 784–85 (2009); RONEN PALAN, RICHARD MURPHY & CHRISTIAN CHAVAGNEUX, TAX HAVENS: HOW GLOBALIZATION REALLY WORKS 2, 17 (2010); SASSEN, *supra* note 8, at 43 n.3.

[17] Steven A. Dean, *Philosopher Kings and International Tax: A New Approach to Tax Havens, Tax Flight, and International Tax Cooperation*, 58 HASTINGS L.J. 911, 928–29 (2007).

[18] *See* PALAN ET AL., *supra* note 16, at 9–10; Anna Manasco Dionne & Jonathan R. Macey, *Offshore Finance and Onshore Markets: Racing to the Bottom, or Moving toward Efficient?*, *in* OFFSHORE FINANCIAL CENTERS AND REGULATORY COMPETITION 8, 11 (Andrew P. Morriss ed., 2010); *Tax Havens: The Missing $20 Trillion*, ECONOMIST, Feb. 14, 2013, http://www.economist.com/news/leaders/21571873-how-stop-companies-and-people-dodging-tax-delaware-well-grand-cayman-missing-20; Richard Gordon & Andrew P. Morriss, *Moving Money: International Financial Flows, Taxes, and Money Laundering*, 37 HASTINGS INT'L & COMP. L. REV. 1, 23 (2014); International Monetary Fund, Monetary and Exchange Affairs Department, *Offshore Financial Centers*, at pt. II.A (IMF Background Paper, June 23, 2000), https://

it turns on whether the taxpayer is found to have intentionally violated the rules.[19] Hence, although Judge Learned Hand was right to observe that "[a]nyone may so arrange his affairs that his taxes shall be as low as possible,"[20] British Chancellor Denis Healey was also right to remind us that the difference between lawful avoidance and unlawful evasion may effectively amount to "the thickness of a prison wall."[21]

In their in-depth study of the topic, Ronen Palan, Richard Murphy, and Christian Chavagneux isolate the desire of the affluent to avoid paying for public services as the driving force behind tax havens, and identify "a legally backed veil of secrecy" as the means through which tax havens facilitate these efforts.[22] On this view, their salient characteristics include low taxation; confidentiality in banking and entity ownership, reinforced through "bureaucratic hurdles against information exchange with other countries"; ease of incorporation; and regulatory competition prompting "niche strategies" as a means of "legislative differentiation."[23] Prominent examples of abuses include inappropriate transfer pricing (i.e., intra-corporate transactions priced to shift profits into low-tax jurisdictions), and placing royalty-generating intellectual property in low-tax jurisdictions while placing deduction-generating debt in high-tax jurisdictions.[24] Given the availability of such tax-reduction techniques, some observers find it particularly telling that 98 of the FTSE 100 companies have "at least one offshore subsidiary,"[25] and that 72 percent of the Fortune 500 do as well.[26]

---

www.imf.org/external/np/mae/oshore/2000/eng/back.htm; Scott A. Schumacher, *Magnifying Deterrence by Prosecuting Professionals* 27 (Univ. of Wash. Sch. of Law Legal Studies Research Paper No. 2013-17, 2013), http://ssrn.com/abstract=2243093; Gabriel Zucman, *Taxing across Borders: Tracking Personal Wealth and Corporate Profits*, 28 J. ECON. PERSP. 121, 137–39 (2014).

[19] *See* Schumacher, *supra* note 18, at 27–31. *See also* 26 U.S.C.S. §§ 6662, 6694, 7201, 7203, 7206 (2016). Professional consequences for tax practitioners similarly turn on state of mind. *See* 31 C.F.R. §§ 10.21, 10.34–10.35, 10.50–10.52 (2016).

[20] *See* Schumacher, *supra* note 18, at 28 (quoting Hand from Helvering v. Gregory, 69 F.2d 809, 810 (2d Cir. 1934)).

[21] *See The Price Isn't Right: Corporate Profit-Shifting Has Become Big Business,* ECONOMIST, Feb. 14, 2013, http://www.economist.com/news/special-report/21571557-corporate-profit-shifting-has-become-big-business-price-isnt-right (quoting Healey).

[22] PALAN ET AL., *supra* note 16, at 6, 45.

[23] *Id.* at 30–38.

[24] *See* Dharmapala, *supra* note 16, at 667. *See also* BRITTAIN-CATLIN, *supra* note 13, at 47–53; PALAN ET AL., *supra* note 16, at 21, 68–71, 175–79; GABRIEL ZUCMAN, THE HIDDEN WEALTH OF NATIONS: THE SCOURGE OF TAX HAVENS 102–04 (Teresa Lavender Fagan trans., 2015).

[25] *See* ECONOMIST, *supra* note 21.

[26] *See* ROBERT S. MCINTYRE ET AL., OFFSHORE SHELL GAMES 2015: THE USE OF OFFSHORE TAX HAVENS BY FORTUNE 500 COMPANIES 1, 7 (2015) (U.S. PIRG Education Fund and Citizens for Tax Justice report). *See also* ZUCMAN, *supra* note 24, at 105–07.

Bermuda, Dubai, Singapore, Hong Kong, Switzerland, and Delaware have all been identified as tax havens,[27] suggesting that such conceptual framing might provide a useful means of theorizing these jurisdictions' similarly extraordinary successes in cross-border finance. Indeed, research in the area has identified common characteristics that do seem to describe many of the jurisdictions studied here: notably, they are typically islands, small in population and land area, with limited natural resources, yet relatively proximate to major economies; affluent, with predominantly coastal populations enjoying "relatively sophisticated communications infrastructure"; and English-speaking, with legal and political structures reflecting "British legal origins."[28]

As discussed below, Bermuda, Dubai, Singapore, Hong Kong, Switzerland, and Delaware all clearly compete on the basis of tax to attract cross-border capital, and do tend to exhibit the foregoing characteristics associated with tax havens. The "tax haven" concept cannot, however, provide a full account of their successes. A growing body of evidence concerning jurisdictions generally deemed tax havens suggests that they cannot effectively attract mobile capital on the basis of their tax regimes alone. Dhammika Dharmapala and James Hines, for example, find that "tax havens score very well on cross-country indices of governance quality," and report data suggesting that "for a well-governed country, moving from a high to a low tax rate is associated with significantly greater U.S. investment," whereas the association is "considerably weaker" for countries exhibiting lower-quality governance.[29] In other words, reducing or eliminating taxes does not itself guarantee the arrival of cross-border capital. Indeed, as we will see, excessive reliance on tax competition and financial secrecy—to the detriment of real, value-added service orientation—has rendered other jurisdictions highly vulnerable, leading to poor performance as financial centers in the long run.[30] The degree of specialization exhibited by jurisdictions that have actually

---

[27] *See, e.g.,* PALAN ET AL., *supra* note 16, at 1, 41–44, 227, 244; MCINTYRE ET AL., *supra* note 26, at 1, 9, 14–15; ZUCMAN, *supra* note 24, at 2, 105–07; Dharmapala, *supra* note 16, at 676.

[28] *See* Dharmapala, *supra* note 16, at 663. They are also "somewhat more likely to be dependent territories." *Id.* *See also* PALAN ET AL., *supra* note 16, at 3, 19, 184–85; Dhammika Dharmapala & James R. Hines, Jr., *Which Countries Become Tax Havens?*, 93 J. PUB. ECON. 1058, 1058–60 (2009).

[29] Dharmapala & Hines, *supra* note 28, at 1058, 1065. Their indices "include measures of voice and accountability, political stability, government effectiveness, rule of law, and the control of corruption." *Id.* at 1058. *See also* Andrew P. Morriss & Clifford C. Henson, *Regulatory Effectiveness in Onshore & Offshore Financial Centers* 13–15 (Univ. of Ala. Sch. of Law Working Paper, 2012), http://ssrn.com/abstract=2016310 (examining such jurisdictions' incentives to maintain high quality governance); Naren Prasad, *Small but Smart: Small States in the Global System, in* THE DIPLOMACIES OF SMALL STATES: BETWEEN VULNERABILITY AND RESILIENCE 41, 50–51 (Andrew F. Cooper & Timothy M. Shaw eds., 2009) (arguing that "better-governed jurisdictions have a far greater chance of success in creating viable OFCs").

[30] *See infra* Chapter 10.B.

succeeded in attracting substantial foreign capital[31]—spanning fields as complex and diverse as insurance, Islamic finance, wealth management, cross-border banking, and incorporation services among those studied here—suggests that their competitive characteristics extend well beyond their tax codes.[32]

Although tax undoubtedly looms large in these jurisdictions' competitive strategies, the tax haven concept's analytical utility is further undermined by the fact that it does not differentiate these jurisdictions from major economic powers in the categorical manner often suggested. As discussed below, Delaware provides some of the most opaque shell companies available anywhere. And in addition to the fact that Delaware is itself a part of the world's preeminent economic power, the United States (writ large) has, for almost a century, actively competed to attract foreign capital on the basis of taxation as well. As further discussed below, the United States does not tax interest income on nonresident alien accounts, a policy intended to "encourage foreign persons to use U.S. banks and savings institutions,"[33] and as of 2015 the United States represented "one fifth of the global market for offshore financial services."[34] Indeed, as J.C. Sharman has observed, "[a]lmost every country in the world can be used to avoid or evade another country's taxation."[35] Accordingly, the Tax Justice Network has identified both "intermediary havens" and "destination havens," emphasizing that much of the money passing through "the conventional list of 'offshore havens'" ultimately gravitates back to "the primary benefits of 'high-cost' First World capital markets," including the United States and the United Kingdom.[36] Consequently, the tax haven concept cannot categorically differentiate smaller jurisdictions of the sort studied here from larger financial markets.

---

[31] Cf. PALAN ET AL., supra note 16, at 35–38 (observing the development of "niche strategies" in response to competition).

[32] See, e.g., Michael J. Burns & James McConvill, An Unstoppable Force: The Offshore World in a Modern Global Economy, 7 HASTINGS BUS. L.J. 205, 205–08, 217–18 (2011). See also infra Part II; Andrew P. Morriss & Lotta Moberg, Cartelizing Taxes: Understanding the OECD's Campaign against "Harmful Tax Competition" 4–7 (Oct. 27, 2011), http://ssrn.com/abstract=1950627.

[33] CHARLES H. GUSTAFSON ET AL., TAXATION OF INTERNATIONAL TRANSACTIONS: MATERIALS, TEXTS AND PROBLEMS 238 (4th ed. 2011). See also TAX JUSTICE NETWORK, NARRATIVE REPORT ON USA 1–2 (2015) (dating this policy to the Revenue Act of 1921); Tracy A. Kaye, Innovations in the War on Tax Evasion, 2014 BYU L. REV. 363, 385–89 (2014); Ernest R. Larkins, Multinationals and Their Quest for the Good Tax Haven: Taxes Are but One, Albeit an Important, Consideration, 25 INT'L LAW. 471, 483 (1991); Jose Martínez, How the U.S. Became a Top Secrecy Jurisdiction, TAX JUST. BLOG (Nov. 3, 2015), http://www.taxjusticeblog.org/archive/2015/11/how_the_us_became_a_top_secrec.php.

[34] TAX JUSTICE NETWORK, supra note 33, at 1.

[35] J.C. SHARMAN, HAVENS IN A STORM: THE STRUGGLE FOR GLOBAL TAX REGULATION 27 (2006).

[36] JAMES S. HENRY, THE PRICE OF OFFSHORE REVISITED: NEW ESTIMATES FOR "MISSING" GLOBAL PRIVATE WEALTH, INCOME, INEQUALITY, AND LOST TAXES 12, 43 (July 2012) (report for the Tax Justice Network).

In light of the foregoing—and the charged nature of much of the tax haven literature and associated discourse—it is worth pausing here to emphasize what I am arguing and what I am not. As described below, I remain agnostic regarding whether "tax competition" among jurisdictions offers social benefits exceeding the costs—particularly given the mixed findings of the economic literature on this issue.[37] I nevertheless remain prepared to believe, however, that greater transparency with respect to both tax information and beneficial ownership of legal entities will occur, and that this will indeed be a good thing—if applied in an even-handed manner to both small jurisdictions and major markets alike.[38] As a descriptive and theoretical matter, the more modest claim advanced in this book is that tax policy and financial secrecy cannot fully explain the MDSJs' successes relative to other outward-oriented small jurisdictions, and likewise do not categorically differentiate the MDSJs from their larger competitors.

## II. OFFSHORE FINANCIAL CENTERS

The "offshore financial center" (OFC) concept avoids this exclusive focus on tax, but the term remains similarly imprecise—in part because it is so closely associated with the term "tax haven" that the two concepts are sometimes used interchangeably.[39] Although the term "OFC" remains similarly difficult to define comprehensively,[40] what appears to distinguish it is a more general focus on cross-border services. A common approach defines OFCs as those jurisdictions exhibiting "incommensurate" reliance on financial services for nonresidents (to which reduced regulatory and tax burdens may, to be sure, contribute)[41]—which would clearly include all six jurisdictions studied here.[42] Accordingly, although commentators studying OFCs

---

[37] *See infra* Chapter 2.C.

[38] *See infra* Chapters 2.C, 11.

[39] *See, e.g.*, BRITTAIN-CATLIN, *supra* note 13, at 42; PALAN ET AL., *supra* note 16, at 21; Andrew K. Rose & Mark M. Spiegel, *Offshore Financial Centers: Parasites or Symbionts?* 9, 11 (NBER Working Paper No. 12044, 2006); J.C. Sharman, *Canaries in the Coal Mine: Tax Havens, the Decline of the West and the Rise of the Rest*, 17 NEW POL. ECON. 493, 496 (2012); Tax Justice Network, *FAQ: Tax Havens*, http://www.taxjustice.net/faq/ (last visited Apr. 2016) (using the terms "tax haven," "offshore," and "secrecy jurisdiction" to describe the same jurisdictions).

[40] *See* Sharman, *supra* note 39, at 496 (observing that "there is no single agreed-upon definition of an OFC").

[41] *See* Ahmed Zoromé, *Concept of Offshore Financial Centers: In Search of an Operational Definition* 3–7, 26 (IMF Working Paper No. WP/07/87, 2007). *See also* Rose-Marie Belle Antoine, *The Legitimacy of the Offshore Financial Sector: A Legal Perspective, in* OFFSHORE FINANCIAL CENTERS AND REGULATORY COMPETITION, *supra* note 18, at 30, 31; S. Corkill Cobb, *Global Finance and the Growth of Offshore Financial Centers: The Manx Experience*, 29 GEOFORUM 7, 9–10 (1998); International Monetary Fund, *supra* note 18, at pt. II.A; Rose & Spiegel, *supra* note 39, at 1.

[42] *See, e.g.*, Zoromé, *supra* note 41, at 8–10, 14–15; International Monetary Fund, Monetary and Capital Markets Department & Legal Department, *Offshore Financial Centers: A Report on the Assessment Program*

emphasize characteristics very similar to those ascribed to tax havens, these commentators additionally emphasize characteristics directly pertinent to development of financial services capacity, including collaborative private- and public-sector interactions, depoliticization of finance, and efforts to generate innovative regulatory and market structures.[43]

Although the OFC concept offers greater capacity to account for institutional and competitive features not related to tax policy, this approach cannot provide a compelling account of the salient features setting apart those smaller jurisdictions that flourish in cross-border finance. As a threshold matter, the fact that some places described figuratively as "offshore" jurisdictions reside "onshore" in a literal geographic sense[44]—including Dubai, Switzerland, and Delaware—ought to give us pause; the misnomer suggests that the OFC concept may exhibit not merely an excessive preoccupation with islands, but a more general and troubling assumption that they (offshore) are categorically distinguishable from us (onshore).

In fact, the offshore/onshore distinction may obscure more than it illuminates. Just as the tax haven literature itself concludes, tax may be important to OFCs but is not the sole determinant of success.[45] As Anna Manasco Dionne and Jonathan Macey observe, "[s]uccessful OFCs are now complete alternative markets."[46] And just as the tendency of the major economic powers to compete on the basis of tax tends to undermine the analytical utility of the tax haven concept, so the tendency of "onshore" financial centers to compete to provide various financial services to nonresidents tends to undermine the analytical utility of the OFC concept. Indeed, an International Monetary Fund background paper on OFCs rightly observes that if we define the concept to mean "any financial center where offshore activity takes place," then the category "would include all the major financial centers in the world."[47] This reality has led the Tax Justice Network to question the geographic

---

and *Proposal for Integration with the Financial Sector Assessment Program* 18 (May 8, 2008) (characterizing Dubai as an OFC following development of the Dubai International Financial Centre).

[43] *See, e.g.*, BRITTAIN-CATLIN, *supra* note 13, at 9–14, 21, 27–32, 37, 97; Cobb, *supra* note 41, at 13–18; Philip R. Lane & Gian Maria Milesi-Ferretti, *Cross-Border Investment in Small International Financial Centers* 4–5, 10–11 (IMF Working Paper No. WP/10/38, 2010); Andrew P. Morriss, *The Role of Offshore Financial Centers in Regulatory Competition, in* OFFSHORE FINANCIAL CENTERS AND REGULATORY COMPETITION, *supra* note 18, at 102, 130–31. *See also* CHRISTOPHER BICKLEY, BERMUDA, BRITISH VIRGIN ISLANDS AND CAYMAN ISLANDS COMPANY LAW ix (4th ed. 2013).

[44] *See, e.g.*, BRITTAIN-CATLIN, *supra* note 13, at 78–79; Morriss, *supra* note 43, at 130.

[45] *See* Lane & Milesi-Ferretti, *supra* note 43, at 4–5. *See also* BICKLEY, *supra* note 43, at xi; Cobb, *supra* note 41, at 11, 19; Dionne & Macey, *supra* note 18, at 13–16; International Monetary Fund, *supra* note 18, at pt. II.A; Morriss, *supra* note 43, at 104, 107, 112–13.

[46] Dionne & Macey, *supra* note 18, at 16.

[47] International Monetary Fund, *supra* note 18, at pt. II.A. *Cf.* MARK YEANDLE & NICK DANEV, THE GLOBAL FINANCIAL CENTRES INDEX 14 at 8–9 (2013) (index sponsored by the Qatar Financial Centre

categorization implicit in the offshore/onshore distinction, concluding rather that the term "offshore" more meaningfully refers to "networks of legal and quasi-legal entities and arrangements that manage and control private wealth," whether located in small jurisdictions such as those studied here or global economic powers such as the United States.[48] The OFC concept accordingly offers at best limited value in seeking to identify what is truly distinctive about those smaller jurisdictions achieving global dominance in cross-border finance.

## III. MICROSTATES AND GLOBAL CITIES

Although the "tax haven" and "OFC" frameworks represent the most prominent extant means of theorizing the role of such jurisdictions, it is well worth considering other frameworks and the insights they might offer—notably, "microstates" and "global cities."

As the "microstate" moniker suggests, this concept focuses on very small jurisdictions and the peculiar challenges they face. "Because they are so small, and often so isolated," the Global Policy Forum explains, "the world's microstates are very vulnerable to social, economic and environmental disturbances in the global system." They face not only "the threat of hurricanes, rising sea levels and global climate change," but also unique economic and financial challenges. Notably, given the small size of their domestic economies they are "dangerously exposed to the vagaries of the global marketplace, including price shifts of their primary exports." Correlatively, they face great challenges in developing "educational and technical capacity," placing them "in danger of being left behind by a fast-evolving world."[49]

Although the substantial economic-development challenges faced by jurisdictions with small populations, limited land areas, and few natural resources figure prominently in the account developed below,[50] the microstate concept cannot provide a full account of the successes achieved by the likes of Bermuda, Dubai, Singapore, Hong Kong, Switzerland, and Delaware. The microstate concept functions principally to draw attention in global policy fora to unique challenges faced by small states, placing less emphasis on potential strengths in areas such as finance.[51] At the

---

Authority and produced by the Z/Yen Group) (evaluating various financial centers—both offshore and onshore—by reference to "connectivity").

[48] *See* HENRY, *supra* note 36, at 9, 13, 44 (emphasis removed).

[49] *Microstates,* GLOBAL POLICY FORUM, http://www.globalpolicy.org/nations-a-states/what-is-a-state/microstates.html (last visited Apr. 2016).

[50] *See infra* Chapter 3.

[51] *See* Godfrey Baldacchino, *Governmentality Is All the Rage: The Strategy Games of Small Jurisdictions,* 101 ROUND TABLE 235, 237–38 (2012); Godfrey Baldacchino, *The Power of Jurisdiction in Promoting Social Policies in Small States* 1–3, 6 (U.N. Soc. Policy and Dev. Paper No. 45, 2011).

same time, neither component of the "microstate" concept adequately captures the range of jurisdictions studied here. Switzerland, for example, though small relative to major economic powers, cannot fairly be described as "micro."[52] The same might be said of Singapore and Hong Kong (at least in terms of population).[53] Bermuda, Dubai, and Delaware, meanwhile, cannot be described as "states" under international law, as they do not possess full territorial sovereignty (though they do possess lawmaking authority in their respective areas of specialization—a capacity critical to their successes in cross-border finance).[54]

Unlike the "microstates" concept, the "global cities" concept focuses quite intently on the comparative advantages enjoyed by relatively small places in a globalizing financial world. This approach—most prominently developed by Saskia Sassen—builds on the insight that the world economy functions predominantly through regional and global "circuits" consisting of cities, which collectively reflect a "division of functions" rather than pure competition.[55] Although increased capital mobility might lead one to predict "the dispersal of firms and markets worldwide," Sassen observes that "this dispersal itself generates a demand for specific types of production needed to ensure the management, control, and servicing of this new organization of manufacturing and finance."[56] The concentration of finance not merely in cities, but in distinct financial districts within cities, vividly reflects the fact that "the risk, complexity, and speculative character of much of this activity raises the importance of face-to-face interaction," facilitating trust and augmenting the potential for innovative new ventures to arise spontaneously—functions that technology cannot effectively replicate.[57] At the same time, these places serve as "entry points into national and/or regional economies" for global businesses, performing a critical "bridging" function.[58] Accordingly, such places take on a dual character as both regional and global sites. Although global cities "have been and still are deeply embedded in the economies of their region," they simultaneously "tend, in part, to disconnect from their region" in favor of cosmopolitan connectedness through associated global circuits.[59]

---

[52] *See infra* Chapter 8.

[53] *See infra* Chapters 6–7.

[54] *See, e.g.,* MALANCZUK, *supra* note 2, at 75 ("The control of territory is the essence of a state."). *See also infra* Chapters 4–5, 9.

[55] *See* Saskia Sassen, *The Specialised Differences of Cities Matter in Today's Global Economy, in* REFORMING THE CITY: RESPONSES TO THE GLOBAL FINANCIAL CRISIS 209, 209–10 (Sam Whimster ed., 2009). *See also* SASSEN, *supra* note 8, at 83–84, 112–15, 126.

[56] SASSEN, *supra* note 8, at 5. *See also id.* at 34–36, 127–28, 138–39, 155.

[57] *Id.* at 192, 222.

[58] *See* Sassen, *supra* note 55, at 212.

[59] SASSEN, *supra* note 8, at 92.

Other scholars have similarly explored various "centripetal" forces favoring concentration of financial services. Thomas Gehrig, for example, emphasizes economies of scale in payments systems, the value of "information spillovers" in complex financial contexts, liquidity benefits, and the attractiveness of deep labor markets for financial professionals, all of which reinforce "the agglomeration of financial activity."[60] Like Sassen, Gehrig further observes the persistent value of "face-to-face communication" in settings characterized by informational complexity, where multiple iterations can help "prevent misinterpretations [and] guarantee a certain degree of confidentiality."[61]

The global cities literature offers a descriptively rich account of factors fostering concentration in finance and related professional services, providing a powerful answer to the globalization literature's claims regarding homogenization and the purported erasure of geography and place.[62] As Sassen rightly emphasizes, "[t]he deep economic history of a place and the specialized economic strengths it can generate increasingly matter in a globalized economy"[63]—dynamics vividly illustrated in the jurisdictions studied here. This literature cannot, however, fully describe a category of jurisdictions so various as Bermuda, Dubai, Singapore, Hong Kong, Switzerland, and Delaware.

The global cities literature has focused predominantly on where transnational firms choose to locate,[64] exhibiting what might be termed a "demand-side" orientation that offers at best limited and indirect insights regarding what might correlatively be termed the "supply side"—that is, what jurisdictions seeking to attract such activity choose to offer, and how they go about developing attractive regulatory regimes and services capacities. Singapore has certainly been described as a "city-state"[65]—leading at times to heated debates among Singaporeans themselves

---

[60] *See* Thomas Gehrig, *Cities and the Geography of Financial Centers, in* Economics of Cities: Theoretical Perspectives 415, 425–28 (Jean-Marie Huriot & Jacques-François Thisse eds., 2000). *See also* Richard Roberts & David Kynaston, City State: A Contemporary History of the City of London and How Money Triumphed 64–65, 191 (2002); TheCityUK, Key Facts about the UK as an International Financial Centre 7 (July 2015).

[61] Gehrig, *supra* note 60, at 440. *See also* Edward L. Glaeser, *Urban Colossus: Why Is New York America's Largest City?*, FRBNY Econ. Pol'y Rev., Dec. 2005, at 7, 22; Darryl S.L. Jarvis, *Race for the Money: International Financial Centres in Asia*, 14 J. Int'l Rel. & Dev. 60, 62–66 (2011).

[62] *See, e.g.*, Sassen, *supra* note 55, at 210–11. *See also* Ronen Palan, *International Financial Centers: The British-Empire, City-States and Commercially Oriented Politics*, 11 Theoretical Inquiries L. 149, 158 (2010) (characterizing Sassen's work as "an interesting synthesis of the two debates, globalization and the city, suggesting that globalization has engendered a hierarchy among cities and regions").

[63] Sassen, *supra* note 8, at 126.

[64] *See, e.g.*, Neil M. Coe et al., *Integrating Finance into Global Production Networks*, 48 Regional Stud. 761, 764 (2014) ("Early research on [world cities] has focused on their roles as 'basing points' for capital and 'command and control centres' of the global economy as TNCs organize global production on larger and more complex scales. . . .").

[65] *See, e.g.*, Palan et al., *supra* note 16, at 185.

regarding which provides the better paradigm for Singapore's society[66]—and Singapore's success in developing a vibrant financial center is certainly amenable to analysis through the global cities lens.[67] However, the focus of this literature on metropolitan centers renders it ill-suited to grapple with dynamics of legislative authority and the global regulatory competition to which the dispersal of such authority over recent decades has given rise. Indeed, none of the jurisdictions investigated in this book are "cities," as such; all embody higher, non-municipal levels of government that depend critically on regulatory autonomy vastly exceeding that typically exhibited by municipalities. Accordingly, although the global cities literature offers important insights into the apparent paradox of financial services concentration in an era of globalization, it cannot provide a full account of the types of jurisdictions studied here and the principal forms of competition in which they engage.

## IV. ENGLISH LEGAL ORIGINS

The apparent predominance of English legal origins across those small jurisdictions active in cross-border finance has been so frequently remarked upon that it is worth exploring, at least briefly, how far this might take us in describing and evaluating this category of jurisdictions.

Scholars investigating tax havens and OFCs alike have observed the prevalence of British ties. As Dhammika Dharmapala explains, tax havens "are more likely to have British legal origins . . . than is the typical country," and are "more likely to use English as an official language."[68] Palan, Murphy, and Chavagneux similarly remark on the utility of English legal structures, observing that "trust arrangements"— which "remain peculiar to Anglo-Saxon jurisdictions"—provide substantial secrecy for beneficial owners of assets because trustees are substituted as legal owners, and most jurisdictions require no publicly accessible record of the trust's existence.[69] Similarly Michael Burns and James McConvill, lawyers practicing in the British Virgin Islands, observe that a "number of OFCs are British Overseas Territories . . . or Crown Dependencies," meaning that "the law [is] heavily influenced by English common law decisions" and "the Privy Council in England is the final court of appeal"—features said to convey "political and legal stability" attractive to mobile capital.[70] These observations broadly resonate with the so-called "law matters"

---

[66] *See* Mong Palatino, *Singapore: Is It a City or Country?*, GLOBAL VOICES (Nov. 30, 2009, 9:37 GMT), http://globalvoicesonline.org/2009/11/30/singapore-is-it-a-city-or-country/.

[67] *See, e.g.*, Sassen, *supra* note 55, at 213.

[68] Dharmapala, *supra* note 16, at 663.

[69] *See* PALAN ET AL., *supra* note 16, at 92.

[70] Burns & McConvill, *supra* note 32, at 219–20. *See also* Lane & Milesi-Ferretti, *supra* note 43, at 8.

theory, arguing (among other things) that common-law legal systems better protect investors than civil-law systems do, leading the former to develop more robust capital markets than the latter.[71] From this perspective it is unsurprising that the United Kingdom, including financial centers that remain under its control, "accounts for a whopping 29.6 percent of international market transactions,"[72] and that "[m]ore than half of the companies implicated in the leaked Panama Papers are registered in UK overseas territories and crown dependencies."[73]

Although British ties may loom large in this context, this cannot possibly form the basis for a comprehensive theory of small jurisdictions achieving success in cross-border finance. Important cases clearly do not fit this description—notably Switzerland, a civil-law system lacking close analogs for English-law structures such as trusts, yet which has long flourished as a financial center. The Swiss example suggests that there is something more fundamental driving the peculiar prevalence of smaller jurisdictions in the highest echelons of cross-border finance.[74] Similarly, Dubai has a mixed system based on civil law and Sharia law, notwithstanding exposure to the British Empire and legal system as a so-called "Trucial state." The Dubai International Financial Centre has, to be sure, adopted a unique finance-specific legal structure based on English common law, yet as we will see, what is truly at the heart of Islamic finance is its hybridization with Islamic sharia law—a distinct legal system that itself offers forms of agency, trust, and partnership relations, undercutting claims that these structures are unique to the Anglo-American common-law tradition.[75]

More generally, however, the notion that English legal origins could form the basis for a full description and evaluation of smaller jurisdictions in cross-border finance encounters some of the same problems that the "law matters" theory does. As I have explored elsewhere, "the fixed historical fact of a [jurisdiction's] association with a given legal family" cannot explain the observed phenomenon of stability or change

---

[71] *See generally* Rafael La Porta et al., *Legal Determinants of External Finance*, 52 J. FIN. 1131 (1997); Rafael La Porta et al., *Law and Finance*, 106 J. POL. ECON. 1113 (1998).

[72] Palan, *supra* note 62, at 156. *See also* TAX JUSTICE NETWORK, NARRATIVE REPORT ON UNITED KINGDOM 1, 4–8 (2015).

[73] Patrick Wintour, *Overseas Territories Spared from UK Law on Company Registers*, GUARDIAN, Apr. 12, 2016, http://www.theguardian.com/business/2016/apr/12/overseas-territories-spared-from-uk-law-on-company-registers.

[74] Switzerland certainly is not the only small civil-law jurisdiction achieving success in cross-border finance without English-law structures such as trusts. *See, e.g.*, CENTRAL INTELLIGENCE AGENCY, THE WORLD FACTBOOK: LIECHTENSTEIN, https://www.cia.gov/library/publications/the-world-factbook/geos/ls.html (last updated Apr. 26, 2016); George E. Glos, *The Analysis of a Tax Haven: The Liechtenstein Anstalt*, 18 INT'L LAW. 929 (1984); Max Riderer von Paar, *Liechtenstein Foundation and Anstalt*, http://mrlawnet.com/news-and-articles/liechtenstein-foundation-and-anstalt/ (last visited Apr. 2016).

[75] *See infra* Chapters 5, 8.

in policy over time.[76] Nor can it explain variations across the category of jurisdictions with common-law legal origins,[77] which is vividly illustrated by four of the six jurisdictions studied here. Bermuda, Singapore, Hong Kong, and Delaware have, for example, focused their efforts on different areas of financial services, performing different functions in global markets—a reality defying explanation solely by reference to their common historical roots in English law. Grappling with the predominance of English legal origins may prove necessary to a thorough account of smaller jurisdictions in cross-border finance, but it by no means exhausts the inquiry.

As the foregoing discussion demonstrates, none of these theoretical frameworks can provide a full account of the range of small jurisdictions that have achieved positions of market dominance in cross-border finance. Each, however, offers important insights contributing to the alternative framework that I develop in this book. Before taking up that task in earnest, I turn first to a couple of related approaches offering perspectives and insights that will contribute to our understanding of such jurisdictions—specifically, the literatures on capital mobility and regulatory competition.

## C. Capital Mobility and Regulatory Competition

Bermuda, Dubai, Singapore, Hong Kong, Switzerland, and Delaware differ in a number of respects that defy compelling description and insightful evaluation through prevailing theoretical lenses. Yet even the little said about these jurisdictions thus far reveals clear commonalities—notably, each is a small jurisdiction that has achieved extraordinary global market dominance in a specialized area of cross-border finance. In this light, it is well worth exploring their differences and commonalities in greater detail to determine what can be said about the strengths and competitive characteristics that may have contributed to their successes. Before turning to the more detailed discussion in the next chapter, however, it is helpful to consider first some of the historical developments that created a marketspace for such jurisdictions to inhabit.

The potential for capital to move across borders in response to the perceived favorability of another jurisdiction's regulatory environment has long been recognized. Montesquieu, writing in the eighteenth century, observed that the expansion of European commerce had generated increasingly mobile forms of wealth—notably

---

[76] CHRISTOPHER M. BRUNER, CORPORATE GOVERNANCE IN THE COMMON-LAW WORLD: THE POLITICAL FOUNDATIONS OF SHAREHOLDER POWER 118 (2013).

[77] Id. at 117–18. For further discussion of problems with the "law matters" theory, see id. at 116–19 and sources cited therein.

"money, notes, bills of exchange, stocks of companies, ships, all commodities and merchandise"—and he well perceived that, unlike real property, such wealth need not remain within any particular jurisdiction. Indeed, Montesquieu identified this growing capital mobility as a potential constraint upon the sovereign, writing that the capacity of commerce to "elude violence, and maintain itself everywhere" had "compelled [rulers] to govern with greater wisdom than they themselves might have intended."[78] In a similar manner, Adam Smith suggested that the growing mobility and intangibility of capital imposed a practical constraint on potentially "vexatious" taxation. Whereas the "proprietor of land is necessarily a citizen of the particular country in which his estate lies," the "proprietor of stock is properly a citizen of the world, and is not necessarily attached to any particular country." Accordingly, Smith explained, he "would be apt to abandon the country in which he was exposed to a vexatious inquisition, in order to be assessed to a burdensome tax, and would remove his stock to some other country where he could either carry on his business, or enjoy his fortune more at his ease." This, Smith concluded, "would so far tend to dry up every source of revenue, both to the sovereign and to the society," that forward-looking sovereigns would "content themselves with some very loose . . . estimation" of taxable stock in order to preserve productivity.[79]

As economist Albert Hirschman observed in his classic essay on "Exit, Voice, and the State," the "fears and hopes aroused by the rise of movable capital in the seventeenth and eighteenth centuries offer many interesting parallels" to our own era, in which "the international mobility of capital is infinitely greater . . . than at the time of Montesquieu and Adam Smith."[80] Broadly, there are two pertinent threads of history in the late nineteenth and early twentieth centuries that set the stage for the acceleration of capital mobility that characterizes modern finance, one relating to incorporation and the other to taxation. By the early twentieth century, the potential for corporations to move their legal homes from one state to another within the United States became fully apparent—a new reality reflected in their steady migration down the East Coast from New York and Massachusetts, which "had the highest concentration of company headquarters in the country" as of the 1880s; to New Jersey, which liberalized its corporate law in the late 1880s and 1890s in an effort to raise revenue; and finally to Delaware—which followed New Jersey's lead

---

[78] Albert O. Hirschman, *Exit, Voice, and the State*, in ALBERT O. HIRSCHMAN, ESSAYS IN TRESPASSING: ECONOMICS TO POLITICS AND BEYOND 246, 253–55 (1981) (essay originally published in 1978) (quoting Montesquieu).

[79] *See id.* at 256 (quoting Smith).

[80] *Id.* at 253, 257.

by liberalizing its own corporate law around the turn of the twentieth century, yet did not later backtrack (as New Jersey did).[81]

Around the same period, a similar dynamic arose with respect to private capital, spurred by perceived excessive taxation and the growing technological ease with which money could be moved from one place to another. Both in Europe and (somewhat later) in the United States, high individual tax rates were imposed in the late nineteenth and early twentieth centuries in response to wars and other crises. On both sides of the Atlantic, the affluent responded by moving their money to lower-tax jurisdictions.[82] Similar dynamics emerged with respect to corporate taxes, the constitutionality of a distinct tax on corporate income being firmly established in the United States by 1909.[83]

Later in the twentieth century, two important developments further accelerated movements of money across borders—growth in the number of sovereigns with capacity to set their own tax rates, due principally to decolonization, and growing technological capacity to move people and their money around the world quickly and at low cost.[84] When major economies sought "in the 1960s and the 1970s to control capital flows through the imposition of restrictive domestic regulation"—mainly in an effort to exert greater control over monetary policy—the result was "a shift of deposits and borrowing to less regulated institutions . . . exempt from such restrictions" in other jurisdictions.[85] As described more fully below,[86] the consequence was the emergence (notably in London, but also in other European financial centers) of so-called "Euromarkets"—essentially "financial activity . . . denominated in a currency other than the currency of the jurisdiction in which the institution is located," of which the modern "offshore" world initially represented an extension.[87] Tacitly

---

[81] *See* PALAN ET AL., *supra* note 16, at 110; ERIN A. O'HARA & LARRY E. RIBSTEIN, THE LAW MARKET 10, 110–11 (2009); Frederick Tung, *Before Competition: Origins of the Internal Affairs Doctrine*, 32 J. CORP. L. 33, 74–97 (2006). For additional background, see *infra* Chapter 9.

[82] *See, e.g.*, PALAN ET AL., *supra* note 16, at 115–22; Jeffrey A. Winters, *Oligarchy and Democracy*, 7 AM. INT., Sept. 28, 2011, http://www.the-american-interest.com/2011/09/28/oligarchy-and-democracy/. *See also* Craig M. Boise, *Regulating Tax Competition in Offshore Financial Centers, in* OFFSHORE FINANCIAL CENTERS AND REGULATORY COMPETITION, *supra* note 18, at 50, 52.

[83] *See* PALAN ET AL., *supra* note 16, at 109.

[84] *See id.* at 140–41; Morriss, *supra* note 43, at 124–25.

[85] Zoromé, *supra* note 41, at 24. Such restrictions included "reserve requirements, interest rate ceilings, restrictions on the range of financial products that supervised institutions could offer, capital controls, and high effective taxation in many OECD countries." International Monetary Fund, *supra* note 18, at pt. II.C.

[86] *See infra* Chapter 10.C.

[87] *See* Salim M. Darbar, R. Barry Johnston & Mary G. Zephirin, *Assessing Offshore: Filling a Gap in Global Surveillance*, FIN. & DEV., Sept. 2003, at 32. *See also Enduring Charms: A Brief History of Tax Havens*, ECONOMIST, Feb. 14, 2013, http://www.economist.com/news/special-report/21571550-brief-history-tax-havens-enduring-charms; International Monetary Fund, *supra* note 18, at pt. II.C; Winters, *supra* note 82; Zoromé, *supra* note 41, at 24–25.

accepted by both the U.K. and U.S. governments notwithstanding their own existing capital controls, both the United Kingdom and the United States "unilaterally liberalized capital flows during the middle and late 1970s,"[88] and capital mobility would soon thereafter become firmly established as a core tenet of the so-called "Washington Consensus" policy mix,[89] fueling competition to attract that newly freed capital.[90] Greater ease of moving money across borders, increased trade, decreased communication and transportation costs, a growing number of sovereigns, and growing policy consensus in favor of capital mobility in major markets set the stage for greatly intensified competition to attract capital and to profit from the movement of that capital—principally through provision of financial services to nonresidents.[91]

These dynamics appear to represent a straightforward example of what Erin O'Hara and Larry Ribstein have termed "the law market," by which they refer to "ways that governing laws can be chosen by people and firms rather than mandated by states."[92] That selection of one's jurisdiction might be broadly analogized to selection of goods or services in a private marketplace has long been recognized.[93] "Just as the consumer may be visualized as walking to a private market place to buy his goods, the prices of which are set," as economist Charles Tiebout expressed it in his seminal 1956 article, the consumer may likewise be characterized as "walking to a community where the prices (taxes) of community services are set."[94] As O'Hara and Ribstein explore, however, the services that communities offer can effectively be unbundled, creating more granular markets for discrete forms of regulatory regimes—in other words, a literal "law market"—to the degree that the selection process can be divorced from any requirement of actual physical mobility.[95]

---

[88] RAWI ABDELAL, CAPITAL RULES: THE CONSTRUCTION OF GLOBAL FINANCE 7–8 (2007).

[89] *See* Harvard University Center for International Development, *Washington Consensus,* http://www.cid.harvard.edu/cidtrade/issues/washington.html (last visited Apr. 2016).

[90] *See* Reuven S. Avi-Yonah, *Globalization, Tax Competition, and the Fiscal Crisis of the Welfare State,* 113 HARV. L. REV. 1573, 1575–86 (2000); Adam H. Rosenzweig, *Why Are There Tax Havens?,* 52 WM. & MARY L. REV. 923, 931 (2010) (describing the "capital neutrality paradox" fueling tax competition).

[91] *See* Avi-Yonah, *supra* note 90, at 1575–86; Morriss, *supra* note 43, at 124–25; Rosenzweig, *supra* note 90, at 931.

[92] *See* O'HARA & RIBSTEIN, *supra* note 81, at 65. *See also* Morriss, *supra* note 43, at 103.

[93] *See* Charles M. Tiebout, *A Pure Theory of Local Expenditures,* 64 J. POL. ECON. 416, 418–23 (1956).

[94] *Id*. at 422. *See also* O'HARA & RIBSTEIN, *supra* note 81, at 66–73.

[95] *See* O'HARA & RIBSTEIN, *supra* note 81, at 14–15, 27–29, 73–74. O'Hara and Ribstein's principal aim is to promote adoption of a U.S. federal statute "that compels states to enforce choice-of-law clauses," subject to state override. *See id*. at 200–01, 206–08. *See also* Bruce G. Carruthers & Naomi R. Lamoreaux, *Regulatory Races: The Effects of Jurisdictional Competition on Regulatory Standards* 45 (2013), http://www.econ.ucla.edu/people/papers/Lamoreaux/Lamoreaux484.pdf. For a discussion of complications that can arise when

Intriguingly, O'Hara and Ribstein observe that smaller jurisdictions lacking substantial endowments (e.g., labor pools, consumer markets, and natural resources) will tend to be more sensitive to this form of law market. "The discipline that mobility exerts on state politicians depends," they explain, "on the benefits that states can offer firms to offset bad laws." Consequently they "expect large and rich states like California to be less responsive to the law market than small states like Delaware," which lack non-regulatory means of competing.[96] O'Hara and Ribstein, however, focus on advancing a normative argument in the domestic choice-of-law context, gesturing only briefly (and equivocally) toward international expressions of the competitive dynamics they describe.[97]

Application of such ideas to the growing cross-border competition for capital has given rise to heated policy debate over recent decades regarding the social desirability of "tax competition," but the economic literature on the subject remains inconclusive. As J.C. Sharman describes it, "there is remarkably little expert consensus on the issue," rendering tax competition debates partly "normative rather than technical" in nature.[98] Styling cross-border efforts to lure mobile business firms as Tieboutian regulatory competition gained purchase in the 1970s, but critics of this approach emphasized the potential for cross-border "fiscal externalities"—notably tax base erosion, the potential for inefficient allocation of capital across jurisdictions, and the potential for inefficiently low taxes if, for example, beneficial government spending were forgone due to fear that requisite taxation would prompt capital flight. Others, then, responded to these critiques from a "public choice" perspective, rejecting "the assumption, common to Tiebout and his critics alike, that governments act as selfless, benevolent dictators immune to the charms of rent-seeking coalitions and the temptation to 'interfere' in the economy for political gain." These commentators offered an alternative depiction of government as a "Leviathan" focused first and foremost on tax revenue maximization, and only secondarily, if at all, on social benefit—in which light tax competition might be styled as a critical market discipline constraining tax-happy governments, along the lines noted above. Sharman, for his part, plausibly suggests that tax competition likely "exerts different effects

---

discrete forms of regulatory regimes cannot be unbundled—notably, when a move aimed at reducing tax requires "shifting to a different, possibly inferior, corporate law regime"—see Mitchell A. Kane & Edward B. Rock, *Corporate Taxation and International Charter Competition*, 106 MICH. L. REV. 1229 (2008).

[96] O'HARA & RIBSTEIN, *supra* note 81, at 68. *See also* Carruthers & Lamoreaux, *supra* note 95, at 7.

[97] *Compare* O'HARA & RIBSTEIN, *supra* note 81, at 225 ("Nations can self-coordinate, just as can states in a federal system.") *with id.* at 13 (observing that the international context "raises concerns about the extent to which firms can flee to low-tax, low-regulation havens while still enjoying the benefits of the more orderly jurisdictions in which they do much of their business").

[98] SHARMAN, *supra* note 35, at 36–37.

simultaneously"[99]—a nuanced view finding support in the literature[100]—in which case "the net benefit or harm caused by tax competition is almost impossible to predict."[101] To be sure, it is empirically documented "that tax considerations strongly influence the choices that firms make,"[102] yet the policy implications of such findings remain unclear—particularly given that such trends are unaccompanied by evidence of any marked decrease in corporate or individual income tax revenue among the world's major industrial powers (for which commentators have offered numerous potential explanations).[103]

In light of the mixed findings of the economic literature, I remain agnostic for purposes of the analyses that follow regarding the relative policy merits of tax competition[104] (while at the same time broadly accepting the claim that greater transparency regarding tax information and beneficial ownership of legal entities—applied in an even-handed manner—would prove beneficial[105]). There remains more to be said, however, about cross-border regulatory competition in order to develop a more complete account of how small jurisdictions have successfully attracted cross-border financial activity, and how tax policy interacts with other forms of regulatory competition. In his study of the "corporate inversion" trend, Eric Talley develops a model of "multi-attribute" regulatory competition involving both tax and non-tax dimensions. In Talley's model, jurisdictions competing to attract mobile firms

---

[99] *See id.* at 37–38. For broadly similar accounts of the economic literature and its evolution regarding tax competition, see Avi-Yonah, *supra* note 90, at 1611–14; John Douglas Wilson, *Theories of Tax Competition,* 52 NAT'L TAX J. 269, 271–98 (1999).

[100] *See, e.g.,* Avi-Yonah, *supra* note 90, at 1615–16 (describing "a more plausible model, in which policymakers value both the welfare of their citizens and the surplus they extract from them for their own uses"); Wilson, *supra* note 99, at 298 (concluding that "competition among governments has both good and bad aspects").

[101] SHARMAN, *supra* note 35, at 39.

[102] *See* James R. Hines, Jr., *Lessons from Behavioral Responses to International Taxation,* 52 NAT'L TAX J. 305, 313–18 (1999).

[103] *See, e.g.,* SHARMAN, *supra* note 35, at 39–40; Avi-Yonah, *supra* note 90, at 1597, 1619–21; Avi-Yonah, *supra* note 16, at 791–92; Reuven S. Avi-Yonah, *Tax Competition and the Trend toward Territoriality* 2 (Univ. of Mich. Law Sch. Pub. Law and Legal Theory Research Paper No. 297, 2012), http://ssrn.com/abstract=2191251; Kenneth Stewart & Michael Webb, *International Competition in Corporate Taxation: Evidence from the OECD Time Series,* 221 ECON. POL'Y 153, 170–72 (2006). *See also* Lans Bovenberg, *Discussion,* 221 ECON. POL'Y 193, 194 (2006) (responding to Kenneth Stewart & Michael Webb, *International Competition in Corporate Taxation: Evidence from the OECD Time Series,* 221 ECON. POL'Y 153 (2006)) (arguing that corporate tax competition might manifest itself in reduced individual, rather than corporate, tax revenue if falling corporate tax rates lead more businesses to incorporate, such that "the corporate tax base expands at the expense of the personal tax base"); Zucman, *supra* note 18, at 133 (arguing that U.S. corporate tax revenue has remained stable notwithstanding a fall in the effective corporate tax rate because "corporate profits have risen as a share of national income").

[104] *See infra* Part II.

[105] *See infra* Chapter 11.

"endeavor to maximize their expected tax revenues net of their costs of installing their [non-tax regulatory regime]," whereas for mobile firms the payoff of locating in a particular jurisdiction is "(a) the firm's baseline profits, *plus* (b) the value contributed by the chosen jurisdiction's [non-tax regulatory regime], *less* (c) the tax levy imposed by the chosen jurisdiction."[106] Although Talley focuses on corporate inversion transactions—in which U.S. multinational corporations' preferences to maintain U.S. corporate governance regulation, on the one hand, and to escape U.S. tax regulation, on the other, constitute the operative incentives[107]—his analytical framework appears more broadly applicable, and offers general insights borne out by the analyses developed in Part II of this book. Notably, Talley demonstrates that "when jurisdictions can bundle [non-tax] and tax regulations, they will tend to differentiate themselves in their offerings, with some jurisdictions serving as market 'leaders' . . . while others serve as market 'laggards.'" He concludes that the leaders' "market power" permits them "to moderate their responses to tax competition from other jurisdictions," and that "a leader's optimal response to another jurisdiction's aggressive tax policies may be muted" in light of their capacity to pull other policy levers.[108] Pitched at a mid-level of abstraction, the intuitively appealing suggestion that jurisdictions offering more diversified suites of tax and non-tax regulatory attributes possess greater flexibility—and consequently face less vulnerability—in

---

[106] *See* Eric L. Talley, *Corporate Inversions and the Unbundling of Regulatory Competition,* 101 VA. L. REV. 1649, 1705–06 (2015). Talley builds on the broader regulatory competition literature while "drawing inspiration from more general theories of oligopolistic competition in multidimensional product space." *See id.* at 1700 n.166. *See also* Andrew Caplin & Barry Nalebuff, *Aggregation and Imperfect Competition: On the Existence of Equilibrium,* 59 ECONOMETRICA 25 (1991); Andrew S. Caplin & Barry J. Nalebuff, *Multi-Dimensional Product Differentiation and Price Competition,* 38 OXFORD ECON. PAPERS, SUPPLEMENT 129 (1986); Avner Shaked & John Sutton, *Relaxing Price Competition through Product Differentiation,* 49 REV. ECON. STUD. 3 (1982).

[107] An inversion—through which a U.S. multinational corporation seeks to move its tax residence to "a jurisdiction offering a more favorable tax environment" (e.g., lower taxes, territorial taxation, and so on)—has historically required sacrificing access to Delaware's sophisticated corporate law and courts upon reincorporation elsewhere. Talley argues, however, that the cost of an inversion has fallen over time as securities regulation has increasingly federalized U.S. corporate governance, permitting companies to move their tax residence while retaining U.S.-style corporate governance by maintaining a U.S. exchange listing. *See* Talley, *supra* note 106, at 1650–1700. For discussion of anti-inversion efforts and corporate responses, see MCINTYRE ET AL., *supra* note 26, at 15; *Experts Expect Corporate Tax Inversions to Survive New Rules,* CHICAGO TRIB., Apr. 7, 2016, http://www.chicagotribune.com/business/ct-corporate-tax-inversions-new-rules-20160407-story.html; *Taxing America Inc: Pfiasco,* ECONOMIST, Apr. 9, 2016, at 63–64; Victor Fleischer, *On Inversions, the Treasury Department Drops the Gloves,* N.Y. TIMES, Apr. 5, 2016, http://www.nytimes.com/2016/04/06/business/dealbook/on-inversions-the-treasury-department-drops-the-gloves.html?_r=0. Accordingly Talley argues that, rather than sweeping tax reforms, the U.S. regulatory response to inversions should involve either "a means for 'pricing out' the governance services that it increasingly gives away to public companies," or backing away from federalization of corporate governance. *See* Talley, *supra* note 106, at 1726.

[108] *See* Talley, *supra* note 106, at 1701.

the face of stiff competition and changing market landscapes is vividly borne out in the contrast between the MDSJs, offering substantial value-added services, and their less successful competitors, relying far more heavily on low taxes and financial secrecy.[109]

Cally Jordan, meanwhile, has explored similar dynamics in the context of a broader study of international capital markets, drawing conclusions generally consistent with the foregoing and resonant with the MDSJ paradigm developed in the following chapters. Jordan observes that certain specialized markets emerge in the gaps between the major economies—so-called "niche markets," a category in which she groups Dubai, Singapore, and Switzerland. These jurisdictions, she observes, "demonstrate linguistic advantages in their diversity," and may be "resource poor" yet "people rich." They have thrived, she argues, through a brand of "state capitalism" aimed at cooperative public-private facilitation of "an international financial infrastructure," and these jurisdictions well understand the competition they face. "Nimbleness and opportunism are hallmarks of niche markets," Jordan explains. "They must innovate or perish."[110]

Others go further, both in analogizing international to domestic regulatory competition and in emphasizing the degree to which U.S. states and foreign jurisdictions compete with one another. For example, Dionne and Macey argue that there is "no qualitative difference" between regulatory competition within the United States, on the one hand, and across international borders, on the other.[111] Rose-Marie Belle Antoine likewise argues that offshore jurisdictions are often "copied wholesale by onshore jurisdictions, even by their archenemies" with which they compete directly. Various U.S. states, she emphasizes, have enacted "trust, banking, insurance, and tax laws that borrow heavily from offshore legal paradigms."[112] Indeed, Andrew Morriss reiterates the analogy between interstate and international regulatory competition[113] and identifies poignant examples of direct competition between U.S. states and foreign jurisdictions—including between Delaware and the British Virgin Islands in business entity registration,[114] and between Vermont and Bermuda in captive insurance.[115]

---

[109] *See infra* Part II and Chapter 10.B.

[110] CALLY JORDAN, INTERNATIONAL CAPITAL MARKETS: LAW AND INSTITUTIONS 202–04 (2014).

[111] *See* Dionne & Macey, *supra* note 18, at 8.

[112] *See* Antoine, *supra* note 41, at 41.

[113] *See* Morriss, *supra* note 43, at 108–09, 114–15.

[114] *See* Morriss & Henson, *supra* note 29, at 23.

[115] *See* Morriss, *supra* note 43, at 136–38; Morriss & Henson, *supra* note 29, at 28; TAX JUSTICE NETWORK, NARRATIVE REPORT ON USA 7 (2015).

In the next part of the book I focus on precisely this form of jurisdictional competition, seeking to explain and evaluate the rise of certain small jurisdictions—both within the United States and elsewhere—to positions of global dominance within specialized fields of cross-border finance. My approach draws upon insights of each of the theoretical frameworks discussed above to advance a new paradigm that I term the "market-dominant small jurisdiction" (MDSJ).[116] I strike out in this new direction—rejecting the extant concepts discussed above—because I believe the approach embodied in the MDSJ concept offers substantial advantages unavailable to the others. Notably, the MDSJ concept remains normatively neutral, avoiding the pejorative overtones of labels such as "tax haven" and "offshore financial center";[117] it more effectively embraces the considerable diversity exhibited by those small jurisdictions achieving global dominance in cross-border finance; and it emphasizes those commonalities that appear highly consequential in their rise to dominance and their subsequent resilience in the face of recurrent challenges.

Although a number of jurisdictions might have been selected for such a study, I have settled upon six in order to contain the comparative analysis[118] while canvassing the diversity and commonalities exhibited by the category of jurisdictions identified. The jurisdictions selected present different types of legal jurisdiction, exhibit substantial specialization in cross-border finance, rose to prominence over different time frames, are situated in different geographies, exhibit different cultural affinities, and vary in the magnitude of their domestic economies.[119] Notwithstanding the very real idiosyncrasies and divergences among them, however, distinct and illuminating patterns do emerge across these jurisdictions, permitting generalizations to be offered regarding the role and strengths of small jurisdictions in cross-border finance, and hypotheses to be generated regarding how they managed to achieve and sustain their extraordinary successes.

---

[116] *See infra* Chapter 3.

[117] *See The Good, the Bad and the Ugland: Havens Serve Clean as Well as Dirty Money*, ECONOMIST, Feb. 14, 2013, http://www.economist.com/news/special-report/21571551-havens-serve-clean-well-dirty-money-good-bad-and-ugland.

[118] *See* BRUNER, *supra* note 76, at 24 and n.45 (observing the "geometric growth in complexity" of comparative analysis as the number of jurisdictions grows).

[119] *See infra* Chapters 4–9.

# II Market-Dominant Small Jurisdictions (MDSJs)

# 3 | What Is an MDSJ?

CLOSE EXAMINATION OF Bermuda, Dubai, Singapore, Hong Kong, Switzerland, and Delaware reveals that, notwithstanding very real differences, they nevertheless exhibit distinctive geographic and cultural commonalities, have faced similar economic development challenges, and have sought to compete in cross-border finance in similar ways. In this part of the book I first set out an "ideal type" of "market-dominant small jurisdiction" (MDSJ), and then examine the degree to which the jurisdictions studied reflect the salient features of the MDSJ paradigm.

For the reader's convenience, the features of the ideal type described below, along with their principal consequences and certain related traits that tend to reinforce them, are summarized in Figure 3.1.

## A. An Ideal Type

All of the theoretical paradigms discussed above contribute to our understanding of how small jurisdictions compete in cross-border finance, yet none of them offers a fully compelling account. Here I build on each of them to develop an alternative—the MDSJ.

To refine the discussion that follows, I first set forth an "ideal type," adopting a mode of analysis well familiar to comparative sociologists. An "ideal type"

| Feature | Consequences | Reinforcement |
|---|---|---|
| *small population and land area, limited natural resources* | • limits development options<br>• credible legal/financial innovation | • dependence on cross-border finance for economic development |
| *legislative autonomy (though not necessarily sovereignty)* | • enables authoritative legal/financial innovation | • territorial financial regulation, incorporation, taxation |
| *cultural proximity, favorable geography vis-à-vis major powers* | • entrepôt/trade financial institutions<br>• regional/global "bridging" capacity | • multilingualism<br>• neutrality |
| *heavy investment in human capital, professional networks, institutions* | • fosters professional community to develop specialized services | • early-mover advantage<br>• accommodating immigration |
| *balancing collaboration with, and oversight of, financial community* | • private-sector regulatory input<br>• flexibility, stability, credibility | • low perceived corruption<br>• low political salience of finance |

FIGURE 3.1 Ideal Type of Market-Dominant Small Jurisdiction.

is essentially a form of archetype or paradigm that aims to express vividly certain consequential features of a social phenomenon that are pertinent to a given scholar's research interest. As Stephen Kalberg explains in his analysis of Max Weber's seminal work,[1] "ideal types aim neither to provide an exhaustive description of empirical reality nor to introduce general laws or theories." Rather, they "accentuate those aspects of the empirical case of particular interest to the researcher."[2] Although empirically grounded in their design, they reflect "conscious exaggeration of *essential* features of the significant action-orientations for the research task at hand." In this manner, an ideal type acknowledges the subjective limitations of the exercise while providing a coherent and empirically grounded "yardstick" or "standard" against which to take the measure of concrete cases, in turn permitting one to assess similarities and differences.[3] Put differently, an ideal type provides

---

[1] *See generally* MAX WEBER, ON THE METHODOLOGY OF THE SOCIAL SCIENCES 90–112 (Edward A. Shils & Henry A. Finch trans., Free Press 1949) (1904).

[2] STEPHEN KALBERG, MAX WEBER'S COMPARATIVE-HISTORICAL SOCIOLOGY 84–85 (1994). *See also* WEBER, *supra* note 1, at 90.

[3] KALBERG, *supra* note 2, at 86–88. *See also* WEBER, *supra* note 1, at 101. For examples of ideal-type analysis of "tax havens" and "small island territories," respectively, see RONEN PALAN, RICHARD MURPHY & CHRISTIAN CHAVAGNEUX, TAX HAVENS: HOW GLOBALIZATION REALLY WORKS 30–38 (2010); Godfrey Baldacchino, *Managing the Hinterland Beyond: Two Ideal-Type Strategies of Economic Development for Small Island Territories*, 47 ASIA PAC. VIEWPOINT 45 (2006).

an empirically grounded "terminology" permitting one to speak more coherently about a given social phenomenon[4]—in this case, a market phenomenon. Although the ultimate goal may be to identify "causal conditions," Weber himself emphasized that ideal types themselves cannot do more than facilitate the "the construction of hypotheses."[5]

What, then, do I regard as the central, consequential features of "market-dominant small jurisdictions"—that is, those small jurisdictions achieving global dominance in cross-border finance? Some reflect the historical, cultural, and geographic circumstances in which the given jurisdiction finds itself, whereas others reflect development strategies consciously pursued in light of those circumstances:[6]

- *MDSJs are small and poorly endowed with natural resources, limiting their economic-development options.* Although there is no generally accepted definition of a "small" jurisdiction,[7] in this context I speak relative to major economic powers. Accordingly, the fact that a given jurisdiction's population exceeds the global median[8] does not disqualify it; by "small" I mean "smaller," as opposed to "smallest."[9] The key is that, lacking the range of endowments and domestic market capacities available to major economic powers, such jurisdictions generally exhibit substantial outward orientation.[10] Among other things, this creates a strong incentive to innovate in

---

[4] KALBERG, *supra* note 2, at 87.

[5] WEBER, *supra* note 1, at 90–92.

[6] *See* Darryl S.L. Jarvis, *Race for the Money: International Financial Centres in Asia*, 14 J. INT'L REL. & DEV. 60, 82–83 (2011) (characterizing favorable geography as necessary but not sufficient in the absence of "a policy framework that encourages cross-border financial transactions").

[7] *See* Godfrey Baldacchino, *Governmentality Is All the Rage: The Strategy Games of Small Jurisdictions*, 101 ROUND TABLE 235, 238 (2012); Naren Prasad, *Small but Smart: Small States in the Global System*, in THE DIPLOMACIES OF SMALL STATES: BETWEEN VULNERABILITY AND RESILIENCE 41, 44 (Andrew F. Cooper & Timothy M. Shaw eds., 2009).

[8] Switzerland's population is approximately 8.1 million, Hong Kong's is approximately 7.1 million, and Singapore's is approximately 5.7 million, whereas the global median is approximately 5.4 million. CENTRAL INTELLIGENCE AGENCY, THE WORLD FACTBOOK: POPULATION, https://www.cia.gov/library/publications/the-world-factbook/rankorder/2119rank.html (last visited Apr. 2016).

[9] *Cf.* Godfrey Baldacchino, *The Power of Jurisdiction in Promoting Social Policies in Small States* 1 n.1 (U.N. Soc. Policy and Dev. Paper No. 45, 2011) ("It is worth considering whether the reference to 'smaller states' is preferable to 'small' in most (though not necessarily all) instances . . . .").

[10] *See, e.g.*, PALAN ET AL., *supra* note 3, at 184–85; Baldacchino, *supra* note 3, at 56; Craig M. Boise, *Regulating Tax Competition in Offshore Financial Centers*, in OFFSHORE FINANCIAL CENTERS AND REGULATORY COMPETITION 50, 62–63 (Andrew P. Morriss ed., 2010); Anna Manasco Dionne & Jonathan R. Macey, *Offshore Finance and Onshore Markets: Racing to the Bottom, or Moving toward Efficient?*, in OFFSHORE FINANCIAL CENTERS AND REGULATORY COMPETITION, *supra*, at 8, 22–23; Andrew P. Morriss, *The Role of Offshore Financial Centers in Regulatory Competition*, in OFFSHORE FINANCIAL CENTERS AND REGULATORY COMPETITION, *supra*, at 102, 130; Prasad, *supra* note 7, at 47.

law and finance, while simultaneously rendering credible their long-term commitment to legal and financial innovations undertaken.[11]

- *MDSJs possess legislative autonomy.* The sine qua non of legal and financial innovation, this capacity represents an MDSJ's critical resource.[12] Sovereigns such as Singapore and Switzerland straightforwardly possess legislative autonomy by reference to the so-called "reserved domain" of domestic jurisdiction. As Ian Brownlie explains, a "corollary of the independence and equality of states is the duty on the part of states to refrain from intervention in the internal or external affairs of other states."[13] Accordingly, the reserved domain amounts to "the domain of state activities where the jurisdiction of the state is not bound by international law."[14] Although the independence and equality of states would seem further to require that "municipal courts accept the validity of the acts of foreign states and their agents, including legislation,"[15] there is a countervailing principle of particular value to MDSJs—"the non-enforcement" in domestic courts of other jurisdictions' "penal or revenue laws."[16]

Critically, however, full-blown sovereignty is not required. Depending on the domain of activity, U.S. states such as Delaware may possess sufficient legislative autonomy under the Tenth Amendment to the U.S. Constitution, which provides that "powers not delegated to the United States by the Constitution, nor prohibited by it to the States, are reserved to the States."[17] Consequently, the scope of financial regulatory authority possessed by Delaware depends largely on the breadth of constitutional grants of such authority to the federal government itself—notably the commerce clause, giving Congress power to "regulate Commerce with foreign Nations, and among the several States" (a topic discussed further below).[18]

---

[11] *See, e.g.,* CALLY JORDAN, INTERNATIONAL CAPITAL MARKETS: LAW AND INSTITUTIONS 203–04 (2014); PALAN ET AL., *supra* note 3, at 184–85; Baldacchino, *supra* note 3, at 46; Dionne & Macey, *supra* note 10, at 22–23; Morriss, *supra* note 10, at 130–31; Scott A. Schumacher, *Magnifying Deterrence by Prosecuting Professionals* 10–11 (Univ. of Wash. Sch. of Law Legal Studies Research Paper No. 2013-17, 2013), http://ssrn.com/abstract=2243093.

[12] *See, e.g.,* WILLIAM BRITTAIN-CATLIN, OFFSHORE: THE DARK SIDE OF THE GLOBAL ECONOMY 37 (2005); PALAN ET AL., *supra* note 3, at 3, 8, 78–80, 185. *See also* Baldacchino, *supra* note 3, at 50–51.

[13] IAN BROWNLIE, PRINCIPLES OF PUBLIC INTERNATIONAL LAW 292 (7th ed. 2008).

[14] *Id.* at 293. As a consequence, Brownlie elaborates, "the extent of this domain depends on international law and varies according to its development." *Id.*

[15] *Id.* at 323.

[16] *Id.* at 324. *See also id.* at 323 n.6; Rose-Marie Belle Antoine, *The Legitimacy of the Offshore Financial Sector: A Legal Perspective, in* OFFSHORE FINANCIAL CENTERS AND REGULATORY COMPETITION, *supra* note 10, at 30, 33.

[17] U.S. CONST. amend. X.

[18] *Id.* art. I, § 8, cl. 3. *See also infra* Chapter 9.

Similarly Dubai, a UAE emirate, possesses substantial economic and financial policy autonomy through a combination of reserved powers and federal delegations.[19]

Other sub-sovereign jurisdictions, such as Bermuda and Hong Kong, may be granted legislative autonomy outright by act of a national legislative body. For Bermuda, an Overseas Territory of the United Kingdom, legislative autonomy derives from a broad U.K. delegation of authority.[20] For Hong Kong, a Special Administrative Region of China since 1997, legislative autonomy derives from Hong Kong's governing "Basic Law," which provides for "a high degree of autonomy" and establishes that "the previous capitalist system and way of life shall remain unchanged for 50 years."[21]

- *MDSJs are culturally proximate to multiple economic powers, and favorably situated geographically vis-à-vis those powers.* Whether such ties arise from colonialism, common histories, or purely by dint of geographic location, MDSJs have often served as way stations or entrepôts[22] along commercial trade routes of larger economies, leaving them predisposed toward the development of financial services and creating natural opportunities to add value in cross-border transactions.[23] At the same time, their simultaneous identification—and capacity to interact closely—with multiple political and economic powers positions them to perform important regional and global "bridging" functions in cross-border financial services.[24] In some cases such functions are enhanced by capacity to transact in multiple languages,[25] perhaps bolstered by a formal neutrality policy.

---

[19] *See infra* Chapter 5.A.

[20] *See* FOREIGN AND COMMONWEALTH OFFICE, THE OVERSEAS TERRITORIES: SECURITY, SUCCESS AND SUSTAINABILITY 14, 85 (June 2012).

[21] The Basic Law of the Hong Kong Special Administrative Region of the People's Republic of China (promulgated by Order No. 26 of the President, Apr. 4, 1990, effective July 1, 1997), arts. 2, 5 (China). *See also Some Facts about the Basic Law,* http://www.basiclaw.gov.hk/en/facts/index.html (last updated Mar. 17, 2008).

[22] *See* OXFORD ENGLISH DICTIONARY ONLINE, entrepôt, *n.,* 1.-2. ("A commercial centre; a place to which goods are brought for distribution to various parts of the world.").

[23] *See, e.g.,* PALAN ET AL., *supra* note 3, at 130–35, 140–41; Baldacchino, *supra* note 3, at 46; S. Corkill Cobb, *Global Finance and the Growth of Offshore Financial Centers: The Manx Experience,* 29 GEOFORUM 7, 14–15 (1998); Philip R. Lane & Gian Maria Milesi-Ferretti, *Cross-Border Investment in Small International Financial Centers* 8–11 (IMF Working Paper No. WP/10/38, 2010); Andrew K. Rose & Mark M. Spiegel, *Offshore Financial Centers: Parasites or Symbionts?* 6–7 (NBER Working Paper No. 12044, 2006).

[24] *Cf.* Saskia Sassen, *The Specialised Differences of Cities Matter in Today's Global Economy, in* REFORMING THE CITY: RESPONSES TO THE GLOBAL FINANCIAL CRISIS 209, 212 (Sam Whimster ed., 2009) (arguing that global cities perform such a function, reflecting their dual character as both regional and global sites).

[25] On potential economic advantages of multilingualism and associated ethnic ties, see generally Michael Anderson et al., *Ethnic Ties and Price Dispersion* (Oct. 2013); Jean-Louis Arcand & François Grin, *Language*

- *MDSJs heavily invest in human capital, professional networks, and related institutional structures.* The aim is to foster a financial professional community with the incentives and capacity to develop centers of specialization in cross-border finance.[26] This effort is often facilitated by early-mover advantages,[27] accommodating immigration regimes designed to attract foreign professional talent,[28] and the jurisdiction's small size—which tends to facilitate the development of consensus and policy adjustment in the face of changing market conditions.[29]

- *MDSJs consciously balance close collaboration with and robust oversight of the financial professional community, seeking at once to convey flexibility, stability, and credibility.* Over- and under-regulation, simply put, represent "Scylla and Charybdis" to small jurisdictions competing for cross-border financial business.[30]

Tax policy inevitably represents an important component of the overall regulatory package they offer, and MDSJs typically seek to balance attractive tax rates with adherence to cooperative tax enforcement initiatives. But tax policy alone will not suffice.[31] MDSJ governments aim more broadly

---

in *Economic Development: Is English Special and Is Linguistic Fragmentation Bad?* (2013), http://graduateinstitute.ch/files/live/sites/iheid/files/sites/international_economics/shared/international_economics/prof_websites/arcand/publications/LIED-7(3)-1.pdf; Teresa L. Cyrus, *Cultural Distance and Bilateral Trade,* 12 GLOBAL ECON. J. 1 (2012); Peter Egger & Andrew Lassman, *The Causal Impact of Common Native Language on International Trade: Evidence from a Spatial Regression Discontinuity Design* (Ctr. for Econ. Policy Research, Discussion Paper No. 9441, 2013); Alfred Lameli et al., *Same Same but Different: Dialects and Trade* (Ctr. for Econ. Studies & Ifo Inst. Working Paper No. 4245, 2013). *See also* JORDAN, *supra* note 11, at 202. This perspective contrasts sharply with studies emphasizing linguistic "fragmentation," which typically "conclude that societal multilingualism is detrimental to economic performance." Arcand & Grin, *supra,* at 6.

[26] *See, e.g.,* PALAN ET AL., *supra* note 3, at 12, 20, 100–04; Baldacchino, *supra* note 3, at 52–54; Cobb, *supra* note 23, at 14–18; Jarvis, *supra* note 6, at 65; Lane & Milesi-Ferretti, *supra* note 23, at 4–5. *See also* Dariusz Wójcik, *Where Governance Fails: Advanced Business Services and the Offshore World,* 37 HUM. GEOGRAPHY 330, 341 (2012) (arguing that financial power in fact resides with professional providers of "advanced business services," as opposed to the jurisdictions they inhabit).

[27] *See, e.g.,* Jarvis, *supra* note 6, at 85. On early-mover advantages in the business context, see DAVID BESANKO ET AL., ECONOMICS OF STRATEGY 465–76 (2000).

[28] *See, e.g.,* CHRISTOPHER BICKLEY, BERMUDA, BRITISH VIRGIN ISLANDS AND CAYMAN ISLANDS COMPANY LAW x (4th ed. 2013).

[29] *See, e.g.,* JORDAN, *supra* note 11, at 203–04. *Cf.* Robert O. Keohane, *The Big Influence of Small Allies,* FOREIGN POL'Y, No. 2, Spring 1971, at 161, 162–63 (characterizing small states' ability "to concentrate on a narrow range of vital interests" as a bargaining strength in international relations).

[30] Tony Freyer & Andrew P. Morriss, *Creating Cayman as an Offshore Financial Center: Structure & Strategy since 1960* at 4 (Sept. 22, 2013), http://ssrn.com/abstract=2329827.

[31] *See* Dhammika Dharmapala, *What Problems and Opportunities Are Created by Tax Havens?,* 24 OXFORD REV. ECON. POL'Y 661, 665 (2008); Dhammika Dharmapala & James R. Hines, Jr., *Which Countries Become Tax Havens?,* 93 J. PUB. ECON. 1058, 1065–66 (2009); Dionne & Macey, *supra* note 10, at 16.

to bring private-sector insights and experience to bear upon the creation, maintenance, and marketing of cutting-edge regulatory regimes in high value-added areas of cross-border financial services, while at the same time conveying stability and credibility to global markets and their foreign regulatory counterparts.[32]

The effort to maintain this delicate balance typically manifests itself throughout the regulatory state and policymaking process. MDSJs exhibit low levels of perceived public corruption, cultivating trust among market actors and foreign regulatory counterparts alike.[33] At the same time, they endeavor to minimize the salience of cross-border finance—in both domestic politics and diplomacy—to bolster confidence in market stability. In domestic politics this may take the form of multiparty support for development of the financial center, and in international relations this may take the form of cooperative participation in global standard-setting efforts. In each context, such efforts reflect the MDSJ's substantial dependence upon cross-border finance in the pursuit of economic-development goals.[34]

Although the MDSJ concept clearly exhibits commonalities with the alternative frameworks described above, it just as clearly differs from them in important respects. Critically, by focusing on those jurisdictions achieving market dominance in cross-border financial services, the MDSJ concept directs attention to a category of jurisdictions narrower than those explored by the alternatives. Accordingly, a given jurisdiction might well fit the prevailing conception of a "tax haven," an "OFC," a "microstate," or a "global city," yet not fall within the MDSJ category that I envision. Important examples include those jurisdictions that have excessively relied on tax competition and financial secrecy to the detriment of real, value-added service orientation. As I explore in Chapter 10, this renders such jurisdictions highly vulnerable,

---

[32] *See, e.g.,* BICKLEY, *supra* note 28, at ix–x; Cobb, *supra* note 23, at 13–14; Dharmapala, *supra* note 31, at 665. *See also* BRITTAIN-CATLIN, *supra* note 12, at 9–10; PALAN ET AL., *supra* note 3, at 12; Michael J. Burns & James McConvill, *An Unstoppable Force: The Offshore World in a Modern Global Economy*, 7 HASTINGS BUS. L.J. 205, 207, 211–12, 219–20 (2011); Morriss, *supra* note 10, at 131–32.

[33] *See* Martha Harris Myron, *The Craft of Creating a Lasting Reputation*, ROYAL GAZETTE, Sept. 21, 2013, http://www.royalgazette.com/article/20130921/COLUMN07/130929952. *See also* Lynn Sharp Paine & Christopher M. Bruner, *Bribery in Business: A Legal Perspective* 1–2 (Harv. Bus. Sch. case no. 9-306-012, 2006); Shang-Jin Wei, *How Taxing Is Corruption on International Investors?*, LXXXII REV. ECON. & STAT. 1, 4–8 (2000).

[34] *See, e.g.,* WILLIAM W. BOYER & EDWARD C. RATLEDGE, DELAWARE POLITICS AND GOVERNMENT 27, 66–69 (2009); Morriss, *supra* note 10, at 131. *See also* SWITZERLAND TRADE & INVESTMENT PROMOTION, HANDBOOK FOR INVESTORS: BUSINESS LOCATION IN SWITZERLAND 13–15, 25 (Apr. 2012 ed.); ORGANISATION FOR ECONOMIC CO-OPERATION AND DEVELOPMENT, THE GLOBAL FORUM ON TRANSPARENCY AND EXCHANGE OF INFORMATION FOR TAX PURPOSES 2 (Apr. 16, 2012).

leading to poor performance as financial centers in the long run. Accordingly, such jurisdictions could aptly be described as "tax havens"—understood to include minimally those jurisdictions relying heavily on low taxes and financial secrecy, with little else to offer—yet clearly could not be described as MDSJs.

In this light, it bears emphasizing that the MDSJ concept does not purport to render these other concepts redundant. Nor, for that matter, does it purport to embrace the universe of circumstances and incentives that might lead a given jurisdiction to seek to compete in cross-border finance.[35] I do, however, argue that the MDSJ concept more comfortably embraces a seemingly disparate category of small jurisdictions achieving prominence in this field than any of the alternatives. The MDSJ concept avoids the exclusive focus on tax embedded within the tax haven concept, transcends the jurisdictional limitations of the microstate and global city concepts, and rejects the artificial geographic distinction drawn between offshore and onshore financial centers.

Of the alternatives canvassed above, the characteristics that I associate with MDSJs most closely resemble those associated with OFCs, but there are important distinctions. Although similarly focusing on small jurisdictions with limited resources turning to financial and legal innovation as a means of attracting cross-border financial activity, the OFC literature places greater emphasis on "relatively new" entrants to this form of regulatory competition,[36] reflecting these commentators' strong focus upon the global acceleration of cross-border financial activity since the late 1960s.[37] Less preoccupied with recent history, the MDSJ concept accordingly remains more open to a broader historical inquiry,[38] and thus more easily accommodates long-standing competitors in cross-border finance—including Switzerland and Delaware. The MDSJ concept's breadth is reinforced by its abandonment of the artificial offshore/onshore distinction, permitting fuller recognition of the degree to which characteristics and competitive strategies popularly associated with far-flung tropical islands manifest themselves squarely within the

---

[35] Aside from efforts of the United States and other major economic powers to attract cross-border finance, see *infra* Chapters 9–11, various jurisdictions partially (though not fully) resembling the MDSJ concept do so as well—a prime example being Alaska's effort to compete in the area of asset protection trusts. *See* Jocelyn Margolin Borowsky & Richard W. Nenno, *A Comparison of the Leading Trust Jurisdictions*, 37 BNA TAX MGM'T EST., GIFTS & TR. J. 233 (2012), http://www.duanemorris.com/articles/static/borowsky_taxmg-mtjrnl_0712.pdf; Robert T. Danforth, *Rethinking the Law of Creditors' Rights in Trusts*, 53 HASTINGS L.J. 287, 312–15 (2002); Duncan E. Osborne & Mark E. Osborne, *Asset Protection Trust Planning*, SU002 ALI-CLE 1, pt. IV.B.1 (2013). Although Alaska is the largest U.S. state in area, it is among the smallest in population. *See Population of USA States*, WORLDATLAS.COM, http://www.worldatlas.com/aatlas/populations/usapoptable.htm (last visited Apr. 2016) (providing state populations and land areas).

[36] *See* Morriss, *supra* note 10, at 131.

[37] *See supra* Chapter 2.B.ii, 2.C.

[38] In this respect, the MDSJ approach resembles the tax haven literature. *See supra* Chapter 2.B.i.

major economic powers of Europe and North America themselves—again, including Switzerland and Delaware. Additionally, the MDSJ concept places greater emphasis on the cultural and geographic "bridging" functions performed by such jurisdictions, a unique capacity to add value in cross-border financial activity exemplified in various ways by each of the core jurisdictions studied in this book.[39]

## B. Comparative Methods

Notwithstanding the real advantages of the approach described above, its methodological limitations must be acknowledged. To suggest that these jurisdictions represent a "type" is to imply a typology of multiple types—minimally, contrasting with those jurisdictions that are not "small" and/or not "market-dominant" in the relevant respects.[40] Such contrasts are implicitly drawn, but not developed, in Part II of the book.

Limiting the analysis exclusively to jurisdictions that are both "small" and "market-dominant" in the pertinent respects, however, would amount to selection upon the dependent variable, precluding strong causal claims.[41] To be sure, the analysis provided in Part II does permit pursuit of more modest claims as a preliminary matter. As political scientist Barbara Geddes observes, "cases selected on the dependent variable" remain "important as generators of insights and hypotheses." She elaborates:

> They are ideal for digging into the details of how phenomena come about and for developing insights. They identify plausible causal variables. They bring to light anomalies that current theories cannot accommodate. In so doing, they contribute to building and revising theories.[42]

This effectively outlines the task undertaken in Part II of the book. Bermuda, Dubai, Singapore, Hong Kong, Switzerland, and Delaware plainly differ in their respective geographies, cultural affinities, economic spheres, financial specializations, regulatory postures, and legal traditions. Yet, as analysis through the MDSJ lens demonstrates, all exhibit strikingly similar suites of cultural and geographic circumstances,

---

[39] In this respect, the MDSJ approach resembles the global cities literature. *See supra* Chapter 2.B.iii.

[40] *Cf.* David Collier et al., *Putting Typologies to Work: Concept Formation, Measurement, and Analytic Rigor,* 65 POL. RES. Q. 217, 218, 222–23 (2012) (describing "conceptual typologies" by reference to a table in which "the rows and columns in the typology" reflect an explored concept's various "dimensions").

[41] *See* Barbara Geddes, *How the Cases You Choose Affect the Answers You Get: Selection Bias in Comparative Politics,* 2 POL. ANALYSIS 131, 132–34, 140 (1990).

[42] *Id.* at 149.

competitive strengths, and development strategies not comfortably accommodated by extant theoretical lenses.

Part III, however, pushes the analysis further. The book concludes with a broader mode of comparative analysis, building upon the identification of commonalities among the MDSJs studied through comparison of this category of jurisdictions with others that are not "small" and/or not "market-dominant" (Chapter 10). The first category of comparisons tends to bolster the explanatory power of the MDSJ concept to the extent that their failures correspond with deviations from the ideal type described above, whereas the second category of comparisons helps illuminate the boundaries of my explanatory domain by revealing the degree to which the characteristics and strategies that I associate with MDSJs are in fact peculiar to such jurisdictions.

# 4 Bermuda

SETTLED IN 1609 by shipwrecked colonists en route from England to Virginia,[1] Bermuda has long represented a mid-Atlantic waypoint between England and America. Although an Overseas Territory of the United Kingdom (the oldest, in fact),[2] Bermuda remains closely linked to the United States economically. Indeed, the Bermudian dollar is pegged (1:1) to the U.S. dollar.[3]

Notwithstanding its inauspicious origins, remote location, limited domestic economy, and lack of natural resources, this mid-Atlantic island group has managed to develop one of the world's largest and most important centers for insurance and risk management. How did tiny Bermuda achieve this significant, and surprising, success? As this chapter explores, Bermuda has cultivated and managed a unique suite of geographic, cultural, economic, and legal characteristics and strengths in

---

[1] *See* CHRISTOPHER BICKLEY, BERMUDA, BRITISH VIRGIN ISLANDS AND CAYMAN ISLANDS COMPANY LAW 3 (4th ed. 2013); BUSINESS BERMUDA, BUSINESS BERMUDA REVIEW 2012, at 20 (2012); CENTRAL INTELLIGENCE AGENCY, THE WORLD FACTBOOK: BERMUDA, https://www.cia.gov/library/publications/the-world-factbook/geos/bd.html (last updated Apr. 26, 2016). The episode is thought to have inspired William Shakespeare's *The Tempest. See* BICKLEY, *supra*, at 3 n.2; BUSINESS BERMUDA, *supra*, at 20.

[2] *See* BICKLEY, *supra* note 1, at 3; BUSINESS BERMUDA, *supra* note 1, at 19; CENTRAL INTELLIGENCE AGENCY, *supra* note 1.

[3] *See* CENTRAL INTELLIGENCE AGENCY, *supra* note 1. *See also* BICKLEY, *supra* note 1, at 4; Standard & Poor's Ratings Services, *Supplementary Analysis: Bermuda,* June 3, 2015 (dating the peg to 1981).

order to establish itself as a dominant player in global insurance markets—a process exemplifying the MDSJ economic development strategy.

## A. Bridging the Atlantic

Bermuda clearly exhibits a number of core attributes associated with the MDSJ concept. Bermuda is very small; the estimated population of 70,196 (as of July 2015) occupies an island group totaling just 54 square kilometers (roughly one-third the size of Washington, DC) providing only very limited natural resources—indeed, they are fortunate to receive "ample rainfall," as they have "no rivers or freshwater lakes."[4] Notwithstanding its small population and lack of resources, however, Bermuda has achieved extraordinary economic successes through concerted efforts to develop a vibrant professional services sector.

Bermuda's 2013 per capita GDP of $85,700 placed them number six in the world, and as of 2016 they had "the fourth highest per capita income in the world, about 70 percent higher than that of the US"—a position achieved principally through services, estimated to account for over 93 percent of GDP in 2015.[5] Financial services—particularly insurance-related services directed toward North American markets—have loomed very large in Bermuda's economy,[6] an orientation reflected in the fact that "75 percent of the Fortune 100 and their European equivalents" have subsidiaries in Bermuda.[7] Indeed, it has been estimated that "international financial services" amounted to "about 25 percent of the country's nominal GDP in 2013," but that this figure "substantially understates the Bermudian economy's reliance on the sector, as it is essentially limited to the employment income of residents working in the sector" (and accordingly does not account for the "indirect impact" of the sector's expenditures there).[8] Bermuda's AA- credit rating was placed on negative outlook by Standard & Poor's in March 2013 due to post-crisis economic "contraction,"

---

[4] See CENTRAL INTELLIGENCE AGENCY, *supra* note 1. According to the CIA's *World Factbook*, Bermuda ranks 204th globally in population and 232nd in area, falling well below the median in both (approximately 5.4 million people and approximately 57,000 square kilometers, respectively). *See* CENTRAL INTELLIGENCE AGENCY, THE WORLD FACTBOOK: POPULATION, https://www.cia.gov/library/publications/the-world-factbook/rankorder/2119rank.html (last visited Apr. 2016); CENTRAL INTELLIGENCE AGENCY, THE WORLD FACTBOOK: AREA, https://www.cia.gov/library/publications/the-world-factbook/rankorder/2147rank.html (last visited Apr. 2016). *See also* BICKLEY, *supra* note 1, at 3; BUSINESS BERMUDA, *supra* note 1, at 20; FOREIGN AND COMMONWEALTH OFFICE, THE OVERSEAS TERRITORIES: SECURITY, SUCCESS AND SUSTAINABILITY 92 (June 2012).

[5] CENTRAL INTELLIGENCE AGENCY, *supra* note 1. *See also* BUSINESS BERMUDA, *supra* note 1, at 22.

[6] *See* BICKLEY, *supra* note 1, at 3–4; CENTRAL INTELLIGENCE AGENCY, *supra* note 1.

[7] FOREIGN AND COMMONWEALTH OFFICE, *supra* note 4, at 92. *See also* BICKLEY, *supra* note 1, at 3–4.

[8] Standard & Poor's Ratings Services, *supra* note 3.

although S&P added that their strong rating remained "supported by our view of the country's ongoing achievements in attracting and retaining foreign financial services companies (largely reinsurance)."[9] In 2015 S&P in fact lowered Bermuda's rating to A+, reflecting "continuing weak economic performance and weak public finances," while adding that their "stable outlook reflects . . . expectations that positive economic growth will return in the next two years."[10]

Although Bermuda possesses clear legislative autonomy, the United Kingdom maintains formal sovereignty—a constitutional reality rendering the U.K. posture toward Bermuda paramount in evaluating their competitive position in cross-border finance.[11] As the U.K. Foreign and Commonwealth Office explained in a 2012 report on the Overseas Territories, "[a]s a matter of constitutional law the UK Parliament has unlimited power to legislate," but this authority has been "devolved to the elected governments of the Territories to the maximum extent possible consistent with the UK retaining those powers necessary to discharge its sovereign responsibilities."[12] As a sub-sovereign, Bermuda requires U.K. permission to enter treaties, which it has received in the form of a "general entrustment" providing latitude "to engage with regional organisations and governments across a range of issues."[13] Bermuda has its own Supreme Court (discussed below), but the Judicial Committee of the Privy Council remains "their final court of appeal in both civil and criminal matters."[14]

The Overseas Territories maintain their U.K. affiliations by choice—because they find it advantageous to do so. "Any decision to sever the constitutional link between the UK and a Territory," the Foreign and Commonwealth Office explains, "should be on the basis of the clear and constitutionally expressed wish of the people of the Territory"[15]—a step the people of Bermuda have expressly declined to take, rejecting independence in a 1995 referendum.[16] This suggests that the relationship remains a mutually beneficial one, and that is certainly how the United Kingdom describes it.

---

[9] Standard & Poor's Ratings Services, *Bermuda Outlook Revised to Negative on Higher Economic, Fiscal, and Banking-Sector Risks; "AA-/A-1+" Ratings Affirmed,* Mar. 28, 2013.

[10] Standard & Poor's Ratings Services, *Bermuda Ratings Lowered to "A+" from "AA-" as Weak Economic Performance Continues; Outlook Stable,* Apr. 29, 2015.

[11] *See* TAX JUSTICE NETWORK, NARRATIVE REPORT ON UNITED KINGDOM 5–8 (2015).

[12] FOREIGN AND COMMONWEALTH OFFICE, *supra* note 4, at 14. Britain's Overseas Territories steadily gained legislative autonomy following World War II. *See* Tony Freyer & Andrew P. Morriss, *Creating Cayman as an Offshore Financial Center: Structure & Strategy since 1960,* at 3–4 (Sept. 22, 2013), http://ssrn.com/abstract=2329827.

[13] FOREIGN AND COMMONWEALTH OFFICE, *supra* note 4, at 85.

[14] *Id.* at 54. *See also* BICKLEY, *supra* note 1, at 5.

[15] FOREIGN AND COMMONWEALTH OFFICE, *supra* note 4, at 15.

[16] *See* CENTRAL INTELLIGENCE AGENCY, *supra* note 1.

The United Kingdom provides aid and defense to Bermuda and the other Territories, lending them greater economic and strategic stability than they could muster on their own.[17] At the same time the United Kingdom bolsters its "global presence," while benefiting from financial services activities in the Territories thought to be "complementary" to those in London, given the Territories' linkages with "fast growing markets in Asia and the Americas."[18] Robust financial services in Bermuda and other Territories further benefit the United Kingdom by permitting them to achieve greater self-sufficiency.[19] Accordingly, although the United Kingdom has called for strong financial regulation, it has done so primarily as a means of fostering international financial centers in the Territories[20]—and the U.K. government expressly defends their capacity to compete in cross-border finance, including through taxation.[21] In this light it is unsurprising that Prime Minister David Cameron has "push[ed] for beneficial ownership registries for the UK, the Crown Dependencies and the Overseas Territories," but at the same time has "rejected the 'tax haven' label."[22] The fact that "Britain's self-governing overseas territories, especially the British Virgin Islands, proved a favored location for companies" revealed by the Panama Papers[23] has led some to call for a requirement that these jurisdictions' registries be publicly accessible (as contemplated for the United Kingdom itself), but as of this writing the U.K. government has indicated that it remains content with their agreement "to set up central registries of beneficial ownership that would be open to law enforcement agencies." These efforts, the U.K. government observed, already compared quite favorably with the lack of beneficial ownership registries among U.S. states active in corporate formations.[24]

---

[17] *See* FOREIGN AND COMMONWEALTH OFFICE, *supra* note 4, at 14. *See also* Godfrey Baldacchino, *Managing the Hinterland Beyond: Two Ideal-Type Strategies of Economic Development for Small Island Territories*, 47 ASIA PAC. VIEWPOINT 45, 49–50 (2006); Godfrey Baldacchino, *Governmentality Is All the Rage: The Strategy Games of Small Jurisdictions*, 101 ROUND TABLE 235, 239–41 (2012); Godfrey Baldacchino, *The Power of Jurisdiction in Promoting Social Policies in Small States* 14–15 (U.N. Soc. Policy and Dev. Paper No. 45, 2011).

[18] FOREIGN AND COMMONWEALTH OFFICE, *supra* note 4, at 13.

[19] *See id.* at 5, 8, 32–33, 36. *See also* Freyer & Morriss, *supra* note 12, at 15, 26.

[20] *See* FOREIGN AND COMMONWEALTH OFFICE, *supra* note 4, at 6, 9, 58.

[21] *See id.* at 32, 58, 60–61. *See also* Freyer & Morriss, *supra* note 12, at 52.

[22] Andrew Morriss, *The End of Offshoring?*, ACCOUNTANCY, Sept. 2014, at 49, 49–50. *See also* Letter from Prime Minister David Cameron to the Overseas Territories (Apr. 25, 2014), https://www.gov.uk/government/publications/prime-ministers-letter-on-beneficial-ownership/prime-ministers-letter-to-the-overseas-territories-on-beneficial-ownership.

[23] Steven Erlanger et al., *Iceland's Prime Minister Steps Down amid Panama Papers Scandal*, N.Y. TIMES, Apr. 5, 2016, http://www.nytimes.com/2016/04/06/world/europe/panama-papers-iceland.html.

[24] Patrick Wintour, *Overseas Territories Spared from UK Law on Company Registers*, GUARDIAN, Apr. 12, 2016, http://www.theguardian.com/business/2016/apr/12/overseas-territories-spared-from-uk-law-on-company-registers. *See also infra* Chapters 9, 11.

As a practical matter, this arrangement leaves Bermuda relatively free of direct pressure from the U.K. government, while providing the ballast of association with the sophisticated and highly developed English legal system. Under the Supreme Court Act 1905, Bermuda applies "the common law, the doctrines of equity, and the Acts of the Parliament of England of general application" in force as of July 11, 1612 (i.e., the date of settlement), unless modified by subsequent Bermuda legislation.[25] The Bermuda Supreme Court has elaborated that, although not literally binding, U.K. Supreme Court opinions "will as a general rule be followed by a court in Bermuda" unless "local conditions dictate a path different from that charted by the House of Lords"—an approach partly reflecting the view that appeal to the Privy Council would be pointless given the Privy Council's "common membership" with the U.K. Supreme Court.[26]

Bermudians have long been aware of the substantial advantages that their geographic, cultural, and historical proximity to major north-Atlantic powers provide, emphasizing the benefits associated with Bermuda's relative proximity to both the United Kingdom and North America. A 2012 "Business Bermuda" marketing piece states that "its close proximity to North America and easy access from the UK" render Bermuda "quite possibly one of the world's most convenient destinations," adding that "more than 75 percent of the Fortune 500 companies have set up businesses here."[27] The piece includes a contribution from Henry Bellingham, U.K. Minister for the Overseas Territories, underscoring "the relationship between Bermuda and the UK, now over 400 years old," and the strong insurance ties between the jurisdictions—Bermuda being viewed "as a partner—not a competitor— to Lloyds of London," for which "Bermuda-based reinsurers provide 25 percent of premiums."[28] The piece also includes a contribution from Grace Shelton, U.S. Consul General to Bermuda, stating that Bermuda and the United States are "close geographical neighbours" sharing "the same language, culture and values." She emphasizes the flow of goods and tourists from the United States, and the flow of financial services from Bermuda, representing "the leading foreign source of insurance and reinsurance services to the United States." As Shelton sums it up, "Bermuda is conveniently close to US financial and capital markets"; its "laws and regulations are compatible with the United States; its final legal recourse is with the Privy Council

---

[25] Supreme Court Act 1905, 1905:4, § 15 (Berm.). *See also* P.T. O'NEILL & J.W. WOLONIECKI, THE LAW OF REINSURANCE IN ENGLAND AND BERMUDA 23 (2d ed. 2004).

[26] In the Matter of Saad Investments Company Limited, [2013] SC (Bda) 28 Com (15 Apr. 2013), paras. 19–28. *See also* O'NEILL & WOLONIECKI, *supra* note 25, at 23–24; *The Judicial Committee*, https://www.jcpc. uk/about/judicial-committe.html (last visited Apr. 2016); *The Supreme Court: Appellate Committee of The House of Lords*, https://www.supremecourt.uk/about/appellate-committee.html (last visited Apr. 2016).

[27] BUSINESS BERMUDA, *supra* note 1, at 100 (contribution from William Griffith, Director of Tourism, Government of Bermuda).

[28] *Id.* at 27.

in London; . . . its regulatory regime . . . is well respected; its infrastructure is first class; and its pool of human talent is innovative and experienced."[29]

Not surprisingly, the professional community and the government alike have aggressively marketed Bermuda's substantial investment in human and institutional capital catering to cross-border finance, as well as the development of a competitive regulatory regime in close coordination with the private sector. Indeed, a strong "brand" consciousness pervades these efforts.[30] As Paula Cox, Premier and Minister of Finance, explains in the aforementioned marketing piece, Bermuda's "country wide 'At your Service' attitude enables us to offer less red tape and more red carpet."[31] Bermuda is indeed home to an extraordinary concentration of financial services professionals, "including on a per capita basis the largest number of chartered financial analysts in the world."[32]

This orientation toward cross-border finance renders Bermuda vulnerable to charges of harmful regulatory competition. Accordingly, they walk a fine line in presenting their financial regulatory regime as "flexible" yet "strong."[33] The endeavor, as we will find with other MDSJs, is to convey business-friendly capacity to innovate, on the one hand, and legitimacy and stability, on the other—a complex message aiming to attract cross-border finance while at the same time mitigating regulatory concerns. As one Bermuda press commentator expressed it, "Bermuda wants to increase international business, but we can never, even by implication, send a message that Bermuda will do business at any cost." The analysis adds that "we must continue to increase, refine, and upgrade our compliance procedures, anti-money laundering laws, corruption prevention, and good corporate governance legislation."[34] In this light, it is hardly surprising that Bermudians would tout their "low-corruption country score" from Transparency International, which "is right up there next to the United States, France, Canada, and the United Kingdom."[35]

---

[29] *Id.* at 29–30.

[30] *See, e.g., id.* at 13. *See also* J.C. SHARMAN, HAVENS IN A STORM: THE STRUGGLE FOR GLOBAL TAX REGULATION 112–14, 123 (2006).

[31] BUSINESS BERMUDA, *supra* note 1, at 11. *See also id.* at 46 (contribution from Jessel Mendes of Ernst & Young Ltd.).

[32] *Id.* at 39 (contribution from Nir Sadeh of N.T. Butterfield & Son Limited).

[33] *See* Erica Robinson-McLeod, *Bermuda Reinsurance Market—Recent Trends,* IFC CARIBBEAN REV. 2012, at 53, 54. *See also* BUSINESS BERMUDA, *supra* note 1, at 11, 31, 39, 45–46, 52 (contributions from various public- and private-sector leaders); Ross Webber, *Bermuda Is a No-Brainer for Captives,* CAPTIVE REV., Mar. 2015, at 44, 45.

[34] *See* Martha Harris Myron, *The Craft of Creating a Lasting Reputation,* ROYAL GAZETTE, Sept. 21, 2013, http://www.royalgazette.com/article/20130921/COLUMN07/130929952.

[35] *Id. See also* Transparency International, *Corruption by Country/Territory: Bermuda,* http://www.transparency.org/country#BMU (last visited Apr. 2016). Transparency International is "a non-profit, non-governmental organisation dedicated to fighting corruption." *See* Transparency International, *FAQs on Transparency International: What Does Transparency International Do?,* http://www.transparency.org/

A legal structure exemplifying Bermuda's dual marketing aim is the "Private Act" process, which permits "the general laws of Bermuda to be tailored to the needs of a particular institution." For example, in the 1980s and 1990s Hong Kong corporate groups establishing Bermuda holding companies for listing applied for and received one-off exemptions from then-existing requirements regarding Bermuda-resident directors. These Private Acts ultimately led to broader changes in Bermuda's Companies Act—a development suggesting that "the Private Act procedure in the 1990s essentially became the testing ground for new or innovative regulation."[36] Similar dynamics would unfold with "segregated portfolio legislation," which "extend[s] the concept of limited liability of a company to certain of its assets"—an innovation of significance to Bermuda's insurance industry, as discussed below.[37]

To be sure, Bermuda has competed aggressively in taxation as well. The aforementioned marketing piece emphasizes that Bermuda has "no corporate or capital gains taxes," and income-based taxes are "limited to a payroll tax of 14 percent on a tranche of income earned on the island"—a principal revenue source for Bermuda, along with "import duties and a wide range of consumption-based and real estate taxes."[38] Christopher Bickley elaborates that Bermuda "levies no tax on its offshore companies based upon profits, income, gains or appreciations," adding that "there is no taxation in the nature of inheritance tax or estate duty in respect of the shares of such companies." Bermuda even offers "procedures whereby applications can be made for express undertakings that a vehicle will not be taxed for a period of time from the date of the undertaking"—currently extending until 2035—"even if such taxing legislation were to be enacted."[39]

---

whoweare/organisation/faqs_on_transparency_international/2/ (last visited Apr. 2016). Note, however, that Bermuda does not appear in the Corruption Perceptions Index. As Transparency International explains, "to be included in the ranking, [a country/territory] must be included in a minimum of three of the CPI's data sources." Transparency International, *What Is the Corruption Perceptions Index?*, http://cpi. transparency.org/cpi2012/in_detail/ (last visited Apr. 2016).

[36] BICKLEY, *supra* note 1, at ix–x.

[37] *See id.* at x, 393; *infra* Chapter 4.B.

[38] BUSINESS BERMUDA, *supra* note 1, at 22. *See also* Standard & Poor's Ratings Services, *supra* note 3 (" . . . Bermuda has none of the conventional significant tax levers available to it, such as income . . . and sales taxes. Almost 40 percent of revenue comes from payroll taxes . . . ; about 20 percent from customs duties; and the rest from various other sources, including company fees, land taxes and stamp duties, vehicle license fees and taxes on hotel occupancy, passenger departures, and a small foreign currency purchase tax. . . .").

[39] BICKLEY, *supra* note 1, at x–xi, 17. *See also* BUSINESS BERMUDA, *supra* note 1, at 72–73 (contribution from David Cooke and Jason Piney of Conyers, Dill & Pearman); Standard & Poor's Ratings Services, *supra* note 3 (describing "Bermuda's recently renewed Exempted Undertakings Tax Protection Amendment Act 2011, which extends to 2035," permitting the Minister of Finance "to assure international companies operating from Bermuda that, were Bermuda ever to introduce certain types of taxes . . . these would not apply to them").

As a small mid-Atlantic island jurisdiction, it is hardly surprising that Bermuda would favor import duties and the like; given their low public expenses and the relative ease of monitoring their port, such measures provide a more efficient means of raising revenue than income-based taxes, which involve "extensive printing, reporting, auditing, and recordkeeping requirements."[40] By the same token, it is hardly surprising that Bermuda's success in attracting cross-border financial activity, coupled with its competitive tax regime, would lead the OECD to brand Bermuda a "tax haven."[41] Bermuda sought to shed the associated stigma through the 2000s, mainly by entering into a sufficient number of tax information exchange agreements and participating in the OECD's "Global Forum on Transparency and Exchange of Information for Tax Purposes." In June 2009 Bermuda "proudly announced . . . that it had made it on to the OECD's white list of benign tax regimes."[42]

Today Bermudians vocally reject the offshore/onshore distinction—suggesting that it is "perhaps a more significant distinction to differentiate between well regulated and poorly run financial centres"[43]—and, as noted above, aim to market a balanced regulatory posture[44] to convey legitimacy and stability to the marketplace while deflecting criticisms from foreign regulators. Although lacking a sovereign's total control over foreign policy, their ties to the United Kingdom nevertheless reinforce the desired image by association with British legal and financial institutions. Cox nicely summarizes Bermuda's suite of competitive characteristics in emphasizing efforts "to provide a strong advanced infrastructure; a strong regulatory system; and the very best in human capital"—an approach "enhanced by [Bermuda's] geography and accessibility to the major markets of the world," as well as the government's cooperative relationship with "experienced industry professionals."[45]

---

[40] Craig M. Boise, *Regulating Tax Competition in Offshore Financial Centers*, *in* OFFSHORE FINANCIAL CENTERS AND REGULATORY COMPETITION 50, 62–63 (Andrew P. Morriss ed., 2010).

[41] *See* Organisation for Economic Co-operation and Development, *List of Unco-operative Tax Havens*, http://www.oecd.org/countries/monaco/listofunco-operativetaxhavens.htm (last visited Apr. 2016); Organisation for Economic Co-operation and Development, *Jurisdictions Committed to Improving Transparency and Establishing Effective Exchange of Information in Tax Matters*, http://www.oecd.org/countries/monaco/jurisdictionscommittedtoimprovingtransparencyandestablishingeffectiveexchangeofinformationintaxmatters.htm (last visited Apr. 2016).

[42] *See Britain's Offshore Financial Centres Race for Respectability*, ECONOMIST, June 18, 2009, http://www.economist.com/node/13863399/print. *See also* ORGANISATION FOR ECONOMIC CO-OPERATION AND DEVELOPMENT, THE GLOBAL FORUM ON TRANSPARENCY AND EXCHANGE OF INFORMATION FOR TAX PURPOSES 2 (Apr. 16, 2012).

[43] *See, e.g.*, BUSINESS BERMUDA, *supra* note 1, at 42 (quoting Mary K. Duke of HSBC Bank Bermuda Ltd).

[44] *See supra* note 33 and accompanying text.

[45] BUSINESS BERMUDA, *supra* note 1, at 11.

This aim to create what Anna Manasco Dionne and Jonathan Macey describe as a "complete alternative market"[46] is exemplified by Bermuda's predominance in insurance-related services, rendering the mid-Atlantic island group (in Cox's words) "the risk capital of the world."[47]

## B. (Re)Insurance and "Captives"

Although actively competing in a number of areas of cross-border finance,[48] Bermuda has achieved its greatest successes in the insurance industry. In addition to primary insurance, Bermuda's insurance industry includes "reinsurance"— essentially insurance for insurers[49]—as well as "captive" insurance—essentially a sophisticated form of self-insurance of a parent company through a subsidiary in-surer.[50] Bermuda now represents "the third largest insurance market in the world,"[51] with total assets of $524 billion in 2011.[52] By the end of 2013 "there were more than 1,200 active insurance companies in Bermuda," and "their total assets were US$505 billion at year-end 2012 and their gross premiums total more than US$120 billion."[53] Bermuda "is now considered the second biggest re-insurance market in the world after New York,"[54] and "the largest global captive domicile,"[55] with captive assets exceeding $80 billion in 2012.[56] S&P reports that "Bermuda reinsurers represent

---

[46] *See* Anna Manasco Dionne & Jonathan R. Macey, *Offshore Finance and Onshore Markets: Racing to the Bottom, or Moving toward Efficient?, in* Offshore Financial Centers and Regulatory Competition, *supra* note 40, at 8, 16.

[47] Business Bermuda, *supra* note 1, at 11.

[48] *See, e.g.,* Business Bermuda, *supra* note 1, at 37, 45, 52–53 (contributions from various private-sector leaders); Mary G. Zephirin & Jorge Chan-Lau, Bermuda: Assessment of Financial Sector Supervision and Regulation 8–10 (IMF Country Report No. 08/336, 2008).

[49] *See* Barlow Lyde & Gilbert LLP, Reinsurance Practice and the Law 3–5 (2009); O'Neill & Woloniecki, *supra* note 25, at 3–4, 25–36.

[50] *See* O'Neill & Woloniecki, *supra* note 25, at 420.

[51] Business Bermuda, *supra* note 1, at 35 (contribution from Greg Wojciechowski, Chief Executive Officer of the Bermuda Stock Exchange).

[52] Robinson-McLeod, *supra* note 33, at 53.

[53] Standard & Poor's Ratings Services, *supra* note 3.

[54] Bickley, *supra* note 1, at 3–4. *See also* Barlow Lyde & Gilbert LLP, *supra* note 49, at 66; *Storm Survivors,* Economist, Feb. 16, 2013, http://www.economist.com/news/special-report/21571549-offshore-financial-centres-have-taken-battering-recently-they-have-shown-remarkable.

[55] Business Bermuda, *supra* note 1, at 61 (contribution from Steven Chirico of A.M. Best Co.). *See also* Marsh Risk Management Research, 2013 Captive Benchmarking Report: Discovering Opportunity in the Shifting Captive Landscape 5 (2013); O'Neill & Woloniecki, *supra* note 25, at 56–57.

[56] Bermuda Insurance Development Council, Bermuda: How and Why to Form a Captive 15 (2012).

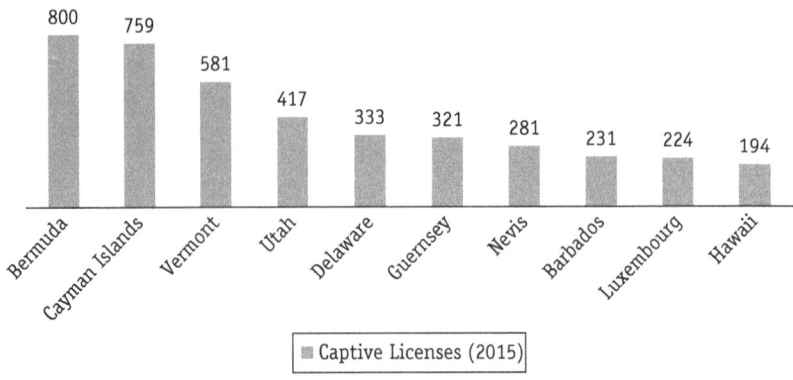

FIGURE 4.1 Captive Insurance Domiciles: Captive Licenses, 2015.*
* See Richard Cutcher, *Domicile Review,* CAPTIVE REV., Mar. 2015, at 29, 30–31.

about 36 percent of the global reinsurance market by net premiums earned," and that Bermuda "is the largest center of captive insurance in the world."[57]

Although facing stiff competition from other jurisdictions in each field—including within the United States,[58] as the data on captive domiciles provided in Figure 4.1 reflect—Bermuda can plausibly claim to occupy a unique market position given its strength across all three components of the insurance industry,[59] and S&P "believe[s] that Bermuda will remain a center of excellence in property and catastrophe reinsurance and that its reinsurers will represent a significant share of the global market."[60] This may seem anomalous given Bermuda's tiny permanent population, but unlike other forms of financial services, which "operate customer service businesses" and thus "have significant fixed assets and enormous workforces," the insurance industry works differently. As Edward Kleinbard explains, "independent agents and brokers play a major role in activities ranging from arranging

---

[57] Standard & Poor's Ratings Services, *supra* note 3.

[58] *See, e.g.,* BARLOW LYDE & GILBERT LLP, *supra* note 49, at 65–70; BUSINESS BERMUDA, *supra* note 1, at 55 (contribution from Allison Towlson, Chairman of the Bermuda Insurance Development Council). In the field of captive insurance, for example, Vermont is a principal competitor within the United States. *See* RONEN PALAN, RICHARD MURPHY & CHRISTIAN CHAVAGNEUX, TAX HAVENS: HOW GLOBALIZATION REALLY WORKS 127 (2010); Andrew P. Morriss, *The Role of Offshore Financial Centers in Regulatory Competition, in* OFFSHORE FINANCIAL CENTERS AND REGULATORY COMPETITION, *supra* note 40, at 102, 137; TAX JUSTICE NETWORK, NARRATIVE REPORT ON USA 7 (2015). Likewise, the Cayman Islands capitalized on Bermuda's initial "reluctance to expand into medical malpractice captives." *See* Freyer & Morriss, *supra* note 12, at 34–35.

[59] BUSINESS BERMUDA, *supra* note 1, at 55 (contribution from Allison Towlson, Chairman of the Bermuda Insurance Development Council). *See also* BERMUDA INSURANCE DEVELOPMENT COUNCIL, *supra* note 56, at 16; Edward D. Kleinbard, *Competitive Convergence in the Financial Services Markets,* 81 TAXES 225, 234–36 (2003); Webber, *supra* note 33, at 44.

[60] Standard & Poor's Ratings Services, *supra* note 3.

retail or institutional insurance to intra-industry reinsurance treaties and facultative contracts."[61]

The emergence and development of the captive insurance industry clearly illustrates Bermuda's substantial capacity for legal and financial innovation. First developed in Bermuda in the 1960s, a "captive" is an insurance company "formed to insure or reinsure the risks of its parents and affiliates."[62] Bermuda is a global leader in captive insurance, with 800 captives in 2015.[63] As Figure 4.1 reflects, however, several competitors have entered the field. Bermuda, the Cayman Islands, and the U.S. state of Vermont are today regarded as the "three traditional captive giants," having become "the go-to captive destinations for some of the world's biggest companies."[64] But other jurisdictions have managed to attract growing numbers of captive registrations as well over recent years, including both "offshore" and "onshore" jurisdictions. Indeed, as of 2015 the top 10 captive domiciles according to *Captive Review* (measured by total licenses) included four U.S. states,[65] a competitive trend thought to promote "both higher standards and specialised jurisdictions" over time.[66]

Self-insuring in this manner can offer substantial benefits, including stabilizing premiums; avoiding commercial insurers' advertising, brokerage, and marketing expenses; making available "niche coverage for a unique or specific risk that would not otherwise be transferable in the commercial insurance market"; control over the captive's investment portfolio; and, in the absence of claims, retention of "underwriting profit . . . which would otherwise be lost to a commercial insurer."[67] Captives can also "access the reinsurance markets, which operate on a lower cost structure than direct insurers."[68]

To be sure, the tax advantages are considerable as well. Bermuda captives can easily secure exemption "from any Bermuda tax on profits or income (except for

---

[61] Kleinbard, *supra* note 59, at 230–31 (emphasis removed).

[62] BERMUDA INSURANCE DEVELOPMENT COUNCIL, *supra* note 56, at 1–2. *See also* PALAN ET AL., *supra* note 58, at 96.

[63] *See* Richard Cutcher, *Domicile Review,* CAPTIVE REV., Mar. 2015, at 29, 30–31.

[64] *Id.* at 31.

[65] *See id.* at 30–31.

[66] *See Final Word,* CAPTIVE REV., Mar. 2015, at 70 (interview with Charles Lavelle of Bingham Greenebaum Doll LLP).

[67] *See* Beckett G. Cantley, *Steering Into the Storm: Amplification of Captive Insurance Company Compliance Issues in the Offshore Tax Crackdown,* 12 HOUS. BUS. & TAX L.J. 224, 225, 231 (2012). *See also* Rent-A-Center, Inc. v. Comm'r, 142 T.C. No. 1, 2014 U.S. Tax Ct. LEXIS 1, *6, *20 (2014); BARLOW LYDE & GILBERT LLP, *supra* note 49, at 43; BERMUDA INSURANCE DEVELOPMENT COUNCIL, *supra* note 56, at 1–3; O'NEILL & WOLONIECKI, *supra* note 25, at 56–57; Robert E. Bertucelli, *The Benefits of Captive Insurance Companies,* J. ACCT., Mar. 2013, http://www.journalofaccountancy.com/Issues/2013/Mar/20126102.htm.

[68] BERMUDA INSURANCE DEVELOPMENT COUNCIL, *supra* note 56, at 2. *See also* BARLOW LYDE & GILBERT LLP, *supra* note 49, at 20; Bertucelli, *supra* note 67.

annual government fees, local land taxes and employment taxes should the cap-tive have a work force present in Bermuda),"[69] and the U.S. Internal Revenue Code (IRC) allows their American owners to deduct premium payments and the captive to receive those payments tax-free (with the premiums giving rise to tax only once the captive pays a dividend or the stock in the captive is sold).[70] The IRS has ex-pressed concern regarding abusive marketing of captives utilizing the foregoing IRC provision to smaller closely held companies,[71] prompting a heated debate within the U.S. captive industry itself. Some argue that this tax election provides a cost-effective means for small businesses to insure against "low-frequency and high-impact" risks that might otherwise bankrupt them, such as "natural hazards, accidents, acts of vi-olence and acts of terrorism."[72] Others, meanwhile, counter that although "existing insurers [have] perfectly valid reasons for electing to be taxed under Section 831(b)," some promoters of these structures "attract customers by downplaying the insur-ance requirements and ginning up the value of the tax benefits."[73]

In response to such concerns, the U.S. Congress amended Section 831(b) in 2015 (generally taking effect in 2017). In addition to raising the ceiling on premiums that an eligible captive can receive from $1.2 million to $2.2 million, the amendments impose a new diversification requirement that can be met in either of two ways. Either the captive must receive no more than 20 percent of its premiums from any single policyholder, or no more than 2 percent of the captive can be owned by the spouse or heirs of the owner of the operating company insured by the captive. The latter approach would allow, for example, the son of a 100 percent owner of the oper-ating company to own no more than 2 percent of the relevant captive (but the son's permitted captive ownership would increase proportionate to his own direct owner-ship stake in the insured operating company).[74] This provision is apparently directed toward those "who attempt to abuse 831(b) captives by using them as a wealth-transfer

[69] BERMUDA INSURANCE DEVELOPMENT COUNCIL, *supra* note 56, at 8.

[70] *See* Cantley, *supra* note 67, at 225–26, 229–31 (describing consequences of a § 831(b) election, permitting receipt of up to $1.2 million in premiums tax-free, but requiring that the captive qualify as an "insurance company" and that the arrangement in question qualify as an "insurance contract"). *See also* Bertucelli, *supra* note 67. For further discussion of offshore captives' U.S. tax exposure, see *Rent-A-Center, Inc.,* 2014 U.S. Tax Ct. LEXIS; Cantley, *supra* note 67, at 267–70; Craig Pichette et al., *Tax Court Allows Deduction for Payments to Captive Insurance Company,* [Mar.] Daily Tax Rep. (BNA) (Mar. 7, 2014).

[71] *See 831(b) Captives Labelled a "Charade" by IRS,* CAPTIVE REV., Mar. 2015, at 9, 9–10.

[72] *See* Sean G. King, *The Big Debate: Should the Captive Industry Be Concerned about the Proliferation of Entities Making the 831(b) Tax Election? No,* CAPTIVE REV., Mar. 2015, at 18, 19.

[73] *See* Donald Riggin, *The Big Debate: Should the Captive Industry Be Concerned about the Proliferation of Entities Making the 831(b) Tax Election? Yes,* CAPTIVE REV., Mar. 2015, at 18.

[74] *See* Jay Adkisson, *Congress Makes 831(b) Captives Much Better and Deals with (Some) Abuses in 2015 Appropriations Bill,* FORBES, Dec. 19, 2015, http://www.forbes.com/sites/jayadkisson/2015/12/19/congress-makes-831b-captives-much-better-and-deals-with-some-abuses-in-2015-appropriations-bill/

vehicle, by allowing Dad to move tax-deductible premiums to Son, outside of Dad's taxable estate,"[75] but such regulatory developments are not expected to hurt the captive insurance industry because most formations are thought to reflect legitimate insurance needs rather than wealth transfer-related tax dodges.[76] Indeed, use of offshore captive insurance structures by entities not themselves subject to U.S. income tax strongly suggests that these structures must offer substantial non-tax benefits.[77] The IRS is widely expected to continue to aggressively pursue abusive captive structures, but observers expect the crackdown ultimately to benefit the industry, and of course legitimate captives "can celebrate . . . raising the 831(b) limit to $2.2 million."[78]

Meanwhile, the quality and integrity of Bermuda's own insurance regulation has been assessed quite positively. International Monetary Fund staff have concluded that "the concentration of professional insurance skills in Bermuda now appear to be of dominant importance in attracting both firms and their customers." They add that "[p]roximity to New York markets and association with the U.K. . . . have enhanced Bermuda as a location."[79] Describing his own company's choice to establish a Bermuda captive, one executive explained that a "key focus for us was reputation. A good domicile will have a good legal framework, so the rules you have to follow are clear." He added that their "evaluation of Bermuda found the Island had transparency and regulatory stability, was favoured by the [OECD], had world-class service providers and easy access to reinsurance, and was also home to other captives in [our] sector."[80] Bermuda's credentials were further burnished in 2015 when the European Commission found "Bermuda's prudential framework for (re)insurance and group supervision [to be] fully equivalent to regulatory standards applied to European reinsurance companies and insurance groups in accordance with the requirements of the Solvency II Directive."[81] Under this directive, insurers must have

---

#533495263be5; Charles Lavelle, *Changes to 831(b)—What Now?*, CAPTIVE REV., Feb. 3, 2016, http://captivereview.com/features/changes-to-831b-what-now/.

[75] *See* Adkisson, *supra* note 74.

[76] *See id.*; Lavelle, *supra* note 74. *Cf.* Cantley, *supra* note 67, at 228.

[77] *See* Morriss, *supra* note 22, at 50 (observing that "Harvard's non-profit hospital must put its medical malpractice insurer in the Caymans for non-tax reasons since Harvard is exempt from US income taxes").

[78] *See* Adkisson, *supra* note 74.

[79] *See* ZEPHIRIN & CHAN-LAU, *supra* note 48, at 1, 4, 12. *See also* BARLOW LYDE & GILBERT LLP, *supra* note 49, at 68; Robinson-McLeod, *supra* note 33, at 53–54; Standard & Poor's Ratings Services, *supra* note 3 (observing "generally positive external reviews of the quality of the Bermuda Monetary Authority's . . . financial sector regulation," as well as the persistence of advantages including "proximity to the U.S., zero income tax, and critical mass of talent").

[80] Myron, *supra* note 34 (quoting "Tommaso Mascarucci, president of Black Gold Re Ltd, the Bermuda-based captive of Colombian oil giant Ecopetrol").

[81] Press Release, Bermuda Monetary Authority, E.C. Declares Bermuda's Commercial (Re)insurance Regime Fully Equivalent to Solvency II (Nov. 26, 2015). Captive insurers and "special purpose insurers" (described below) "remained out of scope of the Solvency II equivalence assessment." *Id.*

"enough capital to have 99.5 percent confidence they could cope with the worst expected losses over a year,"[82] and being "one of the first jurisdictions to receive full Solvency II equivalence"[83] clearly enhanced Bermuda's regulatory reputation. In addition to facilitating competition for European business, the designation more generally enhances Bermuda's global capacity to compete effectively with jurisdictions lacking such recognition.[84] As one Bermuda-based insurance lawyer observed, "now we're having clients who would not initially fall into a bucket of Solvency II equivalency saying, I want to be Solvency II equivalent, I want the additional regulation"—a development attributed to the reputational benefits of association with a well-regulated marketplace.[85]

Bermuda's core insurance legislation actively facilitates collaboration with private-sector professionals and continual innovation. The reach of the Insurance Act 1978 was "deliberately drawn widely,"[86] defining "insurance business" to mean "the business of effecting and carrying out contracts . . . protecting persons against loss or liability to loss in respect of risks to which such persons may be exposed," or "to pay a sum of money or render money's worth upon the happening of an event," expressly including "re-insurance business."[87] The Act requires the Minister of Finance to appoint an Insurance Advisory Committee, including "not fewer than three members . . . appearing to the Minister to be knowledgeable about insurance business in Bermuda." The Committee has a broad mandate to advise the Bermuda Monetary Authority "on any matter relating to the development of the insurance industry in Bermuda which the Authority may refer to it," and may also advise the Minister directly regarding "the development and promotion of [Bermuda's] insurance industry."[88] A marketing piece of the Bermuda Insurance Development Council describes this "consultative process between regulators and industry" as a "unique factor of the Bermuda system of insurance regulation," adding that "various sub-committees regularly review the law and practice of insurance in Bermuda."[89]

---

[82] Oliver Ralph, *Q&A: How Solvency II Works*, FIN. TIMES, Jan. 3, 2016, http://www.ft.com/intl/cms/s/0/51bc0c08-aa38-11e5-9700-2b669a5aeb83.html.

[83] *Solvency II Equivalence: Why It Matters*, BERMUDA REINSURANCE MAG., Feb. 2, 2016, http://www.bermudareinsurancemagazine.com/article/solvency-ii-equivalence-why-it-matters. Others designated as fully or partially equivalent include Switzerland and the United States. Ralph, *supra* note 82.

[84] *See* Bermuda Monetary Authority, *supra* note 81; BERMUDA REINSURANCE MAG., *supra* note 83.

[85] *Bermuda's Regulation Enhances Business Opportunities: Brad Adderley*, ARTEMIS, Feb. 10, 2016, http://www.artemis.bm/blog/2016/02/10/bermudas-regulation-enhances-business-opportunities-brad-adderley-2/ (quoting Brad Adderley of Appleby's).

[86] O'NEILL & WOLONIECKI, *supra* note 25, at 422–23.

[87] Insurance Act 1978, 1978:39, § 1(1) (Berm.).

[88] *Id.* § 2C.

[89] BERMUDA INSURANCE DEVELOPMENT COUNCIL, *supra* note 56, at 6.

Although Bermuda's legal and political links with the United Kingdom remain critical to its success for reasons explored above, the lion's share of Bermuda's insurance business lies in the United States. According to an IMF staff report, "[o]wnership in the Bermuda insurance sector is geographically diverse but dominated by U.S. companies, which owned 60 percent of the 589 active commercial insurers at end-2005." The report adds that approximately "one in three commercial insurers were publicly-listed companies, of which two-thirds were listed in U.S. exchanges."[90] Indeed, although other markets are emerging, the United States remains "the biggest, single source of captive business for Bermuda, accounting for some 60 percent of the Island's insurance formations"—reflecting, among other things, a trend toward increasing use of "healthcare or medical malpractice captives."[91] More broadly, "Bermuda's carriers provide up to one third of US crop insurance in key states and support 25 percent of the US medical liability insurance and reinsurance market."[92]

The fact that Bermuda insurers ably responded to losses resulting from the 9/11 attacks in 2001 "led to a further infusion of capital," resulting in "a position where the island is believed to reinsure around 40 percent of all US risks."[93] Indeed, Bermuda played a big role in responding to catastrophic losses in recent years, paying "nearly 30 percent of the insured losses from 2005 Hurricanes Katrina, Rita and Wilma; . . . $22 billion to rebuild the US Gulf and Florida coasts from the horrific hurricanes seasons of 2004 and 2005; and today provid[ing] more than 60 percent of the hurricane reinsurance in Florida and Texas."[94] In addition to the nine new reinsurance companies established in Bermuda in the wake of 9/11, "a further dozen companies were established in the wake of Hurricane Katrina."[95]

Meanwhile Bermuda continues to innovate, building on its dominant insurance position and competitive strengths. As noted above, Bermuda's considerable capacity for legislative experimentation gave rise to "segregated portfolio legislation" in the early 1990s.[96] This legal structure permits creation of the so-called "protected cell company"—essentially "a modern extension of the captive concept" allowing

---

[90] Zephirin & Chan-Lau, *supra* note 48, at 13.

[91] Bermuda Insurance Development Council, *supra* note 56, at 14–15. *See also* Bermuda Monetary Authority, Bermuda Captive Market 2010 at 4–5 (Oct. 2011).

[92] Business Bermuda, *supra* note 1, at 57 (contribution from Allison Towlson, Chairman of the Bermuda Insurance Development Council).

[93] Barlow Lyde & Gilbert LLP, *supra* note 49, at 68–69. *See also* O'Neill & Woloniecki, *supra* note 25, at 59.

[94] Business Bermuda, *supra* note 1, at 57 (contribution from Allison Towlson, Chairman of the Bermuda Insurance Development Council). *See also* Zephirin & Chan-Lau, *supra* note 48, at 15.

[95] Bickley, *supra* note 1, at 4.

[96] *See supra* note 37 and accompanying text.

each cell within the company to have its own assets and liabilities (creditors of the cell having recourse only to that cell's assets) and issue its own shares. In this manner, cells permit more granular and lower-cost management of risks within a single larger entity.[97]

Similarly, Bermuda's prominence as an insurance center has prompted hybrid structures linking insurance and capital markets. In 2008 the Insurance Act was amended to create a new category of "Special Purpose Insurer" that can fully fund its liabilities through the proceeds of "a debt issuance where the repayment rights of the providers of such debt are subordinated to the rights of the person insured."[98] This development facilitated the emergence of insurance-market/capital-market hybrids such as "catastrophe bonds"—a form of investment "expanding risk-bearing capacity beyond the limited capital held by insurers and reinsurers"[99] by appealing to institutions seeking investments "not co-related to financial markets risk."[100] Special Purpose Insurer registrations "represented 43 percent and 51 percent of all [Bermuda Monetary Authority] company registrations" in 2011 and 2012, respectively.[101] As of 2013 Bermuda represented "about a third of the global cat bond market,"[102] and the market value of such "insurance-linked securities" (ILS) listed on the Bermuda Stock Exchange exceeded $7 billion.[103] By late 2015, the total outstanding catastrophe bond and ILS market stood at an estimated $25.02 billion,

---

[97] See BARLOW LYDE & GILBERT LLP, *supra* note 49, at 43–44, 420. *See also* Bertucelli, *supra* note 67. For additional background, see BICKLEY, *supra* note 1, at 393–415.

[98] Insurance Act 1978, 1978:39, § 1(1) (Berm.). *See also id.* § 5(2)(b) (requiring the Bermuda Monetary Authority to assess, among other things, "the sophistication of the parties to a debt issuance" in considering whether to register such a Special Purpose Insurer). *See also* Rebecca Zuill, *Dr. Gibbons: Bermuda Sees Steady Rise in ILS Formation,* ROYAL GAZETTE, June 18, 2013, http://www.royalgazette.com/article/20130618/BUSINESS03/706189992.

[99] BUSINESS BERMUDA, *supra* note 1, at 56 (contribution from Allison Towlson, Chairman of the Bermuda Insurance Development Council).

[100] *Id.* at 59–60 (contribution from Tim Faries of Appleby's). Investors in a CAT bond issuance "take on the risks of a specified catastrophe or event in return for attractive rates of investment," but lose principal should such an event occur. *Id.* at 60. For additional background see BARLOW LYDE & GILBERT LLP, *supra* note 49, at 44–47; O'NEILL & WOLONIECKI, *supra* note 25, at 44–45; *Bermuda Is a Central Player in ILS Market,* ROYAL GAZETTE, Mar. 12, 2013, http://www.royalgazette.com/article/20130312/BUSINESS04/703129967; *Investor Demand for Insurance-Linked Securities Far Exceeds Supply: A.M. Best,* ARTEMIS, June 21, 2013, http://www.artemis.bm/blog/2013/06/21/investor-demand-for-insurance-linked-securities-far-exceeds-supply-a-m-best/; Kleinbard, *supra* note 59, at 226–27; Robinson-McLeod, *supra* note 33, at 53–54.

[101] Zuill, *supra* note 98.

[102] ROYAL GAZETTE, *supra* note 100.

[103] Rebecca Zuill, *Insurance-Linked Securities Surpass $7 Billion Mark on BSX,* ROYAL GAZETTE, June 20, 2013, http://www.royalgazette.com/article/20130620/BUSINESS/706199904. "Of the ILS class, cat bonds are the largest component, accounting for more than 40 percent." ROYAL GAZETTE, *supra* note 100.

and recent activity—including a "$275 million catastrophe bond providing insurance protection to US train company Amtrak" for "storm surge," "storm wind," and "earthquake" protection in the northeast United States—provided "further evidence that the demand for cat bonds and ILS is a trend set to continue."[104]

Ultimately for Bermuda, much comes down to wedding the reputation for high quality regulatory oversight described earlier with a reputation for openness to such innovations. The same Bermuda-based insurance lawyer quoted above, citing Solvency II equivalence as a competitive advantage, further cited capacity for innovation as equally important to preservation of Bermuda's overall status as a globally significant insurance center. "There's already a history of this: segregated accounts, Special Purpose Insurers, collateralised reinsurance, the cat bonds in Bermuda. . . . Bermuda has a history of fostering new ideas and bringing them to fruition. We have to hope that door continues to exist next time we come along with new structures or innovative products."[105] Based on the foregoing discussion, the co-operative public and private investment required to maintain this balance would appear to be broadly supported by Bermuda's regulators and financial professional community alike.

---

[104] Scott Neil, *Amtrak behind New $275m Cat Bond*, ROYAL GAZETTE, Oct. 9, 2015, http://www.royalgazette.com/article/20151009/BUSINESS04/151009702. The "variable rate notes" issued were "admitted for listing on the Bermuda Stock Exchange." *Id. See also* Standard & Poor's Ratings Services, *supra* note 3 (observing that Bermuda is "a leading jurisdiction for . . . insurance-linked securities, a market with good growth potential").

[105] ARTEMIS, *supra* note 85 (quoting Brad Adderley of Appleby's).

# 5    Dubai

DUBAI, ONE OF seven emirates that together constitute the United Arab Emirates (UAE), occupies a forbidding terrain along the Arabian (Persian) Gulf consisting of a "flat, barren coastal plain merging into rolling sand dunes of vast desert."[1] Yet, visitors to contemporary Dubai arrive at the busiest airport in the world—in all likelihood via Emirates, "Dubai's flagship carrier" and "one of the world's leading airlines"—to find a bustling modern metropolis featuring, among other things, the tallest building and the largest shopping center in the world.[2]

The small emirate's diversified modern economy includes a "major transport hub" with highly developed infrastructure and growing professional capacities,[3] including a financial center rapidly achieving regional and even global significance. Indeed, Dubai is widely recognized today as one the world's three most significant centers (along with Kuala Lumpur and London) for Islamic finance—that is, financial

---

[1] CENTRAL INTELLIGENCE AGENCY, THE WORLD FACTBOOK: UNITED ARAB EMIRATES, https://www.cia.gov/library/publications/the-world-factbook/geos/ae.html (last updated Apr. 27, 2016).

[2] *Rise of the Gulf: Soaring Ambition,* ECONOMIST, Jan. 8, 2015, http://www.economist.com/news/middle-east-and-africa/21638154-economic-power-and-political-influence-are-shifting-gulf-can-it. *See also* Jennifer Urban, *Islamic Financing—A Successful Takeoff or a Crash Landing? Whether or Not Islamic Financing Should Be Used to Finance and Lease Aircraft* 16–17 (Oct. 13, 2015), http://ssrn.com/abstract=2673290.

[3] *See* ECONOMIST, *supra* note 2.

products and services structured to ensure compliance with Sharia law.[4] Although undoubtedly reflecting an approach to financial and commercial relations differing starkly from conventional Western financial structures, this chapter nevertheless reveals the striking degree to which Dubai's geographic and cultural characteristics, competitive strengths, and development strategies reflect the MDSJ paradigm.

## A. The Crossroads of Europe, Africa, and Asia

Like Bermuda and the jurisdictions discussed in subsequent chapters—though perhaps less straightforwardly than some—Dubai fundamentally exhibits geographic, historical, and cultural features that typify MDSJs. Like Bermuda, Dubai is a sub-sovereign jurisdiction—one of seven distinct emirates that joined together in the early 1970s to form the UAE.[5] Critically, however, Dubai possesses "a large degree of independence" within the UAE's federal structure,[6] "with many crucial policy areas having often remained outside of federal control"[7]—including in the economic sphere.[8] Although committed to unity with its neighboring emirates, Dubai in particular has long favored a relatively "looser federation" in order to retain latitude to pursue policies consistent with its particular circumstances.[9]

The UAE's federal structure gestures toward important contextual complexities that require a distinction to be drawn between Dubai and the UAE generally in terms of economic development options. Although the UAE as a whole possesses substantial oil and gas reserves[10]—suggesting that the MDSJ paradigm might be a poor conceptual fit—the vast majority in fact belong to Dubai's larger neighbor,

---

[4] *See, e.g.,* Robert W. Wood & Rafi W. Mottahedeh, *Islamic Debt-Equivalents Take Center Stage,* 11 J. Tax'n Fin. Products 17, 17 (2014). *See also* Thomson Reuters, State of the Global Islamic Economy: 2014–2015 Report 38–39 (2014) (developed and produced in collaboration with DinarStandard, supported by Dubai The Capital of Islamic Economy); Abdul Karim Aldohni, *Reclaiming Islamic Finance: Dubai's Race to the Top and the Challenges Ahead,* 29 J. Int'l Banking L. & Reg. 542, 542 (2014).

[5] *See* Government of the United Arab Emirates, *Governance,* http://government.ae/en/web/guest/governance (last visited Apr. 2016). *See also* Central Intelligence Agency, *supra* note 1; Qatar National Bank, UAE Economic Insight 2 (2013).

[6] BBC News, United Arab Emirates Profile, http://www.bbc.com/news/world-middle-east-14703998 (last updated Nov. 18, 2015).

[7] Christopher M. Davidson, The United Arab Emirates: A Study in Survival 200 (2005).

[8] *See* Tax Justice Network, Narrative Report on Dubai 2 (2015). *See also* Tax Justice Network, *Financial Secrecy Index—2015 Results,* http://www.financialsecrecyindex.com/introduction/fsi-2015-results.

[9] *See* Davidson, *supra* note 7, at 204–05.

[10] *See* Central Intelligence Agency, *supra* note 1.

Abu Dhabi.[11] And although the UAE has a total land area of approximately 83,600 square kilometers (roughly the size of Maine) and a total estimated population (as of 2015) of approximately 9.2 million,[12] Dubai itself represents a small fraction in each case, with a population of approximately 2.4 million (as of 2015) and land area of 3,885 square kilometers.[13] Inhabiting desert terrain without substantial oil or gas reserves of its own, Dubai in fact finds itself sharply resource-constrained[14] in a manner resembling the other jurisdictions investigated in this part of the book. In this light, it is hardly surprising that Dubai would cultivate substantial outward orientation, both culturally and economically.

Abu Dhabi's predominance in size and resources, Dubai's status as a distant number two by these metrics, and the differing incentives and policy preferences stemming from their divergent circumstances all manifest themselves in the UAE's political structure. The Federal Supreme Council (FSC), comprised of the rulers of the seven emirates, constitutes the UAE's "highest constitutional authority" and "establishes general policies and sanctions federal legislation."[15] Although the FSC's substantive decisions require a vote of five rulers, that majority must include the votes of both Abu Dhabi and Dubai, giving these emirates veto power at the highest level of federal decision-making.[16] Dubai's veto power reflects its prominence relative to the remaining emirates, yet other dimensions of federal governance clearly reflect Abu Dhabi's preeminence. Notably, Abu Dhabi is the UAE capital, and the UAE's President and Vice President, though nominally elected by the FSC, have consistently been the rulers of Abu Dhabi and Dubai, respectively[17]—an arrangement that would appear to reflect an oil-driven political equilibrium.[18] As of this writing, Dubai's ruler—His Highness Sheikh Mohammed bin Rashid Al Maktoum—holds the federal positions of Vice President and Prime Minister.[19]

---

[11] *See* QATAR NATIONAL BANK, *supra* note 5, inside front cover and 2.

[12] *See* CENTRAL INTELLIGENCE AGENCY, *supra* note 1.

[13] *See* Government of Dubai, Dubai Statistics Center, *Dubai in Figures 2015,* https://www.dsc.gov.ae/en-us/Pages/dubaiinfigure-details.aspx; Government of Dubai, *Dubai Nature,* http://www.dubai.ae/en/about-dubai/Pages/DubaiNature.aspx (last visited Apr. 2016).

[14] *See* QATAR NATIONAL BANK, UAE ECONOMIC INSIGHT 17, 21–22 (2012); Stephen J. Ramos, *The Blueprint: A History of Dubai's Spatial Development through Oil Discovery* 2 (Dubai Initiative, Belfer Ctr. for Sci. and Int'l Affairs, John F. Kennedy Sch. of Gov't, Harvard Univ., June 2009).

[15] CENTRAL INTELLIGENCE AGENCY, *supra* note 1. *See also* DIB Tier 1 Sukuk (2) Ltd., Prospectus, U.S.$1,000,000,000 Tier 1 Capital Certificates (Jan. 19, 2015), at 131.

[16] *See* DIB Tier 1 Sukuk (2) Ltd., *supra* note 15, at 131.

[17] *See id.*; CENTRAL INTELLIGENCE AGENCY, *supra* note 1.

[18] *See, e.g.,* DAVIDSON, *supra* note 7, at 189–91; QATAR NATIONAL BANK, *supra* note 5, at 2; BBC NEWS, *supra* note 6.

[19] *See* Government of Dubai, *Dubai Rulers,* http://www.dubai.ae/en/aboutdubai/Pages/DubaiRulers.aspx (last visited Apr. 2016).

Consistent with the foregoing, federal powers and responsibilities remain circumscribed—yet within that limited federal domain, Abu Dhabi predominates. The seven emirates remain autonomous with respect to oil policy, and each maintains its own budget.[20] With respect to finance, although the UAE does have a Central Bank, there is "no formal deposit protection scheme" and the Central Bank "does not act as a lender of last resort, a role which tends to fall on the individual Emirates."[21] The relatively limited federal budget, "of which defence is an important part," is funded almost entirely by Abu Dhabi—"Dubai is the only other Emirate that contributes, accounting for 3 percent of federal budget revenue in 2011."[22] Accordingly, federal power has remained concentrated in the presidency. As Christopher Davidson observed in 2005, "with Abu Dhabi being by far the largest contributor to both the federal budget and the UAE's GDP, this historical association of the presidency with the ruler of Abu Dhabi has now been informally accepted by the other emirates."[23] Given the foregoing, it is unsurprising that a 2002 identity survey found that those in Abu Dhabi tend to identify themselves as "UAE/Emirati" (86 percent) whereas those from Dubai tend to identify more strongly with their own emirate (60 percent).[24] Likewise it is unsurprising that nontrivial commercial and financial rivalry endures—perhaps most visible in their conspicuous duplication of major infrastructural investments such as airlines and airports,[25] and the sheer number of banks operating across the UAE. Even though the Muslim world largely remains under-banked (as discussed below), the UAE itself "may be seen as being over-banked with 51 banks" serving the domestic market—reflecting in part "the individual Emirates wishing to retain their own national banks."[26]

To be sure, Dubai has benefited substantially from Abu Dhabi's oil and gas revenue in times of crisis[27]—a point to which I return below—but at the same time Dubai has felt an acute need to diversify well beyond its own quite limited oil and gas reserves.[28] This is indeed a long-standing trend—Dubai's concerted efforts to

---

[20] See QATAR NATIONAL BANK, *supra* note 14, at 11, 29.

[21] DIB Tier 1 Sukuk (2) Ltd., *supra* note 15, at 132–33, 136.

[22] QATAR NATIONAL BANK, *supra* note 14, at 29. Dubai maintained its own defense force until the mid-1990s. *See* Christopher M. Davidson, *Dubai and the United Arab Emirates: Security Threats* 5 (Durham Research Online, 2009), http://dro.dur.ac.uk/7091/ (accepted version, published in 36 BRIT. J. MIDDLE E. STUD. 431 (2011)).

[23] DAVIDSON, *supra* note 7, at 189.

[24] *See id.* at 84.

[25] *See id.* at 166–67.

[26] DIB Tier 1 Sukuk (2) Ltd., *supra* note 15, at 133–35.

[27] *See, e.g.*, TAX JUSTICE NETWORK, *supra* note 8, at 3.

[28] *See* QATAR NATIONAL BANK, *supra* note 14, at 1–2, 10–14. *See also* DAVIDSON, *supra* note 7, at 155, 158–62, 174.

diversify its economy date back at least to the 1980s,[29] and the project has only become more urgent since the late 1990s as Dubai's limited oil and gas production has fallen off.[30] As the BBC explains, whereas "Abu Dhabi remained relatively conservative in its approach, Dubai, which has far smaller oil reserves, was bolder in its diversification policy," seeking in the 2000s "to turn itself into the financial gateway and cosmopolitan hub of the Middle East."[31] Lacking Abu Dhabi's natural resources, "the other emirates have had to look at services and industry to boost their GDP," and Dubai has developed a model emphasizing "a favourable business environment that attracts foreign businesses and workers."[32] By 2008, Dubai "was drawing over 97 percent of its GDP from non-oil sectors."[33] Accordingly, in terms of resource endowments and development strategies, Dubai resembles the MDSJ paradigm more closely than many would guess.

In pursuing such a diversification strategy, Dubai clearly builds upon a long history of bridging major economies from East to West, and North to South. As *The Economist* expresses it, "[p]art of Dubai's success is down to its location—between Europe, Asia and Africa—and its stability in a region plagued by war and stagnant politics."[34] Although evidence of trading activity in Dubai dates back 3,000 years, the historical record predating the arrival of European powers remains quite limited. Broadly speaking, the two principal cultures of the region revolved around the sea and the desert, respectively—the former emphasizing maritime trade and the latter involving "nomadic Bedouin communities based on agriculture and animal husbandry."[35] Venetian traders are thought to have been active in the Gulf region by the fifteenth century, but the Portuguese were the first Europeans "able to take control of the Gulf through maritime dominance" in the sixteenth century. A period of Dutch domination over trade routes in the region followed in the seventeenth century, but they were gradually displaced by the British through the eighteenth and early nineteenth centuries.[36] By 1819 the British established various regional maritime powers, and "a mixture of treaties, truces, indirect rule, and canon diplomacy would maintain this rule until their departure from the region 150 years later."[37]

---

[29] *See* DAVIDSON, *supra* note 7, at 131–37.

[30] *See* QATAR NATIONAL BANK, *supra* note 5, at 2.

[31] BBC NEWS, UNITED ARAB EMIRATES PROFILE—OVERVIEW, http://www.bbc.co.uk/news/mobile/world-middle-east-14703998 (last updated Feb. 24, 2015).

[32] *See* QATAR NATIONAL BANK, *supra* note 14, at 1–2. *See also* Aldohni, *supra* note 4, at 543–44.

[33] Davidson, *supra* note 22, at 1.

[34] ECONOMIST, *supra* note 2. *See also* TAX JUSTICE NETWORK, *supra* note 8, at 1.

[35] Ramos, *supra* note 14, at 1–3. *See also* DAVIDSON, *supra* note 7, at 10–11.

[36] *See* Ramos, *supra* note 14, at 3–4; DAVIDSON, *supra* note 7, at 21–22.

[37] Ramos, *supra* note 14, at 4; DAVIDSON, *supra* note 7, at 22–29.

In 1833, a group of settlers from the desert-dwelling Bani Yas tribe led by the Maktoum family settled by "the creek"—a harbor on Dubai's Gulf coast—and Dubai's modern history and development effectively date from British recognition of the Maktoum family's rule over the region in 1835.[38] British presence in the Gulf region stabilized maritime trade and commerce through a series of truces requiring local rulers to surrender armaments and pirate vessels in exchange for British protection and access to British ports—hence the moniker "Trucial states" in the lower Gulf.[39] Although British policy favored exerting only informal control to the degree possible, "Britain's policing role inevitably expanded to include the arbitration of local disputes"—particularly as British recognition increasingly became a de facto legitimator of local power. In 1892 Britain would assume "control over the region's foreign affairs" in order to fend off "interference from external powers" and "discourage any 'playing off' between the local powers and Britain's rivals."[40] By the early twentieth century, Dubai and other Trucial states had effectively become "rentier" economies substantially dependent upon British payments for "imperial air landing rights" and "oil exploration concessions"—income accruing to the rulers, including the Maktoum family, who consolidated their power by reducing dependence upon pearl merchants and other commercial interests.[41]

Dubai's relationship with the British clearly conditioned attitudes in the emirate regarding economic development, encouraging strong trade orientation and diversification. While pearl exports grew substantially from the 1870s through the turn of the century—with 7,000 of Dubai's 10,000 inhabitants by that time "involved in the pearling sector"[42]—Dubai was already assuming broader significance in regional trade. The emirate had become "the principal commercial port on the Gulf coast," and "Dubai's first free port was born at the turn of that Century" when "Sheikh Maktum bin hasher Al-Maktum ... removed as many trade barriers as possible, including customs fees and licenses for vessels."[43] This move "quickly attracted re-export activities from Lingah"—the previously dominant Persian port that had itself imposed "restrictive Imperial Customs tariffs and controls for re-exported goods, which reached up to 400 percent on some goods, particularly for

---

[38] See Ramos, *supra* note 14, at 6; Government of Dubai, *Dubai History,* http://www.dubai.ae/en/about-dubai/Pages/DubaiHistory.aspx (last visited Apr. 2016); Government of Dubai, *supra* note 19.

[39] See DAVIDSON, *supra* note 7, at 29–30; Ramos, *supra* note 14, at 4–5. For a timeline, see BBC NEWS, UNITED ARAB EMIRATES PROFILE—TIMELINE, http://www.bbc.com/news/world-middle-east-14704414 (last updated Apr. 21, 2015).

[40] DAVIDSON, *supra* note 7, at 30–32. *See also* BBC NEWS, *supra* note 39.

[41] See DAVIDSON, *supra* note 7, at 34–41.

[42] See Ramos, *supra* note 14, at 6–8.

[43] TAX JUSTICE NETWORK, *supra* note 8, at 2.

Arab traders." As Stephen Ramos explains, "[a]ll commerce between Great Britain and India would then pass through Dubai, such that by 1905, some 34 steamers were calling regularly, raising the annual volume of cargo to 70,000 tons." Ramos adds that the "prominent British India Steam Navigation Company essentially shifted its distribution center, firmly establishing Dubai's vocation as a strategic *entrepôt* for British imperial trade routes," following which "large sectors of the Lingah Persian and Indian trading communities migrated to Dubai along with the trade route business."[44] As of the 1930s Dubai's population had already reached 20,000, "a quarter of whom were expatriates."[45] Such developments left the emirate better positioned to weather the decline of the pearling industry in the 1930s following the global market crash and the advent of cultured pearls.[46] Indeed, such developments effectively strengthened the ruling Maktoum family, in that merchant wealth based on pearling declined just as British-centric sources of wealth accruing to the ruler grew—a symbiosis that may help explain why the British remained a presence in the region decades longer than in India.[47]

Throughout the mid-twentieth century, aggressive infrastructural development projects would augment Dubai's trade capacities and, ultimately, the emirate's professional services and financial capacities as well. The Dubai government observes that dredging the creek in the 1950s—"an ambitious, costly, and visionary project"—brought "increased volumes of cargo handling" and "strengthened Dubai's position as a major trading and re-export hub."[48] As Ramos notes, Dubai's growing business took "both legal and illicit" forms, the latter notably including transshipment of "all international gold trade with India," which had prohibited the sale of gold by Indian merchants following India's independence.[49] To a substantial extent for Abu Dhabi and to a lesser extent for Dubai, the discovery and export of oil in the 1950s and 1960s supported further infrastructural investments.[50] The Dubai government observes that what oil they had, initially discovered in 1966, was used

> . . . to spur infrastructure development in Dubai. Schools, hospitals, roads, a modern telecommunications network . . . the pace of development was frenetic. A new port and terminal building were built at Dubai International Airport. A runway extension that could accommodate any type of aircraft was

---

[44] Ramos, *supra* note 14, at 7.

[45] Government of Dubai, *supra* note 38.

[46] *See* DAVIDSON, *supra* note 7, at 7.

[47] *See* Ramos, *supra* note 14, at 9–11.

[48] Government of Dubai, *supra* note 38.

[49] *See* Ramos, *supra* note 14, at 12. *See also* TAX JUSTICE NETWORK, *supra* note 8, at 2.

[50] *See* BBC NEWS, *supra* note 6; DAVIDSON, *supra* note 7, at 137–44.

implemented. The largest man-made harbor in the world was constructed at Jebel Ali, and a free zone was created around the port.[51]

Such initiatives, pursued over the course of decades, exemplify "Dubai's formula for development," involving (again in the government's words) "visionary leadership, high-quality infrastructure, an expatriate-friendly environment, zero tax on personal and corporate income and low import duties," promoting "a business and tourism hub" of growing regional significance.[52]

The accelerating pace of infrastructural investment in Dubai mapped onto the gradual attenuation of the British economic and financial role in the lower Gulf, the two together culminating in the UAE's independence. Whereas the British Bank of the Middle East played a role in development initiatives during the 1940s and 1950s, reflecting its banking monopoly in Dubai during this period, the National Bank of Dubai commenced operations in May 1963, and several foreign banks were subsequently permitted to open offices in the 1960s.[53] Meanwhile, as Davidson explains, "by the mid-1950s Britain began to become more directly involved in the region's institutional development" as a way to promote regional security without requiring "repeated and expensive deployments"—efforts that critically included "setting up a Trucial council." Though "merely an advisory body" at first, the Trucial Council nevertheless promoted "some degree of unity and 'corporate sense' between the previously disparate shaikhdoms." Over time, however, the Trucial Council came to function as a proto-federal government, a development prompted by growing recognition of Britain's impending withdrawal from the lower Gulf and correlative fears of "the expansionary ambitions of neighboring Saudi Arabia and nearby Iran." The late 1960s accordingly saw "more rapid development, especially in the coordination of actions between the various Trucial states, with many of what were soon to become the UAE's federal institutions being set up."[54] With British support, the rulers increasingly "perform[ed] jointly many of the functions that had previously been Britain's responsibility," and starting in 1969 the emirates moved increasingly toward "jointly conducting foreign affairs, defense, security, social services, and a common immigration policy."[55] Full independence came in 1971 with the formal creation of the UAE.[56]

In light of the trade history, infrastructural investments, and diversification strategy described above, the unusual profile of the economy and workforce of the UAE

---

[51] Government of Dubai, *supra* note 38.
[52] *Id.*
[53] *See* Ramos, *supra* note 14, at 12–15.
[54] DAVIDSON, *supra* note 7, at 42–45.
[55] *See id.* at 45–51.
[56] *See* BBC NEWS, *supra* note 39; Government of Dubai, *supra* note 38.

generally, and Dubai specifically, become more comprehensible. According to an analysis by the Qatar National Bank in 2010, "the vast majority of jobs (73 percent) are in the services sector, which at an emirate level reaches as high as 82 percent for Dubai." Services in turn were thought to account for 44 percent of the UAE's GDP in 2011, and Dubai was "the largest contributor to the services sector, accounting for around 46 percent of the overall services GDP"—a divergence attributed to Dubai's lack of oil and consequent focus on diversification through development of "a business friendly environment, services and trade." As to the composition of the workforce, expatriates represented "an estimated 93 percent of the total workforce in 2010," generating substantial remittances. Participation of Emiratis themselves in the labor force was "concentrated in the public sector with 85 percent of employed nationals working in federal and local government," and "participation of nationals in the private sector [being] only 7.4 percent of those employed."[57] It must be acknowledged that such statistics vary from one source and measure to another—for example, the *CIA World Factbook* reports that as of 2015 services accounted for an estimated 49.8 percent of GDP and expatriates accounted for an estimated 85 percent of the workforce.[58] In any event, the substantial reliance on services and a largely expatriate workforce is clear. According to the Dubai government, in the first half of 2014, 12.3 percent of Dubai's GDP was attributable to the "Financial Corporations Sector" alone, a figure exceeded only by "Manufacturing" (13.9 percent), "Real Estate and Business Services" (14.0 percent), "Transports, Storage and communication" (14.8 percent), and "Wholesale, Retail Trade and Repairing Services" (28.2 percent).[59] Unsurprisingly, Dubai's imports far exceed their exports.[60]

Overall, the UAE's economic performance and financial position are impressive. As of 2015, the UAE's per capita GDP was estimated to be $67,000, ranking twelfth in the world.[61] Neither the UAE nor Dubai has a credit rating, because neither has requested a rating and "their lack of transparency would make [an unsolicited] credit assessment difficult" (though Abu Dhabi has been rated AA by Fitch and Standard & Poor's, and Aa2 by Moody's).[62] This does not appear to have substantially impaired private sector confidence in the UAE public sector, however. For example, according to Transparency International, the UAE is broadly perceived as

[57] *See* QATAR NATIONAL BANK, *supra* note 14, at 3–8, 24.
[58] *See* CENTRAL INTELLIGENCE AGENCY, *supra* note 1.
[59] Government of Dubai, Dubai Statistics Center, *Gross Domestic Product at Constant Prices First Half—Emirate of Dubai* (2014).
[60] *See* Government of Dubai, *Dubai in Figures 2015, supra* note 13.
[61] *See* CENTRAL INTELLIGENCE AGENCY, *supra* note 1.
[62] *Ratings Agencies Have No Plans to Rate UAE, Dubai—Fitch,* REUTERS, Mar. 6, 2012, http://www.reuters.com/article/2012/03/06/uae-rating-fitch-idAFL5E8E63S220120306.

exhibiting relatively low public corruption, ranking twenty-third out of 168 countries and territories included in their 2015 Corruption Perceptions Index.[63] The Tax Justice Network, meanwhile, ranked the UAE tenth on its 2015 Financial Secrecy Index, suggesting a relatively high degree of financial secrecy, though this is better than the United States, which ranked third.[64] In any event, that the UAE's public finances are solid would appear quite clear; as of 2012, the Abu Dhabi Investment Authority was the largest sovereign wealth fund in the world, and this—together with reserve accounts reflecting their oil revenue—substantially stabilize the UAE's public finances.[65] The UAE's public debt is considered "manageable and moderate," and although Dubai's public debt is higher (of which more below),[66] markets have appeared broadly comfortable with their debt levels in recent years.[67] Overall the UAE generally, and Dubai in particular, are broadly viewed as an island of stability in a turbulent region, characterized by moderate cultural attitudes, politics, and foreign policy,[68] as well as a stable currency (the UAE dirham) that has been pegged since 1978 to the U.S. dollar—the currency in which global markets price oil and gas.[69]

There is a paradox to this relative stability, however, in that cultural openness and policy moderation coexist with a high degree of social stratification and centralized control. In its profile of the country, the BBC rightly observes that "the UAE is one of the most liberal countries in the Gulf, with other cultures and beliefs generally tolerated, especially in Dubai"[70]—indeed, Dubai's ruler has "worked to make his state the most tolerant in the UAE for foreigners."[71] The Dubai government, for its part, justly touts the emirate's "warm hospitality," that "the Emirati people are welcoming and generous in their approach to visitors," that "Dubai is tolerant and cosmopolitan and all visitors are welcome," and that Dubai in fact "receives millions of leisure and business visitors each year from around the world."[72] It bears emphasizing in this respect that this openness extends not only toward the

---

[63] *See* Transparency International, *Corruption Perceptions Index 2015* (2015). By contrast, the United Kingdom and the United States ranked tenth and sixteenth, respectively. *See id.*

[64] *See* Tax Justice Network, *supra* note 8.

[65] *See* QATAR NATIONAL BANK, *supra* note 14, at 25, 29.

[66] *See id.* at 25, 31–32.

[67] *See* QATAR NATIONAL BANK, *supra* note 5, at 4.

[68] *See* CENTRAL INTELLIGENCE AGENCY, *supra* note 1.

[69] *See* QATAR NATIONAL BANK, *supra* note 14, at 26. *See also* CENTRAL INTELLIGENCE AGENCY, *supra* note 1; Government of Dubai, *About Dubai,* http://www.dubai.ae/en/AboutDubai/Pages/default.aspx (last visited Apr. 2016).

[70] BBC NEWS, *supra* note 31. *See also* HARRIS IRFAN, HEAVEN'S BANKERS 9 (2015).

[71] BBC NEWS, UNITE ARAB EMIRATES PROFILE—LEADERS, http://www.bbc.com/news/world-middle-east-14704227 (last updated Feb. 24, 2015).

[72] Government of Dubai, *supra* note 69.

West; unlike the rest of the UAE, "Dubai has historically enjoyed fairly warm relations with Iran," reflecting the aforementioned wave of Persian immigration.[73] Although Arabic is the official language, Persian, English, Hindi, and Urdu are also spoken,[74] with English (predictably) representing the "lingua franca" for much of the private sector.[75] Recall, however, that noncitizen expatriate workers constitute an enormous percentage of the resident population, by one estimate comprised of 50 percent from South Asia, 23 percent from other Arab countries and Iran, and 8 percent from other parts of the world, including "Westerners and East Asians."[76] Although the UAE's low public corruption score presumably represents a source of comfort to business visitors and tourists, the concentration of the "local" citizen minority in the public sector combines with a strongly centralized political and governmental structure to deny most of the resident population a structural voice in public affairs. Political parties are not permitted,[77] and although Dubai was largely unaffected by the Arab Spring—which, if anything, further burnished their reputation for stability[78]—protests elsewhere did prompt the UAE government to impose "Internet restrictions in 2012 to hinder the use of social media to organise protests," and the government has aggressively pursued suspected Islamist militants, reflecting domestic concerns regarding the surrounding region.[79] Similarly, although considered "a regional and international centre for TV and media" with constitutionally recognized freedom of speech, "there is strong regulatory and political control of media content" in the UAE.[80] For much of the working population, then, circumstances are further destabilized by inability to bring their families with them to the UAE (resulting in "a skewed demographic structure" with far more men than women),[81] as well as the fact that "most undesirable expatriates can simply be relieved of their visas and deported."[82] According to Freedom House, while other

---

[73] Davidson, *supra* note 22, at 14.

[74] *See* CENTRAL INTELLIGENCE AGENCY, *supra* note 1.

[75] DAVIDSON, *supra* note 7, at 263–64.

[76] *See* CENTRAL INTELLIGENCE AGENCY, *supra* note 1. Davidson reports that even the UAE's military relies on expatriates (approximately 27 percent), mainly from Yemen and Egypt. *See* Davidson, *supra* note 22, at 10.

[77] *See* CENTRAL INTELLIGENCE AGENCY, *supra* note 1.

[78] *See* TAX JUSTICE NETWORK, *supra* note 8, at 1.

[79] BBC NEWS, *supra* note 31. *See also* ECONOMIST, *supra* note 2.

[80] *See* BBC NEWS, UNITED ARAB EMIRATES—MEDIA, http://www.bbc.com/news/world-middle-east-14704229 (last updated Feb. 24, 2015). *See also* DAVIDSON, *supra* note 7, at 272 (observing "an unwritten but generally recognized ban on criticism of the government" in academia).

[81] DAVIDSON, *supra* note 7, at 148. *See also* Government of Dubai, *Dubai in Figures 2015, supra* note 13 (reporting that 75 percent of Dubai's population were male in 2014).

[82] DAVIDSON, *supra* note 7, at 13. *But see* IRFAN, *supra* note 70, at 200 (observing that Dubai's employment law has been "gradually catching up with more developed parts of the world").

jurisdictions studied here are considered "free" (Switzerland) or at least "partly free" (Hong Kong, Singapore), the UAE is considered "not free."[83]

The foregoing vulnerabilities and instabilities notwithstanding, Dubai's strategic diversification—including its concerted move into finance—has been marketed in terms strongly resonant with the MDSJ paradigm. The Dubai government states that Dubai has "long been recognized as the Middle East region's leading trading hub" and continues to offer "a competitive combination of cost, market and environmental advantages that create an ideal and attractive investment climate" for regional and global businesses—notably "low logistical and operational costs and excellent infrastructure, international outlook and liberal government policies."[84] As to why and how Dubai has pursued this strategy, the Dubai government candidly acknowledges that, "keen to diversify its economy and diminish its reliance upon shrinking oil revenues," the emirate has sought to become "the Arabian Gulf's premier international business center"—and the suite of competitive advantages and strategies cited by the government strongly resonate with the MDSJ paradigm. In terms of location, "Dubai is a time zone bridge between the Far East and Europe on the East-West axis and the [Commonwealth of Independent States] and Africa on the north-south axis," permitting the emirate to act as a "gateway" between these major markets and geographies—a bridging function facilitated by substantial investment in transport links and related infrastructure.[85] Dubai's innate commercial bridging capacities have been enhanced, then, by legal pluralism. Although the UAE has a "mixed legal system of Islamic law and civil law,"[86] Dubai has used the "financial free zone" structure to facilitate financial activity and products drawing upon Anglo-American common law structures (described further below).[87]

More generally, Dubai has endeavored to make its market "open and free to attract investors and business," including by keeping "regulation of private sector

---

[83] FREEDOM HOUSE, FREEDOM IN THE WORLD 2015, at 25–27 (2015). Although Bermuda and Delaware are not separately evaluated, the United Kingdom and the United States are both considered "free." *Id.* at 26. Freedom House evaluates "political rights and civil liberties" through a methodology "derived from the Universal Declaration of Human Rights." *Id.* at 2.

[84] Government of Dubai, *Dubai Economy,* http://www.dubai.ae/en/aboutdubai/Pages/DubaiEconomy.aspx (last visited Apr. 2016).

[85] *See id.*

[86] CENTRAL INTELLIGENCE AGENCY, *supra* note 1. Although "Article 7 of the UAE's constitution proclaims that Islam is the national religion and Islamic *Sharia* is the main source of legislation," UAE courts typically "will rule according to the *Sharia* if there is not specific legislation on the matter." Urban, *supra* note 2, at 19–20. *See also* Jayanth K. Krishnan & Priya Purohit, *A Common Law Court in an Uncommon Environment: The DIFC Judiciary and Global Commercial Dispute Resolution* 5 (Maurer Sch. of Law, Ind. Univ., Bloomington, Legal Studies Research Paper No. 300, 2014), http://ssrn.com/abstract=2482532 (forthcoming, *American Review of International Arbitration*, 2015).

[87] *See* QATAR NATIONAL BANK, *supra* note 14, at 10.

activities . . . to a minimum" and maintaining a low-tax environment. Dubai has "no direct taxes on corporate profits or personal income (except for oil companies that pay a flat rate of 55 percent and branches of foreign banks that pay a flat rate of 20 percent on net profit generated within Dubai)," and customs duties are kept "low at 4 percent with many exemptions." Likewise, Dubai permits repatriation of all capital and profits, maintains no foreign exchange controls, and has "[l]iberal visa policies [that] permit easy importation of expatriate labor of various skill levels from almost all over the world."[88] To the latter point, the Dubai government further touts the UAE's "stable and harmonious industrial relations," their low crime rate and political stability, and their "commitment to pro-business, liberal economic policies" including intellectual property rights and "a clear set of ownership rules" permitting "ownership rights of up to 49 percent for limited liability companies established within the Emirate of Dubai and up to 100 percent for professional companies, branches and representative offices of foreign companies and free zones enterprises."[89]

At the same time, the government has emphasized efforts to balance collaboration with and oversight of the financial community—a posture closely resembling that encountered in other jurisdictions examined in this part of the book. The Dubai Financial Services Authority expressly aims to be "an internationally respected regulator," administering "world-class regulation of financial services within the [Dubai International Financial Centre]," yet to remain "risk-based and to avoid unnecessary regulatory burden" in so doing.[90] To the latter point, the Dubai Islamic Economy Development Centre (DIEDC)—an initiative aimed at promoting Dubai as a hub of Sharia-compliant commerce and finance—expressly envisions public-private cooperative efforts, adding that they seek to "empower and support government and private sector initiatives" and "develop an enabling and empowering environment, including the necessary legislative and regulatory framework, to support growth of the Islamic economy."[91]

Meanwhile, Dubai further emphasizes heavy investment in human capital, professional networks, and related institutions. The government touts substantial investments "in transport, telecommunications, energy and industrial infrastructure,"

---

[88] Government of Dubai, *supra* note 84. *See also* Economist, *supra* note 2; Tax Justice Network, *supra* note 8, at 7.

[89] Government of Dubai, *supra* note 84.

[90] Dubai Financial Services Authority, *Who We Are,* https://www.dfsa.ae/About-Us/Our-Purpose/Who-We-Are (last visited Apr. 2016).

[91] Dubai Islamic Economy Development Centre, Overview 7–8, http://www.iedcdubai.ae/assets/uploads/files/Dubai%20Islamic%20Economy%20Development%20Centre%20Overview_1400145761.pdf (last visited Apr. 2016) (emphasis removed).

including development of "a network of seven industrial areas, one business park and three highly successful, specialized free zones of international distinction, two world class seaports, a major international airport and cargo village, a modern highway network, state-of-the-art telecommunications and reliable power and utilities." They have also developed "a sophisticated service sector" related to these domains "that features leading regional and international freight forwarders, shipping companies, insurers plus major international hotels, banks and financial service firms, lawyers, accounting firms, consultants, advertising agencies, top international exhibition and conference facilities, high quality office and residential accommodation, first class hospitals, schools, shopping centers and recreational facilities." They additionally note their "multi-lingual and skilled" workforce, and the quality of life that the foregoing infrastructural and professional investments facilitate.[92]

As one logistics professional expressed it, Dubai excels in "soft infrastructure." The emirate "has the right laws, and officials treat businesses like clients and implement what they say they will"[93]—characteristics that are often ascribed to MDSJs. Dubai was the first of the emirates to establish a Chamber of Commerce (in 1965),[94] and due to their "greater diversification and the development of its nonoil sectors, there are unsurprisingly a number of additional government departments and authorities at the local level in Dubai," which tend to focus on servicing trade-related and commercial functions.[95] As we will see below, Dubai's financial and regulatory infrastructure have likewise undergone extraordinary development and growth in recent decades. By the mid-2000s, as Harris Irfan summarizes it, Dubai "had a naturally ideal geographic location to act as a gateway between East and West, first world infrastructure, management talent drawn from all parts of the globe, a world-class airline, and a globally recognized brand name built on the back of iconic landmarks to draw in a constant stream of tourists."[96]

Although badly hurt during the recent financial crisis, Dubai's exposure stemmed not from finance, much less Islamic finance—which, as we will see, broadly eschews the highly speculative forms of instruments that led to the crisis in New York and

---

[92] *See* Government of Dubai, *supra* note 84. As of this writing the Dubai government contemplated construction of "Dubai Wholesale City, the largest wholesale hub in the world"—an effort that the ruler of Dubai expressly rooted in the UAE's "strategic plan to diversify the national economy away from a dependence on oil." *Revealed: Dubai Plans New $8.16bn Wholesale City Project,* ARABIANBUSINESS.COM, Mar. 1, 2016, http:// www.arabianbusiness.com/revealed-dubai-plans-new-8-16bn-wholesale-city-project-623454.html. *See also* Vasudevan Sridharan, *Dubai Setting Up World's Largest Wholesale City Worth £5.9bn,* INT'L BUS. TIMES, Mar. 2, 2016, http://www.ibtimes.co.uk/dubai-setting-worlds-largest-wholesale-city-worth-5-9bn-1547006.

[93] *See* ECONOMIST, *supra* note 2 (quoting "Fadi Ghandour, the founder of Aramex, a Dubai-based logistics company").

[94] *See* DAVIDSON, *supra* note 7, at 209.

[95] *Id.* at 198.

[96] IRFAN, *supra* note 70, at 201.

London.[97] Rather, Dubai was hurt indirectly, as ripple effects of the crisis undercut the emirate's "steroidal property boom."[98] Following a 2006 decree permitting foreigners to own Dubai real estate, "Dubai's real estate projects soared, and additional developments were launched." With the onset of the crisis in the fall of 2008, however, foreigners' interest and confidence in the Dubai real estate market collapsed, and by February 2009 Dubai's government—heavily exposed through its many private-sector ties—"was effectively bankrupt."[99] According to a 2012 report, Dubai had "the highest number of skyscrapers in the Middle East, including the world's tallest building," and with this degree of investment in real estate it is unsurprising that Dubai would have been more heavily impacted by the crisis than surrounding jurisdictions.[100]

Among other things, the crisis and its aftermath for Dubai illuminated the reciprocal interests and incentives of Dubai and Abu Dhabi. In their time of direst need, Abu Dhabi effectively bailed out Dubai to the tune of $10 billion,[101] reflecting Dubai's continued—and presumably humiliating—downside reliance on their larger neighbor's oil and gas revenue. Indeed, in the wake of this bailout, the "828-metre-high Burj Dubai tower was quickly renamed Burj Khalifa, after the savior, Sheikh Khalifa" of Abu Dhabi.[102] Although no doubt reflecting Abu Dhabi's heft and continued dominance within the federation, however, Abu Dhabi's beneficence likely represents a keen and forward-looking appreciation of the need to diversify in preparation for a post-oil economy—a future in which the substantial diversification efforts already undertaken by Dubai could offer a mutually stabilizing effect.[103]

---

[97] *See id.* at xii, 116; Dubai Islamic Economy Development Centre, *Finance,* http://www.iedcdubai.ae/page/view/6/finance (last visited Apr. 2016). For background on U.S. and U.K. market dynamics prompting the crisis, see Christopher M. Bruner, *Corporate Governance Reform in a Time of Crisis,* 36 J. CORP. L. 309, 311–17 (2011); Christopher M. Bruner, *Conceptions of Corporate Purpose in Post-Crisis Financial Firms,* 36 SEATTLE U. L. REV. 527, 549–53 (2013).

[98] IRFAN, *supra* note 70, at 197–202.

[99] *See* Christopher M. Davidson, *Dubai: Foreclosure of a Dream,* MIDDLE E. REP., Summer 2009, at 8, 9–13.

[100] *See* QATAR NATIONAL BANK, *supra* note 14, at 15, 34–35. *See also* CENTRAL INTELLIGENCE AGENCY, *supra* note 1.

[101] *See* BBC NEWS, *supra* note 71; CENTRAL INTELLIGENCE AGENCY, *supra* note 1; Davidson, *supra* note 99, at 13.

[102] *See* ECONOMIST, *supra* note 2. *See also* IRFAN, *supra* note 70, at 215–16.

[103] *Cf.* DAVIDSON, *supra* note 7, at 162 (observing that "if the oil industry falters . . . Dubai can provide greater diversification and more diverse employment opportunities"). Such dynamics took on greater urgency in 2015 due to sustained low oil prices. *See* Matt Egan, *Saudi Arabia to Run Out of Cash in Less than 5 Years,* CNNMONEY, Oct. 26, 2015, http://money.cnn.com/2015/10/25/investing/oil-prices-saudi-arabia-cash-opec-middle-east/index.html (reporting that "the UAE has enough fiscal buffers to withstand $50 oil for nearly 30 years"); Caline Malek, *Abu Dhabi Crown Prince Details UAE Leaders' Vision of Future without Oil,* NAT'L, Feb. 9, 2015, http://www.thenational.ae/uae/government/abu-dhabi-crown-prince-details-uae-leaders-vision-of-future-without-oil.

In any event, by 2012 Dubai's economic recovery was well underway, "boosted by a turnaround in the real estate sector,"[104] and since that time the government has focused increasingly on financial development, and Islamic finance in particular. In 2013 Dubai announced the goal to become "the global capital of Islamic economy,"[105] and well appreciated the suite of geographic, cultural, and strategic advantages—strongly resonant with the MDSJ paradigm—that positioned them to prosper in such business. The DIEDC, created to pursue this goal, touts Dubai's geography at "the crossroads of Europe and Asia," capacity to serve as a "Gateway to the Gulf states, the Middle East, the [Commonwealth of Independent States], East Africa and the Asian subcontinent," political stability, well-developed communications and transport linkages (evidenced by more than 11 million tourists visiting in 2013 alone), growing business and financial center offering "virtual absence of taxation" and "virtually no exchange-control regulations," free-trade zones imposing limited bureaucratic hurdles, and of course Dubai's status as "[h]ome to the world's first Islamic bank and financial market."[106] The following section describes Dubai's various initiatives to develop these capacities, focusing particularly on their growing predominance in Islamic finance.

## B. Islamic Finance

The market for "Islamic finance," referring generally to "the practice of financing transactions in compliance with Islamic principles,"[107] has grown substantially over recent years and appears poised for further growth. According to PricewaterhouseCoopers, Islamic financial assets globally amounted to $1.2 trillion in 2012, and were projected to exceed $2.6 trillion by 2017, with the Middle East representing the largest market.[108] By 2013, according to Thomson Reuters, the total had reached $1.66 trillion, including $1.214 trillion in Islamic banks, $280 billion in sukuk (often analogized to bonds), $51 billion in Islamic investment funds, and

---

[104] See QATAR NATIONAL BANK, supra note 5, at 2–4.
[105] Dubai Islamic Economy Development Centre, About the Centre, http://www.iedcdubai.ae/page/view/2/about_the_centre (last visited Apr. 2016).
[106] DUBAI ISLAMIC ECONOMY DEVELOPMENT CENTRE, supra note 91, at 5.
[107] Kilian Bälz, Book Review, 21 ISLAMIC L. & SOC'Y 320, 320 (2014) (reviewing ISLAMIC FINANCE: LAW AND PRACTICE (Craig Nethercott & David M. Eisenberg eds., 2012) and RODNEY WILSON, LEGAL, REGULATORY AND GOVERNANCE ISSUES IN ISLAMIC FINANCE (2012)).
[108] See PRICEWATERHOUSECOOPERS, ISLAMIC FINANCE: CREATING VALUE 6 (2013). See also DUBAI ISLAMIC ECONOMY DEVELOPMENT CENTRE, supra note 91, at 9; Sara Hamdan, Dubai Seeks to Become Islamic Economic Hub, N.Y. TIMES, Apr. 13, 2014, http://www.nytimes.com/2014/04/14/world/middleeast/dubai-seeks-to-become-islamic-economic-hub.html?_r=0.

$28 billion in takaful (offering a form of insurance coverage).[109] Although small in comparison with so-called conventional finance, the growth rate of Islamic financial assets has attracted increasing attention over recent years.[110] (The breakdown is presented graphically in Figure 5.1 below.) Strikingly, sukuk issuances totaled $116 billion in 2014 alone, and rating agency Fitch "expects Islamic banking and finance assets to continue their double-digit growth in coming years due to a combination of growth plans within the [Gulf Cooperation Council] and Asia, and rapidly improving investor confidence."[111] The DIEDC itself reports that "the value of Sukuk is expected to be greater than US $421 billion by 2017."[112]

As a threshold matter, Dubai finds itself very well positioned geographically to pursue these market opportunities. As of 2012 there were an estimated 1.6 billion Muslims worldwide, representing approximately 23 percent of the global population,[113] while "growing at twice the rate of the global population."[114] Approximately 10–13 percent are Shia Muslims (living mainly in India, Iran, Iraq, and Pakistan),

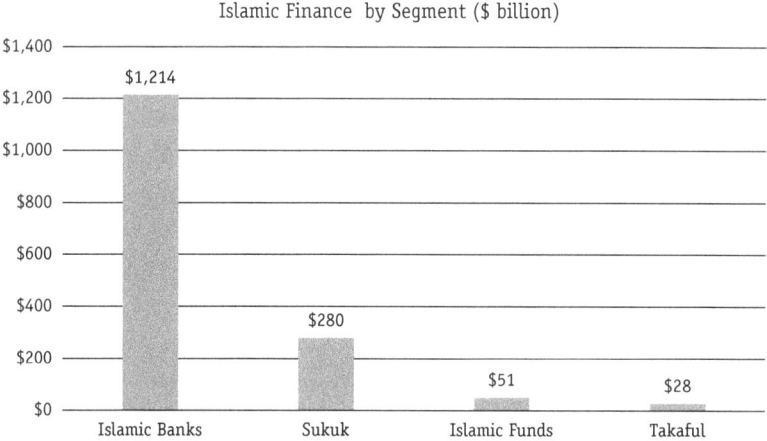

FIGURE 5.1 Islamic Finance by Segment, 2013.*

*See Thomson Reuters, State of the Global Islamic Economy: 2014–2015 Report 79 (2014) (developed and produced in collaboration with DinarStandard, supported by Dubai The Capital of Islamic Economy).

---

[109] See Thomson Reuters, *supra* note 4, at 22, 79. Thomson Reuters clarifies that the total figure excludes "undisclosed assets of most Islamic windows." *See id.* at 79 n.5.

[110] See Irfan, *supra* note 70, at 10–11.

[111] *Fitch Appoints Global Head of Islamic Finance Group,* Reuters, Feb. 16, 2015, http://www.reuters.com/article/2015/02/16/idUSFit91389020150216. *See also* Manu Mair & Mehreen Khan, *Britain to Lead the World in Islamic Finance,* Telegraph, Feb. 26, 2015, http://www.telegraph.co.uk/finance/newsbysector/banksandfinance/11435465/Britain-to-lead-the-world-in-Islamic-finance.html.

[112] Dubai Islamic Economy Development Centre, *supra* note 97.

[113] Pew Research Center Forum on Religion & Public Life, *The Global Religious Landscape: Muslims,* Dec. 18, 2012, http://www.pewforum.org/2012/12/18/global-religious-landscape-muslim/.

[114] Dubai Islamic Economy Development Centre, *supra* note 91, at 2.

whereas the "overwhelming majority" are Sunnis. Although almost 62 percent of Muslims live in the Asia-Pacific region, there are also substantial populations in the Middle East and Africa, and the "Middle East-North Africa region contains the highest percentage of Muslim-majority countries."[115] In light of this geography it has been suggested that Dubai's "access (within a short flight) to a large share of the global Muslim population may hold the key to its dominance of the industry,"[116] and that advantage will only continue to grow. "The world's Islamic population is projected to grow by 35 percent by 2030," prompting industry observers to predict substantial growth in demand for financial services compliant with Islamic law— notably banking and retirement savings products.[117] Indeed, substantial swathes of the global Muslim population remain "underbanked" due to religious objections to conventional banking described below.[118] Although financial literacy and "consumer awareness" remain challenges, additional growth opportunities for Islamic finance are thought to include the socially responsible investing market, "Hajj financing," infrastructure financing, and financing for the emerging "halal" food and lifestyle markets.[119]

Appreciating these market dynamics and opportunities requires recognizing that Islam, as a faith, represents a comprehensive life system. The word "Islam" literally means "submission," and is aptly described as presenting "a system built around an ideal"—ordering one's life in conformity with Allah's will, as revealed to the Prophet Muhammad and recorded in the Quran.[120] The word "Sharia," although often translated as "Islamic law," literally means "path"—that is, how to live in conformity with Islam. Accordingly, from the Islamic perspective, Sharia inextricably

---

[115] See Pew Research Center Forum on Religion & Public Life, supra note 113; Pew Research Center Forum on Religion & Public Life, Mapping the Global Muslim Population, PEW RESEARCH CENTER, Oct. 7, 2009, http://www.pewforum.org/2009/10/07/mapping-the-global-muslim-population/. The Sunni-Shia distinction arose from "a dispute over leadership succession soon after the death of the Prophet Muhammad in 632 A.D.," and over time they came to "differ over conceptions of religious authority and interpretation as well as the role of the Prophet Muhammad's descendants." See id.

[116] IRFAN, supra note 70, at 10.

[117] PRICEWATERHOUSECOOPERS, supra note 108, at 10–11. See also DUBAI ISLAMIC ECONOMY DEVELOPMENT CENTRE, supra note 91, at 2; THOMSON REUTERS, supra note 4, at 25.

[118] See IRFAN, supra note 70, at xii; PRICEWATERHOUSECOOPERS, supra note 108, at 11; Bloomberg, Banking Holes Seen by IMF Study Threaten Growth, BUS. TIMES, Feb. 19, 2015, http://www.businesstimes.com.sg/banking-finance/banking-holes-seen-by-imf-study-threaten-growth.

[119] See THOMSON REUTERS, supra note 4, at 102–03. "Hajj" refers to the requirement that Muslims able to do so undertake a pilgrimage to Mecca at least once in their lives. "Halal" food and lifestyle markets cater to consumers aiming to conform such consumption to Islamic law. See id. at 103.

[120] See RAJ BHALA, UNDERSTANDING ISLAMIC LAW (SHARĪ'A) xxii–xxiii (2011). See also IRFAN, supra note 70, at 21. While only the Classical Arabic Quran is considered authentic, the "vast majority of Muslims do not speak Arabic," and "aside from the call to prayer and certain readings . . . most non-Arab Muslims live their religious and secular life in the vernacular." BHALA, supra, at xxvi–xxvii.

links law, politics, morality, and lifestyle.[121] "The central concern," Rodney Wilson explains, "is with what is *halal*," or "permissible under Islamic law," and "what is *haram*, or impermissible."[122]

In this light, it is unsurprising that Islamic law has long imposed limitations on financial transactions—though it bears emphasizing that Islam is not inherently anti-finance. Indeed, Muhammad himself "was a successful merchant" with a keen interest in "strengthening mercantile institutions," and early Islamic financial structures are thought to have contributed to the spread of Islam through expanding trade networks in Africa and Asia.[123] Sharia does, however, include restrictions that are fundamentally inconsistent with core activities and functions of conventional banking and investment—notably the prohibitions of "gharar" and "riba." Rooted in concerns regarding "gambling, uncertainty, deception and speculation," the gharar prohibition precludes significant "uncertainties and ambiguity" in financial transactions.[124] Although itself amounting to a rather blurry distinction, Raj Bhala observes that "gharar" literally means "trick," underscoring historical concerns regarding fraudulent or deceptive conduct, and that Sharia today prohibits only "major" gharar—notably, financial transactions involving "excessive" uncertainty in "the principal components" of a contract.[125] The riba prohibition, then, reflects concerns regarding usury and oppression of the financially desperate—a wrong deemed particularly offensive when perpetrated by a financially stronger party performing no useful work (although a transaction involving riba does not become permissible simply because both parties are informed and possess bargaining capacity).[126] The word "riba" literally means "increase," and Sharia today broadly prohibits "the earning of money upon money"—critically, including financial transactions that involve payment or receipt of interest.[127] Together, the gharar and riba prohibitions further preclude use of derivative instruments in Islamic finance, as well as investment structures predicated on their use—notably, hedge funds.[128]

---

[121] *See* BHALA, *supra* note 120, at xix–xxii.

[122] RODNEY WILSON, LEGAL, REGULATORY AND GOVERNANCE ISSUES IN ISLAMIC FINANCE 20–21, 235 (2012).

[123] *See* TIMUR KURAN, THE LONG DIVERGENCE: HOW ISLAMIC LAW HELD BACK THE MIDDLE EAST 7, 45, 52–59, 273 (2011).

[124] Aldohni, *supra* note 4, at 542–43. *See also* Abdul Karim Aldohni, *Soft Law, Self-Regulation and Cultural Sensitivity: The Case of Regulating Islamic Banking in the UK*, 15 J. BANKING REG. 164, 169 (2014).

[125] *See* BHALA, *supra* note 120, at 654–57. *See also* IRFAN, *supra* note 70, at 67.

[126] *See* BHALA, *supra* note 120, at 679–80, 691–92, 696.

[127] IRFAN, *supra* note 70, at 35–38, 59–64. *See also* BHALA, *supra* note 120, at 667–72; Mohammad Fadel, *Riba, Efficiency, and Prudential Regulation: Preliminary Thoughts*, 25 WIS. INT'L L.J. 655, 655–57 (2008). Limited exceptions have been permitted, however, where deemed welfare-enhancing. The term "qard," meaning "loan," has been applied exclusively in charitable contexts. *See* Fadel, *supra*, at 666–72.

[128] *See* BHALA, *supra* note 120, at 658–62, 688–89; IRFAN, *supra* note 70, at 125–31, 141–62, 167–70.

So what is left of finance, as conventionally practiced in the West, once instruments and investment structures running afoul of the gharar and riba prohibitions are omitted? What remains are essentially various forms of equity. Representative contractual structures are described below, but as a general matter Islamic finance embodies the normative view that "the proper way to make money . . . is to earn it, for instance by investing or trading for gain."[129] Wilson elaborates that Sharia views financing "as a tool and not an end in itself," such that returns require justification by reference to "work and effort or risk sharing." Consequently, core principles of permissible Islamic financial arrangements include transparency, risk sharing, and channeling productive resources toward halal (rather than haram) activities.[130]

This is not to suggest, however, that Islam provides anything approaching a clear and detailed set of codes on finance. Sharia law "for most types of legal contracts . . . is concerned with general principles," and in the financial context focuses particularly on general concepts of justice and equity.[131] Indeed, as Abdul Karim Aldohni has observed, "the term *gharar* was not referred to in the Quran in the commercial context," and although "the prohibition of *riba* was generally and explicitly stated in the Quran," this central text "does not explain what qualifies as *riba*."[132] Accordingly, much has been left to scholarly interpretation—and in addition to distinct Shia thinking regarding the compatibility of a given financial structure with Sharia, there are four Sunni schools of "fiqh," essentially "jurisprudence," that may arrive at inconsistent conclusions among themselves.[133] Although effectively precluding a "general theory of contract or obligation" based on classical Islam,[134] the foregoing interpretive latitude, combined with the fact that "a proposal is permissible unless proven otherwise" under Sharia law, creates substantial capacity for financial innovation.[135]

These dynamics clearly animate contemporary Islamic finance—a distinctly modern phenomenon arising from the encounter between conventional Western banking and changing social and religious attitudes in the Muslim world. The emergence of a distinctly modern Islamic finance movement maps closely onto the mid-twentieth-century rise of "Islamic revivalism," which prompted an effort to mediate profit-driven capitalism and Islamic "social justice" orientation.[136] "As far

---

[129] BHALA, *supra* note 120, at 695.
[130] *See* WILSON, *supra* note 122, at 2–4.
[131] *See id.* at 1.
[132] Aldohni, *supra* note 124, at 169.
[133] *See* BHALA, *supra* note 120, at 388–89; IRFAN, *supra* note 70, at 57–58.
[134] *See* Haider Ala Hamoudi, *The Muezzin's Call and the Dow Jones Bell: On the Necessity of Realism in the Study of Islamic Law,* 56 AM. J. COMP. L. 423, 434–38 (2008).
[135] *See* BHALA, *supra* note 120, at 853.
[136] *See* Hamoudi, *supra* note 134, at 452–60. *See also* IRFAN, *supra* note 70, at 11–12; KURAN, *supra* note 123, at 297, 300–01.

as is known," Timur Kuran observes in his economic history of the Middle East, "no Muslim polity has had a genuinely interest-free economy."[137] Indeed, it has been argued that interest-based lending, "regardless of its impact on social welfare, was only marginally related to the pre-modern doctrines of *riba*," and that "it was the *moral* criticism of lending at interest by religious scholars . . . that gave rise to the birth of Islamic finance in the latter-half of the twentieth century."[138]

In its endeavor to mediate—or bridge—such radically different systems, Islamic finance involves enormous legal, financial, cultural, and organizational complexities. Kilian Bälz describes Islamic finance as "a *business practice* that operates in several overlapping and interacting legal fields," including not only Sharia principles but also secular legal and regulatory frameworks operative in Muslim and Western financial markets alike.[139] Accordingly, writes Bälz, this field is fundamentally about the "intricate interplay between Islamic legal structures, transnational contractual practices and national legal rules."[140] As we will see, a single "Islamic" financial transaction might implicate not only Sharia law, but also the civil-law UAE and Dubai legal systems; the common-law legal system of the Dubai International Financial Centre (DIFC), a "free trade zone" granted substantial legal and regulatory autonomy in the domain of finance; and the common-law legal system of England, the standard choice of law for transnational Islamic financial contracts.[141]

Interestingly, Sharia law and English common law share strong affinities, including adherence to precedent, the general permissibility of transactions unless shown to be forbidden, and financially useful legal concepts including agency, trusts, and partnerships.[142] Indeed, some historians have speculated that English common law may have been impacted by Sharia law via the Normans, "the last invaders of England in the Middle Ages, [who] also ruled the island of Sicily," which itself bore the imprint of geographic proximity to North Africa and "had been previously under Muslim rule."[143] This is not to suggest, however, that Islamic finance transactions encounter no hurdles in the English legal system. English regulators have

---

[137] KURAN, *supra* note 123, at 147–50. *See also* IRFAN, *supra* note 70, at 31.

[138] Fadel, *supra* note 127, at 678.

[139] *See* Bälz, *supra* note 107, at 322–23; Kilian Bälz, *A* Murābaha *Transaction in an English Court—The London High Court of 13th February 2002 in Islamic Investment Company of the Gulf (Bahamas) Ltd. v. Symphony Gems N.V. & Ors.*, 11 ISLAMIC L. & SOC'Y 117, 117–18 (2004). *See also* IRFAN, *supra* note 70, at 16.

[140] Bälz, *supra* note 139, at 119. *See also* WILSON, *supra* note 122, at 17–21.

[141] *See, e.g.*, DIB Tier 1 Sukuk (2) Ltd., *supra* note 15, at 135, 143–44; CENTRAL INTELLIGENCE AGENCY, *supra* note 1; WILSON, *supra* note 122, at 28, 32, and at 23 (observing that most Islamic finance contracts are drafted by Western law firms).

[142] *See* WILSON, *supra* note 122, at 24–31; IRFAN, *supra* note 70, at 25–32; Bälz, *supra* note 107, at 321.

[143] WILSON, *supra* note 122, at 25. *Cf.* Bälz, *supra* note 107, at 321 (describing "the tradition of Anglo-Mohammedan law").

made real efforts to accommodate Islamic finance, as discussed below, but when disputes involving such transactions are litigated in England, the English courts assess their validity solely under English law, treating Sharia principles not as law, but rather as terms incorporated into the contract.[144] The potential for legal "dislocation" between English and Sharia principles naturally introduces risk that investors must price in one way or another.[145] Additional risks arise, of course, to the extent that legal structures such as trusts—well familiar to Sharia, England, and now the DIFC—could conceivably end up litigated in general courts of the UAE, where trust concepts are not recognized under the civil law.[146]

Such complexities also manifest themselves within individual financial institutions as they endeavor to wed conventional banking methods with Sharia ethical and financial principles. Whether it be a dedicated Islamic financial institution or a conventional financial institution conducting limited Islamic financial business through a distinct "Islamic window," the institution generally must retain the services of Islamic legal scholars to confirm that their products, services, and use of funds are Sharia-compliant—a judgment taking the form of a "fatwa," or religious order, of an independent "Sharia board" within the financial institution.[147] As we will see, this role is a multifaceted one, being equal parts law, corporate governance, and audit, essentially resulting in multiple tiers of institutional governance reflecting very different perspectives—a "management board, often consisting of trained bankers with rather limited knowledge of Islamic legal principles," and a Sharia board focusing on compatibility with Islam.[148]

Conventional equity investments are generally considered unproblematic from a Sharia perspective (as long as they do not finance haram activities),[149] but a variety of distinctive Islamic financial products have developed—the overarching aim being to meet customers' financial needs through instruments not running afoul of the gharar and riba prohibitions. Although a distinctly innovative and dynamic field,[150]

---

[144] *See* WILSON, *supra* note 122, at 33–35. *See also generally* Bälz, *supra* note 139 (examining "the complex interaction between and among Islamic contractual structures, English style contractual drafting and principles of international commercial law").

[145] *See* IRFAN, *supra* note 70, at 17.

[146] *See id.* at 213–14.

[147] *See* BHALA, *supra* note 120, at 737, 853–55; WILSON, *supra* note 122, at 4. As of 2012, only two countries— Iran and the Sudan—required fully Islamic banking systems. *See* WILSON, *supra* note 122, at 90. In the Islamic investment fund context, meanwhile, there are "three major index specialists who provide Islamic screening: the S&P Global Benchmark *Shari'ah* Index Series, the Financial Times FTSE Global Islamic Index Series and the Dow Jones Islamic Indexes." WILSON, *supra* note 122, at 187–89. For an example, see S&P Dow Jones Indices, *Screens for Shari'ah Compliance,* http://www.djindexes.com/islamicmarket/ ?go=shariah-compliance (last visited Apr. 2016) (describing industry and financial ratio screens).

[148] Bälz, *supra* note 139, at 129–30.

[149] *See* WILSON, *supra* note 122, at 4, 185.

[150] *Cf.* Bälz, *supra* note 107, at 322–23.

many such instruments are built on the foundation of Islamic partnership and trust forms that date to the eighth and ninth centuries.[151] Some prominent examples and contemporary uses are described below.

In a mudaraba partnership, a passive financier called the "rabb al-mal" provides funds to another called the "mudarib," who manages the venture as an agent of the rabb al-mal until a profit is generated, at which point the mudarib becomes a partner and the two share the profits.[152] (By contrast, in a "musharaka" partnership, "all the partners subscribe to the capital required by the business."[153]) The mudaraba partnership structure has been employed in a wide range of financial and commercial contexts, including banking, investment funds, securities brokerage and underwriting, and construction financing.[154] In the banking context, for example, deposit accounts generally employ mudaraba structures, and the lack of any fixed return obligation to depositors generally prompts Islamic banks to compete aggressively through services and to set aside reserves in order to maintain consistent profit distributions.[155] For corporations and "high net worth" individuals, meanwhile, banks often provide "treasury deposit" accounts employing different structures.[156]

A murabaha contract is essentially a "cost-plus" sales contract in which a financier buys a desired asset—say, a home or a car in the consumer context, or inventory in the trade finance context—and then resells it to the ultimate purchaser, the key being that the ultimate purchaser pays a higher price to the financier in exchange for delayed payment. Although the markup obviously compensates the financier for the time value of money just as interest does, the risk borne by the financier arguably exceeds that borne by a conventional lender because, for some period of time, the financier literally owns the asset, and further "retains purchaser and seller responsibilities."[157] Doubts have been expressed regarding this structure, however, given the close resemblance to interest charges and the ability of the financier to transfer

---

[151] *See* KURAN, *supra* note 123, at 10, 33.

[152] *See* BHALA, *supra* note 120, at 710–12.

[153] WILSON, *supra* note 122, at 83.

[154] *See* BHALA, *supra* note 120, at 728; WILSON, *supra* note 122, at 11–14; Aldohni, *supra* note 4, at 546–47.

[155] *See* WILSON, *supra* note 122, at 11–14, 40–50. *See also* Dubai Islamic Bank, *Business Alerts Keep Track of Your Finances on the Go,* Form No. 1313/1—Rev.0 (brochure as of June 2015).

[156] These may include "wakala" treasury deposits under which the bank "serves as an agent by investing the sum deposited on behalf of the client" in exchange for an "arrangement fee" and residual profits beyond a stated target rate, and "murabaha" treasury deposits, a more complex form in which deposited sums are used to buy and sell commodities on the client's behalf in exchange for fees, with instructions to the bank's broker to sell on a particular date at a higher stated price. *See* WILSON, *supra* note 122, at 53–56. Other structures, meanwhile, combine insurance and investment features. *See* Dubai Islamic Bank, *Al Islami Takaful Savings & Investment Programmes with Capital Protection (Dynamic Protection Programme),* Form No. 1206/1—Rev.0 (brochure as of June 2015).

[157] *See* BHALA, *supra* note 120, at 728–33; WILSON, *supra* note 122, at 62–67.

ownership immediately while retaining "a legal charge" over the assets.[158] A more comfortable alternative embraced by the Islamic mortgage industry involves a form of "sale and leaseback" transaction—termed "ijara plus diminishing musharaka"— in which the financier and the customer enter a partnership (the musharaka component) with interests proportionate to their respective contributions toward the home's purchase price. Title to the home initially remains with the financier, and the customer leases the property (the ijara component) while simultaneously buying out the financier's partnership interest over time (hence "diminishing" musharaka).[159]

Sukuk offerings, in particular, have taken on "increasing global prominence" over recent years, and reflect constant innovation in the Islamic financial marketplace[160]—notably "to finance heavy infrastructure spending in the [Gulf] region."[161] Although often described colloquially as a bond equivalent, it is critical to recognize that sukuk fundamentally differ from bonds and other debt obligations. Whereas bonds straightforwardly involve riba in the form of interest and may finance forbidden haram activities, sukuk investments involve ownership of real assets and may finance only halal activities.[162] Broadly, the structure of a sukuk financing resembles conventional securitization; investors purchase tradable certificates from a bankruptcy-remote special purpose vehicle organized for the offering, which in turn purchases revenue-generating assets—held in trust, typically subject to English law—that produce the return to certificate holders. For example, in a sukuk offered to finance the purchase of a major business asset, the asset may be leased to the business, generating a stream of lease payments that in turn support the payment of a return to the certificate holders.[163] Unlike conventional bonds, however, which obligate the issuer to make scheduled payments to bondholders, sukuk by design involve no such obligation—the certificate holders receive payments "only if the securitized asset produces a revenue stream." Hence in the above example, if the lessee were to default, payments to certificate holders would cease, unless some form of guarantee were in place.[164] Sukuk tend to be priced, however, in a manner resembling conventional bonds—typically by reference to a benchmark rate such as

---

[158] *See* WILSON, *supra* note 122, at 66–67.

[159] *See* IRFAN, *supra* note 70, at 229–31.

[160] BHALA, *supra* note 120, at 736–37, 790–91. *See also* IRFAN, *supra* note 70, at 15–18.

[161] *See* Hamdan, *supra* note 108.

[162] *See* WILSON, *supra* note 122, at 163–66, 178–79; Robert W. Wood & Rafi W. Mottahedeh, *Taxation of Islamic Finance: Part I,* Ijara *and* Sukuk al-Ijara, TAX NOTES, July 21, 2014, at 349, 349–50.

[163] *See* BHALA, *supra* note 120, at 771–76; WILSON, *supra* note 122, at 166–73. Sukuk may not, however, create "different levels of risk from the same investment pool" through different tranches, as this would violate the "bar on risk shifting." Wood & Mottahedeh, *supra* note 162, at 350.

[164] *See* BHALA, *supra* note 120, at 756–59, 763–64, 775. *See also* IRFAN, *supra* note 70, at 33–34 (observing that guarantees may eliminate true risk sharing).

LIBOR—and "the spreads . . . are relatively similar."[165] Sukuk can be constructed through a number of Islamic contractual forms—including murabaha, musharaka, and mudaraba.[166] The permissibility of secondary market trading depends on the structure employed, trading being permissible where "the composition of the group of assets . . . consists of a majority of physical assets and financial rights." If, on the other hand, the assets were predominantly "cash and interpersonal debts," secondary market trading would violate the riba prohibition.[167]

Although such Islamic financial structures continue to gain traction, problems and criticisms have certainly arisen. First and foremost, many suggest that the Islamic finance industry has elevated form over substance, generating financial instruments that are economically indistinguishable from conventional interest-based counterparts[168]—and it is certainly not difficult to identify examples. Islamic banks, for example, may offer "Islamic credit cards" that effectively charge a fee for late payment by building in a predetermined financing period (say, a year) and then reducing the charges for earlier payment[169]—a transparent restyling of interest as the sacrifice of a discount. In yet other contexts—including murabaha financings—the riba prohibition might be avoided by dividing a single noncompliant transaction into multiple transactions that comply if viewed in isolation.[170] The gharar-based objection to conventional insurance as involving excessive uncertainty, meanwhile, has been avoided in Sharia-compliant "takaful" structures through "semantic re-classification" of premium payments as "gifts" (to which the gharar prohibition does not apply), said to reflect "solidarity" among participants in times of hardship.[171] The concept of "hilah"—a "legal trick"—reflects recognition of the general form-over-substance problem,[172] yet as Bhala explains, "the Sacred Law is concerned with the outward aspect of a transaction," and "there is a stress in Islamic Law on following the letter, as distinct from the spirit, of that Law." Accordingly, "form matters, and it can and does triumph over substance" in significant cases.[173]

---

[165] *See* BHALA, *supra* note 120, at 792–93.

[166] *See id.* at 783–90; WILSON, *supra* note 122, at 166–73.

[167] *See* BHALA, *supra* note 120, at 782–83 (quoting the Fiqh Council of the Organization of Islamic Countries). *See also id.* at 791 (describing regional differences regarding the tradability of certain sukuk structures).

[168] *See, e.g.,* KURAN, *supra* note 123, at 147–50, 289–90.

[169] *See* BHALA, *supra* note 120, at 694. Alternatively, the bank might charge a fee for late payment but "channel those collected fees to charity foundations as determined by the Fatwa and Sharia Supervisory Board," as Dubai Islamic Bank does. Dubai Islamic Bank, *Terms & Conditions of Al Islami Credit Card*, CREDIT/T&C/04/2012, para. 4.10. Note that Dubai Islamic Bank's application requires the customer to promise to use the card "only for Sharia compliant purposes." Dubai Islamic Bank, *Al Islami Credit Cards*, Form No. 898/1—Rev.0 (application form as of June 2015).

[170] *See* IRFAN, *supra* note 70, at 135–41; Fadel, *supra* note 127, at 655–57; Hamoudi, *supra* note 134, at 448.

[171] *See* Hamoudi, *supra* note 134, at 447.

[172] *See* IRFAN, *supra* note 70, at 135–41.

[173] *See* BHALA, *supra* note 120, at 704–08.

In fairness, however, it has to be acknowledged that such dynamics have been greatly exacerbated by the dominant role of Western financial institutions and law firms, who have sought to tap attractive new markets by dressing up conventional products in Islamic garb—sometimes termed "reverse engineering" or "Sharia arbitrage."[174] Meanwhile, eagerness within Muslim-majority countries to court global capital, combined with competitive pressures exerted upon local Islamic financial institutions by their much larger Western counterparts, has exacerbated form-over-substance problems.[175] Accordingly, it is unsurprising that practitioners of Islamic finance report substantial "cognitive dissonance."[176]

Another critical challenge facing the industry relates to the process for ascertaining Sharia-compliance. Although Muslims naturally consider Sharia law "God given and universal," there is no single authoritative global Islamic institution.[177] Consequently, there is great potential for inconsistencies across regions, Sharia schools, and of course individual scholars—a problem heightened by the fact that Sharia-compliance opinions generally remain unpublished.[178] Such inconsistencies naturally incentivize opinion "shopping,"[179] which may exert considerable downward pressure on standards—particularly in combination with the global competitive pressures described above.[180] Promoting standardization has rightly been identified as important to maintenance of Islamic "consumer confidence,"[181] and initiatives have been pursued in various fora[182]—notably the Accounting and Auditing Organization for Islamic Financial Institutions (AAOIFI), judgments of which have come to be regarded "in the same vein as regulatory edicts."[183] Comprehensive standardization remains difficult to achieve, however, due to the inherent challenge of identifying singular correct answers in many areas. Meanwhile,

---

[174] See IRFAN, *supra* note 70, at 16, 40–41, 155–62, 221–23, 244. Deutsche Bank's strained efforts to create Sharia-compliant derivatives provide a poignant example. *See id.* at 143–62. On the difficulty of squaring derivatives with the gharar and riba prohibitions, see BHALA, *supra* note 120, at 761–62.

[175] See WILSON, *supra* note 122, at 89–90; Hamoudi, *supra* note 134, at 460–63. *See also* IRFAN, *supra* note 70, at 163–65 (observing that, with no Sharia-compliant hedging options, Islamic financial institutions have had no option but to rely on conventional banking tools).

[176] See IRFAN, *supra* note 70, at 274–80.

[177] See WILSON, *supra* note 122, at 17–19.

[178] See Anjuli Davies & Mirna Sleiman, *"Rock Star" Scholars a Risk for Islamic Finance*, REUTERS, Mar. 1, 2012, http://www.reuters.com/article/2012/03/01/us-finance-islamic-scholars-idUSTRE8200LE20120301.

[179] See Wood & Mottahedeh, *supra* note 162, at 350.

[180] See, e.g., IRFAN, *supra* note 70, at 160–61.

[181] See Aldohni, *supra* note 124, at 172–73.

[182] See WILSON, *supra* note 122, at 123–31; Davies & Sleiman, *supra* note 178; Accounting and Auditing Organization for Islamic Financial Institutions, *About AAOIFI*, http://aaoifi.com/about-aaoifi/?lang=en (last visited Apr. 2016).

[183] IRFAN, *supra* note 70, at 32–33.

opponents of such efforts respond that standardization will undercut potentially valuable innovations.[184]

Meanwhile, reliance on Sharia scholars to assess Sharia compliance raises other issues. Notably, there is an acute shortage of scholars sufficiently versed in both Sharia and modern finance to credibly deliver such judgments—and the perceived credibility of the entire industry may be compromised by conflicts of interest that arise when highly sought-after scholars are paid by those whose products they evaluate, and occupy seats on multiple boards. Although there are reportedly "over 400 sharia scholars worldwide [there are] only around 15 to 20 prominent and experienced ones,"[185] resulting in extraordinary concentration. Indeed, a 2011 survey found that "only the top 20 Shariah scholars hold 619 Board positions representing more than half of the 1,141 positions available," creating obvious "independence and succession issues."[186] Unsurprisingly, the handful of top scholars receive "sky-high fees" for their services, thought to amount to "$1,000 to $1,500 per hour of consultation" plus "an annual bonus of between $10,000 and $20,000 per board seat." This remuneration—paid by the architects of the rated products—gives rise to straightforward conflict-of-interest concerns that are only exacerbated when the given scholar simultaneously occupies other board positions, including for standard-setters such as AAOIFI.[187] For example, Sheikh Hussein Hamed Hassan—a highly respected figure in Islamic finance who has been dubbed the "Billion-Dollar Scholar"[188]—has chaired "no fewer than 22 [Sharia] boards," including that of Dubai Islamic Bank (discussed below), and has sat on other boards including that of AAOIFI.[189] Such dynamics are widely regarded as growth inhibiters, and efforts to address them include development of programs to train other qualified scholars to serve on Sharia boards, as well as to expand the pool of personnel with sufficient financial expertise to work in Islamic banks and financial institutions.[190]

---

[184] *See* WILSON, *supra* note 122, at 227–28; Davies & Sleiman, *supra* note 178.

[185] Davies & Sleiman, *supra* note 178.

[186] PRICEWATERHOUSECOOPERS, *supra* note 108, at 14.

[187] Davies & Sleiman, *supra* note 178.

[188] IRFAN, *supra* note 70, at 74–100.

[189] Davies & Sleiman, *supra* note 178. *See also* Accounting and Auditing Organization for Islamic Financial Institutions, *Shari'ah Board: Members,* http://aaoifi.com/members-2/?lang=en (last visited Apr. 2016); Dubai Islamic Bank, *Sharia Board,* http://www.dib.ae/about-dib/sharia-board (last visited Apr. 2016).

[190] *See* PRICEWATERHOUSECOOPERS, *supra* note 108, at 10, 14; Davies & Sleiman, *supra* note 178; Dubai Islamic Economy Development Centre, *Dubai Centre for Islamic Banking and Finance,* http://www.iedcdubai.ae/initiatives/dubai_center_for_islamic_banking_and_finance (last visited Apr. 2016); Emirates Institute for Banking and Financial Studies, *Islamic Banking Diploma,* http://www.eibfs.com/eibfs/IslamicDiploma.aspx (last visited Apr. 2016); Hamdan, *supra* note 108.

The foregoing issues certainly present real challenges, though promoters of Islamic finance are likely correct in asserting that they will not prove fatal to the project. Deepening the pool of trained Sharia scholars and advancing standardization efforts may—in combination with thoughtful regulatory initiatives[191]—substantially allay concerns regarding conflicts of interest. And although form-over-substance concerns remain entirely legitimate and readily substantiated in the current marketplace, they do not fully capture the entirety of the industry or its potential for development. For example, an Islamic bank financing a home acquisition really does face differing legal risks by virtue of acting as a buyer and seller, or alternatively as a partner in a diminishing partnership;[192] sukuk lacking guarantee features really do place certificate holders in a legal position differing markedly from that of conventional bondholders;[193] and so on. Moreover, even if much of contemporary Islamic finance arguably remains too debt-like to meet strictly construed Sharia standards, there is reason to believe that standards are in fact tightening over time, and it does happen that product structures favored by powerful conventional banks are rejected on Sharia grounds.[194] Finally, and perhaps most critically, one must recall that the true driver of Islamic finance remains the demand side—underserved Muslim populations seeking banking and investment products consistent with deeply held beliefs. For this customer base, Islamic finance—imperfect though it may be—presents "a real alternative to contracts based on *riba.*"[195]

As described above, there is no gainsaying the market potential for Islamic finance, and Dubai has not only established itself as an innovator, but has pursued a global leadership position in this field.[196] Dubai Islamic Bank (DIB), established in 1975, was the world's first Islamic bank, and continues to be regarded as an industry leader.[197] Describing themselves as "champions of morality, equality and transparency in everything we do," and with the aim of being "the world's leading Islamic bank" and "most progressive Islamic Financial Institution,"[198] DIB clearly plays an

---

[191] *See, e.g.,* Aldohni, *supra* note 4, at 545 (advocating regulatory rules limiting multiple Sharia board positions, and regulatory oversight of bank boards' decisions regarding the composition of Sharia boards).

[192] *See* IRFAN, *supra* note 70, at 229–31; WILSON, *supra* note 122, at 62–67.

[193] *See* BHALA, *supra* note 120, at 756–59, 763–64, 775; IRFAN, *supra* note 70, at 33–34.

[194] *See* IRFAN, *supra* note 70, at 118–22, 243–59, 270–87.

[195] WILSON, *supra* note 122, at 18.

[196] *See* Aldohni, *supra* note 4, at 544.

[197] *See* WILSON, *supra* note 122, at 62, 107–08; DIB Tier 1 Sukuk (2) Ltd., *supra* note 15, at 89; Dubai Islamic Bank, *Overview,* http://www.dib.ae/about-dib/overview (last visited Apr. 2016); *World's First Islamic Bank Continues to Drive Industry,* WORLD FIN., Jan. 13, 2014, http://www.worldfinance.com/banking/worlds-first-islamic-bank-continues-to-drive-industry.

[198] Dubai Islamic Bank, *supra* note 197; Dubai Islamic Bank, *Vision and Mission,* http://www.dib.ae/about-dib/vision-and-mission (last visited Apr. 2016).

important role in Dubai's economic development[199] and appears to have catalyzed the development of banking regulation in the UAE.[200] As of 2016, DIB was the UAE's largest Islamic bank by assets, had a customer base of over 1.5 million with respectable ratings of Baa1 from Moody's and A from Fitch,[201] and staked out a strong regional presence with aspirations of global expansion.[202] At the same time, per the government's goal to "Emiratize" finance—that is, to encourage more Emiratis themselves to join the financial workforce[203]—DIB reported "an Emiratisation level" of 43.8 percent as of September 2014.[204]

DIB has been involved in "watershed" cross-border Islamic financing deals with Western banks—notably where the Dubai government was the buyer and "stipulated" DIB's involvement[205]—and they now work in "all areas of commercial and investment banking."[206] Their deposit and investment accounts employ profit-linked mudaraba relationships, under which "account holders agree to share the profit or loss made by DIB's Mudaraba asset pool over a given period," and their "Retail & Business Banking Group" is their largest division.[207] Their self-identified advantages include "a strong and trusted brand," their "proven track record" in Islamic finance including "a wide range of innovative products," their reputable Sharia board, well-trained staff and management experienced in both conventional and Islamic banking, and "a diversified deposit base" of private and public customers reflecting strong relationships in both domains. Additionally, they note that "DIB is not subject to tax in Dubai or the UAE, whether corporate or otherwise."[208]

The composition of the DIB Board of Directors reflects the institution's close connections with the Dubai government. As of this writing, the Board is chaired by H.E. Mohammed Al Shaibani, who also serves as Director General of His Highness the Ruler's Court, as well as CEO and Executive Director of the Investment

[199] *See* WORLD FIN., *supra* note 197.

[200] WILSON, *supra* note 122, at 107–11.

[201] *See* Dubai Islamic Bank, *Company Overview,* http://www.dib.ae/investor-relations/company-information/company-overview/overview (last visited Apr. 2016).

[202] *See* DIB Tier 1 Sukuk (2) Ltd., *supra* note 15, at 96, 104–06; Dubai Islamic Bank, *Operational Footprint,* http://www.dib.ae/investor-relations/company-information/company-overview/operational-footprint#tab-section (last visited Apr. 2016); Dubai Islamic Bank, *Distribution Network,* http://www.dib.ae/investor-relations/company-information/company-overview/distribution-network#tab-section (last visited Apr. 2016).

[203] *See* DAVIDSON, *supra* note 7, at 150–54.

[204] DIB Tier 1 Sukuk (2) Ltd., *supra* note 15, at 98, 130, 135.

[205] *See* IRFAN, *supra* note 70, at 88–100.

[206] *See* WORLD FIN., *supra* note 197.

[207] DIB Tier 1 Sukuk (2) Ltd., *supra* note 15, at 100–02, 118.

[208] *See id.* at 97–98, 123.

Corporation of Dubai, among other high-profile positions.[209] The Ruler's Court, in particular, "is the Prime Government Body of Dubai," to which other divisions of government including the Department of Finance and the courts are subordinate, while the Investment Corporation of Dubai "consolidates the commercial and business assets of Dubai Government." These include a stake of almost 28 percent in DIB, making the government by far the single largest shareholder.[210] Al Shaibani is also the President of the Dubai Office, "a Private Management office for the Royal Family of Dubai,"[211] underscoring DIB's close connection with the ruling Maktoum family.

DIB does, however, express strong commitment to financial transparency,[212] and has adopted a Western-style "Code of Corporate Governance" that further expresses commitment to ensuring some degree of board independence and multiple levels of operational oversight. Objectives include protecting "Stakeholders" (broadly construed), promoting "transparent and efficient management," and ensuring "timely and accurate disclosure" to all shareholders on a nonexclusive basis.[213] Although the Board of Directors need only be one-third independent, the Code does provide for independent external and internal auditors.[214] The Code further requires a Board-appointed "Fatwa and Sharia'a Supervisory Board" (FSSB), reporting to the shareholders, to "oversee and verify the Sharia'a aspects of the Bank's business and ensure that they are Sharia'a compliant," as well as a "Sharia'a Supervisor" to "be responsible for monitoring and auditing the entire Bank's business transactions" for Sharia compliance.[215]

---

[209] See id. at 124–26; Dubai Islamic Bank, *Board of Directors,* http://www.dib.ae/about-dib/board-of-directors (last visited Apr. 2016).

[210] DIB Tier 1 Sukuk (2) Ltd., *supra* note 15, at 17, 89–91; Dubai Islamic Bank, *supra* note 209; Dubai Islamic Bank, *Ownership,* http://www.dib.ae/investor-relations/company-information/ownership (last visited Apr. 2016); Investment Corporation of Dubai, *About ICD,* http://www.icd.gov.ae/about-icd/ (last visited Apr. 2016). Al Shaibani also sits on the Board of Directors of the Investment Corporation of Dubai, which is chaired by the ruler himself. *See* Investment Corporation of Dubai, *Board of Directors,* http://www.icd. gov.ae/about-icd/board-of-directors/ (last visited Apr. 2016). DIB's articles of association prohibit entities other than the Dubai government from owning more than 10 percent of DIB's shares, and likewise prohibit non-UAE nationals from owning an aggregate of more than 25 percent. *See* DIB Tier 1 Sukuk (2) Ltd., *supra* note 15, at 91.

[211] Dubai Islamic Bank, *supra* note 209.

[212] This may reflect the fact that the government became the largest shareholder "following discovery of a significant fraud" in 1998, and subsequently overhauled DIB's leadership "to improve its management and processes." DIB Tier 1 Sukuk (2) Ltd., *supra* note 15, at 89.

[213] See DUBAI ISLAMIC BANK, CODE OF CORPORATE GOVERNANCE, §§ 1.7, 4, 4.3(h) (promulgated Dec. 30, 2010).

[214] See id. §§ 4.3(a), 7.2, 10.1–10.2.

[215] Id. § 5.

The FSSB, for its part, would appear to possess substantial authority, including the ability to issue fatwas binding on the Board of Directors.[216] Reflecting the "rock star" scholar phenomenon described above, the FSSB is chaired as of this writing by Sheikh Hussein Hamed Hassan and includes four other highly regarded scholars.[217] According to the DIB's website, the FSSB "supervises" development of products and services, and is further "empowered to issue [fatwa] and sharia guidance on routine matters as required by different business units of the bank." Additionally, the FSSB oversees a "team of Sharia Auditors [that] regularly audits the transactions conducted by the Bank."[218]

In addition to DIB's pioneering role in Islamic banking, Dubai has taken other dramatic steps to cultivate the field of Islamic finance, including "the first modern *takaful* [insurance] provider" in 1979,[219] as well as "the world's first Islamic Shari'a compliant stock exchange, the Dubai Financial Market (DFM) in 2007, which also launched the first of its kind Islamic standard for the issuing, acquiring and trading of shares in the same year, and was followed by another DFM standard for sukuk in April 2014."[220] As of the fourth quarter of 2015, the market capitalization of the DFM stood at about AED 308 billion, and the market capitalization of NASDAQ Dubai was over AED 67 billion.[221] Perhaps most consequential for Dubai's financial development, however, has been the creation of the Dubai International Financial Centre (DIFC)—an independent and autonomous legal and regulatory environment for financial services.[222]

The DIFC presents its advantages in terms strongly resonant with the MDSJ paradigm, describing itself as "strategically located between the east and west" and "fill[ing] the time-zone gap for a global financial centre between the leading financial centres of London and New York in the west and Hong Kong and Tokyo in the east," while providing "reach into and out of the emerging markets of the region." They further emphasize the DIFC's "independent risk-based regulator"; their "legislative system consistent with English Common law"; their regulatory and judicial

---

[216] *See* WILSON, *supra* note 122, at 212.

[217] *See* Dubai Islamic Bank, *supra* note 189; Davies & Sleiman, *supra* note 178.

[218] Dubai Islamic Bank, *supra* note 189.

[219] *See* WILSON, *supra* note 122, at 143.

[220] *See* THOMSON REUTERS, *supra* note 4, at 80. *See also id.* at 83 (observing that the growing volume of sukuk issuances supports the development of exchange trading).

[221] *See* Government of Dubai, *Dubai in Figures 2015, supra* note 13. Equity listings on NASDAQ Dubai "were operationally consolidated into the DFM in July 2010 after the DFM bought a majority stake (67 percent) in NASDAQ Dubai in May 2010." QATAR NATIONAL BANK, *supra* note 14, at 39. Note also that in 2007 Dubai and Qatar became "the two biggest shareholders of the London Stock Exchange." BBC NEWS, *supra* note 39.

[222] Dubai International Financial Centre, *About Us,* https://www.difc.ae/about (last visited Apr. 2016).

"autonomy," including courts with "exclusive jurisdiction" to interpret distinct DIFC-specific civil and commercial laws; their "supportive infrastructure," including "a large pool of skilled professionals" and advanced transportation and communications capabilities; and of course their "Zero percent tax rate on income and profits (guaranteed for a period of 50 years)" and absence of exchange controls.[223] The DIFC does in fact enjoy "the highest international profile in the region,"[224] and the ability of its courts to hear non-DIFC disputes (granted in 2011) will likely further raise the DIFC's profile as a comfortable choice of law and judicial forum for foreign investors and companies doing business in the region.[225] Overall, Dubai ranked twenty-ninth in the 2014 Global Financial Centres Index and third among Middle Eastern and African centers. By 2016, Dubai had risen to thirteenth overall and first among Middle Eastern and African centers. In each case, Dubai was listed among the top centers globally considered likely to grow in significance.[226]

The process that gave rise to the DIFC clearly reflects the capacity for legal innovation, the value placed upon regulatory autonomy, the cultivation of professional capabilities and networks, and the emphasis placed upon public-private cooperative efforts that are hallmarks of the development of financial services capacity among MDSJs. As a threshold matter, creating the DIFC required a complex structure of federal and Dubai laws.[227] Pursuant to a 2003 amendment to the Constitution of the UAE, the UAE has "exclusive legislative jurisdiction" over areas including banking, insurance, and "major legislations relating to . . . civil and commercial transactions and company law," yet also expressly has jurisdiction regarding "the order and

---

[223] See id. See also Paul Lee, *The Regulation of Securities and Islamic Finance in Dubai: Implications for Models of Shari'ah Compliance* 5–6 (Mar. 17, 2016), http://ssrn.com/abstract=2720737 (forthcoming, *UCLA Journal of Islamic and Near Eastern Law*) (observing that "the DIFC provides for the laws of England and Wales as a residual source of law").

[224] WILSON, *supra* note 122, at 137.

[225] See Amgad Husein & Jonathan Burns, *Choice of Forum in Contracts with Saudi Arabian Counterparties: An Analysis of the DIFC Common Law Courts from a Saudi Arabian Perspective*, 48 INT'L LAW. 179, 180, 185 (2015). *See also* Krishnan & Purohit, *supra* note 86, at 9–15, 22–28 (observing that international lawyers express skepticism regarding the enforcement of DIFC judgments outside the DIFC, but that in-house lawyers nevertheless favor the DIFC courts, in part due to the high settlement rate). Note the further advantage that the UAE (like Malaysia) adheres to the Shafii school of Sunni jurisprudence, "often regarded as the most liberal, including in matters of finance." WILSON, *supra* note 122, at 31.

[226] See MARK YEANDLE & NICK DANEV, THE GLOBAL FINANCIAL CENTRES INDEX 15 at 5, 8, 25 (2014) (index sponsored by the Qatar Financial Centre Authority and produced by the Z/Yen Group); Z/Yen Group Limited, *Global Financial Centres Index 19: Information Pack*, http://www.longfinance.net/global-financial-centre-index-19/992-gfci-19.html (last visited Apr. 2016); Press Release, Z/Yen Group Limited, Global Financial Centers Index: London Remains on Top and Singapore Climbs to Third Place (Apr. 6, 2016).

[227] See Dubai Financial Services Authority, *Laws & Rules*, http://dfsa.ae/laws-and-rules (last visited Apr. 2016).

the manner of establishing Financial Free Zones and the boundaries within which they are exempted from having to apply rules and regulations of the [UAE]."[228] Accordingly, such Free Zones may be created by "Federal Decree," and pursuant to federal law remain "subject to all Federal laws," including anti-money-laundering regulations, but are exempted from "Federal civil and commercial laws." Otherwise, their regulation is left to "the concerned Emirate"[229]—a substantial delegation of financial regulatory authority, in this case, to Dubai. Federal law does provide, however, that licensing within any such Free Zone must require "a strong financial position and systems and controls," that licensed entities be physically located "within the boundaries" established, and that they refrain from "deal[ing] in deposit taking from the State's markets" or "deal[ing] in the UAE Dirham,"[230] underscoring that such Free Zones are aimed solely at international finance. Pursuant to this federal law, the DIFC was decreed into existence in June 2004.[231]

Per the foregoing structure, the DIFC's substantive regulation arises under Dubai law. Although the governance structure is formally quite centralized—with a President, Higher Board of Directors, Governor, Chief Justice, and Deputy Chief Justices all appointed by the ruler[232]—the DIFC, its regulator, and its dispute resolution mechanism are expressly intended to maintain "independence."[233] The DIFC's Higher Board of Directors is to consist of "persons renowned for their competence and expertise in the fields of financial services, banking, insurance, and capital markets," and the DIFC's objectives are to "promote the position of the Emirate as a leading international financial centre," to contribute to Dubai's economic development, and to operate according to "principles of efficiency, transparency and integrity with a view to making an effective contribution to the international financial services industry"[234]—an aspiration aided by the UAE's relatively low level of perceived public corruption.[235] Meanwhile the Dubai Financial Services Authority (DFSA), the DIFC's sole regulator, has a distinct

---

[228] Constitutional Amendment No (1) of 2003, Art. One (U.A.E.) (replacing Article 121 of the Constitution of the UAE).

[229] Federal Law No. 8 of 2004 Regarding the Financial Free Zones, Arts. 2–3, 7 (U.A.E.). *See also* Cabinet Resolution No. 28 of 2007 On the Implementing Regulations of Federal Law No. 8 of 2004 concerning Financial Free Zones, Arts. 2–3, 7 (U.A.E.).

[230] Federal Law No. 8 of 2004, *supra* note 229, Art. 4. *See also* Cabinet Resolution No. 28, *supra* note 229, Art. 4.

[231] *See* Federal Decree No. 35 of 2004 To Establish Financial Free Zone in Dubai, Art. One (U.A.E.).

[232] *See* Dubai Law No. 9 of 2004 In Respect of the Dubai International Financial Centre, Arts. 3, 5 bis, 8 Second (U.A.E.). *See also* TAX JUSTICE NETWORK, *supra* note 8, at 5–7.

[233] *See* Dubai Law No. 9 of 2004, *supra* note 232, Art. 3.

[234] *See id.* Arts. 3–4.

[235] *See* Transparency International, *supra* note 63.

board of directors who "may be removed only by reason of their gross negligence, incapacity or misconduct in performance of their duties."[236] The DIFC's courts, for their part, have "exclusive jurisdiction to interpret the Centre's Laws and the Centre's Regulations," authority that extends to a wide range of civil and commercial claims.[237] Critically, these laws pertaining to the DIFC expressly trump any other conflicting Dubai laws.[238]

The DFSA clearly recognizes the need to cultivate the perception of balance between robust, effective regulation and enforcement on the one hand, and flexible, market-conscious facilitation of financial services on the other. In addition to its broad financial regulatory mandate, the DFSA also "strives to detect and prevent money laundering activities within the DIFC, and will work closely with the UAE Central Bank in this vital area,"[239] reflecting awareness of cross-border regulatory scrutiny. The DFSA's board includes "leading industry, legal and regulatory experts drawn from major international financial jurisdictions,"[240] and the DFSA's rule-making process clearly conveys a commitment to private-sector input; "policy proposals" may be drawn "from DIFC firms" (among others), and proposed legislation remains open for public consultation "for at least 30 days."[241] The ultimate aim is a "regulatory regime . . . tailor-made to suit the DIFC, to the highest international standards," striking a balance that MDSJs all endeavor to convey to the global marketplace—"uncompromisingly high standards in a clear, succinct and flexible regulatory framework based on international best practices." The DFSA endeavors to maintain "confidence," "financial stability," and "the reputation of the DIFC"— including through cooperation with foreign regulators—yet to ensure that "the cost of regulation is proportionate to its benefit."[242] They elaborate that "compliance obligations should be proportionate to the mitigation of . . . risks within a framework that enables regulated entities to effectively and efficiently meet their compliance obligations,"[243] while emphasizing their wide-ranging licensing and enforcement

---

[236] Dubai Law No. 9 of 2004, *supra* note 232, Art. 7.

[237] *See id.* Art. 8 Second; Dubai Law No. 12 of 2004 In Respect of the Judicial Authority at Dubai International Financial Centre, Arts. 5–6 (U.A.E.) (amended through Oct. 31, 2011).

[238] *See* Dubai Law No. 9 of 2004, *supra* note 232, Art. 20; Dubai Law No. 12 of 2004, *supra* note 237, Art. 10.

[239] Dubai Financial Services Authority, *Who We Are*, https://www.dfsa.ae/About-Us/Our-Purpose (last visited Apr. 2016). *See also* Dubai Financial Services Authority, *Legislation*, https://www.dfsa.ae/Laws-and-Rules/LEGAL-RESOURCES#Legislation (last visited Apr. 2016).

[240] *See* Dubai Financial Services Authority, *Board of Directors*, https://www.dfsa.ae/About-Us/Our-Structure#Board-of-Directors (last visited Apr. 2016).

[241] Dubai Financial Services Authority, *Consultation Papers*, https://www.dfsa.ae/Your-Resources/Consultation-Papers (last visited Apr. 2016).

[242] Dubai Financial Services Authority, *Who We Are, supra* note 239.

[243] Dubai Financial Services Authority, *What We Do*, https://www.dfsa.ae/what-we-do (last visited Apr. 2016).

powers.[244] As noted above, the DFSA reports that it "strives to detect and prevent money laundering activities within the DIFC"[245]—a critical priority for the DIFC, and Dubai generally, given that the same stability, service capabilities, and infrastructure so attractive to legitimate investment can be expected to attract illicit funds and activity as well.[246] In 1987 the UAE became "one of the first countries to adopt specific anti-money-laundering articles," but such initiatives took on renewed vigor following the 9/11 attacks, due to U.S. accusations of a Dubai nexus with terrorism financing.[247]

Dubai's aim to establish itself as "the global capital of Islamic economy" is clearly a wide-ranging endeavor, but developing Islamic finance capabilities will just as clearly prove central to its fruition. Accordingly, the strategies pursued by the Dubai Islamic Economy Development Centre (DIEDC) closely dovetail with those pursued by the DIFC. The DIEDC's Board of Directors includes prominent members from both public and private spheres—including from the DIFC[248]—and they style the endeavor as a public-private partnership. DIEDC management aims to "work closely with relevant stakeholders" to create "a dynamic interactive climate drawing the participation of the public and private sectors to collectively achieve the strategy's objectives."[249] They anticipate the effort being facilitated by Dubai's "diversified, open, and flexible economy," the "advanced technical and logistic infrastructures," as well as Dubai's early-mover advantage reflected in the emergence of "the first Islamic bank in the world" and "the first Islamic financial market."[250]

Reflecting both Dubai's finance-oriented aspirations, on the one hand, and its Islamic economy-oriented aspirations on the other, it is unsurprising that initiatives

---

[244] *See, e.g.,* Dubai Financial Services Authority, *About Authorisation,* https://www.dfsa.ae/What-We-Do/AUTHORISATION (last visited Apr. 2016); Dubai Financial Services Authority, *About Enforcement,* https://www.dfsa.ae/What-We-Do/ENFORCEMENT (last visited Apr. 2016); Dubai Financial Services Authority, *About Recognition,* https://www.dfsa.ae/What-We-Do/RECOGNITION (last visited Apr. 2016); Dubai Financial Services Authority, *About Registration,* https://www.dfsa.ae/What-We-Do/REGISTRATION (last visited Apr. 2016); Dubai Financial Services Authority, *About Supervision,* https://www.dfsa.ae/What-We-Do/SUPERVISION (last visited Apr. 2016).

[245] Dubai Financial Services Authority, *Who We Are, supra* note 239. *See also* Dubai Financial Services Authority, *About Supervision, supra* note 244.

[246] *See* CENTRAL INTELLIGENCE AGENCY, *supra* note 1; TAX JUSTICE NETWORK, *supra* note 8, at 1, 4–5; Davidson, *supra* note 22, at 4, 11–13, 27–30.

[247] *See* DAVIDSON, *supra* note 7, at 223.

[248] *See* Dubai Islamic Economy Development Centre, *Centre Governance,* http://www.iedcdubai.ae/page/view/3/centre_governance (last visited Apr. 2016).

[249] Dubai Islamic Economy Development Centre, *Centre Management,* http://www.iedcdubai.ae/page/view/4/centre_management (last visited Apr. 2016).

[250] Dubai Islamic Economy Development Centre, *Dubai the Capital of Islamic Economy,* http://www.iedcdubai.ae/page/view/5/dubai_the_capital_of_islamic_economy (last visited Apr. 2016) (emphasis removed).

to develop Islamic finance capacities would be pursued with such vigor. Indeed, the DIFC's architects envisioned from the beginning that its financial activities would include "Islamic financing and business" subject to DFSA regulation,[251] and "development of a thriving international Islamic finance market would be a cornerstone of the DIFC."[252] Dubai, like the UAE generally, has a "dual banking system" permitting both conventional and purely Islamic financial institutions,[253] but in either case a license from the DFSA is required in order to carry on "Islamic Financial Business"—the regulatory designation being an "Islamic Window" for a conventional financial institution only partly engaging in Sharia-compliant finance, and an "Islamic Financial Institution" for institutions engaging solely in Sharia-compliant finance.[254]

In either case, Dubai law requires appointment of a "Shari'a Supervisory Board" (SSB) and authorizes the DFSA to make rules governing "appointment, formation, conduct and operation of [an SSB]."[255] To date, however, the DFSA has "focus[ed] its regulatory efforts in relation to Sharia governance at the institutional level," avoiding involvement in substantive dimensions of Sharia-consistency.[256] The DFSA's "Islamic Finance Rules" require that an SSB have "at least three members" who are "competent to perform their functions," but who are neither directors nor controllers of the institution; that appointment policies and decisions be documented; that the institution have a policy regarding disclosure and management of conflicts of interest; that the SSB have reasonable access to accurate information and ability to pursue its work without interference; and that the SSB produce an annual report. The DFSA's rules further require an "internal Shari'a review" process, and disclosure to clients regarding the institution's Sharia-compliance process. In the case of an "Islamic Window," the institution must further disclose any commingling of Sharia-compliant funds "with funds attributable to conventional financial business."[257] The rules require that "appointments, dismissals or changes" in SSB membership be approved by the institution's "Governing Body,"[258] an approach that has

---

[251] *See* Dubai Law No. 9 of 2004, *supra* note 232, Art. 9; Dubai Law No. 13 of 2004 Regulating Islamic Financial Business, Art. 7 (U.A.E.) (amended through Aug. 2014).

[252] IRFAN, *supra* note 70, at xiv.

[253] *See* BHALA, *supra* note 120, at 679.

[254] Dubai Law No. 13 of 2004, *supra* note 251, Art. 9.

[255] *Id*. Art. 13.

[256] Aldohni, *supra* note 4, at 544–47. Paul Lee contrasts this "systems-based" approach with Malaysia's "centralized" approach, in which public regulators make substantive determinations of Sharia compliance. Lee suggests that the former reflects a preference for "autonomy" in an internationally oriented market whereas the latter reflects the greater value of consistency in a domestically oriented market. *See* Lee, *supra* note 223, at 11, 19–24, 35–37.

[257] DUBAI FINANCIAL SERVICES AUTHORITY, DFSA RULEBOOK: ISLAMIC FINANCE RULES, IFR/VER10/04-16, Rules 3.5–3.8 (U.A.E.).

[258] *See id.*, Rule 3.5.1(c).

been critiqued as insufficiently insulating SSB decision-making from conventional financial business imperatives.[259] With respect to Islamic financial products themselves, the rules include various procedural and disclosure-oriented requirements for "Profit Sharing Investment Accounts" involving various forms of Islamic contractual structures, "Islamic Collective Investment Funds," Islamic securities offerings, and takaful insurance.[260]

The strategic initiatives, infrastructural investments, and legal and regulatory developments described above have supported major Dubai-based advances toward mainstreaming Sharia-compliant investment. One notable example is the NASDAQ Dubai Murabaha Platform established in 2014. NASDAQ Dubai, a DIFC-based exchange majority owned by the Dubai government, is touted as "bring[ing] together the best of international standards with regional knowledge and understanding," providing a regional listing option with global reach.[261] The Murabaha Platform, then, "provides Islamic financing services to a rapidly growing number of individual and institutional customers" and "is playing a key role in Dubai's growth as the Capital of the Islamic Economy globally," completing "more than AED 21 billion of transactions" by November 2014. NASDAQ Dubai explains that the Murabaha Platform "makes use of Sharia'a-compliant Certificates that have been developed for the underlying assets of the financing transactions," facilitating such transactions by "Islamic banks, Islamic windows of conventional banks, and Islamic finance companies and their clients."[262] Overall, NASDAQ Dubai's sukuk listings have helped Dubai "make up ground on Kuala Lumpur and London,"[263]

---

[259] *See* Aldohni, *supra* note 4, at 545.

[260] *See* Dubai Financial Services Authority, *supra* note 257, Chapters 5–8.

[261] NASDAQ Dubai, *Overview,* http://www.nasdaqdubai.com/exchange/about-us/overview (last visited Apr. 2016) (explaining that NASDAQ Dubai is two-thirds owned by the DFM and one-third owned by Borse Dubai). *See also* Borse Dubai, *Borse Dubai,* http://www.borsedubai.ae/about_us.htm (last visited Apr. 2016) (explaining that Borse Dubai was created in 2007 "to consolidate the Government of Dubai's two stock exchanges"); Borse Dubai, *Frequently Asked Questions,* http://www.borsedubai.ae/faq.htm (last visited Apr. 2016) (same); Borse Dubai, *Borse Dubai Exchange Portfolio,* http://www.borsedubai. ae/borse-dubai-exchange-portfolio.htm (last visited Apr. 2016) (explaining that Borse Dubai holds a 79.63 percent stake in the DFM, as well as a 17 percent stake in NASDAQ itself); Dubai Financial Market, *About DFM,* http://www.dfm.ae/about-dfm/about-dfm (last visited Apr. 2016) (explaining that the DFM was established "as a public institution," but that 20 percent of its shares were "offered through an IPO"). Unsurprisingly, the same individual—H.E. Essa Abdulfattah Kazim—serves as Governor of the DIFC, Chairman of Borse Dubai, and Chairman of the DFM, as well as "Deputy Chairman of Supreme Legislation Committee in Dubai and a member in Dubai Supreme Fiscal Committee." Borse Dubai, *Chairman,* http://www.borsedubai.ae/chairman.htm (last visited Apr. 2016).

[262] NASDAQ Dubai, *Aafaq—Islamic Finance Begins Transacting on NASDAQ Dubai Murabaha Platform for Islamic Financing,* Nov. 3, 2014, http://www.nasdaqdubai.com/press/ aafaq-islamic-finance-begins-transacting-on-nasdaq-dubai-murabaha-platform-for-islamic-financing.

[263] Frank Kane, *Dubai Closer to Becoming Islamic Finance Hub,* Nat'l, Dec. 30, 2014, http://www.the-national.ae/business/economy/dubai-closer-to-becoming-islamic-finance-hub.

establishing Dubai as "the world's largest centre for Sukuk listings" and NASDAQ Dubai as "the world's largest single exchange."[264] In 2013 the DIEDC established the "Dubai Global Sukuk Centre," an initiative aimed at promoting Dubai's growing capacity in this field, and since its launch sukuk valued at approximately $5.4 billion have listed on the DFM and NASDAQ Dubai, raising the total to $12.6 billion.[265] By July 2015 Dubai had become the top listing venue for sukuk, reaching a total of $36.7 billion.[266] (Figure 5.2 provides comparative data.)

Dubai is indeed regarded today as one of the three leading centers for Islamic finance,[267] and the foregoing discussion identifies substantial strengths in this field—though of course Dubai will face stiff competition not only from Kuala Lumpur, the clear "global leader" in Islamic finance,[268] but also increasingly from London. The United Kingdom in fact was "the first non-Muslim country to issue Sukuk at the national level" in 2014,[269] and British regulators and lawmakers have undertaken substantial financial and tax reforms aimed at clarifying the treatment of Islamic financial products and services under U.K. law.[270] As of 2015, with "six Islamic

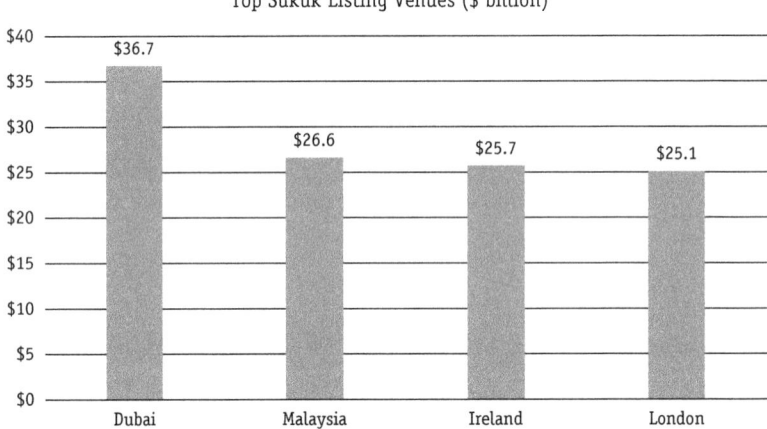

FIGURE 5.2 Top Sukuk Listing Venues, 2015.*

* *See* Andrew Torchia, *Dubai Plans New Sukuk Channels as Listings Top Other Centres,* REUTERS, July 8, 2015, http://www.nasdaqdubai.com/products/dubai-tops-sukuk-listing.

---

[264] NASDAQ Dubai, *Sukuk & Islamic Products,* http://www.nasdaqdubai.com/products/islamic-securities (last visited Apr. 2016).

[265] *See* Dubai Islamic Economy Development Centre, *Dubai Global Sukuk Centre,* http://www.iedcdubai.ae/initiatives/dubai_global_sukuk_centre (last visited Apr. 2016).

[266] *See* Andrew Torchia, *Dubai Plans New Sukuk Channels as Listings Top Other Centres,* REUTERS, July 8, 2015, http://www.nasdaqdubai.com/products/dubai-tops-sukuk-listing.

[267] *See supra* note 4 and accompanying text.

[268] *See* Kane, *supra* note 263.

[269] THOMSON REUTERS, *supra* note 4, at 95. *See also* Mair & Khan, *supra* note 111.

[270] *See* WILSON, *supra* note 122, at 115–19. *See also generally* Aldohni, *supra* note 124; Lee, *supra* note 223, at 25–29, 35 n.168. Although taxation presents no issues in the Gulf region "given the absence of income tax,

banks [and] another 20 lenders currently offer[ing] Islamic financial products and services," the United Kingdom has more Islamic banks "than any other Western country."[271] Such efforts, combined with the natural affinities between Islamic and English law discussed above and Islamic financial institutions' continuing need for conventional banking partners as a means of global market access,[272] suggest that the United Kingdom may prove to be a formidable competitor indeed.

Many of the dynamics discussed in this chapter—the tensions that arise as Islamic finance encounters global capital markets, the competitive challenges facing Dubai, and the opportunities moving forward—are illustrated by two prominent sukuk offerings conducted in 2015. The first, for Dubai Islamic Bank (DIB), was a clear success, raising $1 billion to finance DIB's "general business activities"[273] through an offering that was substantially oversubscribed.[274] The sukuk offering employed a mudaraba partnership structure, involving a mudaraba agreement governed by Dubai law, a declaration of trust and issued certificates governed by English law, and a Cayman trustee—a common feature in sukuk offerings.[275] The offering occurred through a syndicate in which regional banks certainly participated, but under the leadership of HSBC and Standard Chartered[276]—a clear reflection of continued reliance on conventional banks for global market access. The sukuk is perpetual with scheduled distributions per year, but payments are supported by the bank's profits and technically occur "at the sole discretion of DIB (as Mudareb),"[277] reflecting the profit-sharing structure of the mudaraba arrangement. Indeed, the prospectus

---

transfer taxes and capital gains tax," WILSON, *supra* note 122, at 117–18, sukuk and other Islamic investment structures can create "virtually limitless" issues elsewhere—notably under tax systems favoring debt over equity. *See* Wood & Mottahedeh, *supra* note 4, at 18–20. As of 2014, the United States was "the only major developed economy that fails to provide any useful information on how these instruments should be taxed." Wood & Mottahedeh, *supra* note 162, at 350–53.

[271] Mair & Khan, *supra* note 111.

[272] *See* WILSON, *supra* note 122, at 29–30, 139; THOMSON REUTERS, *supra* note 4, at 85.

[273] DIB Tier 1 Sukuk (2) Ltd., *supra* note 15, at 1, 57, 144.

[274] *See* Reuters, *Dubai Islamic Bank Sukuk May Open Window for Gulf Bond Issues,* GULF BUSINESS, Jan. 17, 2015, http://gulfbusiness.com/2015/01/dubai-islamic-bank-sukuk-may-open-window-gulf-bond-issues/; *Dubai Islamic Bank Launches $1bln Tier 1 Sukuk at 6.75 pct—Leads,* REUTERS, Jan. 14, 2015, http://www.reuters.com/article/2015/01/14/dib-sukuk-pricing-idUSL6N0UT25920150114.

[275] *See* DIB Tier 1 Sukuk (2) Ltd., *supra* note 15, at 1, 27–29, 35–37, 42, 77, 84–85, 143–47. *See also DIB Tier 1 Sukuk (2) Ltd.,* SUKUK.COM, https://www.sukuk.com/sukuk-new-profile/dib-tier-1-sukuk-2-ltd-3711/ (last visited Apr. 2016). The predominance of Cayman trustees in sukuk offerings has been attributed to the Cayman Islands' highly developed trust law, tax neutrality, ease of incorporation, professional sophistication, and (as a British Overseas Territory) grounding in English law—"generally the law of choice for Sukuk transactions." Ciaran Bohnacker, *Cayman SPVs in Sukuk Structures,* ISLAMIC FIN. NEWS, Sept. 23, 2015, at 24. They have further sought to attract sukuk business by amending their trust legislation to reduce associated regulatory costs and by developing "an Arabic language facility to enable companies to register and issue certificates in both English and Arabic." Bohnacker, *supra.*

[276] *See* DIB Tier 1 Sukuk (2) Ltd., *supra* note 15, at 1, 37.

[277] *See id.* at 27, 35–38.

clearly explains that an issued certificate does not constitute debt, but rather represents "an undivided ownership interest" in the trust assets, and that if DIB were to fail the certificates and associated payment rights would be "cancelled and not restored under any circumstances."[278]

Accordingly, the potential DIB sukuk investor finds risk disclosures reflecting this structure, along with others relevant to Islamic finance generally and Dubai as a jurisdiction, including the lack of any guarantee feature; DIB's inability, as an Islamic bank, to employ the "range of hedging products" available to conventional banks; uncertainties regarding enforceability of the terms of an English law trust in a UAE court, given that "UAE law does not recognise the concept of trust or beneficial interests"; lingering 9/11-related litigation (though "DIB believes that it has meritorious defences"); potential for the Dubai government, as the largest shareholder, "to influence DIB's business significantly"; and potential impacts of "regional geopolitical instability."[279] Perhaps most interesting of all, however, are the risk disclosures and disclaimers regarding the reliability of Sharia board approvals. Although DIB's "highly reputed Fatwa and Sharia Supervisory Board" is identified as a competitive advantage,[280] and their approval of the sukuk offering is confirmed (along with approvals of Sharia boards at other institutions involved with the offering), potential investors are nevertheless warned that they "should not rely on such approvals in deciding whether to make an investment in the Certificates and should consult their own *Shari'a* advisers as to whether the proposed transaction described in such approvals is in compliance with their individual standards of compliance with *Shari'a* principles"[281]—a stark reminder that Sharia compliance remains contested intellectual terrain, and that Islamic finance remains a long way from the clarity and standardization that many argue will be necessary to support further growth.

Another interesting example involved an ijara-based issuance of over $913 million in sukuk to finance acquisition of four Airbus A380-800 aircraft for Emirates Airlines.[282] Under this structure the trustee (again a Cayman entity) bought the aircraft, which it then leased to Emirates.[283] The issued certificates—similarly sold through a syndicate

---

[278] *See id.* at 1, 20, 25, 39–40, 54.

[279] *See id.* at 12, 16–17, 19, 29, 107–09, 118–20.

[280] *See id.* at 97, 128–30, 159–60.

[281] *Id.* at 1, 3, 30, 158–59.

[282] *See* Khadrawy Limited, Prospectus, U.S.$913,026,000 2.471 per cent. Certificates due 2025 (Mar. 26, 2015), at iii, 8; Press Release, Emirates Group, Emirates Set to Close US$913 Million Sukuk, Marking a World's First for Utilising UKEF-Backed Sukuk for Aircraft Financing (Mar. 30, 2015), http://www.emirates.com/no/english/about/media-centre/2363864/emirates-set-to-close-us-913-million-sukuk-marking-a-world-s-first-for-utilising-ukef-backed-sukuk-for-aircraft-financing; *Khadrawy Limited,* Sukuk.com, https://www.sukuk.com/sukuk-new-profile/khadrawy-limited-3935/ (last visited Apr. 2016).

[283] *See* Khadrawy Limited, *supra* note 282, at iii, 7–11; Emirates Group, *supra* note 282. For a discussion of Islamic aviation finance transactional structures, see Urban, *supra* note 2, at 17–19.

including regional banks but predominantly led by conventional banks—again represent "an undivided ownership interest" in trust assets, with payments ultimately funded by Emirates' lease payments.[284] Once again the offering finances activities of a government-controlled business, the declaration of trust and the certificates are governed by English law, and very similar disclaimers regarding Sharia compliance appear in the prospectus.[285] The offering represented yet another tremendous success for Islamic finance in Dubai, "recording an oversubscription of 3.6 times"[286] and representing "the first time a sukuk has been used to pre-fund an aircraft acquisition."[287]

The Emirates sukuk exhibits critical differences from the DIB sukuk, however, that reflect looming competitive threats. Aside from the limited duration of this sukuk,[288] the most consequential distinction relates to the financial terms and parties involved. Some have speculated that sovereigns and sovereign-controlled entities might offer sukuk as a political imperative to achieve greater prominence in Islamic finance[289]—which may have been at work in both of these offerings. In the Emirates offering, however, there is an additional player jockeying for position— the U.K. government, which provided a guarantee.[290] In this light, the Emirates offering represents another milestone—"the first sukuk to be guaranteed by UK Export Finance."[291] The U.K. government's willingness to accept this exposure most certainly reflects the fact that Airbus A380 wings are built in Broughton, yet commentators also link the move with "a real drive in the UK to promote and nurture Islamic finance"—a move dovetailing nicely with the legal and regulatory efforts to this end described above.[292] Accordingly, these prominent sukuk offerings highlight Dubai's continuing initiative and growing prominence in Islamic finance, while at the same time reflecting persistent structural and competitive challenges.

---

[284] *See* Khadrawy Limited, *supra* note 282, at v, 8, 13, 20, 28–31, 123. For a discussion of UAE law regarding aviation financing, see Urban, *supra* note 2, at 19–27.

[285] *See* Khadrawy Limited, *supra* note 282, at 18, 24, 81, 90.

[286] Emirates Group, *supra* note 282.

[287] Tim Burke, *Corporates Slow to Take Plunge on Sukuk*, Fin. News, Aug. 20, 2015, http://www.efinancial-news.com/story/2015-08-20/corporates-slow-to-take-plunge-on-sukuk.

[288] The Emirates sukuk has a 10-year duration and Emirates has an option to buy the aircraft outright. *See* Khadrawy Limited, *supra* note 282, at 14, 71–72.

[289] *See* Burke, *supra* note 287.

[290] *See* Khadrawy Limited, *supra* note 282, at 9, 25–27.

[291] Burke, *supra* note 287.

[292] Barry Cosgrave, *Islamic Finance in the UK: Recent Developments Building on Strong Foundations*, Mondaq, Aug. 10, 2015, http://www.mondaq.com/x/418842/islamic+finance/Islamic+Finance+In+The+UK+Recent+Developments+Building+On+Strong+Foundations. *See also* Andrew Critchlow, *UK Government Guarantees Its First Islamic Bond for Emirates*, Telegraph (UK), Mar. 30, 2015, http://www.telegraph.co.uk/finance/newsbysector/banksandfinance/11504180/UK-government-guarantees-its-first-Islamic-bond-for-Emirates.html.

# 6 Singapore

OF THE JURISDICTIONS studied here, Singapore has undergone the most dramatic transformation in recent decades. As economist Joseph Stiglitz observes, it is
"hard to believe how far this city-state has come in the half-century since it attained
independence from Britain," when "a quarter of Singapore's work force was unem-
ployed or underemployed" and "per-capita income (adjusted for inflation) was less
than a tenth of what it is today."[1] In 2015 Singapore's unemployment rate stood at
just 2 percent while per capita GDP reached $85,700—fifth highest in the world.[2]
By 2015 Singapore ranked "eighth in the world in terms of personal wealth per adult,
the highest ranking of all countries in Asia," with mean wealth of $269,408.[3]

---

[1] Joseph E. Stiglitz, *Singapore's Lessons for an Unequal America*, N.Y. TIMES, Mar. 18, 2013, http://opinion-
ator.blogs.nytimes.com/2013/03/18/singapores-lessons-for-an-unequal-america/.

[2] *See* CENTRAL INTELLIGENCE AGENCY, THE WORLD FACTBOOK: SINGAPORE, https://www.cia.gov/
library/publications/the-world-factbook/geos/sn.html (last updated Apr. 26, 2016). *See also* IGNATIUS
LOW, FIONA CHAN & GABRIEL CHEN, SUSTAINING STABILITY: SERVING SINGAPORE 13 (2012). By
2014 Singapore was "the world's most expensive city" as well. *Singapore Named the World's Most Expensive
City,* BBC NEWS, Mar. 3, 2014, http://www.bbc.com/news/business-26412821.

[3] ANTHONY SHORROCKS, JIM DAVIES & RODRIGO LLUBERAS, CREDIT SUISSE GLOBAL WEALTH
REPORT 2015, at 54 (2015). Singapore exhibits relatively high income inequality and has seen a growing
number of "needy Singaporeans applying for financial assistance" in recent years, though the government
argues that "A poor person in Singapore fares much better than the poor in Asia or the West," and has increased the "income ceiling for those who are eligible for financial assistance." *See* Choon-Piew Pow,

How did Singapore achieve such staggering successes over so short a period? The MDSJ approach highlights a number of competitive strengths and development strategies facilitating Singapore's rise to global prominence.

## A. East Meets West

Like Bermuda and Dubai, Singapore clearly exhibits a number of core MDSJ attributes. An island group totaling just 697 square kilometers (approximately 3.5 times larger than Washington, DC) with a population of approximately 5.7 million, Singapore similarly lacks substantial natural resources.[4] Accordingly, Singapore has relied heavily on services, which accounted for over 76 percent of 2015 GDP and employ almost 84 percent of the workforce.[5] Singapore today enjoys "a highly developed and successful free-market economy" in which financial services, in particular, loom large,[6] accounting for almost 12 percent of GDP.[7] Singapore receives a sterling AAA credit rating from Standard & Poor's[8]—hardly surprising, given that "the government has not borrowed to finance deficit expenditures since the 1980s"[9]— and the city-state is considered one of the most stable jurisdictions in the world.[10] Singapore's dollar floats[11] (unlike Bermuda's), yet Singapore's monetary policy has focused on exchange rates for reasons resonating with MDSJ status. "Singapore has almost no natural resources and a heavy dependence on imports—which it pays for with its exports—resulting in an uncommonly open economy with negligible

---

"*The World Needs a Second Switzerland*": *Onshoring Singapore as the Liveable City for the Super-Rich, in* GEOGRAPHIES OF THE SUPER-RICH 61, 69, 71–72 (Iain Hay ed., 2013).

[4]  *See* CENTRAL INTELLIGENCE AGENCY, *supra* note 2; Darryl S.L. Jarvis, *Race for the Money: International Financial Centres in Asia*, 14 J. INT'L REL. & DEV. 60, 77 (2011). According to the CIA's *World Factbook,* Singapore ranks 114th globally in population and 192nd in area, falling slightly above the median with respect to the former and far below the median with respect to the latter (approximately 5.4 million people and approximately 57,000 square kilometers, respectively). *See* CENTRAL INTELLIGENCE AGENCY, THE WORLD FACTBOOK: POPULATION, https://www.cia.gov/library/publications/the-world-factbook/rankorder/2119rank.html (last visited Apr. 2016); CENTRAL INTELLIGENCE AGENCY, THE WORLD FACTBOOK: AREA, https://www.cia.gov/library/publications/the-world-factbook/rankorder/2147rank. html (last visited Apr. 2016).

[5]  *See* CENTRAL INTELLIGENCE AGENCY, *supra* note 2.

[6]  *Id.*

[7]  *See* LOW ET AL., *supra* note 2, at 13.

[8]  Standard & Poor's Ratings Services, *Singapore Ratings Affirmed at "AAA/A-1+" on Robust Public Finances; Outlook Stable,* May 3, 2013.

[9]  CENTRAL INTELLIGENCE AGENCY, *supra* note 2.

[10]  *See* World Bank, *Worldwide Governance Indicators,* http://info.worldbank.org/governance/wgi/index. aspx (last visited Apr. 2016) (assigning Singapore a "Political Stability and Absence of Violence/Terrorism" percentile rank of 92.2 out of 100 in 2014).

[11]  *See* CENTRAL INTELLIGENCE AGENCY, *supra* note 2.

import restrictions." Due to "its extremely small size, Singapore has to be a price-taker in the global markets."[12]

Again like Bermuda and Dubai, Singapore benefits from its capacity to serve as a cultural and geographic bridge between major economic and financial powers. Long a "focal point for Southeast Asian sea routes,"[13] Singapore has effectively hybridized Eastern and Western cultures, a posture apparent in their four official languages—Mandarin, English, Malay, and Tamil—which in turn reflect Singapore's legal and economic history.[14] Established as an English colony in the early nineteenth century to secure control over the Straits of Malacca and thereby maintain a "gateway to China from the West,"[15] Singapore's formal legal and constitutional status would change several times before full independence from the United Kingdom arrived in the mid-1960s.[16] The British claim to Singapore was recognized by the rival Dutch through the 1824 Treaty of London, and in 1826 the British combined Singapore with the ports of Malacca and Penang to form the Straits Settlements, which became a crown colony in 1867. Following the traumatic Japanese occupation of 1942–1945, Singapore was granted the status of crown colony in its own right, and in 1959 was granted the status of a state of the British Commonwealth, effectively rendering Singapore "internally self-governing with autonomy in all matters except defense and external relations." Following a brief and tumultuous union with the Federation of Malaysia (a move prompted by fears of "a Communist take-over of the island") in 1963, Singapore left the union and became a fully independent sovereign on August 9, 1965.[17]

Notwithstanding these constitutional convolutions, however, it was well established by the mid-1820s that English law would govern in Singapore.[18] English statutes "of general application and suited to the condition of the place" applied, as did English common law, and modifications grew rare over time due to "the progressive Westernisation of the population and the enactment of statutes grounded firmly on English principles."[19] This high degree of conformity to English law has persisted,

---

[12] Low et al., *supra* note 2, at 38.

[13] Central Intelligence Agency, *supra* note 2. *See also* Jarvis, *supra* note 4, at 82.

[14] *See* Central Intelligence Agency, *supra* note 2. *See also* Walter Woon, *The Applicability of English Law in Singapore, in* The Singapore Legal System 230, 233 (Kevin Y.L. Tan ed., 2d ed. 1999).

[15] Woon, *supra* note 14, at 231. *See also* Kevin Tan, *A Short Legal and Constitutional History of Singapore, in* The Singapore Legal System, *supra* note 14, at 26, 28–30.

[16] *See* Tan, *supra* note 15, at 30–46; Woon, *supra* note 14, at 232–33. Singapore became part of Malaysia in 1963, but following "disagreements between the Federal Government and the Government of Singapore, Singapore was expelled . . . on 9 August 1965," accordingly becoming an independent republic. Woon, *supra* note 14, at 233.

[17] *See* Bank of America, Singapore: A Bank of America Report 5–9 (1968/1969).

[18] *See* Woon, *supra* note 14, at 233–36.

[19] *Id.* at 236–38.

notwithstanding Singapore's establishment of full sovereignty—an approach reflected until 1993 in Section 5 of the Civil Law Act, described by one commentator as "perhaps the most academically-dissected section in the whole statute book,"[20] and subsequently by the Application of English Law Act (AELA).[21]

Even though Singapore ceased to be a British colony in 1963 and became fully independent in 1965, the long-time application of English statutes and common law rendered it necessary to clarify "the extent to which English law is applicable in Singapore."[22] AELA states that English common law survives "so far as it is applicable to the circumstances of Singapore and its inhabitants and subject to such modifications as those circumstances may require."[23] Likewise, certain enumerated English statutes survive "with the necessary modifications."[24] Beyond this, "no English enactment shall be part of the law of Singapore."[25] This technical clarification may implicitly overstate the degree of divergence, however, because as Walter Woon has observed, "English authorities form the overwhelming majority of precedents cited in court" in Singapore[26]—a trend he attributes to statutory similarities, the relative lack of local precedents, ease of access to English authorities, and the fact that the Privy Council remained "Singapore's final court of appeal until the enactment of the Judicial Committee (Repeal) Act in 1994."[27] Woon further observes, however, that this dependence on English precedent has gradually waned due to "the advent of computer databases of cases and statutory materials, and an increased output of cases and textbooks."[28] In any event, the capacity of Singapore's "fair and impartial judiciary to ensure certainty with respect to property rights and contract enforcement" is identified as a competitive strength.[29]

As noted above, Singapore's development since full independence in the mid-1960s has been staggering, and the capacity to bridge different regions and major economies has proven critical in their rise to financial prominence. A 40-year retrospective of the Monetary Authority of Singapore (MAS) quotes a Chinese saying to the effect that "the factors for success are time, place and people" (*tian shi, di li, ren he*)[30]—and in Singapore's case this certainly rings true. Its history as a Southeast

---

[20] *Id.* at 239. *See also* PHILIP N. PILLAI, COMPANY LAW 1–2 (1979).

[21] Application of English Law Act, ch. 7A, Act 35 of 1993, § 6(1) (Sing.) (repealing § 5 of the Civil Law Act).

[22] *Id.*, preamble.

[23] *Id.* § 3.

[24] *Id.* § 4.

[25] *Id.* § 5.

[26] Woon, *supra* note 14, at 230.

[27] *See id.* at 240–42.

[28] *Id.* at 243.

[29] LOW ET AL., *supra* note 2, at 148.

[30] *Id.* at 171.

Asian entrepôt and long-standing commercial culture provided a strong foundation for development of a cross-border financial center beginning in the late 1960s,[31] and their historical and diplomatic ties with regional and global powers positioned them to work collaboratively with well-regarded financial regulators around the world.[32]

Although it is certainly "unusual to find a country's history so closely identified with one man"[33]—Lee Kuan Yew, Singapore's charismatic, energetic, and authoritarian Prime Minister from 1959 to 1990, widely regarded as the "father of the nation"[34]—Lee "was not generally the driving force on economic policy."[35] Lee was, however, a critical supporter of developing cross-border financial services capacity, and has provided in his memoir of the period a description of the origins of the initiative sufficiently vivid—and evocative of the dynamics explored in this book—to merit examination. Looking back, Lee emphasizes the broad goal "to create a First World oasis in a Third World region," explaining that "[i]f Singapore could establish First World standards in public and personal security, health, education, telecommunications, transportation and services, it would become a base camp for entrepreneurs, engineers, managers and other professionals who had business to do in the region."[36] Yet, he acknowledges that "[a]nyone who predicted in 1965 when we separated from Malaysia that Singapore would become a financial centre would have been thought mad."[37]

Singapore's extraordinary successes in cross-border finance are, in the first instance, attributed to two nongovernmental individuals—Dr. Albert Winsemius, a Dutch economist dispatched by the United Nations in the early 1960s, who would long advise the Singapore government in its economic and financial development efforts,[38] and J.D. Van Oenen, a Bank of America executive then involved with the bank's Singapore operations. Lee recounts:

> It had a most improbable start in 1968. In his oral history, Dr Winsemius recalls his telephone call to his friend, the vice-president of the Bank of America branch in Singapore, who was then in London. "Look here, Mr Van Oenen,

[31] *Id.* at 102, 143–46.

[32] *Id.* at 203–10.

[33] MICHAEL D. BARR, LEE KUAN YEW: THE BELIEFS BEHIND THE MAN 127 (2000).

[34] *See id.* at 7–38. In his in-depth study, Barr identifies progressivism, elitism, and cultural evolutionism as the central tenets of Lee's worldview and governance philosophy. *See id.* at 49–184.

[35] *Id.* at 145.

[36] LEE KUAN YEW, FROM THIRD WORLD TO FIRST—THE SINGAPORE STORY: 1965–2000, at 76 (2000).

[37] *Id.* at 89.

[38] *See* Sumiko Tan, *Dr. Albert Winsemius: Singapore's Trusted Guide,* http://ourstory.asia1.com.sg/dream/lifeline/win2.html (first published in *The Straits Times,* Dec. 7, 1996). *See also* LEE, *supra* note 36, at 66, 78–79.

we (Singapore) want, within ten years, to be the financial centre in Southeast Asia." Van Oenen replied, "All right, you come to London. In five years you can develop it." Winsemius immediately went to London where Van Oenen took him to a large globe standing in a boardroom, and said, "Look here, the financial world begins in Zurich. Zurich banks open at 9 o'clock in the morning, later Frankfurt, later London. In the afternoon Zurich closes, then Frankfurt and London. In the meantime, New York is open. So London hands over financial money traffic to New York. In the afternoon New York closes; they had already handed over to San Francisco. When San Francisco closes in the afternoon, the world is covered with a veil. Nothing happens until next day, 9:00 am Swiss time, then the Swiss banks open. If we put Singapore in between, before San Francisco closes, Singapore would have taken over. And when Singapore closes, it would have handed over to Zurich. Then, for the first time since creation, we will have a 24-hour round-the-world service in money and banking."[39]

Van Oenen might have added that Singapore, situated a bit further west than Hong Kong, offers the additional benefit of being "the last major Asian market to close" (improving its overlap with European business hours),[40] but of greater significance for present purposes are the themes of this account, which strongly resonate with the MDSJ concept—early-mover advantage, favorable geography, ability to bridge major global markets, and coordinated public-private initiative aimed at developing a favorable regulatory and market environment for cross-border financial services activity. Indeed, the MAS retrospective noted above confirms the impact that these advantages and geographically rooted strategies would have on the country's development, explaining that this "time zone advantage"[41] had in fact positioned Singapore to "bridge the gap between East and West at a time when funds were flowing strongly into a rapidly industrialising Asia."[42] This, in turn, gestures toward a further bridging function that would prove important for Singapore—the ability to mediate developed and developing worlds, having themselves "made the leap from a Third World economy to First World status" within the lifetime of many Singaporeans.[43]

---

[39] LEE, *supra* note 36, at 89.

[40] *See* Jagjit Kaur Meetook, *A Survey of Banking Laws and Policies in Hong Kong and Singapore,* 1986 BYU L. REV. 835, 837, 852 (1986).

[41] LOW ET AL., *supra* note 2, at 145.

[42] *Id. See also id.* at 152–53.

[43] *See id.* at 13, 220–21.

The earliest, and perhaps most vivid, illustration of these dynamics took the form of the "Asian Dollar Market" (ADM). Capitalizing at once on Singapore's favorable geography amidst global financial markets and the growing pool of dollars in East Asia in the late 1960s (due, among other things, to growing U.S. trade deficits and military expenditures in the region),[44] the ADM effectively represented East Asia's answer to the "Eurodollar" market[45]—a market where dollars outside the U.S. regulatory ambit could be borrowed, pooled, and on-lent to finance economic development in the region.[46]

In light of the background provided above, it is perhaps unsurprising that the first mover in developing Singapore's ADM would be Bank of America, which received a license from the government in 1968 to operate an "Asian Currency Unit" (ACU)—a unit within the bank that would pursue ADM operations distinct from the bank's domestic banking business (in order to insulate monetary policy and help ensure domestic price stability).[47] Tellingly, within months of receiving this license, Bank of America appears to have adopted the promotion of Singapore's nascent financial center as its own marketing imperative. In a report published during the winter of 1968–1969, the bank describes Singapore's ancient and modern history; their political development and then-current affairs; the state of infrastructure, industry, trade, transportation and communications capabilities, and tourism potential; and of course the state of financial development. On the latter subject, Bank of America noted "the island's traditional role as a center of trade which has led to the creation of significant financial services for facilitating the movement of goods"—including commercial banking and insurance capacity, as well as legal and accounting services[48]—and emphasizes throughout various other characteristics strongly resonating with the MDSJ paradigm, including Singapore's small size, lack of natural resources, and consequent outward orientation; long-standing status as a "midway point between East and West"; well-educated, multilingual, and English-speaking workforce; and relative political and economic stability.[49]

That Bank of America's report—replete with photos and written in an evocative tone—reads like a business-oriented travel guide is no accident; indeed, the

---

[44] *See* Jarvis, *supra* note 4, at 77; Singapore International Merchant Bankers Limited, The Asian Dollar 3–4 (1973). *See also* Ronen Palan, *International Financial Centers: The British-Empire, City-States and Commercially Oriented Politics*, 11 Theoretical Inquiries L. 149, 171–72 (2010); Tax Justice Network, Narrative Report on Singapore 2–3 (2015).

[45] *See infra* Chapter 10.C.

[46] *See* Singapore International Merchant Bankers Limited, *supra* note 44, at 6.

[47] *See id.*; Meetook, *supra* note 40, at 838–39; Low et al., *supra* note 2, at 143, 149–52. *See also* Jarvis, *supra* note 4, at 77–78.

[48] *See* Bank of America, *supra* note 17, at 22–25.

[49] *See id.* at 1, 6, 11–13.

document states that its "dual purpose" is to "provide the reader with a broad yet succinct background of the Republic of Singapore," and to "inform the potentially interested foreign businessman of the areas of opportunity which Singapore offers."[50] In this light, it is all the more striking that the piece concludes by directing the reader to Singapore's nascent ADM—and Bank of America's role as the sole entry point at that time. Noting Bank of America's three local branches and "bankers who know first-hand the commerce and industry of Singapore," the piece closes by emphasizing that:

> . . . Bank of America now has established an Asian Currency Unit (A.C.U.) in Singapore. A.C.U.'s role is to assist in Singapore's development as a financial center for Asia and to assure the continued expansion of Bank of America as an international corporate financier. Bank of America's Asia Currency Unit serves depositors, borrowers, and investors by attracting and lending funds. The Unit is authorized to operate in the traded currencies in a manner similar to the Euro-Dollar market in London and other European money centers. A.C.U. provides flexibility in the placement and investment of funds and increases accessibility of working capital to industrial ventures.[51]

These efforts were, of course, facilitated and promoted by Singapore's government, as Bank of America took pains to convey. In addition to creating an "Economic Development Board" aimed at providing "a centralized authority which would give potential investors all the information and practical help they could need as quickly and efficiently as possible, cutting 'red tape' to a minimum,"[52] Bank of America emphasizes the "healthy business environment—exemplified in the Government's generous investment incentives, a fairly administered program of realistic taxation, unrestricted remission of profits, enforcement of laws to insure a productive labor force, plus flexibility and a displayed willingness to change where change promises to be advantageous."[53]

It would take little time before a host of banks had established ACUs in Singapore, and other financial institutions would join Bank of America's effort to market Singapore as a financial center—in remarkably similar terms. First National City Bank, for example, in a 1973 report, likewise described Singapore's commercial history, geographic and cultural advantages, political and economic stability, and

---

[50] *See id.* at 2.
[51] *Id.* at 30.
[52] *Id.* at 15–16.
[53] *Id.* at 11.

the government's own efforts, "encouraging Singapore's development as the 'Zurich of the East' by relaxing foreign exchange regulations, strengthening the local money and capital markets and allowing more reputable foreign banks and institutions to come in."[54] Singapore International Merchant Bankers Limited, also writing in 1973, would recount similar advantages, to which it attributed the rapid growth in licensed ACUs and ADM volume.[55]

Meanwhile, Singapore's government introduced a range of incentives aimed at further developing the market. The MAS, explaining that the "impetus" for the ADM "was provided when the Government decided to abolish the withholding tax on interest on foreign currency deposits earned by non-residents," highlighted a number of further inducements to ADM activity in a 1977 report, including lifting exchange controls, reducing the tax on income from loans to nonresidents, and exemption from estate duty on nonresident ACU deposits and balances.[56] Further incentives aimed at promoting the ADM would be emphasized by the MAS in subsequent iterations of this MAS report,[57] as well as by the financial community. In addition to tax incentives and abandonment of exchange controls, other policies thought critical to the development of Singapore's ADM—and the financial center more broadly—included liberalizing interest rates, "a liberal policy to admit reputable international financial institutions into Singapore," and a "liberal immigration policy to allow well-qualified foreign professionals to work in the financial sector in Singapore."[58] As the MAS would summarize its regulatory posture in the aforementioned 1977 report, the "role of the Authority is to create the conditions and the infrastructure to encourage the private sector to participate in Singapore's financial centre development."[59] Accordingly, it is unsurprising that the MAS would follow the banks' lead in emphasizing advantages resonating with the MDSJ paradigm, including Singapore's "sound financial infrastructure, developed communications network, a stable Government and a geographical location with a time zone

---

[54] *See* First National City Bank, The Asian Dollar Market 1–6 (1973 ed.). *See also* First National City Bank, The Asian Dollar Market 2–5 (1975 ed.); Meetook, *supra* note 40, at 847.

[55] *See* Singapore International Merchant Bankers Limited, *supra* note 44, at 7.

[56] *See* Monetary Authority of Singapore, The Financial Structure of Singapore 49–56 (1977 ed.).

[57] *See, e.g.*, Monetary Authority of Singapore, The Financial Structure of Singapore 63–64 (1980 ed.); Monetary Authority of Singapore, The Financial Structure of Singapore 57–58 (1989 ed.).

[58] *See* The Association of Banks in Singapore et al., Singapore: An International Financial Centre 21 (1994). *See also* Lee Sheng Yi, *Financial Structure and Monetary Policy of Singapore* 37 (Nanyang Univ. Inst. of Econ. and Bus. Studies Occasional Paper/Technical Report Series No. 35, 1979).

[59] Monetary Authority of Singapore, *supra* note 56, at 74.

advantage so that transactions with both Europe and the Far East are possible in a trading day."[60]

The growth rate of Singapore's ADM has remained extraordinary from the beginning. Starting with just US$33 million in late 1968, the ADM market would reach US$133 million in 1969, US$423 million in 1970, and over US$1 billion in 1971.[61] The ADM would stand at US$38 billion in 1979,[62] US$280 billion in 1988,[63] and US$386 billion in 1993.[64] By early 2015, the ADM stood at US$1.2 trillion.[65] (Figure 6.1 reflects total assets/liabilities over the last decade.) Although depositors have, from the early days, included multinational corporations, central banks, and individuals as well, with borrowers including multinationals and other companies generating currencies required to repay such loans,[66] interbank transactions would soon come to constitute the lion's share of ADM activity.[67] Although aptly described as a "regional subsidiary" of the Eurodollar market in the early days,[68] it would not be long before ADM interest rates would exert substantial influence. By 1977 the MAS would report "greater interdependence" in ADM and Eurodollar rates,[69] and by 1989 it could be said that over any given trading day "the flow of funds between the two centres tends to bring about a convergence of the two rates."[70]

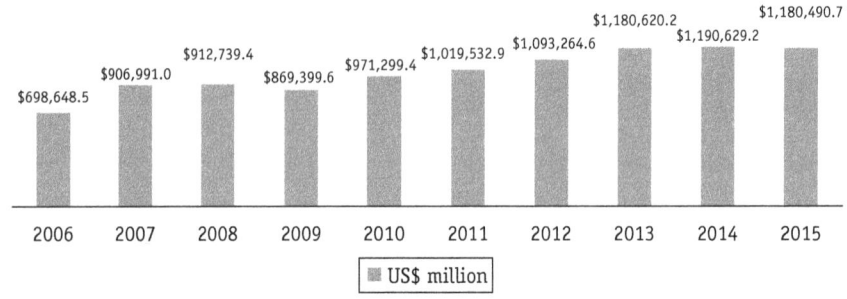

FIGURE 6.1 Asian Dollar Market: Total Assets/Liabilities, 2006–2015.*

*See MONETARY AUTHORITY OF SINGAPORE, ANNUAL REPORT 2014/15, at 121 (2015) (data through March 2015).

---

[60] *Id.* at 49.

[61] *See* FIRST NATIONAL CITY BANK (1973 ed.), *supra* note 54, at 11.

[62] *See* MONETARY AUTHORITY OF SINGAPORE (1980 ed.), *supra* note 57, at 57–58. *See also* Lee, *supra* note 58, at 38–39.

[63] *See* MONETARY AUTHORITY OF SINGAPORE (1989 ed.), *supra* note 57, at 51.

[64] *See* THE ASSOCIATION OF BANKS IN SINGAPORE ET AL., *supra* note 58, at 22.

[65] *See* MONETARY AUTHORITY OF SINGAPORE, ANNUAL REPORT 2014/15, at 121 (2015).

[66] *See, e.g.,* FIRST NATIONAL CITY BANK (1973 ed.), *supra* note 54, at 7–8; SINGAPORE INTERNATIONAL MERCHANT BANKERS LIMITED, *supra* note 44, at 13–14; Lee, *supra* note 58, at 36–37, 42.

[67] *See* MONETARY AUTHORITY OF SINGAPORE, *supra* note 56, at 51.

[68] *See* SINGAPORE INTERNATIONAL MERCHANT BANKERS LIMITED, *supra* note 44, at 5.

[69] *See* MONETARY AUTHORITY OF SINGAPORE, *supra* note 56, at 56.

[70] *See* MONETARY AUTHORITY OF SINGAPORE (1989 ed.), *supra* note 57, at 52.

Over the years, Singapore's investment in developing a credible "alternative to the London eurodollar market"[71] and associated infrastructure[72] generated opportunities in other areas of finance as well. Over the 1970s an "Asian Bond Market" would organically emerge as a longer-term funding alternative to the shorter-term ADM.[73] More generally, then, growing international trade and a wave of deregulation in major economies catalyzed "growth in foreign exchange transactions," and "Singapore's foreign exchange market became part of the round-the-clock market, with several of the leading banks installing a regular night-shift in the dealing room."[74] Singapore branched into capital markets, linking its futures exchange with the Chicago Mercantile Exchange to create "the first global round-the-clock futures trading platform" for Eurodollar futures,[75] further capitalizing on Singapore's time zone advantage, which, as the MAS would observe in 1989, was "acquiring increasing significance" with the move into these new areas.[76] Since that time Singapore has continued to expand into new areas of cross-border finance.[77] By the mid-1990s the ADM remained the "mainstay" of Singapore's financial market, but the financial community could tout "a major foreign exchange trading centre," their "growing importance as a risk management centre for the region," banking and financial services providing "a wide range of facilities for domestic, regional and international trade and investment," and "a complete network of top class ancillary services."[78]

As the foregoing account of the ADM demonstrates, Singapore has from the outset worked collaboratively with the private sector to develop both a competitive financial services infrastructure and a respected regulatory regime. In its early days the MAS held weekly lunches with industry representatives to remain close to the marketplace,[79] and coordination with the private sector—including through

[71] International Monetary Fund, Monetary and Exchange Affairs Department, *Offshore Financial Centers*, at pt. II.C (IMF Background Paper, June 23, 2000), https://www.imf.org/external/np/mae/oshore/2000/eng/back.htm. *See also Enduring Charms: A Brief History of Tax Havens,* ECONOMIST, Feb. 14, 2013, http://www.economist.com/news/special-report/21571550-brief-history-tax-havens-enduring-charms.

[72] *See* LOW ET AL., *supra* note 2, at 146.

[73] *See* Lee, *supra* note 58, at 43–51.

[74] LOW ET AL., *supra* note 2, at 150–51.

[75] *Id*. at 152–53.

[76] *See* MONETARY AUTHORITY OF SINGAPORE (1989 ed.), *supra* note 57, at 4.

[77] *See infra* Chapter 6.B.

[78] *See* THE ASSOCIATION OF BANKS IN SINGAPORE ET AL., *supra* note 58, at 9–12. For additional background on Singapore's efforts to develop additional financial services capacities through the 1970s and 1980s, see *id*. at 29 ("In March 1989, the [Stock Exchange of Singapore] became one of the first in the world to adopt a fully-computerised trading system."); MONETARY AUTHORITY OF SINGAPORE (1989 ed.), *supra* note 57, at 2–3 (describing efforts to develop Singapore's gold market, insurance center, and securities trading, as well as to promote Singapore as a site for multinational corporations' "regional headquarters"); Lee, *supra* note 58, at 81–82 (observing that Singapore had, by 1979, "adopted a diversification policy in financial development strategy").

[79] LOW ET AL., *supra* note 2, at 15.

consultation in the development of MAS regulatory policy—has been identified as a competitive strength.[80] At the same time, the MAS "has been commonly perceived as one of the most careful regulators in the world, instituting prudential limits and policies stricter than the international norm."[81] As "a small, open economy vulnerable to the vicissitudes of international markets," Singapore must ensure "the fairness of [its] regulations, the impartiality of its courts, and the professionalism of its officers," and "cannot afford to have external investors lose confidence in its political or economic stability."[82] Success in this regard is reflected in Singapore's reputation as one of the least corrupt jurisdictions in the world; in Transparency International's 2015 *Corruption Perceptions Index*, ranking 168 countries from lowest to highest perceived corruption, Singapore ranked eighth—exceeding the United States, which ranked sixteenth.[83] Indeed, Singapore has even served as a low-corruption benchmark, one economic study concluding that "an increase in the corruption level from that of Singapore to that of Mexico would have the same negative effect on inward [foreign direct investment] as raising the tax rate by fifty percentage points."[84]

Well aware that Singapore has nevertheless been characterized as a "tax haven" or an "offshore sanctuary," its regulators emphasize a suite of competitive characteristics and strengths strongly resonating with the MDSJ paradigm. An MAS retrospective observes that Singapore has made "concerted efforts to participate in cross-border information sharing agreements" in order to "dispel the tax haven misperception," while emphasizing their "education system, clean and green environment, cosmopolitan and skilled population, and strategic location in Asia" as salient attractions. Regarding their financial successes, a former MAS Managing Director explains that:

> This is a place where serious economic value-add is the name of the game, not regulatory arbitrage or tax arbitrage .... People know that we are not a 'nameplate' jurisdiction. It's a place where financial institutions base substantive activities, because we are part of a growing Asia and have an environment

---

[80] *See id.* at 30–31.

[81] *Id.* at 27. *See also* THE ASSOCIATION OF BANKS IN SINGAPORE ET AL., *supra* note 58, at 15.

[82] LOW ET AL., *supra* note 2, at 148–49.

[83] *See* Transparency International, *Corruption Perceptions Index 2015* (2015); Transparency International, *Corruption by Country/Territory: Singapore*, http://www.transparency.org/country#SGP (last visited Apr. 2016). *See also* Transparency International, *Corruption by Country/Territory: United States of America*, http://www.transparency.org/country#USA (last visited Apr. 2016).

[84] Shang-Jin Wei, *How Taxing Is Corruption on International Investors?*, LXXXII REV. ECON. & STAT. 1, 1 (2000).

that's conducive to high value work in financial services. Our human capital especially.[85]

Consistent with this position, Singapore's market and regulatory system have remained highly regarded among those jurisdictions commonly associated with "offshore" activity,[86] and it is generally conceded that Singapore does not comfortably fit the "tax haven" model.[87]

## B. Wealth Management

Over the last decade, Singapore has focused its efforts on solidifying its position as a "wealth management" center. Although there is "no generally accepted standard definition of wealth management," the term typically refers to various financial services for high net-worth individuals (HNWIs). Aimed at both preservation and growth of private wealth, such services include brokerage, core banking, lending, insurance, asset management, general financial advice, and "concierge-type services."[88] Here, as in other areas of finance, Singapore has sought to capitalize on its capacity to bridge East and West, servicing both the flow of global investment into Asia and the flow of Asian investment elsewhere. Singapore's strategy has proven very successful, with assets under management growing from S$18 billion in 1990 to S$1.4 trillion in 2010.[89]

*The Economist* has remarked on Singapore's "ability to take consistent advantage of global upheavals." Just as they perceived the foreign exchange opportunity that arose from the demise of the Bretton Woods fixed exchange rate regime, they "anticipated the effects of the 1997 handover of Hong Kong," gaining a jump on this regional competitor as "numerous clients took steps to 'book' assets in Singapore."

---

[85] LOW ET AL., *supra* note 2, at 219 (quoting Tharman Shanmugaratnam, Managing Director, Apr.–Oct. 2001).

[86] *See, e.g.,* International Monetary Fund, *supra* note 71, at pt. II.A; *The Rise of the Midshores: The Offshore Industry's Centre of Gravity Is Shifting Eastwards,* ECONOMIST, Feb. 14, 2013, http://www.economist.com/news/special-report/21571555-offshore-industrys-centre-gravity-shifting-eastwards-rise-midshores.

[87] *See* RONEN PALAN, RICHARD MURPHY & CHRISTIAN CHAVAGNEUX, TAX HAVENS: HOW GLOBALIZATION REALLY WORKS 141 (2010).

[88] *Difference between Private Banking and Wealth Management,* AAFM INDIA (Jan. 31, 2012), http://aafmindia.wordpress.com/2012/01/31/difference-between-private-banking-and-wealth-management/. *See also* TAN CHWEE HUAT, FINANCIAL SERVICES AND WEALTH MANAGEMENT IN SINGAPORE 214 (2011); Jek Aun Long & Danny Tan, *The Growth of the Private Wealth Management Industry in Singapore and Hong Kong,* 6 CAP. MARKETS L.J. 104, 104 (2011); Junxu (Jx) Lye, *The Practice of Private Wealth Management in Singapore* 1 (Wharton Research Scholars Journal, 2011), http://repository.upenn.edu/wharton_research_scholars/82.

[89] LOW ET AL., *supra* note 2, at 161–63.

Although Hong Kong remains a more natural "gateway to the Chinese mainland," boosting their equity market—of which more will be said in Chapter 7—Singapore's development of "a legal framework enabling trust accounts," its "strong asset-management," and its well-established "foreign-exchange capabilities" have given Singapore a strong boost in wealth management.[90]

The same desire to establish high value-added "niche" specialization that led Singapore to develop its foreign exchange capabilities in the late 1960s also led it to focus on wealth management around the turn of the millennium.[91] In the late 1990s the government initiated a series of public-private committees and advisory councils to assess the prospects of "various aspects of the financial sector."[92] Recognizing that "the traditional businesses that [had] underpinned Singapore's success as a financial centre, like foreign exchange trading, [had] matured," a 2002 report of the Financial Services Working Group (FSWG)—a government-sponsored group comprised of industry participants[93]—emphasized the "need to look externally and to develop new growth engines for the financial sector."[94] Drawing upon "detailed analyses of . . . niche financial centres such as Bermuda for risk management [and] Zurich and Geneva for private banking,"[95] the FSWG identified wealth management as a promising opportunity for Singapore[96] and emphasized competitive characteristics broadly resonant with the MDSJ concept that would position them well to achieve growth in this area. "A high-quality living environment, a competitive tax regime, a vibrant cultural landscape, and a conducive environment for research and information exchange," the report explains, "will be critical to ensuring that Singapore continues to [be] able to retain and attract top talent."[97] Wealth management, the

---

[90] *Singapore's Financial Rise Going Swimmingly: The City-State Has a Habit of Taking Advantage of Financial Upheaval,* ECONOMIST, Apr. 20, 2011, http://www.economist.com/node/18586804/print. *See also* CALLY JORDAN, INTERNATIONAL CAPITAL MARKETS: LAW AND INSTITUTIONS 219 (2014) (describing Singapore's competition with Hong Kong); HANS TJIO, PRINCIPLES AND PRACTICE OF SECURITIES REGULATION IN SINGAPORE 1, 14 (2d ed. 2011) (observing that "there is far more money . . . in the banking system than is invested in the stock market," and that Singapore's "stock market remains comparatively small, and prone to bouts of consolidation"); Long & Tan, *supra* note 88, at 117–21 (observing Hong Kong's advantageous proximity to China).

[91] *See* FINANCIAL SERVICES WORKING GROUP, POSITIONING SINGAPORE AS A PRE-EMINENT FINANCIAL CENTRE IN ASIA: MAIN REPORT 1, 7–8 (Sept. 2002).

[92] *See* TAN, *supra* note 88, at 22–24.

[93] FINANCIAL SERVICES WORKING GROUP, *supra* note 91, at 41–46.

[94] *Id.* at 4.

[95] *Id.* at 7. *See also* TAN, *supra* note 88, at 215–16; TAN CHWEE HUAT & JOSEPH LIM YOUNG SAIN, SINGAPORE AND HONG KONG AS COMPETING FINANCIAL CENTRES 74 (2007); Pow, *supra* note 3, at 62.

[96] FINANCIAL SERVICES WORKING GROUP, *supra* note 91, at 2, 8.

[97] *Id.* at 5. This point of emphasis presumably reflects the human capital-intensive nature of wealth management. *Cf.* Edward D. Kleinbard, *Competitive Convergence in the Financial Services Markets,* 81 TAXES 225,

report observes, would build on "Singapore's distinctive and self-sustaining competitive advantages of economic and political stability, a highly skilled and largely bilingual workforce, a well-regulated financial sector and an advanced IT platform."[98]

Although differing from their initial specialization in foreign exchange, the FSWG report similarly observes that wealth management would allow Singapore to trade upon its East-West bridging capacity—notably by "managing the Asian investment portfolios of both Asian and Western clients," and by "managing global investments of clients in Asia."[99] The plan involved building a "critical mass" of asset management talent by developing "strong indigenous [asset management] firms" and attracting "small and medium-sized foreign fund management companies."[100] Among other things, the FSWG further recommended tax breaks to incentivize repatriation of Singaporean wealth and to foster the development of private equity investment, legislation to introduce the limited partnership business form, and the modernization of "trust and company legislation."[101] As to the "business environment," the FSWG recommended concerted "branding" of Singapore's financial services, the development of domestic talent, and provision of first-rate "business infrastructure."[102] The report further notes that the U.S. tax environment was more "competitive" than Singapore's in pertinent respects[103]—signaling awareness of the significance of taxation in the competition for mobile financial business, as well as the fact that countries with larger economies and financial markets do not hesitate to compete on this basis themselves.

In little more than a decade since the FSWG's report, Singapore's wealth management strategy has proven very successful. By 2008 "Singapore's star as a haven for the super-rich [was] rising fast" and, "with the highest density of millionaires in the world," Singapore was "seeing its wealth management industry prosper as the United States and Europe grapple[d] with the worst slump in a generation." Although remaining well behind Switzerland, Singapore's assets under management topped $800 billion,[104] reflecting Singapore's "sterling reputation" in global financial markets. By 2010 Singapore had been rated the "world's easiest place to

---

230–31 (2003) (observing that, "because they operate *customer service* businesses," financial services firms "have significant fixed assets and enormous work forces").

[98] FINANCIAL SERVICES WORKING GROUP, *supra* note 91, at 8.

[99] *Id.* at 9.

[100] *Id.* at 11, 14.

[101] *Id.* at 12–18.

[102] *Id.* at 30–38.

[103] *See id.* at 15–16, 34–36.

[104] Neil Chatterjee & John O'Donnell, *Wealth Management Prospers in Singapore,* N.Y. TIMES, Nov. 14, 2008, http://www.nytimes.com/2008/12/14/business/worldbusiness/14iht-singapore.1.18654227.html?g wh=12FE543A181AD9B14EF8749DE77EF7FB.

do business," was "ranked number two worldwide as the city with the best investment potential for 16 consecutive years," was "ranked first for having the most open economy for international trade and investment," and was "cited as having the best business environment in Asia Pacific and worldwide"[105]—accolades reflecting a concerted effort by a range of Singaporean government agencies to achieve efficiencies and appeal to global investors sensitive to these metrics.[106] By 2013 Singapore ranked among the world's most competitive financial centers—trailing only London, New York, and Hong Kong according to one influential index—and ranked first among those financial centers considered "likely to become more significant in the next few years."[107] As of 2016 Singapore remained the financial center considered most likely to grow in significance and narrowly edged out Hong Kong, ranking third behind London and New York.[108] More broadly, Singapore has come to be viewed as a "midshore" jurisdiction, combining "offshore traits (low tax, secrecy) and onshore ones (sophisticated, well-staffed financial centres)"[109]—a characterization highlighting the inability of the onshore/offshore distinction to accommodate MDSJs such as Singapore.

Singapore's tax environment—including "full tax exemption for foreign-sourced income received in Singapore" by nonresidents, as well as "an absence of capital gains, gift or estate taxes"[110]—and its "hard line on bank secrecy" have certainly prompted scrutiny from larger markets.[111] Today, a common law-based duty of confidentiality in banking (historically rooted in English law)[112] has effectively been subsumed by a statutory duty, appearing in Section 47 of the Banking Act, which imposes

---

[105] Long & Tan, *supra* note 88, at 106–07. *See also* Jarvis, *supra* note 4, at 83.

[106] *See* Lin Lin & Michael Ewing-Chow, *The Doing Business Indicators in Minority Investor Protection: The Case of Singapore* 4–21 (Nat'l Univ. of Sing. Faculty of Law Working Paper No. 2014/007, 2014), http://ssrn.com/abstract=2464407. For a discussion of the utility and shortcomings of *Doing Business* indicators—notably their investor protection measures, as applied to Singapore—see *id.* at 21–43.

[107] *See* MARK YEANDLE & NICK DANEV, THE GLOBAL FINANCIAL CENTRES INDEX 14, at 3–4, 7 (2013) (index sponsored by the Qatar Financial Centre Authority and produced by the Z/Yen Group). *See also* MARK YEANDLE & NICK DANEV, THE GLOBAL FINANCIAL CENTRES INDEX 15, at 2–5, 8 (2014) (index sponsored by the Qatar Financial Centre Authority and produced by the Z/Yen Group) (again placing Singapore fourth overall, and third among financial centers "likely to become more significant").

[108] *See* Z/Yen Group Limited, *Global Financial Centres Index 19: Information Pack,* http://www.longfinance.net/global-financial-centre-index-19/992-gfci-19.html (last visited Apr. 2016); Press Release, Z/Yen Group Limited, Global Financial Centers Index: London Remains on Top and Singapore Climbs to Third Place (Apr. 6, 2016); Jeremy Koh, *Singapore Edges Past Hong Kong as World's No 3 Financial Centre: Survey,* STRAITS TIMES, Apr. 8, 2016, http://www.straitstimes.com/business/banking/singapore-overtakes-hong-kong-as-worlds-no-3-financial-centre-survey.

[109] *See* ECONOMIST, *supra* note 86.

[110] *See* TAX JUSTICE NETWORK, *supra* note 44, at 6.

[111] *See* Chatterjee & O'Donnell, *supra* note 104.

[112] *See* POH CHU CHAI, BANKING LAW 543–53 (2d. ed. 2011).

criminal liability for breaches of bank confidentiality, subject to various enumerated exceptions (including disclosures required by law).[113] However, Singapore occupies "a stronger position to resist pressure from the United States" than European competitors such as Switzerland, reflecting Singapore's "close ties to power throughout Asia"—where much of the wealth flowing into Singapore originates.[114] As one London-based asset manager put it, "Hong Kong and Singapore are now such powerful centres that I can't see where else the Asian business is going."[115] This has given Singapore greater capacity simply to avoid U.S. clients.[116] In any event, like Bermuda, Singapore would placate the OECD in 2009 by entering a sufficient number of tax information exchange agreements and participating in the OECD's "Global Forum on Transparency and Exchange of Information for Tax Purposes."[117] Although it is understood that bank secrecy can be abused by those seeking to hide their wealth from tax authorities and others, it is thought that Singapore wealth managers "are cautious about wealth concealers from countries where there is political turmoil and illegal activities are common," and that "wealth developers and builders" engaging in entrepreneurial activity or taking over established family businesses "are the fastest growing segments."[118]

In the intervening years, Singapore's gain on Switzerland as a destination for private wealth has continued.[119] In 2009, assets under management by financial institutions in Singapore stood at S$1.2 trillion, reflecting "a 19 percent per annum growth rate on a rolling 5-year-average basis."[120] By 2011 the figure would exceed S$1.3 trillion,[121] with over 2,880 institutions registered with the MAS to provide financial services in Singapore.[122] Assets under management would reach S$1.63 trillion in

---

[113] *See id.* at 555–73; Banking Act, ch. 19, Act 41 of 1970, § 47 (Sing.).

[114] Chatterjee & O'Donnell, *supra* note 104. *See also* Jean-Rodolphe W. Fiechter, *Exchange of Tax Information: The End of Banking Secrecy in Switzerland and Singapore?*, INT'L TAX J., Nov.–Dec. 2010, at 55, 56–57, 62–63; Sarah Krouse & Mike Foster, *Singapore "to Become New Switzerland,"* WALL ST. J., May 7, 2013, http://blogs.wsj.com/moneybeat/2013/05/07/singapore-to-become-new-switzerland/.

[115] YEANDLE & DANEV 15, *supra* note 107, at 11 (quoting an "Asset Manager based in London"). *Cf.* Z/Yen Group Limited, *supra* note 108 (reporting that, in every iteration of the Global Financial Centres Index, Singapore and Hong Kong have each ranked third or fourth, following only London and New York).

[116] *See* ECONOMIST, *supra* note 90. *See also* Beckett G. Cantley, *Steering Into the Storm: Amplification of Captive Insurance Company Compliance Issues in the Offshore Tax Crackdown,* 12 HOUS. BUS. & TAX L.J. 224, 263 (2012).

[117] *See* ORGANISATION FOR ECONOMIC CO-OPERATION AND DEVELOPMENT, THE GLOBAL FORUM ON TRANSPARENCY AND EXCHANGE OF INFORMATION FOR TAX PURPOSES 2 (Apr. 16, 2012); Fiechter, *supra* note 114, at 61; Long & Tan, *supra* note 88, at 115–16. *See also* Cantley, *supra* note 116, at 263.

[118] TAN, *supra* note 88, at 223–24.

[119] *See* Long & Tan, *supra* note 88, at 104–05.

[120] *Id.* at 107.

[121] *See* Lye, *supra* note 88, at 1.

[122] *See* ECONOMIST, *supra* note 90.

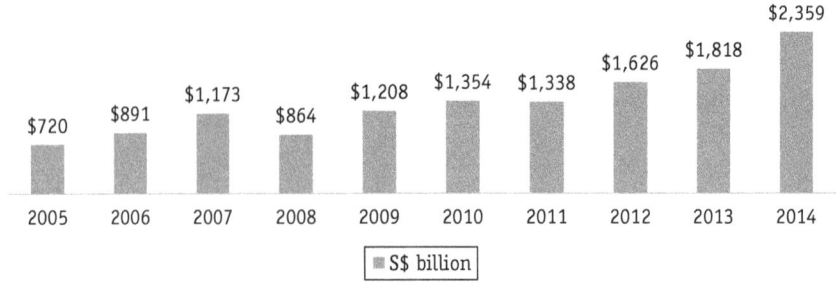

FIGURE 6.2 Singapore Financial Institutions: Assets under Management, 2005–2014.*

* See MONETARY AUTHORITY OF SINGAPORE, 2010 SINGAPORE ASSET MANAGEMENT INDUSTRY SURVEY 1 (2011), 2011 SINGAPORE ASSET MANAGEMENT INDUSTRY SURVEY 1 (2012), 2012 SINGAPORE ASSET MANAGEMENT INDUSTRY SURVEY 1 (2013), 2013 SINGAPORE ASSET MANAGEMENT INDUSTRY SURVEY 2 (2014), 2014 SINGAPORE ASSET MANAGEMENT SURVEY 2, 4 (2015).

2012[123] and S$1.82 trillion in 2013, approximately 77 percent of which "was sourced from outside Singapore."[124] In 2014, assets under management jumped to S$2.4 trillion with 81 percent from outside Singapore, a substantial rise attributed by the MAS to "positive asset inflows arising from Asia's growth dynamism and Singapore's position as a pan-Asian asset management hub." The MAS further notes that of the assets under management sourced outside Singapore in 2014, 54 percent came from the Asia-Pacific region, whereas 19 percent came from Europe, 18 percent came from North America, and 9 percent came from elsewhere.[125] As of May 2013 it was estimated that Singapore would "overtake Switzerland as the biggest offshore wealth center in terms of assets under management by 2020."[126] Figure 6.2 reflects total assets under management by Singapore financial institutions over the last decade.

Two Singaporean lawyers, writing in 2010, observed that the shift toward Singapore was occurring amidst the economic rise of Asian powers such as China and India, and that Asia remained "comparatively unscathed by the sub-prime crisis."[127] Critically, they underscored Singapore's East-West bridging capacity and resulting ability to capitalize on these trends by pursuing the sort of two-way wealth

---

[123] See MONETARY AUTHORITY OF SINGAPORE, 2012 SINGAPORE ASSET MANAGEMENT INDUSTRY SURVEY 1 (2013).

[124] See MONETARY AUTHORITY OF SINGAPORE, 2013 SINGAPORE ASSET MANAGEMENT INDUSTRY SURVEY 1 (2014).

[125] See MONETARY AUTHORITY OF SINGAPORE, 2014 SINGAPORE ASSET MANAGEMENT SURVEY 2, 4, 10 (2015).

[126] Krouse & Foster, supra note 114. See also Cantley, supra note 116, at 262–63; TAX JUSTICE NETWORK, supra note 44, at 1.

[127] Long & Tan, supra note 88, at 105–06. See also Krouse & Foster, supra note 114; Storm Survivors, ECONOMIST, Feb. 16, 2013, http://www.economist.com/news/special-report/21571549-offshore-financial-centres-have-taken-battering-recently-they-have-shown-remarkable.

management strategy discussed in the FSWG's 2002 report. "Within the private wealth management industry," they write, "portfolio allocations shifted toward Asia [following the crisis], private wealth managers sought to forge new relationships in Asia and private banks strengthened their presence in Asia to manage private wealth in an effort to tap the rising population of HNWIs."[128] Others similarly emphasize the significance of this two-way strategy, one observer explaining that "this surge of wealth in Asia has created a sudden increase in demand for wealth management services," but that cultural idiosyncrasies set Asia's HNWIs apart—notably being "more aggressive when it comes to handling their investments" and demanding greater contact with financial services providers.[129] It has also been observed that "Asian HNWIs tend to keep their wealth close to home," preferring Singapore and Hong Kong to Switzerland, and that the "profile of the Asian millionaire is different from those of European HNWIs." The typical Chinese HNWI is "under 40 years old," is likely "a self-made entrepreneur" remaining active in the business, and as such "require[s] a holistic evaluation of their financial needs"—meaning that those advising them will probably have to understand the relevant industry and "offer the whole range of products from corporate banking to capital markets and investment banking."[130]

Accordingly, it is unsurprising that Singapore has pursued various legal reforms to facilitate their development as a full-service wealth management center. More nuanced and flexible banking and securities licensing regimes were implemented through the Banking Act and the Securities and Futures Act to give wealth managers focusing on HNWIs "the ability to choose a licensing or regulatory regime more appropriate to their needs, instead of having to apply for the full bank license or [Capital Markets Services License]"—reforms that have "attracted growth and encouraged development of the wealth management industry."[131]

---

[128] Long & Tan, *supra* note 88, at 106. *See also* ECONOMIST, *supra* note 86; TAN, *supra* note 88, at 222–23; Jonathan V. Beaverstock et al., *Overseeing the Fortunes of the Global Super-Rich: The Nature of Private Wealth Management in London's Financial District, in* GEOGRAPHIES OF THE SUPER-RICH, *supra* note 3, at 43, 46–47.

[129] Lye, *supra* note 88, at 2–4. *See also* Gabriel Zucman, *Taxing across Borders: Tracking Personal Wealth and Corporate Profits*, 28 J. ECON. PERSP. 121, 140–41 (2014); Pow, *supra* note 3, at 63.

[130] TAN, *supra* note 88, at 227.

[131] Long & Tan, *supra* note 88, at 108–10. For additional background on the bank licensing regime and categories of banking activity, see Banking Act, ch. 19, Act 41 of 1970, §§ 2(1), 4, 30 (Sing.); Monetary Authority of Singapore, *Commercial Banks*, http://www.mas.gov.sg/singapore-financial-centre/types-of-institutions/commercial-banks.aspx (last modified May 28, 2013); Monetary Authority of Singapore, *Merchant Banks*, http://www.mas.gov.sg/Singapore-Financial-Centre/Types-of-Institutions/Merchant-Banks.aspx (last modified May 28, 2013). On the securities licensing regime, see Securities and Futures Act, ch. 289, Act 42 of 2001, §§ 2(1), 82, 99, Second Schedule, Third Schedule (Sing.); Securities and Futures (Licensing and Conduct of Business) Regulations, reg. 14 (Sing.).

Similarly, Singapore has sought to implement the English-law trust concept in a manner attractive to Asia's growing number of HNWIs. For example, the Trust Companies Act generally prohibits carrying on "trust business" without being a "licensed trust company," but includes an exemption for the so-called "private trust company" (PTC)—defined to mean a company "the purpose of which is solely to provide trust business services in respect of a specific trust or of specific trusts where" each settlor for that company is a "connected person," including family members, and "each beneficiary of such a trust is a connected person in relation to the settlor of that trust" (so long as a licensed trust company is engaged "to carry out trust administration services" to ensure regulatory compliance).[132] As Jek Aun Long and Danny Tan explain, "HNWIs looking to set up private family-trust structures will usually want a say in the management supervision of their assets and be reluctant to hand over trusteeship wholesale to an external trust company." The private trust company structure permits such individuals "to be involved in the trusteeship through direct ownership of shares in the PTC itself or by sitting on the board of directors of the PTC," and the exemption described above "spares such settlors from the process of having to apply for and obtain a trust business license."[133] Although use of Singapore trusts as a wealth planning device has historically remained limited, statutory developments and a growing body of sophisticated case law have rendered Singapore increasingly attractive in this regard,[134] and Singapore trusts have become "increasingly popular with rich Chinese keen to preserve newly acquired wealth."[135]

Naturally questions have arisen regarding Singapore's future following Lee Kuan Yew's passing in March 2015, a reflection of Lee's enormous impact and

---

[132] Trust Companies Act, ch. 336, Act 11 of 2005, §§ 3(1), 15(1)(d) (Sing.); Trust Companies (Exemption) Regulations, regs. 2, 4(1)(a), 4(2), Schedule (Sing.).

[133] Long & Tan, *supra* note 88, at 111. *See also id.* at 111–13; ECONOMIST, *supra* note 90. On the theoretical and practical difficulty of achieving asset protection through trust structures while retaining control over trust assets—and the global competition to provide trust services—see generally 2 ASSET PROTECTION: DOMESTIC AND INTERNATIONAL LAW AND TACTICS (updated May 2013); Jocelyn Margolin Borowsky & Richard W. Nenno, *A Comparison of the Leading Trust Jurisdictions,* 37 BNA TAX MGM'T EST., GIFTS & TR. J. 233 (2012), http://www.duanemorris.com/articles/static/borowsky_taxmg-mtjrnl_0712.pdf; Robert T. Danforth, *Rethinking the Law of Creditors' Rights in Trusts,* 53 HASTINGS L.J. 287 (2002); Duncan E. Osborne & Mark E. Osborne, *Asset Protection Trust Planning,* SU002 ALI-CLE 1, pt. IV.B.1 (2013).

[134] *See, e.g.,* ALAN BINNINGTON & LIONEL CHOI (RBC WEALTH MANAGEMENT), SINGAPORE COMES OF AGE AS A TRUST JURISDICTION (2012).

[135] ECONOMIST, *supra* note 86. Note, however, that Singapore trusts would appear less popular in North America. *See, e.g.,* 2 ASSET PROTECTION: DOMESTIC AND INTERNATIONAL LAW AND TACTICS, *supra* note 133 (assessing the merits of a number of "offshore" trust jurisdictions, though not including Singapore).

controversial approach to governance that required of Singaporeans a "trade-off between liberty and prosperity"—effectively creating "a secure and predictable regime for business, while not extending the same to dissidents and journalists."[136] Reflections on his "blending [of] capitalistic modernity with a state-directed economy and authoritarianism"[137] have prompted various and mixed responses, ranging from high praise for Singapore's stability and rapid economic development to criticism for the stifling of press freedoms and political opposition.[138] It is worth recognizing, however, that social and political change appears to have been coming, if slowly, prior to Lee's passing—to some degree reflecting a generational shift. In the 2011 election, Lee's People's Action Party (PAP) received just 60 percent of the vote, and his son, the current Prime Minister Lee Hsien Loong, "has said he will hand over power by 2020."[139] *The Economist* suggests that "[h]aving grown up in a rich country, young Singaporeans increasingly chafe at restrictions their grandparents willingly accepted," and *The Wall Street Journal* similarly reports that the younger generation, "better-educated and more-affluent than generations past, [has] begun calling for wider political freedoms."[140] Although tentative to date, "the government of the younger Mr. Lee has moved to loosen the state's control," permitting "plays that poke fun at the government" and giving citizens "more leeway, through blogs and social media, to criticize the PAP's hold on power." Perhaps tellingly, Lee Kuan Yew himself, "in his memoirs, concluded that Singapore was unlikely to

---

[136] *See* Michael Skapinker, *Singapore's Law Sets It Apart and Makes It Hard to Imitate*, Fin. Times, Apr. 2, 2015, at 8.

[137] *See* Joel Kotkin, *Singapore after Lee Kuan Yew: Future Is Uncertain for the Utilitarian Paradise He Created*, Forbes, Mar. 22, 2015, http://www.forbes.com/sites/joelkotkin/2015/03/22/lee-kuan-yew-dead-singapore/. *See also Asia's City-Statesman*, Economist, Mar. 28, 2015, at 29, 29–30.

[138] *See, e.g.*, Thomas Fuller & Austin Ramzy, *Teary Mourners in Singapore Remember Lee Kuan Yew*, N.Y. Times, Mar. 23, 2015, http://www.nytimes.com/2015/03/24/world/asia/lee-kuan-yew-of-singapore-prasied-by-world-leaders.html; Kirsten Han, *Lee Kuan Yew Is Gone. Where Does Singapore Go Now?*, Guardian, Mar. 23, 2015, http://www.theguardian.com/world/2015/mar/23/lee-kuan-yew-is-gone-where-does-singapore-go-now; David Stout, *Global Leaders Pay Respects after the Passing of Singapore's Lee Kuan Yew*, Time, Mar. 23, 2015, http://time.com/3753703/lee-kuan-yew-death-global-reaction/; *The Wise Man of the East*, Economist, Mar. 28, 2015, at 18. *See also* Skapinker, *supra* note 136, at 8 ("The trade-off between liberty and prosperity seems to have widespread, if not universal, support there."); Calvin Cheng, *The Legacy of Lee Kuan Yew and the Myth of Trade-Offs*, HuffingtonPost.com, Mar. 27, 2015, http://www.huffingtonpost.com/calvin-cheng/lee-kuan-yew-legacy-myths_b_6950646.html ("object[ing] that there has been any such trade-off" and arguing that "the things you cannot do in Singapore are precisely the sort that civilized people should not do anyway").

[139] *See* Reuters, *As Lee Era Ends, Singapore Braces for Change as Young Worry about Future*, Japan Times, Mar. 25, 2015, http://www.japantimes.co.jp/news/2015/03/25/asia-pacific/politics-diplomacy-asia-pacific/lee-era-ends-singapore-braces-change-young-worry-future/#.VVtNjWdAS2w.

[140] *See Singapore after Lee Kuan Yew: After the Patriarch*, Economist, Mar. 28, 2015, at 44; Chun Han Wong & P.R. Venkat, *Lee Kuan Yew, Singapore's Founding Father, Dies at 91*, Wall St. J., Mar. 22, 2015, http://www.wsj.com/articles/lee-kuan-yew-singapores-founding-father-dies-at-91-1427056223.

remain static in a fast-moving globalized world: 'Will the political system that my colleagues and I developed work more or less unchanged for another generation? I doubt it.' "[141]

Ultimately, Singapore retains an impressive suite of characteristics, strengths, and strategies—resonating strongly with the MDSJ concept described above— that augur well for their future. In their analysis of Singapore's wealth management industry, Long and Tan emphasize the salience of Singapore's proximity to major Asian economies; the "sound legal and regulatory framework coupled with a pro-business and tax-friendly environment for wealth managers, private banks and HNWIs"; cognizance of international standard-setting processes regarding tax evasion and information exchange; a "pragmatic" regulatory approach, aiming "to strike a balance so that any regulatory enhancements do not unduly deter the growth pattern" achieved to date; and proactive efforts to attract "human capital" by ensuring that Singapore remains a desirable place to live, a reputation reinforced by maintaining "amongst the least restrictive immigration laws in Asia for foreign talent."[142] In this light, predictions of Singapore's future preeminence as a global center of private wealth management[143] appear well justified.

---

[141] See Wong & Venkat, supra note 140 (quoting Lee). See also ECONOMIST, supra note 140 (reporting that in "recent years the PAP has overcome its aversion to welfare programmes, expanding financial aid to the elderly and directing more benefits to poorer Singaporeans," and increasingly used "persuasion rather than bullying" in meeting political challenges).

[142] Long & Tan, supra note 88, at 105–10, 116–17. See also ECONOMIST, supra note 90; JORDAN, supra note 90, at 217; TAN & LIM, supra note 95, at 74; Jarvis, supra note 4, at 84; Pow, supra note 3, at 61–62, 64–65.

[143] See supra note 126 and accompanying text.

# 7   Hong Kong

OF ALL THE jurisdictions examined in Part II of this book, Hong Kong has achieved perhaps the greatest sustained prominence in cross-border finance. Consisting of the Kowloon Peninsula and 263 islands at the mouth of the Pearl River Delta in the South China Sea,[1] Hong Kong is regarded as one of the most significant financial centers in the world, consistently trailing only London and New York, while alternately edging out or (as in 2016) slightly trailing Singapore.[2] Perhaps more so than any other jurisdiction examined here, Hong Kong has exemplified the "bridging" function associated with MDSJs—particularly as a gateway to the enormous domestic market and production capabilities of the Chinese Mainland. At the same

---

[1] *See* CENTRAL INTELLIGENCE AGENCY, THE WORLD FACTBOOK: HONG KONG, https://www.cia.gov/library/publications/the-world-factbook/geos/hk.html (last updated Apr. 26, 2016); Survey and Mapping Office, Lands Department, Government of the Hong Kong Special Administrative Region, *Hong Kong Geographic Data* (Feb. 2015), http://www.landsd.gov.hk/mapping/en/publications/hk_geographic_data_sheet.pdf.

[2] *See* MARK YEANDLE & NICK DANEV, THE GLOBAL FINANCIAL CENTRES INDEX 15, at 3–5 (2014) (index sponsored by the Qatar Financial Centre Authority and produced by the Z/Yen Group); Z/Yen Group Limited, *Global Financial Centres Index 19: Information Pack,* http://www.longfinance.net/global-financial-centre-index-19/992-gfci-19.html (last visited Apr. 2016); Press Release, Z/Yen Group Limited, Global Financial Centers Index: London Remains on Top and Singapore Climbs to Third Place (Apr. 6, 2016).

time, however, their substantial dependence upon and continuing integration with the Mainland has introduced challenges and risks that many fear could destabilize Hong Kong's financial center moving forward.

## A. The Gateway to China

Like the other jurisdictions examined in Part II of this book, Hong Kong is small and poorly endowed in natural resources. Their total land area amounts to just over 1,100 square kilometers (approximately six times larger than Washington, DC), and as of 2015 the population stood at just over 7.1 million.[3] Hong Kong's "harbor, deep and sheltered by steep granite hills, is one of the best in the world,"[4] a geographic advantage exerting enormous impact on Hong Kong's development (discussed below). Natural resources as such, however, "are limited, and food and raw materials must be imported." Hong Kong today relies heavily on services, which constitute approximately 93 percent of GDP.[5] Overall, Hong Kong's economy remains "highly dependent on international trade and finance," reflecting the outward orientation common among MDSJs, and the Hong Kong dollar remains pegged to the U.S. dollar under an arrangement dating back to 1983.[6]

Hong Kong currently enjoys a AAA rating from Standard & Poor's, reflecting "the economy's above-average growth prospects for a high-income economy, consistently healthy fiscal performance, sizable fiscal reserves, and strong external position."[7] As of 2015, per capita GDP stood at $57,000, seventeenth highest in the world.[8] As Standard & Poor's has observed, however, Hong Kong's prosperity derives substantially from its proximity to and connections with the Mainland—a double-edged reality presenting substantial opportunities and substantial risks. Although Hong Kong benefits enormously from its "key role in facilitating the international use of the Chinese currency and foreign investment in China," the rating agency has rightly warned that "increasing economic and administrative integration with the mainland has also increased Hong Kong's exposure to changes in administrative policies and weaker civil institutions in China."[9]

---

[3] CENTRAL INTELLIGENCE AGENCY, *supra* note 1.

[4] JOHN M. CARROLL, A CONCISE HISTORY OF HONG KONG 1 (2007).

[5] CENTRAL INTELLIGENCE AGENCY, *supra* note 1.

[6] *Id. See also* Standard & Poor's Ratings Services, *Hong Kong Ratings Affirmed at "AAA/A-1+" and "cnAAA/cnA-1+"; Outlook Stable,* Aug. 20, 2014; Financial Services Development Council, *Strengthening Hong Kong as a Leading Global International Financial Centre* 4, 8–13 (FSDC Research Paper No. 01, 2013) (reporting that financial services represented 16 percent of GDP in 2011).

[7] *See* Standard & Poor's Ratings Services, *supra* note 6.

[8] *See* CENTRAL INTELLIGENCE AGENCY, *supra* note 1.

[9] Standard & Poor's Ratings Services, *supra* note 6.

Hong Kong's history and economic development have long been defined by relationships with global powers—notably China, England, and the United States[10]—which have left Hong Kong uniquely positioned to mediate these engines of global production and finance. As John Carroll explains, "Hong Kong was founded primarily for trade," and "its promise of free trade, along with easy access to markets in China, attracted a wide range of foreign merchants involved mainly in the China trade in silk, tea, and opium; in the international trade; and in insurance and shipping."[11] The British took control of Hong Kong in 1839, and the 1842 Treaty of Nanking (which ended the First Opium War) "ceded the island of Hong Kong to Britain 'in perpetuity.'" Hong Kong formally became a British colony in 1843,[12] and as "a haven for Western traders engaged in commerce with China . . . Hong Kong developed into the most important entrepot in East Asia."[13] The colony hosted "the Asian headquarters for many British firms that had powerful economic and political connections with London," while at the same time providing "a commercial base for trade with Southeast Asia" conducted by Chinese merchants[14]—a two-way strategy reminiscent of that employed by Singapore.

Notwithstanding the stark terms of the Treaty of Nanking, the potential for a reassertion of Chinese rule long loomed over Hong Kong, adding a dimension of geopolitical complexity to their role as an intermediary between East and West. When Britain, in 1898, leased a 365-square-mile area from Kowloon to the Shenzhen River (the so-called "New Territories") for a 99-year period, they inadvertently established the expiration date of June 30, 1997, as a historical focal point—a convenient date to revisit Britain's presence in the region. As Carroll sums it up, by signing the Convention of Peking "the British had not ensured the future of Hong Kong; rather, they had made 'an appointment with China.'"[15]

As discussed further below, China long tolerated Hong Kong's independent identity, economy, and global linkages in a spirit of pragmatic self-interest,[16] but over the latter half of the twentieth century China increasingly pressed for Hong Kong's return. Although Chinese interest in asserting control over Hong Kong grew during World War II,[17] the postwar Communist government "remained consistently

---

[10] *See* CARROLL, *supra* note 4, at 35, 140–43.

[11] *Id.* at 33.

[12] *See id.* at 12–16.

[13] CATHERINE R. SCHENK, HONG KONG AS AN INTERNATIONAL FINANCIAL CENTRE: EMERGENCE AND DEVELOPMENT 1945–65, at 1 (2001).

[14] *Id.* at 34.

[15] *See* CARROLL, *supra* note 4, at 67–72. *See also* P.Y. LO, THE HONG KONG BASIC LAW 6 (2011).

[16] *See infra* Chapter 7.B.

[17] *See* CARROLL, *supra* note 4, at 126–29.

levelheaded and sophisticated" in its approach, reflecting the regime's recognition that aggressive moves might provoke responses from the United Nations and associated powers, and perhaps more pertinently that Hong Kong "could be of great use to China, just as it had been for more than a century, as a window to the outside world."[18] During the period of the Cultural Revolution, "foreign currency acquired through colonial Hong Kong financed much of the PRC's imports"—indeed, the Mainland "earned almost half of its hard currency from selling food and water to Hong Kong." And just as Hong Kong served as "a British and American listening post on China," the colony "served a similar function for Chinese Communist Party cadres and activists" vis-à-vis the West.[19]

Following China's admission to the United Nations in 1971, however, the Mainland began to exert greater pressure, pushing for Hong Kong's (and Macau's) removal from the U.N.'s list of colonies—a move prompting the British government to change Hong Kong's status from "Crown Colony" to "Dependent Territory." Although the precise timing of the Chinese government's decision to wrest Hong Kong from British rule remains unknown, their intentions became eminently clear during Prime Minister Margaret Thatcher's visit to China in 1982.[20] Formal negotiations followed, leading to the 1985 "Sino-British Joint Declaration" under which Hong Kong would formally become part of China on July 1, 1997—though with a unique status encapsulated in the principle of "one country, two systems."[21]

Although a part of China today, the architects of Hong Kong's government and regulatory status went to great pains to preserve the region's value to the Mainland as a nexus with global economic and financial markets.[22] The "Basic Law of the Hong Kong Special Administrative Region of the People's Republic of China" was adopted in 1990 and took effect in 1997 upon the commencement of Chinese rule.[23] Though a Chinese legislative act, the Basic Law effectively serves as Hong Kong's "constitutional document."[24] Under the Basic Law, Hong Kong "is an inalienable part of the People's Republic of China," yet is authorized "to exercise a high degree of autonomy and enjoy executive, legislative and independent judicial power,"[25] as

---

[18] Id. at 136–37. See also id. at 217.

[19] Id. at 176.

[20] Id. at 176–78.

[21] See id. at 179–83.

[22] TAX JUSTICE NETWORK, NARRATIVE REPORT ON HONG KONG 4 (2015).

[23] See Decree of the President of the People's Republic of China, No. 26, Apr. 4, 1990; XIANGGANG JIBEN FA Annex III, instruments 9–10 (H.K.) (unofficial translation of the Basic Law of the Hong Kong Special Administrative Region of the People's Republic of China), http://www.basiclaw.gov.hk/en/basiclawtext/index.html (last visited Apr. 2016) [hereinafter Basic Law].

[24] Some Facts about the Basic Law, http://www.basiclaw.gov.hk/en/facts/index.html (last updated Mar. 17, 2008).

[25] Basic Law, supra note 23, arts. 1–2. See also id. arts. 12, 16–19.

well as limited capacity to "maintain and develop relations and conclude and implement agreements with foreign states and regions and relevant international organizations in the appropriate fields."[26] The Basic Law further states that the "laws previously in force in Hong Kong, that is, the common law, rules of equity, ordinances, subordinate legislation and customary law shall be maintained," subject to any amendments of local law promulgated by the Hong Kong legislature, and of course further subject to the Basic Law itself.[27] The upshot is effectively a "mixed legal system of common law based on the English model and Chinese customary law."[28] Ultimately, however, the Basic Law trumps in a conflict with local law,[29] and powers of interpretation and amendment of the Basic Law remain firmly with the National People's Congress.[30]

Like other MDSJs (and numerous other jurisdictions around the world), Hong Kong has sought to attract financial business through low taxation. InvestHK touts their "simple, predictable and low tax system," characterizing Hong Kong as "one of the most tax-friendly economies in the world." Indeed, Hong Kong has no sales, withholding, capital gains, dividends, or estate taxes. Moreover, their three direct taxes (a profits tax of 16.5 percent, a salaries tax of 15 percent, and a property tax of 15 percent) have "generous allowances and deductions" reducing effective tax rates.[31] Hong Kong's advantages extend well beyond tax, however, strongly resembling the MDSJ paradigm.

Hong Kong's fortunes have long remained fundamentally rooted in their proximity to and relationship with the Mainland, and the centrality of this relationship has only grown over recent decades. "Whereas in 1972 the United States and Britain were Hong Kong's first and second most important markets," as of 1986 "Hong Kong was doing more business with China than with any other country."[32] Indeed, by 1997 Hong Kong "handled half of China's exports and almost 60 percent of its total foreign investment and provided one-third of its foreign exchange reserves," and the Mainland itself was

---

[26] *Id.* art. 151.

[27] *Id.* art. 8.

[28] CENTRAL INTELLIGENCE AGENCY, *supra* note 1.

[29] *See* Basic Law, *supra* note 23, art. 11.

[30] *See id.* arts. 158–59. For in-depth, article-by-article discussion of the Basic Law, see Lo, *supra* note 15.

[31] InvestHK, *Low and Simple Tax Regime,* http://www.investhk.gov.hk/why-hong-kong/low-and-simple-tax-regime.html (last visited Apr. 2016). *See also* TAX JUSTICE NETWORK, *supra* note 22, at 7; Jefferson P. Vanderwolk, *The Role of Hong Kong's Tax Policies, in* DAVID C. DONALD, A FINANCIAL CENTRE FOR TWO EMPIRES: HONG KONG'S CORPORATE, SECURITIES AND TAX LAWS IN ITS TRANSITION FROM BRITAIN TO CHINA 171, 171–73 (2014). *But see* Vanderwolk, *supra,* at 173–74, 183–87 (adding that Hong Kong does impose "stamp duty on purchases and sales of Hong Kong stock . . . and on conveyances of Hong Kong real estate," a form of taxation that is "unusual in major financial centres," and that taxpayers fare particularly badly in tax disputes with the Hong Kong government relative to other financial centers).

[32] CARROLL, *supra* note 4, at 163.

by 1994 the largest investor in Hong Kong.[33] Accordingly, Hong Kong has increasingly branded itself as "the premier gateway to China," capitalizing on a "geographical and geopolitical" position that "makes it the logical first stop for overseas enterprises keen to access the Mainland, and for Mainland businesses keen to go global"[34]—a two-way strategy vis-à-vis China itself strongly reminiscent of that pursued by Singapore in the broader Asian wealth management business. As Hong Kong-based lawyer Melissa Pang observes, "China has become the world's premier destination for foreign investment," and "Hong Kong has become a conduit to funnel capital, high-caliber talent, and technology into China from all over the world, while also introducing China's enterprises, products, and services to the global market."[35] InvestHK, a government branding initiative, elaborates that Hong Kong further offers proximity to the Pearl River Delta—"China's largest and most productive manufacturing region," and "home to tens of thousands of factories owned or managed by Hong Kong and overseas companies."[36] According to BrandHK, Hong Kong "is the mainland's most important entrepot, handling about one-fifth of China's foreign trade," representing "the single largest source of foreign capital for Mainland enterprises," and playing "a key role in the internationalisation of the Mainland currency," the renminbi (RMB).[37]

Hong Kong has invested heavily in human capital, professional networks, and related institutional structures—in each case reinforcing Hong Kong's substantial cultural and geographic capacities to perform important regional and global bridging functions in cross-border finance. The Basic Law establishes that "[i]n addition to the Chinese language, English may also be used as an official language,"[38] and well-educated and bilingual public and private workforces have enhanced Hong Kong's ability to navigate global finance efficiently and effectively.[39] More generally, InvestHK emphasizes the "strong pool of local talent," adding that "business-friendly immigration policies make it simple to recruit professionals from overseas." Hong Kongers combine "international savvy and knowledge of Western/Chinese business culture," and "[a]lmost all business professionals speak excellent English," with many also speaking Cantonese and Mandarin.[40]

---

[33] *Id.* at 211.

[34] BRANDHK, GATEWAY TO CHINA (Aug. 2013). *See also* DOUGLAS W. ARNER ET AL., ASSESSING HONG KONG AS AN INTERNATIONAL FINANCIAL CENTRE 171 (2014).

[35] Melissa Kaye Pang, *Hong Kong as a Base for Doing Business in Mainland China*, BUS. L. TODAY, June 2013, at 1, 1.

[36] InvestHK, *Strategically Located for Business in Asia,* http://www.investhk.gov.hk/why-hong-kong/strategic-location.html (last visited Apr. 2016). *See also* BRANDHK, *supra* note 34.

[37] BRANDHK, *supra* note 34.

[38] Basic Law, *supra* note 23, art. 9. *See also* CENTRAL INTELLIGENCE AGENCY, *supra* note 1.

[39] CARROLL, *supra* note 4, at 232; Pang, *supra* note 35, at 3.

[40] InvestHK, *Easy Recruitment of Skilled Staff,* http://www.investhk.gov.hk/why-hong-kong/easy-recruitment-of-skilled-staff.html (last visited Apr. 2016). *See also* InvestHK, *Living in Hong Kong,*

Carroll, in his history of Hong Kong, observes that following the revolution of 1949 on the Mainland, Hong Kong students learned Chinese culture "in the abstract"[41]—essentially cultivating a unique hybrid identity lying somewhere between East and West. Indeed, by the mid-1980s, "three-fifths of Hong Kong's Chinese population preferred to see themselves as Hong Kongese rather than Chinese."[42] Over the intervening decades, this in-between status has served them well. BrandHK observes that "Hong Kong is an international city," well-connected globally, but that at the same time "Hong Kong entrepreneurs . . . share the same culture as their counterparts in the Mainland."[43] Pang elaborates that, armed at once with "Hong Kong's regulatory framework" and knowledge of "the Mainland China market," Hong Kong's legal establishment can "facilitate transactions involving parties from China by acting as a bridge between clients from the international and China capital markets."[44]

At the same time—and in a manner that further resembles the approach of other MDSJs—Hong Kong strongly cultivates and markets a regulatory balance of close collaboration with and robust oversight of the financial professional community, seeking at once to convey flexibility, stability, and credibility to market participants and foreign regulators alike. To substantiate its claim that Hong Kong is "one of the world's most business-friendly cities," InvestHK cites "[f]ree market policies, the rule of law and free flow of information," creating "a level playing field for all companies." They further emphasize Hong Kong's "political stability," the ability to conduct business in English, and their status as "[o]ne of the world's most open, and corruption-free economies." Their marketing efforts further emphasize that their "legal system is based on the British Common Law system [with] a fully independent judiciary," supplemented by "extensive mediation and arbitration services"— and more generally cultivate the perception that their "one country, two systems" arrangement with the Mainland offers the best of both worlds. "This has helped [Hong Kong] to retain all the fundamental strengths that underpin its success as an international business city, while enhancing its appeal with unrivalled access to opportunities in Mainland China."[45]

---

http://www.investhk.gov.hk/why-hong-kong/hong-kong-lifestyle.html (last visited Apr. 2016). For additional accounts similarly ascribing Hong Kong's success to the foregoing factors, see FINANCIAL SERVICES AND THE TREASURY BUREAU, GOVERNMENT OF THE HONG KONG SPECIAL ADMINISTRATIVE REGION, HONG KONG: CHINA'S GLOBAL FINANCIAL CENTRE 4 (2013), http://www.fstb.gov.hk/fsb/topical/doc/pitchbook_brochure(Nov%202013)_e.pdf; Financial Services Development Council, *supra* note 6, at 16–17, 30.

[41] CARROLL, *supra* note 4, at 148.

[42] *Id.* at 170.

[43] BrandHK, *supra* note 34.

[44] Pang, *supra* note 35, at 2.

[45] InvestHK, *International, Transparent, and Efficient,* http://www.investhk.gov.hk/why-hong-kong/international-transparent-and-efficient.html (last visited Apr. 2016). *See also* InvestHK, *Government*

It bears emphasizing that, notwithstanding their connection with China, Hong Kong itself is broadly viewed as a very low-corruption jurisdiction, ranking a respectable eighteenth in the world in Transparency International's 2015 *Corruption Perceptions Index.*[46] Starting in the 1970s, Hong Kong's government made a concerted effort to root out systemic corruption,[47] an effort that has paid substantial dividends in the cultivation of cross-border financial business. BrandHK, for example, observes that the hundreds of Mainland companies listed for trading in Hong Kong—accounting for about 56 percent of market capitalization in Hong Kong— "are subject to rigorous international standards of accounting and transparency,"[48] suggesting that Hong Kong's regulatory credibility in global markets is of substantial value to China itself. As Andrew Morriss has observed, "[a]ccess to jurisdictions that offer sophisticated and honest courts, certainty of legal interpretation and up-to-date statutory and regulatory frameworks enables businesses to invest in those countries despite flaws in the legal systems of investment targets"—Hong Kong, vis-à-vis China, representing a prime example.[49]

## B. Mainland Finance

Over the last several decades, Hong Kong has gradually established itself as the most important financial "gateway" to and from China, and Hong Kong's prosperity has become increasingly dependent upon its capacity to play that role effectively. Carroll suggests that "Hong Kong's status as both a British colony and an Asian entrepôt . . . laid the foundation for its emergence as an international financial center, while the political instability in other parts of East Asia [in the postwar decades] increased Hong Kong's economic competitiveness."[50] This is surely right as a general matter—particularly given the "considerable level of administrative and financial autonomy" that had been granted to Hong Kong by the 1950s.[51] But Catherine Schenk has rightly emphasized the role of historical idiosyncrasy as well, arguing that Hong Kong truly became an international financial center in the two postwar

---

Support for Companies, http://www.investhk.gov.hk/why-hong-kong/government-support-for-companies. html (last visited Apr. 2016); InvestHK, *World-Class Business Infrastructure,* http://www.investhk.gov.hk/ why-hong-kong/world-class-business-infrastructure.html (last visited Apr. 2016).

[46] *See* Transparency International, *Corruption Perceptions Index 2015* (2015). China, by contrast, ranked eighty-third. *Id.*

[47] *See* Carroll, *supra* note 4, at 172–76.

[48] BrandHK, *supra* note 34.

[49] *See* Andrew Morriss, *The End of Offshoring?*, Accountancy, Sept. 2014, at 49, 50.

[50] Carroll, *supra* note 4, at 144. *See also* Schenk, *supra* note 13, at 133.

[51] Carroll, *supra* note 4, at 171.

decades between 1945 and 1965 due to their unique capacity to mediate major geographies and components of the global economy in two critical respects—they mediated China and the world, while at the same time mediating the sterling area and the dollar area.[52] Hong Kong increased manufacturing in the 1950s and 1960s, to be sure,[53] but over the same time period began to "transition from an exclusively commercial to an increasingly financial focus."[54]

Under the Bretton Woods fixed exchange rate regime, the Hong Kong dollar was pegged to the British pound sterling—reflecting their participation in the "sterling area" group of jurisdictions—which was in turn pegged to the U.S. dollar (exchangeable for gold at a fixed rate). At the same time, however, a "freely floating exchange market for US dollars" was tolerated by British authorities to allow Hong Kong "to function as a trade entrepot." The "official fixed exchange rates of the HK dollar to sterling and to the US dollar co-existed with a parallel free market exchange rate set by demand and supply"—the only such free exchange market in the sterling area. In essence, "Hong Kong's regulatory system fell into the cracks between the tightly controlled sterling area arrangements and the free markets which persisted in Asian trade"—such that Hong Kong "attracted customers from the West as well as elsewhere in Asia." According to Schenk, "this combination of being a British colony and an Asian entrepot [provided] the foundation for Hong Kong's emergence as an international financial centre" in the immediate postwar decades.[55]

The consequences of this "Hong Kong Gap" were profound, creating trade and arbitrage opportunities unavailable elsewhere. As Schenk explains, Hong Kong's free exchange market

> . . . allowed Americans and Europeans to sell sterling securities for dollars, which they could not do in London or New York or any other financial centre. Australians, British and other residents of the sterling area could use the market to convert their sterling to US dollar securities within the rules of the exchange control. Again, this was a transaction that was not possible in the usual international financial centres.[56]

One of the important consequences of this unique role is that it effectively globalized Hong Kong's banks during a period when exchange controls applied throughout most of the world. "Hong Kong straddled the sterling area and the non-sterling

---

[52] *See generally* SCHENK, *supra* note 13.

[53] *Id.* at 6.

[54] *Id.* at 121.

[55] *Id.* at 8–9, 72–73, 80.

[56] *Id.* at 82.

area which meant that banks had intimate connections with the City of London, as well as operating on a large scale in US dollars," Schenk observes. "This was the primary source of Hong Kong's global rather than regional advantage in international finance."[57]

It is critical to observe the mutual value of this arrangement to both China and Hong Kong. Hong Kong's dependence on China for imported food and water generated much-needed foreign exchange for China, the Hong Kong dollar being "convertible to most other currencies through the free exchange markets in Hong Kong." At the same time, China's trade surplus generated "a demand for sterling among Hong Kong banks that linked them to foreign exchange markets in New York and London, and created arbitrage opportunities for international investors."[58]

Notwithstanding the idiosyncratic nature of the advantage that Hong Kong enjoyed during this period as a free exchange market, however, Schenk herself emphasizes attributes and advantages that strongly resonate with the MDSJ paradigm developed in this book. First, financial regulation in Hong Kong long reflected an ethos of "positive non-interventionism," creating an attractive marketplace facilitating transactions that were difficult and costly to achieve elsewhere. "Exchange controls were limited to a few imposed by the UK, . . . there were no controls on international flows of capital," and the "government was stubbornly resistant to regulating the banking system."[59] Indeed, Hong Kong's banking system was effectively "unregulated in the 1950s," with robust regulation taking shape over subsequent decades.[60] Greater room to maneuver proved attractive to American banks already expanding abroad in the late 1950s and early 1960s due to "restrictions on international banking in the USA," and a boom in Hong Kong's bank assets occurred during this period.[61] Schenk further emphasizes the significance of Hong Kong's ability to conduct business in English, as in Singapore, as well as their relative political stability,[62] and concludes that the "number of foreign banks in Hong Kong [during this period] is an important indicator of the nature of international financial and commercial business that attracted them to open offices."[63]

---

[57] *Id.* at 136–37.

[58] *Id.* at 12–14, 41–42.

[59] *Id.* at 15.

[60] *Id.* at 45, 154–55. *See also* TAN CHWEE HUAT & JOSEPH LIM YOUNG SAIN, SINGAPORE AND HONG KONG AS COMPETING FINANCIAL CENTRES 20–21 (2007).

[61] SCHENK, *supra* note 13, at 50, 58. *See also infra* Chapter 10.C (discussing the origins of Euromarkets in London).

[62] *See* SCHENK, *supra* note 13, at 133–34.

[63] *Id.* at 52–53.

Schenk makes a strong case that Hong Kong truly became a global financial center in the postwar decades, and that the government's posture of "positive non-interventionism" heavily conditioned the financial center's development. It is important to recognize, however, that Hong Kong's MDSJ advantages were apparent and operative considerably earlier, and that government support of Hong Kong's financial development did in fact play a critical role—if a less direct one than we have observed elsewhere. These dynamics are perhaps nowhere more apparent than in the establishment and growth of the Hong Kong and Shanghai Banking Corporation—now known globally as HSBC but historically referred to in Hong Kong as "the Hong Kong Bank," or even more succinctly as "the Bank," reflecting its strong local identification and predominance in the marketplace.[64]

Though the Bank would eventually move its headquarters to London in 1993, "following its takeover of Midland Bank, and four years before the handover of Hong Kong to China,"[65] HSBC has long represented Hong Kong's most prominent financial institution,[66] and its establishment in the 1860s largely foreshadows the MDSJ characteristics and strategies now reflective of Hong Kong more generally. The purpose of the Bank was "to finance the growing trade between Asia and Europe,"[67] and this aim is clearly expressed in the Bank's July 1864 prospectus, observing that the "local and foreign trade in Hongkong and at the open ports in China and Japan has increased so rapidly . . . that additional Banking facilities are felt to be required." Critically, then, the prospectus distinguishes the contemplated institution from competitors "whose headquarters are in England and India," and who were thus "scarcely in a position to deal satisfactorily with the local trade," adding that "the largest profits are obtained by those Public Companies which

---

[64] *See* 1 Frank H.H. King, The History of the Hongkong and Shanghai Banking Corporation 67 (1987); HSBC, The Hongkong and Shanghai Banking Corporation: 1865–1965 (1965) (remarks of the Governor of Hong Kong, Sir David Trench).

[65] Giles Turner, *HSBC Threatens to Leave London, Again*, Wall St. J., Apr. 24, 2015, http://blogs.wsj.com/moneybeat/2015/04/24/hsbc-threatens-to-leave-london-again/. For a time HSBC actively considered moving its headquarters back to Hong Kong—a possibility prompted by discontent with the U.K. "bank levy" that had "cost HSBC $1.1 billion in 2014, more than any other bank," and that was "expected to rise to $1.6 billion" in 2015. *See id.* Following a relaxation of the levy, and in light of "gyrations in Chinese markets coupled with concerns about China's growing influence over Hong Kong," HSBC decided in February 2016 to remain headquartered in London, while indicating that a U.K. vote to leave the European Union would require the board to rethink the matter. *See* Rachel Armstrong & Lisa Jucca, *HSBC Keeps Headquarters in London, Rejects Move to Hong Kong*, Reuters, Feb. 15, 2016, http://www.reuters.com/article/us-hsbc-headquarters-idUSKCN0VN11P.

[66] *See* Schenk, *supra* note 13, at 46; Svetlana Andrianova, Panicos Demetriades & Chenggang Xu, *Political Economy Origins of Financial Markets in Europe and Asia*, 39 World Dev. 686, 694 (2011).

[67] *HSBC's History*, https://www.hsbc.com.hk/1/2/about/home/hsbc-s-history (last visited Apr. 2016). *See also* HSBC, *supra* note 64 (remarks of the Governor of Hong Kong, Sir David Trench); King, *supra* note 64, at 47, 51, 53; Carroll, *supra* note 4, at 30–31; Andrianova et al., *supra* note 66, at 694.

possess an interested local body of Proprietors or Shareholders, whose support naturally forms a chief element of remunerative success."[68]

These expectations were quickly borne out, as the minutes of an August 1866 report of the "Court of Directors" (as it was termed) observes that "[w]ith comparatively few exceptions, the entire mercantile community, and very many native merchants are now interested in the Bank, and have given it their full support."[69] A year later, in August 1867, the Directors would underscore the value of their roots in the local market, explaining that the Bank had "Established further claims on the sympathies of the mercantile community in not altering like the other competing Banks, the customary usance which has for many years regulated Sterling Exchanges in the East." They add that by "adhering to a liberal policy the [Bank] has realized one of the main objects of its institution, namely, to supply the legitimate requirements of the China trade whose representatives, almost without exception, look upon the maintenance of the six months usance as an object of primary importance especially when applying to shipments of Tea to Europe and America."[70] Economic historian Frank King attributes the Bank's early successes to "the broad international base of its directorate," observing that "eight of the fourteen [initial] members were not from Britain," resulting in a board more broadly representative of Hong Kong's merchant community while at the same time underscoring the Bank's depth of "local" commitments.[71]

The Bank's formal business commenced in 1865, and in 1866 they were formally incorporated,[72] which ultimately had the effect of imbuing the Bank with a quasi-public role and status that proved critical to the institution's growth and development—and, by association, Hong Kong's. Notably, the ordinance of

---

[68] See KING, supra note 64, at 73 (reproducing "The Prospectus of the Hongkong and Shanghae Banking Company, Limited").

[69] Hongkong & Shanghai Banking Company, Limited, Report of the Court of Directors to the Ordinary Half-Yearly General Meeting of Shareholders (Aug. 16, 1866).

[70] Hongkong & Shanghai Banking Corporation, Fourth Report of the Court of Directors to the Ordinary Half-Yearly General Meeting of Shareholders (Aug. 13, 1867). The term "usance" refers to the "time allowed for the payment of a foreign bill of exchange," whether set by law or custom. See BLACK'S LAW DICTIONARY 1540 (7th ed. 1999).

[71] See KING, supra note 64, at 54–57. It must be added, however, that well into the twentieth century the Bank "had a policy of not having any Chinese on its board," a policy reflective of the broader exclusion of Hong Kong's Chinese population from public or private positions of power through much of Hong Kong's history. See CARROLL, supra note 4, at 105.

[72] See KING, supra note 64, at 70–72. See also THE HONGKONG GOVERNMENT GAZETTE, vol. XII no. 31, July 28, 1866, at 281, 282 (reporting the first reading, on July 25, 1866, of an ordinance for the Bank's incorporation); THE HONGKONG GOVERNMENT GAZETTE, vol. XII no. 34, Aug. 18, 1866, at 317, 318 (reporting the second reading and passage with amendment on August 14, 1866); THE HONGKONG GOVERNMENT GAZETTE, vol. XII no. 51, Dec. 15, 1866 (reporting satisfaction of a condition regarding the Bank's capitalization).

incorporation permitted the Bank to issue bank notes that would be accepted by co-lonial governments in the region,[73] which—particularly once enhanced (in 1872) by the exclusive right to issue notes denominated below five dollars—"implied a kind of endorsement by the British government of the Hongkong Bank and its notes."[74] Combined with their ability under the ordinance "to bid for government accounts," which the Bank did successfully, "the Hongkong Bank became, in effect, the banker to both the British Government and the local government." By the close of the nineteenth century, the Bank "had become the virtually permanent banker to the British Government in China and was responsible for over 80 percent of the local note issue."[75] Indeed, for lack of a true central bank, the Hong Kong Bank "would act as Hong Kong's central bank until the last years of the colonial era,"[76] while at the same time enjoying some degree of indirect political power, as its directors "reg-ularly held seats on the Executive Council and the Legislative Council."[77]

Given the local knowledge and commercial ties of its managers, it is hardly sur-prising that the Bank would be called upon to advise "the British Government in political and economic negotiations with the Imperial Government of China," and it is likewise unsurprising that the Bank would be called upon by the Chinese Imperial government to assist them in borrowing on the London capital market.[78] As King observes, "the Bank was obliging and 'understood' China," permitting this unique institution to perform bridging functions that its competitors could not do effectively. He explains that the Bank essentially "operated as an *interface* between two differing financial systems, making it possible for the parties to understand each other," elaborating:

> . . . The Bank did not insist on the Chinese changing their terms to suit the Bank or the public; the Bank, however, understood China—even if the public did not. The Bank also understood both the Hong Kong and Shanghai mar-kets and, note well, the London market; accordingly, having met the terms of the borrower, the Bank translated not only the terms but also the approach to meet the requirements of the lender.[79]

---

[73] *See* Hongkong and Shanghae Bank Ordinance, No. 5 of 1866, §§ XII–XV (H.K.).

[74] Andrianova et al., *supra* note 66, at 694. *See also* SCHENK, *supra* note 13, at 9.

[75] Andrianova et al., *supra* note 66, at 694.

[76] *See* CARROLL, *supra* note 4, at 31. *See also* Andrianova et al., *supra* note 66, at 693 (comparing this indirect government role in financial development through state-granted monopoly privileges to the quasi-public roles of the Dutch and English joint stock companies centuries earlier).

[77] *See* CARROLL, *supra* note 4, at 229.

[78] *See* Andrianova et al., *supra* note 66, at 694.

[79] KING, *supra* note 64, at 536–37. *See also id.* at 541–43.

In stark contrast with this approach, the Bank's competitors headquartered else-where "suffered from the almost missionary, and certainly self-destructive, urge to tell the Chinese (i) what they should borrow for and (ii) how they should go about borrowing."[80] The upshot was that the Bank was called upon to handle "over 70 per-cent of all foreign loans" for the Chinese Imperial government between 1874 and 1890, helping the Bank "to become by the end of the 19th century the most impor-tant foreign financial institution in the East."[81]

In light of the foregoing it is important to recognize that HSBC's—and, by as-sociation, Hong Kong's—MDSJ advantages and strategies were recognized and operative from a very early stage in its commercial and financial history, and that coordinated public-private initiatives were an important part of the formula for suc-cess. As Governor of Hong Kong Sir David Trench would observe in a toast to the Bank on the occasion of their 1965 centennial, "the histories of the Bank and of Hong Kong . . . are so intertwined that it is sometimes hard to distinguish between them." He elaborated that the "China trade, local international support, and the best interests of the area in which it conducted its operations have . . . been the main pillars of the Bank's policies throughout its history. One could express the general policies of Hong Kong throughout *its* history in almost identical terms."[82]

Consistent with Schenk's fundamental claim, however, the Bank itself did increas-ingly pursue a global footprint in the decades following World War II. Expansion began in earnest with the establishment of a California subsidiary in 1955 and, more consequentially, the acquisition of the India-based Mercantile Bank in 1959 and the British Bank of the Middle East in 1960.[83] The "policy of expansion" embodied by

---

[80] *See id.* at 543.

[81] *See* Andrianova et al., *supra* note 66, at 694. *See also* KING, *supra* note 64, at 535, 547–49.

[82] HSBC, *supra* note 64 (remarks of the Governor of Hong Kong, Sir David Trench). An interesting reflection of the Bank's status at the heart of Hong Kong's financial center is its building, located on the same site in the Central district of Hong Kong since its business commenced in the 1860s. *See* KING, *supra* note 64, at 64; *HSBC's History, supra* note 67. Successive iterations of the building have long embodied progress and the Bank's prestige, one shareholder at the 1936 general meeting hailing the 1935 building's construction as a "milestone in the history of our Corporation." *See* Hongkong and Shanghai Banking Corporation, One Hundred and Twentieth Report of the Board of Directors to the Ordinary Yearly General Meeting of Shareholders 28 (Feb. 22, 1936). Among other things attracting attention, this building was at the time thought to contain one of the world's largest air conditioning installations, and "almost certainly the largest for an office building in the British Empire"—an immediately popular workplace innovation in a place renowned for stifling summer heat and humidity. *See* C.A. Middleton Smith, *Air Conditioning in a Hongkong Bank,* FAR E. REV., Nov. 1937, at 389, 395. More recently, the 1985 building "was the world's most expensive building when it was completed." *See* CARROLL, *supra* note 4, at 183.

[83] 4 FRANK H.H. KING, THE HISTORY OF THE HONGKONG AND SHANGHAI BANKING CORPORATION 482–86, 489–90 (1991); SCHENK, *supra* note 13, at 47–48; *HSBC's History, supra* note 67. On the Mercantile Bank acquisition, see KING, *supra,* at 498–517, and on the British Bank of the Middle East acquisition, see KING, *supra,* at 529–39.

these acquisitions[84] reflected HSBC's perception that they needed to diversify due to the growing complexity of regional relations,[85] as well as growing competitive pressures (notably from U.S. banks).[86] As Schenk observes, "the Hongkong Bank was on its way to becoming one of the world's largest banks, helped by the acquisition of the British Bank of the Middle East and the Mercantile Bank."[87] By 1960 HSBC could report to its shareholders that "our group now covers a wide area stretching from the Pacific to the Mediterranean,"[88] and by its 1965 centennial the Bank could tout "a complex network of international banking with a comprehensive chain of over 150 offices stretching from Casablanca through the Near, Middle and Far East to Tokyo and in San Francisco, New York, London, Paris and Hamburg."[89] A year later, after acquiring control of Hang Seng Bank Limited, the number reached 170 offices,[90] and by 1967 it could "truly be said that our Bank is an international one with a world-wide coverage," offering "material benefit to clients to assist them in their efforts to expand trade with all the countries involved."[91] These events at HSBC do map closely onto the internationalization of Hong Kong's banking system, even if building on MDSJ attributes and strategies that were recognized and pursued long before the postwar decades of rapid global expansion.

As the broad similarities in their competitive attributes and strategies suggest, there has been some degree of competition between Hong Kong and Singapore ever since the latter jurisdiction's initial rise to prominence in the late 1960s and early 1970s. "Both were city-states, populated overwhelmingly by Chinese, which flourished under colonial administration in the pre-war period, and found their main activity as trading and financial entrepots."[92] At the same time, both offer common-law

---

[84] *See* KING, *supra* note 83, at 517.

[85] *See id.* at 523, 534–35.

[86] *See id.* at 529; SCHENK, *supra* note 13, at 48; Hongkong and Shanghai Banking Corporation, Report of the Directors and Accounts: 31st December 1958, at 18 (ordinary yearly general meeting of shareholders, Mar. 13, 1959) (reporting the observation of Chairman Michael Turner that "in British exchange banking . . . the tendency must be for consolidation, not only because larger units tend to become stronger and can operate more effectively, but also because they are less vulnerable to takeover bids"). *See also* SCHENK, *supra* note 13, at 60 (observing a rapid expansion of HSBC branches after 1959).

[87] SCHENK, *supra* note 13, at 123–24.

[88] Hongkong and Shanghai Banking Corporation, Report of the Directors and Accounts: 31st December 1959, at 21 (ordinary yearly general meeting of shareholders, Mar. 11, 1960).

[89] Hongkong and Shanghai Banking Corporation, Centenary Report of the Directors and Accounts: 31st December 1964, at 2.

[90] *See* Hongkong and Shanghai Banking Corporation, Report of the Directors and Accounts: 31st December 1965, at 1 (ordinary yearly general meeting of shareholders, Mar. 18, 1966).

[91] Hongkong and Shanghai Banking Corporation, Report of the Directors and Accounts: 31st December 1966 and the Chairman's Survey 3–4 (ordinary yearly general meeting of shareholders, Mar. 17, 1967) (reporting comments of J. Eitzen in seconding the motion to adopt the report and accounts).

[92] SCHENK, *supra* note 13, at 137. *See also* V. Le Leslé et al., *Why Complementarity Matters for Stability—Hong Kong SAR and Singapore as Asian Financial Centers* 9–10 (IMF Working Paper WP/14/119, 2014).

legal systems[93] familiar to Western financial communities and benefited from "a clear 'early mover advantage'" in developing their own financial capacities.[94] There are also substantial differences, however, in terms of their respective geographies and regulatory traditions. Whereas Hong Kong straightforwardly represents the more natural geographic "gateway" to and from China, Singapore may loom larger where corporate and/or investment strategies favor "a location with good access to other Southeast Asian nations."[95] And observers have long remarked on the distinct regulatory postures of the two jurisdictions, Hong Kong's traditional "laissez-faire" approach contrasting sharply with Singapore's greater reliance on centralized state management.[96]

As of the early 1960s, however, Hong Kong far exceeded Singapore in banking activity, benefiting from free markets in gold and foreign exchange. Interestingly, Singapore sought a free foreign exchange market as well, but the British declined to expand this controversial practice beyond Hong Kong (where it was thought "it could not be eliminated" in any event).[97] Singapore would find its niche, however, with the development of the Asian Dollar Market in the 1960s—an initiative aided by Hong Kong's maintenance of its own 15 percent withholding tax. This tax was removed in the early 1980s, and by the mid-1980s "Hong Kong had surpassed Singapore in terms of the size of the Asian dollar market and Asian dollar bond issues."[98] With respect to foreign assets generally, the two have gone back and forth over recent decades, with Hong Kong holding the lead in the 1960s, Singapore surpassing them in the 1970s (due to the Asian Dollar Market), and Hong Kong taking the lead again in the 1990s.[99] Today, Hong Kong exhibits a decided advantage in initial public offerings and equity trading, largely reflecting its proximity to Mainland companies,[100] as well as internationalization of the Chinese renminbi (RMB),[101] whereas Singapore exhibits strength in foreign exchange, commodities, and derivatives trading, as well as overall liveability for those populating the financial center.[102]

---

[93] *See* Jeremy Grant, *Singapore Jostles with Hong Kong for Financial Crown*, FIN. TIMES, Oct. 16, 2014, http://www.ft.com/intl/cms/s/0/b18372a6-5297-11e4-a236-00144feab7de.html.

[94] *See* Le Leslé et al., *supra* note 92, at 5.

[95] *See* Evelyn Cheng, *Bad News in Hong Kong Is Good News for Singapore*, CNBC.COM, Sept. 2, 2014, http://www.cnbc.com/id/101963981. *See also* Grant, *supra* note 93; Le Leslé et al., *supra* note 92, at 12, 26.

[96] *See, e.g.*, LEE KUAN YEW, FROM THIRD WORLD TO FIRST—THE SINGAPORE STORY: 1965–2000, at 97–98 (2000); TAN & LIM, *supra* note 60, at 73; Le Leslé et al., *supra* note 92, at 11; Jagjit Kaur Meetook, *A Survey of Banking Laws and Policies in Hong Kong and Singapore*, 1986 BYU L. REV. 835, 852, 861–62 (1986).

[97] *See* SCHENK, *supra* note 13, at 137–39.

[98] *See id.* at 155. *See also* TAN & LIM, *supra* note 60, at 3; *supra* Chapter 6.A (discussing development of the Asian Dollar Market in Singapore).

[99] *See* SCHENK, *supra* note 13, at 130–31. *See also* TAN & LIM, *supra* note 60, at 36–37.

[100] *See* Financial Services Development Council, *supra* note 6, at 15; Grant, *supra* note 93; Le Leslé et al., *supra* note 92, at 16.

[101] *See* Financial Services Development Council, *supra* note 6, at 15, 28–29; Le Leslé et al., *supra* note 92, at 15.

[102] *See* Reuters, *Singapore Exchange Expands in China, Names Country Chief*, BUS. TIMES, Feb. 11, 2015, http://www.businesstimes.com.sg/companies-markets/singapore-exchange-expands-in-china-names-

Hong Kong's proximity to China gives them a leg up in attracting wealth management business from high-net-worth individuals (HNWIs) on the Mainland. "The private wealth management industry in China is not well developed," Jek Aun Long and Danny Tan explain, "and consequently many HNWIs there choose to have their wealth managed by private banks in Hong Kong." Attractive features in Hong Kong include "the range of investment products and expertise available, its competitive tax regime and the absence of any exchange controls or restrictions on capital flows into and out of Hong Kong."[103] Hong Kong likewise maintains strong (common-law-based) bank secrecy laws, yet managed to avoid the OECD's grey list "[b]y virtue of China's status in the G20" (as well as having "committed to sign at least 12 agreements with other jurisdictions implementing the internationally agreed tax standard on exchange of information").[104] In light of the foregoing it is notable that, although "[m]ore than half of the companies implicated in the leaked Panama Papers are registered in UK overseas territories and crown dependencies,"[105] these records further reveal that the "Hong Kong branch of Mossack Fonseca is the busiest for the Panamanian law firm," and that "[s]hell companies incorporated through the Hong Kong and the mainland offices . . . accounted for 29 percent of [the firm's] active companies worldwide."[106] Increased movements of money outside the Mainland have been attributed to "a falling yuan and a crackdown on corruption," as well as "Chinese citizens' lack of trust in the country's laws and courts."[107]

---

country-chief; Financial Services Development Council, *supra* note 6, at 18, 21, 36–38; Grant, *supra* note 93.

[103] Jek Aun Long & Danny Tan, *The Growth of the Private Wealth Management Industry in Singapore and Hong Kong*, 6 CAP. MARKETS L.J. 104, 118, 121 (2011).

[104] *See id*. at 120, 125. *See also* TAX JUSTICE NETWORK, *supra* note 22, at 1 n.1; Vanderwolk, *supra* note 31, at 177–78.

[105] Patrick Wintour, *Overseas Territories Spared from UK Law on Company Registers*, GUARDIAN, Apr. 12, 2016, http://www.theguardian.com/business/2016/apr/12/overseas-territories-spared-from-uk-law-on-company-registers.

[106] Jun Mai, *Hong Kong Was Busiest Office of Panama Papers Law Firm*, S. CHINA MORNING POST, Apr. 8, 2016, http://www.scmp.com/news/hong-kong/article/1934566/hong-kong-was-busiest-office-panama-papers-law-firm (emphasis removed). *See also The Panama Papers: A Torrential Leak*, ECONOMIST, Apr. 9, 2016, at 59–61; Juliette Garside & David Pegg, *Panama Papers Reveal Offshore Secrets of China's Red Nobility*, GUARDIAN, Apr. 6, 2016, http://www.theguardian.com/news/2016/apr/06/panama-papers-reveal-offshore-secrets-china-red-nobility-big-business; Mia Lamar & Ned Levin, *5 Things to Know about Hong Kong and the "Panama Papers*," WALL ST. J., Apr. 6, 2016, http://blogs.wsj.com/briefly/2016/04/06/5-things-to-know-about-hong-kong-and-the-panama-papers/. In addition to their Hong Kong office, Mossack Fonseca's website lists seven offices on the Mainland. *See* Mossack Fonseca, *Global Presence*, http://www.mossfon.com/contact-our-offices/ (last visited Apr. 2016).

[107] *See* Lamar & Levin, *supra* note 106. Although "Chinese law doesn't bar citizens from investing in offshore firms," *id*., the Communist Party code of conduct prohibits party members "from registering or investing in companies abroad," creating problems for Chinese officials with relatives revealed to have offshore holdings. *See* ECONOMIST, *supra* note 106.

Hong Kong itself "has performed better than most in the midst of the global financial turmoil,"[108] and the Securities and Futures Commission (SFC) adds that Mainland economic growth "has generated huge savings and wealth accumulation," with Mainland financial liberalization permitting Hong Kong to play "an increasingly important role in connecting investors to investment opportunities around the world."[109] Hong Kong now far exceeds Singapore in exchange listings—again, largely reflecting their proximity to and relationship with China. As recently as the 1960s, Hong Kong's stock market "was small in relation to other Asian stock markets," but "turnover increased substantially" in the 1970s.[110] Hong Kong is now a global leader in exchange listings, the Singapore Exchange being "a fraction of the size of its Hong Kong counterpart, raising only one-ninth the amount of capital, offering one-third the amount of liquidity and trading less than one-fifth on average per day."[111]

Given its far more developed corporate legal system, Hong Kong has represented an attractive base for investments into China from abroad.[112] As of 2011, Hong Kong was the global leader in initial public offerings for the third straight year, with "640 China companies listed in Hong Kong, making up 55.5 percent (i.e., US$1.2 trillion) of the market total."[113] By the end of 2012 "there were a total of 721 Mainland companies listed in Hong Kong," representing "47 percent of the total number of listed companies in Hong Kong and . . . 57 percent of the total market capitalisation."[114] The SFC has likewise reported that the stocks of Mainland companies are "the most actively traded stocks, accounting for 54 percent of total market turnover," and that in the first half of 2014 the Hong Kong Stock Exchange remained first in Asia for

---

[108] Long & Tan, *supra* note 103, at 119. *See also* ARNER ET AL., *supra* note 34, at 24.

[109] SECURITIES AND FUTURES COMMISSION, FUND MANAGEMENT ACTIVITIES SURVEY 2013, at 5 (July 2014) (H.K.).

[110] SCHENK, *supra* note 13, at 108–09.

[111] CALLY JORDAN, INTERNATIONAL CAPITAL MARKETS: LAW AND INSTITUTIONS 219–20 (2014). *See also* Reuters, *supra* note 102; *Taiwan and Singapore to Open Stock Market Link in 2015,* CITYINDEX.COM, Nov. 18, 2014, http://www.cityindex.com.sg/market-talk/financial-news/asian-stock-markets-news/79552014/taiwan-and-singapore-to-open-stock-market-link-in-2015/.

[112] *See* Jing Li, *Venture Capital Investments in China: The Use of Offshore Financing Structures and Corporate Relocations,* 1 MICH. J. PRIVATE EQUITY & VENTURE CAP. L. 1, 41–51 (2012); Morriss, *supra* note 49, at 50; Wei Shen, *China's Dilemma: How Can a Weak Company Law Regime Support a Strong Market for International Private Equity Investments? A Real "Piggybacking" Case,* 11:3 BUS. L. INT'L 195, 200, 209–13, 216 (2010). On the evolving legal landscape regarding Hong Kong–based investment vehicles as a means of avoiding application of Chinese corporate law, see generally Gordon Y.M. Chan, *Reforming the Sponsor Regulatory Regime—A Case of Hong Kong's Response to the Impact of Chinese Listings,* 43 HONG KONG L.J. 973 (2013); Li, *supra*; Shen, *supra*.

[113] Pang, *supra* note 35, at 3. *See also* Chan, *supra* note 112, at 973; WORLD ECONOMIC FORUM, THE FINANCIAL DEVELOPMENT REPORT 2012, at 20–22 (2012).

[114] Chan, *supra* note 112, at 977.

"equity funds raised through IPOs," and fourth in the world. "Mainland companies accounted for 68 percent of the total funds raised" through IPOs in the first half of 2014.[115]

By the end of 2015, as Figure 7.1 indicates, the predominance of Mainland companies remained the defining feature of Hong Kong's equity market, representing 62 percent of market capitalization, 51 percent of issuers, and 73 percent of annual trading turnover.[116] In fact, it should be noted that these data may understate the degree of reliance on Mainland business to the extent that they fail to account for de facto Chinese businesses owned and controlled by individuals who have sought citizenship elsewhere under so-called "citizenship-for-sale" programs, such as that promoted by the Caribbean nation of St. Kitts and Nevis—the attractions of which, according to one Hong Kong immigration lawyer, include "freedom of travel, wealth planning and as a place of citizenship if they're doing a foreign listing of a mainland company."[117] As St. Kitts and Nevis does not disclose "who buys passports or how much money has been generated," and "has no freedom of information legislation," there is no way to quantify the impact of this activity.[118]

Douglas Arner and a team of Hong Kong-based researchers, writing in 2014, shed light on the nature of the investment activity occurring in and through Hong Kong. "Hong Kong excels at attracting investment," they conclude, observing that "market capitalisation of Hong Kong's stock markets … eclipses other economies, at roughly 600 percent of GDP." They elaborate that "Hong Kong's market

---

[115] Securities and Futures Commission, *Half-Yearly Review of the Global and Local Securities Markets* 9–10 (Research Paper No. 55, 2014) (H.K.). *But see* Wang Jiangyu, *China's Impact on Hong Kong's Position as an International Financial Centre: The Legal and Policy Dimensions, in* A FINANCIAL CENTRE FOR TWO EMPIRES, *supra* note 31, at 223, 230 (observing, in 2014, that most large Chinese state-owned enterprises had already listed). For a discussion of governance in Chinese state-owned enterprises and the attractions of listing in Hong Kong, see Wang, *supra*, at 234–49.

[116] *See* HONG KONG EXCHANGES AND CLEARING LIMITED (HKEx), MARKET STATISTICS 2015, at 15–19 (2016).

[117] *See* Jason Chow, *The Hot New Immigration Destinations for China's Wealthy,* WALL ST. J., Apr. 18, 2013, http://blogs.wsj.com/chinarealtime/2013/04/18/the-hot-new-immigration-destinations-for-chinas-wealthy/ (quoting Hong Kong immigration lawyer Denny Ko). *See also* Ian Young, *St Kitts and Nevis Recalls Passports over Security Concerns from Canada and US,* S. CHINA MORNING POST, Dec. 9, 2014, http://www.scmp.com/news/world/article/1659120/st-kitts-and-nevis-recalls-passports-over-security-concerns-canada-and-us; Ian Young, *Trouble In Paradise: Chinese "Astronaut" Dads Caught in St Kitts Passport Tangle,* S. CHINA MORNING POST, Dec. 10, 2014, http://www.scmp.com/comment/blogs/article/1659290/trouble-paradise-chinese-astronaut-dads-caught-st-kitts-passport?page=all.

[118] *See* Jason Clenfield, *This Swiss Lawyer Is Helping Governments Get Rich off Selling Passports,* BLOOMBERGBUSINESS, Mar. 11, 2015, http://www.bloomberg.com/news/articles/2015-03-11/passport-king-christian-kalin-helps-nations-sell-citizenship. For additional discussion of concerns prompted by such programs, as well as the inherent vulnerabilities of this mode of economic development, see *infra* Chapter 10.B.

| Year | Market Capitalization (HK$ billion) | | Number of Issuers | | Annual Trading Turnover (HK$ billion) | |
|---|---|---|---|---|---|---|
| | Mainland Enterprises | % of HKEx Equity Market | Mainland Enterprises | % of HKEx Equity Market | Mainland Enterprises | % of HKEx Equity Market |
| 2006 | $6,714.46 | 50% | 367 | 31% | $3,879.36 | 60% |
| 2007 | $12,049.01 | 58% | 439 | 35% | $11,549.41 | 69% |
| 2008 | $6,160.91 | 60% | 465 | 37% | $8,977.30 | 71% |
| 2009 | $10,443.75 | 58% | 524 | 40% | $8,336.55 | 72% |
| 2010 | $11,935.77 | 57% | 592 | 42% | $8,436.13 | 68% |
| 2011 | $9,723.75 | 55% | 640 | 43% | $7,966.62 | 66% |
| 2012 | $12,597.78 | 57% | 721 | 47% | $6,628.42 | 70% |
| 2013 | $13,690.57 | 57% | 797 | 49% | $8,036.62 | 72% |
| 2014 | $15,077.62 | 60% | 876 | 50% | $8,933.20 | 71% |
| 2015 | $15,319.82 | 62% | 951 | 51% | $12,705.53 | 73% |

FIGURE 7.1 Mainland Enterprises Trading on the HKEx, 2006–2015.*

* See HONG KONG EXCHANGES AND CLEARING LIMITED (HKEx), MARKET STATISTICS 2015, at 15–19 (2016) (providing market cap, issuer, and turnover data on "Mainland Enterprises," including H-share issuers, i.e. companies that are "incorporated in the Mainland which are either controlled by Mainland Government entities or individuals"; Red Chip issuers, i.e. companies that are "incorporated outside of the Mainland and are controlled by Mainland Government entities"; and Mainland Private Enterprises, i.e. companies that are "incorporated outside of the Mainland and are controlled by Mainland individuals").

capitalisation combines a large number of small companies with a smaller number of larger companies, mainly Mainland companies, Hong Kong conglomerates and property developers, and HSBC."[119] The explanation for Hong Kong's dominance is, again, proximity to China. They note that "Hong Kong appears easily able to attract cross-border direct investment, despite its indigenous private equity and venture capital resources having expanded only recently," due to "the relatively free access to new and expanding Mainland ventures given to foreign direct investment (FDI), which has resulted since the 1980s in Hong Kong becoming an entrepôt for FDI sourced from Greater China and elsewhere."[120]

---

[119] ARNER ET AL., *supra* note 34, at 23–24.

[120] *Id.* at 25. *See also* JAMES S. HENRY, THE PRICE OF OFFSHORE REVISITED: NEW ESTIMATES FOR "MISSING" GLOBAL PRIVATE WEALTH, INCOME, INEQUALITY, AND LOST TAXES (July 2012) (report for the Tax Justice Network) (discussing the prevalence of "round tripping" via Hong Kong and British Virgin Islands entities, through which Mainland investors endeavor to gain access to tax breaks available only to foreigners); TAX JUSTICE NETWORK, *supra* note 22, at 7 (pointing to round tripping to explain Hong Kong's and the British Virgin Islands' respective status as the first and second largest sources of inward investment into China).

The SFC has observed that "Hong Kong's proximity to and long history of close co-operation with the Mainland has always made it the undisputed forum of choice for Mainland-related companies who wish to gain international exposure."[121] Strikingly, 50 percent of Hong Kong-managed assets in 2013 were invested in Hong Kong or the Mainland.[122] As to the activity supported by this financing, Arner et al. find that real estate investment "represents the lion's share of [outward and inward foreign] investment (more than half in both cases)," and that "[t]hese flows clearly reflect large construction projects by Hong Kong's real estate companies at home and on the Mainland."[123] They conclude that although "Hong Kong attracts a significant amount of portfolio and direct investment," this "seems to fuel Hong Kong's volatile real estate sector rather than more productive sectors"[124]—a trend with potentially negative consequences discussed below.

As the foregoing stock exchange and investment data reflect, Hong Kong effectively has one foot within China and one foot without, a complex economic and financial status carefully cultivated by the Basic Law—because it serves the Mainland's interests. Although Hong Kong constitutes "an inalienable part of the People's Republic of China," they are nevertheless granted "a high degree of autonomy" to manage their own affairs,[125] notably in economic and financial domains. This expresses itself most directly in the Basic Law's assurance that the "socialist system and policies shall not be practised in the Hong Kong Special Administrative Region, and the previous capitalist system and way of life shall remain unchanged for 50 years."[126] Referred to as "the principle of 'one country, two systems,'"[127] this structure clearly advances the pragmatic aim of maintaining Hong Kong's stature as a financial center for the mutual benefit of Hong Kong and the Mainland. Indeed, the Basic Law establishes a mandate to do so in Article 109, which states:

> The Government of the Hong Kong Special Administrative Region shall provide an appropriate economic and legal environment for the maintenance of the status of Hong Kong as an international financial centre.[128]

---

[121] SECURITIES AND FUTURES COMMISSION, *supra* note 109, at 1.

[122] *See id.* at 20.

[123] ARNER ET AL., *supra* note 34, at 25–26.

[124] *Id.* at 27.

[125] *See* Basic Law, *supra* note 23, arts. 1–2.

[126] *Id.* art. 5. It is worth noting that "Deng Xiaoping, meeting members of the Basic Law Drafting Committee on 16 April 1987, emphasized that the policy . . . on Hong Kong would not only remain in force for at least 50 years but also that there would be even less need to change the policy and the Basic Law after the 50-year period." LO, *supra* note 15, at 35–36.

[127] Basic Law, *supra* note 23, Preamble. As P.Y. Lo explains, this principle had previously been developed to facilitate reunification with Taiwan. *See* LO, *supra* note 15, at 7–10.

[128] Basic Law, *supra* note 23, art. 109.

To that end, Hong Kong "shall, on its own, formulate monetary and financial policies, safeguard the free operation of financial business and financial markets, and regulate and supervise them in accordance with law."[129] A background piece on the drafting of the Basic Law emphasizes that the "one country, two systems" principle "is the fundamental policy of the Chinese Government for bringing about the country's reunification," and that the various economic and financial freedoms extended to Hong Kong were those considered "indispensable to ensuring the normal operation of Hong Kong's capitalist economic mechanism and maintaining its status as an international financial centre and free port."[130]

Today, however, the process of Hong Kong's ongoing integration with the Mainland represents a growing source of uncertainty, at once presenting further opportunities and imposing substantial risks. One particularly consequential area is internationalization of the renminbi (RMB), and Hong Kong's role in that process. As the SWIFT data summarized in Figure 7.2 reflects, growth in use of the renminbi in the Asia Pacific for payments with China and Hong Kong has been phenomenal, rising from just 7 percent in early 2012 to 31 percent in early 2015. Indeed, the renminbi now stands as "the fifth most active currency for global payments," accounting for "2.07 percent of payments worldwide."[131]

Hong Kong has made much of being "the world's leading provider of renminbi products outside the Mainland," a role considered "one of the key drivers behind the growth of [Hong Kong's] fund management business." As the SFC explains, "[w]ith the gradual internationalisation of the renminbi, Hong Kong continues to serve as a testing ground for new financial reform initiatives," adding that "Hong Kong serves as a bridge linking the onshore and offshore renminbi markets and promotes the use and circulation of renminbi funds."[132]

---

[129] *Id.* art. 110. *See also id.* arts. 105–06, 112, 115 (requiring protection of property rights, ensuring "independent finances," forbidding "foreign exchange control policies," and requiring pursuit of "free trade," respectively).

[130] *Id.* Annex III, Instrument 8, at 73, 85 (Ji Pengfei, Chairman of the Drafting Committee for the Basic Law of the Hong Kong Special Administrative Region of the People's Republic of China, "Explanations on 'The Basic Law of the Hong Kong Special Administrative Region of the People's Republic of China (Draft)' and Its Related Documents" (Addressing the Third Session of the Seventh National People's Congress, Mar. 28, 1990)). For additional discussion, see Lo, *supra* note 15, at 585–89.

[131] *See* SWIFT, *RMB Ranks #1 in Asia Pacific for Payments with Greater China* (May 27, 2015). *See also* James Kynge, *Renminbi Outstrips Dollar for Asia Transactions with China*, FIN. TIMES, May 29, 2015, at 18. Global currencies standing ahead of the renminbi include the U.S. dollar (at 45.14 percent), the euro (at 27.36 percent), the British pound (at 7.96 percent), and the Japanese yen (at 2.73 percent). *See* SWIFT, *supra*.

[132] SECURITIES AND FUTURES COMMISSION, *supra* note 109, at 1, 7. *See also* CENTRAL INTELLIGENCE AGENCY, *supra* note 1 (observing that the "government is promoting [Hong Kong] as the site for Chinese renminbi (RMB) internationalization"); FINANCIAL SERVICES AND THE TREASURY BUREAU, *supra* note 40, at 5–12.

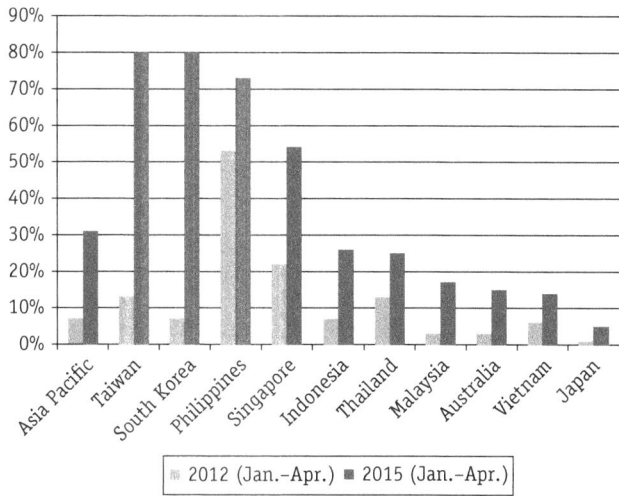

FIGURE 7.2 Renminbi Payments with China and Hong Kong, 2012 v. 2015.*

* *See* SWIFT, *RMB Ranks #1 in Asia Pacific for Payments with Greater China* (May 27, 2015).

Hong Kong does indeed seem to loom larger in China's planning over time in this respect. China's twelfth "Five-Year Plan," adopted in 2011, had "a special significance to Hong Kong," being "the first time that it has incorporated a chapter on Hong Kong." The plan emphasized Hong Kong's role as a financial center and signaled "support for Hong Kong's development into an offshore renminbi ... centre and an international asset management centre," calling for deeper "economic co-operation between the Mainland and Hong Kong."[133] Hong Kong's favorable position "as the choice for holding and using the yuan has eroded overtime," however, falling from approximately 85 percent of offshore holdings in December 2011 to approximately 65 percent in September 2013. Moreover, it has not gone unnoticed that once "China eliminates capital controls, the advantages Hong Kong has will be removed." And of course in the meantime competing jurisdictions continue to target this business as well, notably London[134] and Singapore.

More generally, Hong Kong's degree of exposure to the Mainland's economy presents substantial risks. As Arner et al. observe, Hong Kong's mandate to maintain its financial center is not paired with "a specific financial stability mandate," and financial sector reforms in Hong Kong have lagged those in other financial centers,

---

[133] KPMG, CHINA'S 12TH FIVE-YEAR PLAN: HONG KONG TAX PROPOSALS 1 (May 2011). *See also* Pang, *supra* note 35, at 1.

[134] ARNER ET AL., *supra* note 34, at 89–93. For additional background on China's efforts to internationalize its currency, see Weitseng Chen, *Size Matters? Renminbi Internationalization and the Beijing Consensus*, *in* THE BEIJING CONSENSUS? HOW CHINA HAS CHANGED THE WESTERN IDEAS OF LAW AND ECONOMIC DEVELOPMENT (Weitseng Chen ed., Cambridge University Press, forthcoming 2016);

particularly in the area of systemic risk oversight.[135] Observing that fragility to shock among Hong Kong's banks is greater than typically recognized, Arner et al. explain that the banks have "a far less diversified client base than other jurisdictions such as Singapore."[136] They further argue that "China may at some point . . . experience some form of banking and/or financial crisis" with "significant effects on Hong Kong's securities, real estate and banking sectors," and accordingly that "diversifying the Hong Kong financial sector" would help reduce such risks emanating from "over-reliance on the Mainland."[137] Particularly noteworthy examples of such risks relate to China's apparent real estate bubble and enormous "shadow banking sector."[138] A 2014 IMF research paper voiced a similar perspective, arguing that Singapore's lower reliance on Chinese business offers larger systemic stability benefits insofar as Singapore "could buffer a shock from China that is immediately transmitted to Hong Kong SAR and hence slow the contagion to the rest of Asia."[139]

At the same time, greater exposure to Mainland institutions and governance structures will itself test the viability of the "one country, two systems" principle upon which Hong Kong's prosperity rests. As Carroll has observed, historically "Hong Kong's business knowledge and connections in the capitalist world helped China's economic reforms through investment, finance, and trade."[140] More recently, however, Standard & Poor's has warned that "the increasing economic and administrative integration with the mainland has . . . increased Hong Kong's exposure to changes in administrative policies and weaker civil institutions in China," adding that "Hong Kong cannot be completely insulated from less-developed mainland institutions while economic integration with China continues."[141] In March 2016, then, S&P elaborated that "we do not believe that the credit standing of Hong Kong can be completely disconnected from that of the mainland, given financial and economic linkages, and

---

Weitseng Chen, *China's Long March to Dismantling the Financial Great Wall: RMB Internationalization and Macroprudential Policy, in* SYSTEMIC RISK, INSTITUTIONAL DESIGN AND THE REGULATION OF FINANCIAL MARKETS (Anita Anand ed., Oxford University Press, forthcoming 2016).

[135] *See* ARNER ET AL., *supra* note 34, at 148, 159, 168.

[136] *Id.* at 22–23.

[137] *Id.* at 14. *See also* Financial Services Development Council, *supra* note 6, at 20, 36.

[138] *See* ARNER ET AL., *supra* note 34, at 135, 140. *See also* Securities and Futures Commission, *supra* note 115, at 7–8; Joe Lynam, *Li Ka-shing: The Man Who Wants to Add O2 to Three*, BBC NEWS, Jan. 23, 2015, http://www.bbc.com/news/business-30954764 (reporting that Hong Kong tycoon Li Ka-shing has "been selling off much of his property portfolio in China amid fears of a massive asset bubble there").

[139] Le Leslé et al., *supra* note 92, at 23. *See also* Dezan Shira & Associates, *Hong Kong versus Singapore: A Business Center Loses Its Way,* CFOINNOVATION.COM, May 19, 2015, http://www.cfoinnovation.com/story/9838/hong-kong-versus-singapore-business-center-loses-its-way (observing that Singapore is "less dependent on China," exhibiting greater trade orientation toward ASEAN).

[140] CARROLL, *supra* note 4, at 169–70.

[141] Standard & Poor's Ratings Services, *supra* note 6. *See also* Grant, *supra* note 93; Wang, *supra* note 115, at 223–25 (characterizing integration as "a double-edged sword, making Hong Kong vulnerable to certain economic and political forces originated in China").

the ultimate sovereign authority of China," and revised their outlook on Hong Kong to negative based solely on the fact that they had made the same revision for China.[142] As noted above, the Basic Law trumps in the event of a conflict with local law, and powers of interpretation and amendment remain firmly rooted on the Mainland.[143] Concerns of the sort raised by Standard & Poor's are hardly new—indeed, there is a long history of Mainland-related concerns causing panics in Hong Kong.[144]

China has, by and large, respected Hong Kong's autonomy following the 1997 handover, reflecting long-standing pragmatism regarding Hong Kong's value to China "as a window to the outside world."[145] Nevertheless, potential instabilities loom—most recently stemming from the desire of Hong Kongers for more substantial democratic rule. The Basic Law establishes as an "ultimate aim" the "selection of the Chief Executive by universal suffrage upon nomination by a broadly representative nominating committee in accordance with democratic procedures,"[146] yet the committee process adopted in 2014 imposed "procedural barriers for candidates for the city's leader that would ensure Beijing remained the gatekeeper to that position."[147] Although democracy advocates had pushed for free and direct elections, an August 2014 decision of the National People's Congress Standing Committee rejected that call, concluding that from 2017 Hong Kong's leader would be elected from a slate of candidates endorsed by a Mainland nominating committee.[148] This approach has been said to "reflect a fear among leaders in Beijing that political concessions [in Hong Kong] would ignite demands for liberalization on the mainland, a quarter-century after such hopes were extinguished at Tiananmen Square."[149]

In any event, the "Occupy Central" movement threatened protests "to block the financial district by staging a sit-in . . . just yards from the Asian headquarters of Citi

---

[142] *See* Standard & Poor's Ratings Services, *Hong Kong Outlook Revised to Negative after Same Action on China; "AAA/A-1+" and "cnAAA/cnA-1+" Ratings Affirmed,* Mar. 31, 2016.

[143] *See* Basic Law, *supra* note 23, arts. 11, 158–59.

[144] *See, e.g.,* CARROLL, *supra* note 4, at 178–79, 191–98; SCHENK, *supra* note 13, at 153–54; Meetook, *supra* note 96, at 850–51.

[145] *See* CARROLL, *supra* note 4, at 217–19, 222.

[146] Basic Law, *supra* note 23, art. 45.

[147] Chris Buckley & Michael Forsythe, *China Restricts Voting Reforms for Hong Kong,* N.Y. TIMES, Aug. 31, 2014, http://www.nytimes.com/2014/09/01/world/asia/hong-kong-elections.html?hpw&rref= world&action=click&pgtype=Homepage&version=HpHedThumbWell&module=well-region&region=bottom-well&WT.nav=bottom-well&_r=0.

[148] *See id.*; Chris Dodd, *Beijing Puts Hong Kong Business on Alert,* FINANCEASIA.COM, Aug. 31, 2014, http://www.financeasia.com/News/389846,beijing-puts-hong-kong-business-on-alert.aspx; Laura Hilgers, *Hong Kong's Umbrella Revolution Isn't Over Yet,* N.Y. TIMES, Feb. 18, 2015, http://www.nytimes.com/2015/02/22/magazine/hong-kongs-umbrella-revolution-isnt-over-yet.html?_r=0; Editorial, *Let Wisdom Prevail as Opposing Sides Meet on Hong Kong's Electoral Reform,* S. CHINA MORNING POST, May 27, 2015, http://www.scmp.com/comment/insight-opinion/article/1809980/let-wisdom-prevail-opposing-sides-meet-hong-kongs-electoral.

[149] Buckley & Forsythe, *supra* note 147.

and HSBC," viewed as "a threat to the city's reputation as a stable financial centre." Beijing, for its part, responded in kind, "warn[ing] the city that its status as a premier renminbi trading hub was at risk"[150]—a vulnerability apparent in the October 2014 announcement that "Singapore and China . . . agreed to further strengthen financial cooperation through new path-finding initiatives in the offshore Renminbi . . . market, capital markets and insurance."[151] Ultimately the protests "failed to secure electoral reforms,"[152] but Singapore's attractiveness to multinational companies as a regional headquarters site has meanwhile increased in direct response to lingering tensions between Hong Kong and the Chinese government,[153] and S&P has warned that "we might lower our rating on Hong Kong without a downgrade of China, if Hong Kong's political polarization worsens to a point where it compromises policymaking and the business environment."[154] As of this writing, the emergence of the pro-independence Hong Kong National Party was further stoking tensions. Thought to reflect a marked trend away from self-identification as "Chinese" among Hong Kong's younger population,[155] the establishment of this new party prompted one member of China's Basic Law Committee to state that "large-scale discussion [of independence] in the hope of gathering a large number of like-minded people to act together, this is 'sedition' under the Crimes Ordinance."[156]

---

[150] Dodd, *supra* note 148. *See also* Financial Services Development Council, *supra* note 6, at 19; Mark Hanrahan, *Hong Kong Political Reform: Is "Chinese Democracy" the Best the Region Can Get?*, INT'L BUS. TIMES, Apr. 26, 2015, http://www.ibtimes.com/hong-kong-political-reform-chinese-democracy-best-region-can-get-1897032; Hilgers, *supra* note 148; Twinnie Siu & Christina W.Y. Lo, *Hong Kong's Economy Posts Mild Q1 Growth as Tourism Slowdown Bites*, REUTERS, May 15, 2015, http://in.reuters.com/article/2015/05/15/hongkong-economy-idINL3N0Y54D420150515.

[151] Press Release, Monetary Authority of Singapore, Singapore and China Further Strengthen Financial Cooperation through New Initiatives (Oct. 27, 2014), http://www.mas.gov.sg/News-and-Publications/Media-Releases/2014/Singapore-and-China-further-strengthen-financial-cooperation-through-new-initiatives.aspx. *See also* Jeanne Ong & Yeo Wico, *Singapore, China Launch New Initiatives in Offshore RMB, Capital Markets*, World Sec. L. Rep. (BNA), 2014.

[152] Jessica Macy Yu & Yimou Lee, *Hundreds Gather in Hong Kong to Mark Anniversary of Protests*, REUTERS, Sept. 28, 2015, http://mobile.reuters.com/article/idUSKCN0RS04O20150928.

[153] *See* Cheng, *supra* note 95. *See also* Frank Chen, *Why Shanghai Will Not Gain if Hong Kong Stumbles*, EJINSIGHT, May 4, 2015, http://www.ejinsight.com/20150504-why-shanghai-will-not-gain-if-hong-kong-stumbles/ (arguing that if "Hong Kong falters, the real beneficiary will probably be Singapore, not Shanghai").

[154] Standard & Poor's Ratings Services, *supra* note 142.

[155] Gary Cheung, *Formation of Hong Kong National Party Is the Latest Sign That China Is Losing Hong Kong's Young*, S. CHINA MORNING POST, Apr. 4, 2016, http://www.scmp.com/print/comment/insight-opinion/article/1933451/formation-hong-kong-national-party-latest-sign-china-losing (reporting Hong Kong poll results indicating that "just 13.3 per cent of respondents aged between 18 and 29 identified themselves as 'Chinese' . . . compared with 35.9 per cent among those aged above 30").

[156] Stuart Lau, *Calls for Hong Kong Independence Break the Law, Says Legal Chief of Beijing Liaison Office*, S. CHINA MORNING POST, Apr. 8, 2016, http://www.scmp.com/news/hong-kong/article/1934768/calls-hong-kong-independence-break-law-says-legal-chief-beijing (quoting Wang Zhenmin).

At the same time, Hong Kong faces growing competition from burgeoning financial centers on the Mainland—notably Shanghai (in bond markets), Shenzhen (in IPOs), and Beijing (in banking)[157]—which Mainland authorities might increasingly favor if tensions with Hong Kong were to grow substantially.[158] To date these various centers have functioned in what could fairly be described as a "complementary" manner,[159] and joint endeavors aimed at linking stock markets and facilitating mutual recognition of investment funds[160] may reflect a broader goal of cooperative market integration. Yet certain initiatives pursued by the Chinese government nevertheless tend to signal a desire to diversify China's international financial capacities beyond Hong Kong itself—notably the Shanghai "Free Trade Zone," which aims to introduce on a "pilot" basis a range of economic and financial liberalization policies.[161] Although observers express mixed views regarding the depth and significance of financial liberalization efforts undertaken[162]—and question whether Shanghai could ever surpass Hong Kong without "the rule of law and independent judiciary" so valued by global markets[163]—the initiative's potential impact on Hong Kong has been a live issue since its establishment in 2013,[164] and there is no gainsaying that Shanghai and Shenzhen alike have experienced

---

[157] *See* ARNER ET AL., *supra* note 34, at 69–79.

[158] *Cf.* Chen, *supra* note 153 (reporting that "[m]any mainland Chinese believe that Beijing has spoilt Hong Kong rotten since the 1997 handover").

[159] *See generally* Karen Lai, *Differentiated Markets: Shanghai, Beijing and Hong Kong in China's Financial Centre Network,* 49 URB. STUD. 1275 (2012) (finding "differentiated markets leading to the distinctive development of Shanghai as a commercial centre, Beijing as a political centre and Hong Kong as an offshore financial centre, with all three financial centres performing distinctive and complementary roles within the regional banking strategies of foreign banks").

[160] *See* Neil Gough, *Hong Kong and Mainland China to Partly Open Markets for Investment Funds,* N.Y. TIMES, May 22, 2015, http://www.nytimes.com/2015/05/23/business/dealbook/hong-kong-and-china-to-connect-investment-fund-markets.html?_r=0; Samuel Shen & Pete Sweeney, *Hong Kong, China Stocks Welcome New Cross-Border Investment Scheme,* REUTERS, May 26, 2015, http://www.reuters.com/article/2015/05/26/markets-hongkong-china-stocks-midday-idUSL3N0YH1TW20150526.

[161] *See generally* China (Shanghai) Pilot Free Trade Zone, *Introduction,* http://en.china-shftz.gov.cn/About-FTZ/Introduction/ (last visited Apr. 2016); China (Shanghai) Pilot Free Trade Zone, *Location,* http://en.china-shftz.gov.cn/About-FTZ/Location/ (last visited Apr. 2016); China (Shanghai) Pilot Free Trade Zone, *Regional Advantage,* http://en.china-shftz.gov.cn/About-FTZ/Advantages/ (last visited Apr. 2016).

[162] *See, e.g.,* Shannon Tiezzi, *Can China Save the Shanghai Free Trade Zone?,* DIPLOMAT, Sept. 20, 2014, http://thediplomat.com/2014/09/can-china-save-the-shanghai-free-trade-zone/. *See also* Saikat Chatterjee & James Pomfret, *Shanghai Free Trade Zone No Game-Changer for Hong Kong, For Now,* REUTERS, Sept. 30, 2013, http://www.reuters.com/article/2013/09/30/us-hongkong-shanghai-idUSBRE98T03U20130930; *Shanghai Free Trade Zone: The Next Shenzhen?,* ECONOMIST, Oct. 3, 2013, http://www.economist.com/news/china/21587237-new-enterprise-zone-could-spark-wider-market-reformsbut-only-if-bureaucrats-ease-their-grip; Mandy Zuo, *Shanghai out of Fresh Ideas for Free-Trade Zone,* S. CHINA MORNING POST, Jan. 26, 2015, http://www.scmp.com/news/china/article/1691793/shanghai-out-fresh-ideas-free-trade-zone.

[163] *See* Wang, *supra* note 115, at 255–56.

[164] *See* Chatterjee & Pomfret, *supra* note 162.

substantial economic growth relative to Hong Kong.[165] Meanwhile, the Chinese government has pursued a new legal framework for foreign investment that "aligns with common international practice"[166]—a move that, if successful, could tend to erode Hong Kong's unique advantages as a preferred site for the legal structuring of investments into China. As of 2016 Hong Kong remained on the Global Financial Centres Index listing of financial centers thought likely to grow in significance, but these three Mainland centers appeared alongside Hong Kong—and Shanghai in fact came in ahead of Hong Kong (appearing second, narrowly edged out by Singapore).[167]

Some have even expressed concerns that the falling level of English language proficiency among Hong Kong's adults (partially attributed by experts to "the switch from teaching mainly in English to mainly in Chinese since the handover") could diminish Hong Kong's advantages, including relative to the Mainland, where "English skills have been improving."[168] Similarly, although English remains an official language in Hong Kong, observers have documented diminishing use of English in official and nonofficial government communications alike—a trend prompting speculation that "the government is trying to shut down the use of English in order to emphasise the fact that Hong Kong is a mainland city," and correlative expressions of concern regarding the inconsistency of this trend with maintenance of Hong Kong's status "as an international and financial city."[169]

In these respects, it would appear that the very proximity that has proven so profitable for Hong Kong and the Mainland alike simultaneously threatens potential instabilities that could compromise Hong Kong's status as a premier global financial center moving forward.

---

[165] See Chen, *supra* note 153 (reporting that "Shanghai has raced past Hong Kong on a few key parameters, including annual economic output"); Tim Culpan & Xin Zhou, *Shenzhen Set to Surpass Hong Kong*, AUSTRALIAN FIN. REV., May 12, 2015, http://www.afr.com/news/world/shenzhen-set-to-surpass-hong-kong-20150512-ggzkqz ("The switch to innovation and finance helped almost double the size of the city's economy to 1.6 trillion yuan in the five years to 2014. At that rate it would this year eclipse Hong Kong, whose economy is growing more slowly.").

[166] See Xu Ping et al., *China Breaking Down the Walls—Revolution in Foreign Investment Planned*, Jan. 23, 2015, http://www.kwm.com/en/knowledge/insights/a-new-era-for-the-prc-foreign-investment-regime-20150101.

[167] See Z/Yen Group Limited, *supra* note 2. Overall, the index ranked Shanghai sixteenth, Shenzhen nineteenth, and Beijing twenty-third. *See id.*

[168] See Shirley Zhao, *Hong Kong's English Language Skills Branded "Pathetic" as Chinese Has "Negative Influence,"* S. CHINA MORNING POST, Nov. 5, 2013, http://www.scmp.com/news/hong-kong/article/1348626/hong-kongs-english-language-skills-branded-pathetic-chinese-has?page=all.

[169] See Cannix Yau, *Official Use of English Being "Neglected" by Hong Kong Government*, S. CHINA MORNING POST, June 8, 2015, http://www.scmp.com/news/hong-kong/article/1818260/official-use-english-being-neglected-hong-kong-government (quoting "Civic Party lawmaker Claudia Mo Man-ching," and "[f]ormer civil service chief Joseph Wong Wing-ping," respectively).

# 8 Switzerland

UNLIKE BERMUDA, A U.K. Overseas Territory; Dubai, a UAE emirate; Hong Kong, a Chinese Special Administrative Region; Delaware, a U.S. state (discussed below); and Singapore, which gained independence only in the 1960s, Switzerland is a long-time sovereign. Formed in 1291 "as a defensive alliance," the Swiss Confederation broke away from the Holy Roman Empire in 1499. Switzerland persisted as a confederation until 1848, when its "centralized federal government" was established.[1]

As a landlocked jurisdiction in the heart of Europe, Switzerland would appear to occupy a very different position from the foregoing jurisdictions. Analysis through the MDSJ lens reveals, however, that Switzerland's global predominance in cross-border banking reflects a very similar set of characteristics and competitive strengths.

## A. At the Heart of Europe

Though occupying a very different geography, Switzerland nevertheless exhibits the core features of an MDSJ just as Bermuda, Dubai, Singapore, and Hong Kong do.

---

[1] *See* CENTRAL INTELLIGENCE AGENCY, THE WORLD FACTBOOK: SWITZERLAND, https://www.cia.gov/library/publications/the-world-factbook/geos/sz.html (last updated Apr. 26, 2016).

Although larger than the others, relative to the major economic powers Switzerland is nevertheless comparatively small, with just 41,277 square kilometers in total area (roughly double the size of New Jersey) and a population of approximately 8.1 million people.[2] Likewise, although landlocked, Switzerland resembles the others in its lack of natural resources, similarly prompting heavy reliance on cross-border services as a development strategy. As an investor handbook observes, Switzerland is "strongly committed to foreign countries thanks to its location, lack of resources and limited domestic market."[3] Given "its central location, [Switzerland] has been a major crossroads for various trade routes since the early days of international trade."[4] The fact that the country "has no significant natural resources" meant that "the service sector had an early, continuing importance"—particularly in banking, insurance, and tourism[5]—and that openness and economic integration have long been favored.[6] Today, in addition to a substantial manufacturing industry tied closely to the E.U. market,[7] "Switzerland's economy benefits from a highly developed service sector, led by financial services," and has consistently enjoyed "a per capita GDP among the highest in the world"[8]—a position reinforced through a high degree of government collaboration with the private sector, including in banking.[9] As of 2015, Switzerland's wealth per adult stood at $567,122, "putting Switzerland at the top of the global rankings."[10]

---

[2]  *Id.* According to the CIA's *World Factbook*, Switzerland ranks 97th in population and 136th in area, falling above the median with respect to the former and below the median with respect to the latter (approximately 5.4 million people and approximately 57,000 square kilometers, respectively). *See* CENTRAL INTELLIGENCE AGENCY, THE WORLD FACTBOOK: POPULATION, https://www.cia.gov/library/publications/the-world-factbook/rankorder/2119rank.html (last visited Apr. 2016); CENTRAL INTELLIGENCE AGENCY, THE WORLD FACTBOOK: AREA, https://www.cia.gov/library/publications/the-world-factbook/rankorder/2147rank.html (last visited Apr. 2016).

[3]  SWITZERLAND TRADE & INVESTMENT PROMOTION, HANDBOOK FOR INVESTORS: BUSINESS LOCATION IN SWITZERLAND 19–20, 113 (Apr. 2012 ed.).

[4]  *Id.* at 24, 36.

[5]  Margrit Zinggeler, *Business Languages in Multi-Lingual Switzerland* 2, 8 (Perdue CIBER Working Paper No. 28, 2004), http://docs.lib.purdue.edu/ciberwp/28.

[6]  *See* Thomas J. Jordan, Chairman of the Governing Board, Swiss National Bank, Switzerland at the Heart of Europe: Between Independence and Interdependence, Address at the Université libre de Bruxelles 5 (Feb. 17, 2015).

[7]  *See id.* at 5–6.

[8]  CENTRAL INTELLIGENCE AGENCY, *supra* note 1. *See also* SWITZERLAND TRADE & INVESTMENT PROMOTION, *supra* note 3, at 17, 82. Services account for about 73 percent of Swiss GDP and 73 percent of the workforce, whereas industry accounts for about 27 percent of GDP and 23 percent of the workforce. *See* CENTRAL INTELLIGENCE AGENCY, *supra* note 1. *See also* CALLY JORDAN, INTERNATIONAL CAPITAL MARKETS: LAW AND INSTITUTIONS 208 (2014) (observing Switzerland's "balanced economy").

[9]  *See, e.g.,* Swiss Bankers Association, *Our Association,* http://www.swissbanking.org/en/home/aboutus-link/portrait.htm (last visited Apr. 2016); *infra* Chapter 8.B.

[10]  ANTHONY SHORROCKS, JIM DAVIES & RODRIGO LLUBERASIS, CREDIT SUISSE GLOBAL WEALTH REPORT 2015, at 52 (2015).

As a sovereign, legislative autonomy follows straightforwardly[11]—though Switzerland's confederation of 26 cantons resembles a federal republic in its legislative structure, giving the cantons "a high degree of control."[12] As Thomas Jordan, Chairman of the Governing Board of the Swiss National Bank describes it, "federalism, direct democracy and citizen involvement are seen by the Swiss population as crucial elements of their identity," and "fiscal decentralisation is pervasive: the cantons ... are like sovereigns on a smaller scale, and have extensive taxation and spending powers."[13] It must also be recognized that, given its civil law legal system,[14] Switzerland only awkwardly accommodates certain common-law legal devices highly valued by the cross-border financial marketplace—notably trusts.[15] Nevertheless, "Switzerland excels at comparative law, putting legal concepts from multiple sources to work."[16]

Clearly Switzerland is not literally located "offshore" as Bermuda, Hong Kong, and Singapore are, yet nevertheless occupies a very similar geographic position vis-à-vis major market economies. Notably, Switzerland similarly performs a spatial and cultural bridging function among various regions of Europe. Switzerland is aptly described as occupying "the heart of Europe"[17] and laying at the "crossroads of northern and southern Europe,"[18] and the Swiss fairly boast that "[n]o other country offers such great variety in so small an area."[19] Although the majority of the population speaks German, Switzerland is a highly multicultural and multilingual country, with three other official languages—French, Italian, and Romansch.[20] At the same time there is a very high level of English-language proficiency, reflecting the growing importance of English as a language of international business.[21] Switzerland borders "[t]hree of the four largest European markets and economies," and provides a

---

[11] *See supra* Chapter 3.A.

[12] SWITZERLAND TRADE & INVESTMENT PROMOTION, *supra* note 3, at 10.

[13] Jordan, *supra* note 6, at 4, 7.

[14] *See* CENTRAL INTELLIGENCE AGENCY, *supra* note 1.

[15] *See generally* Kinga M. Weiss, *Switzerland: Treatment of Trusts in Switzerland,* MONDAQ.COM, Oct. 23, 2012, http://www.mondaq.com/x/202962/Trusts/Treatment+of+Trusts+in+Switzerland. *See also* RICHARD HAY ET AL., TOWARDS A LEVEL PLAYING FIELD: REGULATING CORPORATE VEHICLES IN CROSS-BORDER TRANSACTIONS 29, 37–38 (2002) (review commissioned by the International Trade and Investment Organisation and the Society of Trust and Estate Practitioners, and conducted by Stikeman Elliott); SWITZERLAND TRADE & INVESTMENT PROMOTION, *supra* note 3, at 40, 44.

[16] JORDAN, *supra* note 8, at 203.

[17] Jordan, *supra* note 6, at 1.

[18] CENTRAL INTELLIGENCE AGENCY, *supra* note 1.

[19] SWITZERLAND TRADE & INVESTMENT PROMOTION, *supra* note 3, at 9, 36.

[20] *See* CENTRAL INTELLIGENCE AGENCY, *supra* note 1; SWITZERLAND TRADE & INVESTMENT PROMOTION, *supra* note 3, at 10. *See also* Zinggeler, *supra* note 5, at 2–4.

[21] *See* SWITZERLAND TRADE & INVESTMENT PROMOTION, *supra* note 3, at 7, 13, 115; Zinggeler, *supra* note 5, at 15–16. *See also* JORDAN, *supra* note 8, at 202.

critical "[c]ommunications and transportation center between northern and southern Europe," with a highly educated, multilingual and cosmopolitan workforce.[22] Switzerland's status as a meeting point for major powers is reinforced by its strict, long-standing neutrality policy, itself a reflection of Swiss heterogeneity,[23] which has made Switzerland a natural base for a host of international organizations—a unique status that has "strengthened Switzerland's ties with its neighbors."[24] Switzerland joined the United Nations only in 2002, and remains outside the European Union and the eurozone, although "the EU is by far Switzerland's most important trading partner."[25]

On the whole, and notwithstanding clear differences from other jurisdictions studied here, Switzerland's competitive strengths closely adhere to the MDSJ type. The aforementioned investor handbook touts their "[e]fficient official procedures and favorable regulatory environment"; geographic, cultural, and linguistic centrality within Europe; a well-established financial center; diplomatic neutrality; economic and political stability; competitive tax rates; and high-quality infrastructure.[26] Switzerland enjoys a AAA credit rating from Standard & Poor's with a stable outlook,[27] and according to the World Bank exhibits a very high degree of political stability,[28] rendering the Swiss franc an attractive "safe haven."[29] The country's banking center remains "an international leader" with a 27 percent market share in

---

[22] SWITZERLAND TRADE & INVESTMENT PROMOTION, *supra* note 3, at 7. *See also* Peter Egger & Andrew Lassman, *The Causal Impact of Common Native Language on International Trade: Evidence from a Spatial Regression Discontinuity Design* (Ctr. for Econ. Policy Research, Discussion Paper No. 9441, 2013) (examining the impact of common language on trade between Swiss regions and neighboring countries); Alfred Lameli et al., *Same Same but Different: Dialects and Trade* (Ctr. for Econ. Studies & Ifo Inst. Working Paper No. 4245, 2013) (examining the impact of dialect on trade ties within Germany).

[23] TAX JUSTICE NETWORK, NARRATIVE REPORT ON SWITZERLAND 2 (2015) (observing that due to marked geographic and linguistic divisions, "[a]ny taking of sides in a European war would have risked civil war in Switzerland"). *See also* Jordan, *supra* note 6, at 4.

[24] *See* CENTRAL INTELLIGENCE AGENCY, *supra* note 1; JORDAN, *supra* note 8, at 208–09; SWITZERLAND TRADE & INVESTMENT PROMOTION, *supra* note 3, at 7, 13–15; Jordan, *supra* note 6, at 4; Zinggeler, *supra* note 5, at 8.

[25] SWITZERLAND TRADE & INVESTMENT PROMOTION, *supra* note 3, at 13, 36. *See also* Jordan, *supra* note 6, at 2.

[26] *See* SWITZERLAND TRADE & INVESTMENT PROMOTION, *supra* note 3, at 7, 82–83, 89–90, 94, 104. *See also* CENTRAL INTELLIGENCE AGENCY, *supra* note 1; SWISS BANKERS ASSOCIATION & BOSTON CONSULTING GROUP, SUMMARY: BANKING IN TRANSITION—FUTURE PROSPECTS FOR BANKING IN SWITZERLAND 1 (Sept. 2011).

[27] Standard & Poor's Ratings Services, *Swiss Confederation*, http://www.standardandpoors.com/en_US/web/guest/ratings/entity/-/org-details/sectorCode/SOV/entityId/107141 (last visited Apr. 2016).

[28] *See* World Bank, *Worldwide Governance Indicators*, http://info.worldbank.org/governance/wgi/index.aspx (last visited Apr. 2016) (assigning Switzerland a "Political Stability and Absence of Violence/Terrorism" percentile rank of 93.7 out of 100 in 2014).

[29] *See* Jordan, *supra* note 6, at 3.

cross-border private banking as of 2011[30]—a position the Swiss desperately hope to defend against new competitors and challenges.

## B. Cross-Border Banking

The banking sector as a whole clearly remains central to Switzerland's economy in multiple respects. As the Swiss Bankers Association (SBA) emphasizes, financial services are quite significant to Switzerland in terms of economic productivity, employment, and taxes.[31] Indeed, the financial center "accounts [for] more than 14 percent of all taxes paid in Switzerland, [and] over 10 percent is from the banking sector."[32] As the Tax Justice Network has observed, with "total banking assets . . . estimated in 2012 at 460 percent of Swiss GDP," among the world's highest, "it is hardly surprising to find a strong 'financial consensus' that curbs domestic criticism of the financial centre."[33]

Although Switzerland subscribes to "the model of universal banking," meaning that "all banks can provide all banking services," there are several categories of Swiss banks distinguished by the forms of services upon which they focus.[34] The category of "big banks," which "offer essentially every type of transaction," consists of just two banks—Credit Suisse and UBS, which together "account for over 50 percent of the balance sheet total of all banks in Switzerland." The category most strongly associated with Swiss banking, however, is the so-called "private bank." According to the SBA, the "private bankers are among the oldest banks in Switzerland and consist of individual enterprises, collective and limited partnerships," their defining characteristics being the bankers' unlimited personal liability and their focus on "asset management, primarily for private customers."[35] As noted above, Swiss banks had a 27 percent market share in cross-border private banking as of 2011.[36]

---

[30] Swiss Bankers Association & Boston Consulting Group, *supra* note 26, at 1.

[31] Swiss Bankers Association, *The Economic Importance of the Swiss Financial Centre,* http://www.swissbanking.org/en/home/finanzplatz-link/facts_figures.htm (last visited Apr. 2016).

[32] *See id.*

[33] Tax Justice Network, *supra* note 23, at 1.

[34] *See* Swiss Bankers Association, *Banking Groups*, http://www.swissbanking.org/en/home/finanzplatz-link/bankengruppen.htm (last visited Apr. 2016). For a discussion of various public and private "players" in the Swiss financial center (including the Swiss Bankers Association), see Swiss Bankers Association, *Swiss Financial Center—Players*, http://www.swissbanking.org/en/home/finanzplatz-link/akteure.htm (last visited Apr. 2016).

[35] Swiss Bankers Association, *Banking Groups, supra* note 34. *See also* Swiss Private Bankers Association, *Private Bankers, A Breed Apart*, http://www.swissprivatebankers.ch/en/ (last visited Apr. 2016). On the emergence of big banks in Switzerland since the 1980s, see Mitchell J. Larson et al., *Strategic Responses to Global Challenges: The Case of European Banking, 1973–2000*, 53 Bus. Hist. 40, 43–47 (2011).

[36] *See supra* note 30 and accompanying text.

Some confusion persists regarding what "private banking" involves, as the term is often conflated with "wealth management." The two are closely related, with asset management representing the core activity in each setting, but in general parlance private banking involves a narrower set of activities, with greater emphasis placed upon personal service. Traditionally private banking has included "banking services (deposit taking and payments), discretionary asset management, brokerage, limited tax advisory services and some basic concierge-type services, offered by a single designated relationship manager."[37] To be sure, Switzerland's "big banks" do loom large in the provision of such services; according to the Tax Justice Network, as of 2012 UBS and Credit Suisse were the world's top two "private banks" measured by "offshore client assets."[38] (See Figure 8.1 below for these rankings.) The Swiss Private Bankers Association (SPBA) emphasizes, however, that the term "private banker" has legal significance in Switzerland distinct from colloquial usage, applying to those who "invest their own capital in their business and are personally liable for its obligations."[39] This remains critical to the Swiss private banker's identity, the term being (as the SPBA puts it) "synonymous with unbounded responsibility."[40]

In contrast with this noble identity statement stands the image of Swiss banking often invoked abroad—the instrumental use of opaque, numbered accounts to hide foreigners' assets, facilitating evasion of taxes in other countries. As Palan, Murphy, and Chavagneux observe, Switzerland has been considered by many "the archetypal tax haven,"[41] a perception resulting principally from the feature of their banking

---

[37] *Difference between Private Banking and Wealth Management*, AAFM India (Jan. 31, 2012), http://aafmindia.wordpress.com/2012/01/31/difference-between-private-banking-and-wealth-management/. *See also* Jonathan V. Beaverstock et al., *Overseeing the Fortunes of the Global Super-Rich: The Nature of Private Wealth Management in London's Financial District, in* Geographies of the Super-Rich 43, 44 (Iain Hay ed., 2013); Swiss Private Bankers Association, *supra* note 35.

[38] *See* James S. Henry, The Price of Offshore Revisited: New Estimates for "Missing" Global Private Wealth, Income, Inequality, and Lost Taxes 32–33 (July 2012) (report for the Tax Justice Network); James S. Henry, *Revised Estimates of Private Banking Assets under Management and Total Client Assets—Top 50 Global Private Banks, 2005–2010* (July 21, 2012), http://www.taxjustice.net/cms/upload/pdf/Private%20Banking%202012.pdf (update to James S. Henry, The Price of Offshore Revisited: New Estimates for "Missing" Global Private Wealth, Income, Inequality, and Lost Taxes (July 2012)).

[39] Swiss Private Bankers Association, *supra* note 35. *See also* Swiss Private Bankers Association, *Association*, http://www.swissprivatebankers.ch/en/the-association (last visited Apr. 2016) (observing that the SPBA "was founded in 1934, following the enactment of the Federal Act on Banks and Savings Banks, which recognised the special position and status of private bankers").

[40] Swiss Private Bankers Association, *The Values*, http://www.swissprivatebankers.ch/en/the-values (last visited Apr. 2016).

[41] Ronen Palan, Richard Murphy & Christian Chavagneux, Tax Havens: How Globalization Really Works 124 (2010). *See also* Scott A. Schumacher, *Magnifying Deterrence by Prosecuting Professionals* 9 (Univ. of Wash. Sch. of Law Legal Studies Research Paper No. 2013-17, 2013), http://ssrn.com/abstract=2243093.

| Bank | Headquarters Jurisdiction | Rank | International Client Assets (US$ billions) |
|---|---|---|---|
| UBS | Switzerland | 1 | $955.6 |
| Credit Suisse | Switzerland | 2 | $940.1 |
| HSBC | United Kingdom | 3 | $663.0 |
| Deutsche Bank | Germany | 4 | $624.7 |
| BNP Paribas | France | 5 | $574.6 |
| JPMorgan Chase | USA | 6 | $569.0 |
| Morgan Stanley/SSB | USA | 7 | $525.1 |
| Wells Fargo | USA | 8 | $510.0 |
| Goldman Sachs | USA | 9 | $499.8 |
| Pictet | Switzerland | 10 | $459.0 |
| Bank Leumi | Israel | 11 | $426.7 |
| Barclays | United Kingdom | 12 | $405.1 |
| ABN Amro | Netherlands | 13 | $371.2 |
| TD Canada | Canada | 14 | $311.1 |
| Banque Julius Baer | Switzerland | 15 | $307.7 |

FIGURE 8.1 Global Private Banks: International Client Assets, 2010 Rankings.*

*For rankings and international client assets, see James S. Henry, *Revised Estimates of Private Banking Assets under Management and Total Client Assets—Top 50 Global Private Banks, 2005–2010* (July 21, 2012), http://www.taxjustice.net/cms/upload/pdf/Private%20Banking%202012.pdf (defining "international client assets" to include international assets under management, client deposits, client custody, and brokerage assets).

laws for which the Swiss are best known—strict bank secrecy. Article 13 of the Swiss Constitution states that "[e]very person has the right to privacy in their private and family life," as well as "the right to be protected against the misuse of their personal data."[42] Article 47 of the Federal Act on Banks and Savings Banks, then, makes it a crime to disclose "confidential information entrusted to them in their capacity as a member of an executive or supervisory body, employee, representative or liquidator of a bank." Those who violate this provision negligently "shall be penalized with a fine of up to CHF 250,000," and those who do so "intentionally" may be imprisoned for "up to three years."[43]

[42] Federal Constitution of the Swiss Confederation, Apr. 18, 1999, SR 101, art. 13 (Switz.) (unofficial translation as of June 14, 2015), https://www.admin.ch/opc/en/classified-compilation/19995395/201506140000/101.pdf.

[43] Federal Act on Banks and Savings Banks, Nov. 8, 1934, SR 952.0, art. 47 (Switz.) (KPMG unofficial translation as of Jan. 1, 2016), https://assets.kpmg.com/content/dam/kpmg/pdf/2016/02/ch-banking-act-sr952.0-en.pdf; Loi fédérale du 8 novembre 1934 sur les banques et les caisses d'épargne (Loi sur les banques, LB): Modifications (Switz.), http://www.admin.ch/opc/fr/classified-compilation/19340083/changes.html (last visited Apr. 2016). *See also* Sébastien Guex, *The Origins of the Swiss Banking Secrecy Law and Its Repercussions for Swiss Federal Policy,* 74 BUS. HIST. REV. 237, 244 (2000); Schumacher, *supra* note 41, at 9–10; Swiss Bankers Association, *Protection of Privacy,* http://www.swissbanking.org/en/home/dossiers-link/dossiers/bankkundengeheimnis.htm (last visited Apr. 2016).

Although first enshrined in federal banking law in 1934, Swiss bank secrecy in fact emerged considerably earlier.[44] Sébastien Guex has suggested that by the late nineteenth century bank secrecy represented "an instrument with primarily internal functions . . . designed to protect [Swiss businesses] from the domestic tax authorities"[45]—a dynamic illustrating bank secrecy's broad consistency with the long-standing conservatism of Swiss politics.[46] Increased taxes across Europe in the latter decades of the nineteenth century, however, "triggered the first wave of capital flight to neighboring Geneva, Basel, and Zurich,"[47] a development suggesting that bank secrecy could serve as "an instrument with external functions" as well—"a lynchpin in the strategy of attracting foreign capital to Switzerland and hence a major asset in international competition."[48] By 1912 bank secrecy is thought to have been established as "the norm in Switzerland,"[49] and both internal tax competition among Swiss cantons and more concerted cross-border tax competition are thought to have been well underway by the 1920s.[50] Following World War I and a subsequent wave of tax increases across Europe, "foreign capital—especially French, German, Italian, and Austrian—poured into Swiss banks on a scale hitherto unknown." Guex attributes this development to "the solidity of the Swiss franc," "the political stability of the country," "its neutrality," "the mildness of its taxation laws," "the obliging nature of its fiscal authorities, and, last but not least, . . . the existence of banking secrecy."[51]

A prominent "legend" has it that bank secrecy was enshrined in Swiss federal banking law in 1934 to help protect Jewish assets from the Nazis, but the evidence does not bear this out.[52] Aside from the fact that bank secrecy in fact arose much

---

[44] *See* Rolf H. Weber, *Swiss Banking Secrecy in Evolution,* 18 BANKING & FIN. L. REV. 317, 317–18, 322 (2003) (observing that bank secrecy "has its basis in private law, in particular the law of contracts and agency"); TAX JUSTICE NETWORK, *supra* note 23, at 2 (dating bank secrecy in Switzerland to 1713, when "the Great Council of Geneva adopted regulations prohibiting bankers . . . from revealing details about their clients").

[45] Guex, *supra* note 43, at 241.

[46] *Cf.* TAX JUSTICE NETWORK, *supra* note 23, at 2 (arguing that Swiss banking secrecy is in part rooted in Switzerland's "tradition of neutrality and its powerful system of direct democracy").

[47] *See* PALAN ET AL., *supra* note 41, at 115–16.

[48] Guex, *supra* note 43, at 241.

[49] PALAN ET AL., *supra* note 41, at 115. Note that this predates "the 1924 English Court of Appeal decision in *Tournier v. National Provincial and Union Bank of England,*" the basis for "[f]inancial privacy in the common law world." Richard Gordon & Andrew P. Morriss, *Moving Money: International Financial Flows, Taxes, and Money Laundering,* 37 HASTINGS INT'L & COMP. L. REV. 1, 28 (2014).

[50] *See* PALAN ET AL., *supra* note 41, at 111–12, 118. *See also* Jordan, *supra* note 6, at 7.

[51] Guex, *supra* note 43, at 241–42. *See also* Jean-Rodolphe W. Fiechter, *Exchange of Tax Information: The End of Banking Secrecy in Switzerland and Singapore?,* INT'L TAX J., Nov.–Dec. 2010, at 55–56; GABRIEL ZUCMAN, THE HIDDEN WEALTH OF NATIONS: THE SCOURGE OF TAX HAVENS 14–16 (Teresa Lavender Fagan trans., 2015).

[52] *See* Guex, *supra* note 43, at 239–40; R. Vogler, *The Genesis of Swiss Bank Secrecy: Political and Economic Environment,* 8 FIN. HIST. REV. 73, 73–74 (2001). *See also* Weber, *supra* note 44, at 320–21.

earlier, federalizing and criminalizing breaches of bank secrecy appear to have represented a political quid pro quo in exchange for greater regulatory oversight of banks following the crisis that emerged in 1931, and an effort to reinforce confidence following the damaging revelation of the names of a large number of affluent, tax-evading clients that resulted from the French government's 1932 search of the Paris offices of a prominent Swiss bank.[53] As Palan, Murphy, and Chavagneux observe, "Article 47 proved a great success. Foreign deposits in Swiss banks increased by 28 percent during the three years that followed."[54] They continued to grow during the three decades following World War II, a period in which the Swiss faced little cross-border wealth management competition.[55]

In light of the foregoing history—and bearing in mind Switzerland's location and dependence upon commercial relations with the European Union[56]—it is perhaps unsurprising that Switzerland would face greater diplomatic pressure than the other jurisdictions studied here to relax bank secrecy laws and facilitate exchange of tax-relevant information. As Josephine Moulds observes, "Switzerland has long been at the heart of the private banking industry, with its tradition of secrecy," but "since the global economic meltdown, cash-strapped governments are scrambling around for revenue, and Switzerland has been one of the first places they have looked."[57] European Union officials have made no secret of pursuing "the death of bank secrecy,"[58] and at the same time the Swiss find themselves facing greater competition from aspiring financial centers less dependent upon European and North American business,[59] prompting fears of capital flight.[60] Like others, Switzerland has sought

---

[53] *See* Guex, *supra* note 43, at 245–52. *See also* PALAN ET AL., *supra* note 41, at 121–22.

[54] PALAN ET AL., *supra* note 41, at 122.

[55] ZUCMAN, *supra* note 51, at 20–23.

[56] *See, e.g.*, SWITZERLAND TRADE & INVESTMENT PROMOTION, *supra* note 3, at 36–39.

[57] Josephine Moulds, *Private Banking's Cosy World under Seige*, GUARDIAN OBSERVER, July 21, 2012, http://www.theguardian.com/business/2012/jul/22/private-banks-swiss-accounts-coutts-tax. *See also* Raphael Minder, *Pressure Mounts on Vaunted Secrecy of Switzerland's Banks*, N.Y. TIMES, May 23, 2013, http://www.nytimes.com/2013/05/24/business/global/swiss-banking-secrecy-under-pressure-from-europe.html?pagewanted=all.

[58] Andrew Higgins, *Europe Pushes to Shed Stigma of a Tax Haven*, N.Y. TIMES, May 22, 2013, http://www.nytimes.com/2013/05/23/world/europe/europe-pushes-to-shed-stigma-of-tax-haven-with-end-to-bank-secrecy.html?pagewanted=all&_r=0 (quoting Algirdas Semeta, "the European Union's senior official responsible for tax issues").

[59] *See* SWISS BANKERS ASSOCIATION & BOSTON CONSULTING GROUP, *supra* note 26, at 1–2; ZUCMAN, *supra* note 51, at 61; Gabriel Zucman, *Taxing across Borders: Tracking Personal Wealth and Corporate Profits*, 28 J. ECON. PERSP. 121, 143 (2014).

[60] *See The Rise of the Midshores: The Offshore Industry's Centre of Gravity Is Shifting Eastwards*, ECONOMIST, Feb. 14, 2013, http://www.economist.com/news/special-report/21571555-offshore-industrys-centre-gravity-shifting-eastwards-rise-midshores; Minder, *supra* note 57; TAX JUSTICE NETWORK, NARRATIVE REPORT ON HONG KONG 6 (2015).

to assuage the OECD by entering into a sufficient number of tax information exchange agreements and by accepting a withholding tax on Swiss interest income of those subject to E.U. tax,[61] while resisting further incursions.[62]

High-profile scandals, however, have prompted damaging enforcement actions in the United States.[63] In 2009 "UBS, Switzerland's largest bank, agreed to hand over the names of 4,450 of its clients to American judicial authorities, as well as pay a fine of $780 million for facilitating their tax evasion"—a move "seen by many in the Swiss financial sector as a stunning breach of client confidentiality."[64] Perhaps more shocking to the Swiss was the January 2013 announcement that Wegelin, "Switzerland's oldest bank," would close "after pleading guilty to helping American clients evade tax payments on at least $1.2 billion of assets."[65] In May 2014 Credit Suisse pled guilty to a U.S. criminal charge of aiding tax evasion, agreeing to pay $2.6 billion and to provide "information that Deputy Attorney General James Cole said would lead to specific account holders."[66]

In the wake of such events, a cloud of uncertainty has descended upon the Swiss financial center as their bankers face the twin threat of U.S. enforcement proceedings and Swiss prosecution (should they violate bank secrecy laws).[67] One consequence has been the exertion of "pressure from Swiss banks" upon U.S. account-holders to enter "the IRS's limited-amnesty program for undeclared offshore accounts" before the banks themselves are forced to disclose their names and associated account information (which would preclude later entry into the amnesty program).[68] As of

---

[61] See Beckett G. Cantley, *Steering Into the Storm: Amplification of Captive Insurance Company Compliance Issues in the Offshore Tax Crackdown*, 12 HOUS. BUS. & TAX L.J. 224, 254–55 (2012); Fiechter, *supra* note 51, at 60–61.

[62] See, e.g., SWITZERLAND TRADE & INVESTMENT PROMOTION, *supra* note 3, at 39, 84; *Automatic Response: The Way to Make Exchange of Tax Information Work*, ECONOMIST, Feb. 14, 2013, http://www.economist.com/news/special-report/21571561-way-make-exchange-tax-information-work-automatic-response.

[63] See TAX JUSTICE NETWORK, *supra* note 23, at 5.

[64] Minder, *supra* note 57. See also Cantley, *supra* note 61, at 256–59; Schumacher, *supra* note 41, at 18–22.

[65] Minder, *supra* note 57.

[66] See Andrew Grossman et al., *Credit Suisse Pleads Guilty in Criminal Tax Case*, WALL ST. J., May 19, 2014, http://www.wsj.com/articles/SB10001424052702304422704579571732769356894. For additional background on the fallout of these actions, see Tracy A. Kaye, *Innovations in the War on Tax Evasion*, 2014 BYU L. REV. 363, 394–98 (2014).

[67] See John Letzing & John Revill, *Swiss Government Sets Parameters to Settle US Tax Dispute*, DOW JONES, July 3, 2013, http://www.4-traders.com/UBS-AG-9365071/news/UBS-AG-Swiss-Government-Sets-Parameters-to-Settle-US-Tax-Dispute-17067385/; *Swiss Fund Managers, Advisers, Lawyers Decry Proposed Bank Settlement Framework with U.S.*, World Sec. L. Rep. (BNA), 2013; *Swiss Government Proposal Would Facilitate Individual Bank Settlements with U.S. Government*, World Sec. L. Rep. (BNA), 2013. See also Grossman et al., *supra* note 66.

[68] Laura Saunders, *More U.S. Taxpayers Admit to Secret Swiss Accounts: Swiss Bank Clients are Being Pressured to Declare Their Offshore Accounts*, WALL ST. J., Nov. 1, 2013, http://online.wsj.com/news/articles/SB10001424052702303843104579168150805769812. See also Grossman et al., *supra* note 66 (reporting that over

May 2014, approximately "a dozen Swiss banks [were] still subjects of criminal investigations by U.S. authorities,"[69] and a growing number of Swiss private banks had "opted for limited liability, ending the owners' total responsibility for the core bank—mainly because of the risk these days of picking the wrong clients."[70]

Hence, although remaining "the world leader" with $2.1 trillion in assets under management in 2013,[71] Switzerland faces greater near-term challenges than the other jurisdictions studied here. The Swiss Bankers Association's own study (conducted with the Boston Consulting Group) concludes that Switzerland needs to redirect itself toward HNWIs in emerging markets, broaden its asset management offerings,[72] and, in essence, do a better job accentuating various strengths of the sort associated here with MDSJs. To be sure, "Swiss banks have stepped up their efforts in the region," opening Asian offices and increasing staffing.[73] In light of "competitive disadvantages compared to other banking centres," however, the aforementioned study concluded that Switzerland must pursue "both political and regulatory improvements and better cooperation between authorities and the institutions being supervised in the interests of the banking centre," including more deliberate "public-private" efforts to market, and manage the reputation of, the Swiss financial center.[74] At the same time, new regulatory challenges will also have to be addressed, as the banks' shift toward unfamiliar emerging markets has itself given rise to concern that such reorientation may increase their exposure to money laundering.[75]

The Swiss financial center clearly retains substantial strengths. Switzerland "remained relatively unscathed amid a deepening downturn and debt crisis in the surrounding euro zone," underscoring their stability and durability, and the contrast with failed banking centers suggests that "Switzerland's ability to attract money stretches well beyond maintaining secrecy"[76]—a form of contrast extended to MDSJs generally below.[77] Their competitive position is further enhanced by a very low level of perceived corruption, placing them (with Singapore) near the top of

---

43,000 taxpayers have joined the program and "collectively paid more than $6 billion in back taxes, interest, and penalties"); Kaye, *supra* note 66, at 395–96.

[69] Grossman et al., *supra* note 66.

[70] *Swissness Is Not Enough*, ECONOMIST, Mar. 29, 2014, at 77.

[71] ECONOMIST, *supra* note 60.

[72] *See* SWISS BANKERS ASSOCIATION & BOSTON CONSULTING GROUP, *supra* note 26, at 7.

[73] *See* TAN CHWEE HUAT, FINANCIAL SERVICES AND WEALTH MANAGEMENT IN SINGAPORE 223 (2011).

[74] SWISS BANKERS ASSOCIATION & BOSTON CONSULTING GROUP, *supra* note 26, at 7.

[75] *See* Ralph Atkins, *Swiss Supervisor Flags Money-Laundering Risks*, FIN. TIMES, Apr. 8, 2016, at 4.

[76] Minder, *supra* note 57 (comparing Switzerland with Cyprus). *See also* ECONOMIST, *supra* note 70.

[77] *See infra* Chapter 10.B.

Transparency International's scale.[78] As Edouard Cuendet, secretary general of the Geneva Private Bankers' Association, suggested in 2013, "[p]eople will not leave Switzerland to go to places with poor jurisdiction. . . . The competition for us is much more Anglo-Saxon." He elaborated that the "U.S. has become very attractive for nondeclared clients, and New York has been developing as an offshore center, as has London"[79]—at once an expression of confidence in the Swiss financial center's legitimate strengths and a gesture toward the growing perception that the United States imposes a double standard regarding secrecy. This form of comparison is likewise extended to MDSJs generally below.[80]

*The Economist* has suggested that "the next few years will provide a stern test" for Switzerland. The Swiss will have to convey to global financial markets that "political and economic stability, top-notch service and a holistic investment approach . . . count for more than the ability to hide money,"[81] and a shift toward institutional assets has emerged for this reason. Simply put, institutional asset management "is more transparent than private banking and less prone to attracting dodgy clients."[82]

Switzerland's capacity to manage this transition, however, will itself be affected by the cultural significance attached to bank secrecy. As Peter Damisch of the Boston Consulting Group has observed of the predicament facing Swiss private banking, such times present very real difficulties for "an industry with no real history of transformation."[83] Swiss private bankers' inertia is only reinforced by the identity-relevance of bank secrecy to the Swiss people. As Jean-Rodolphe Fiechter observes, bank secrecy has, over the decades, become "so deeply rooted in the Swiss collective conscience that any criticism of the banks and their secrecy was regarded as a critique against the nation as a whole."[84]

Given the diversity of the Swiss financial sector and economy, and "contrary to a common notion, Switzerland does not live off of financial opacity (unlike some microstates), and it would do very well if it completely disappeared."[85] Nevertheless, given the stakes involved, it was entirely predictable that calls to relax bank secrecy

---

[78] *See* Transparency International, *Corruption Perceptions Index 2015* (2015) (ranking Switzerland seventh of 168 countries included); Transparency International, *Corruption by Country/Territory: Switzerland*, http://www.transparency.org/country#CHE (last visited Apr. 2016).

[79] Minder, *supra* note 57 (quoting Cuendet).

[80] *See infra* Chapters 10.C, 11.

[81] ECONOMIST, *supra* note 60.

[82] ECONOMIST, *supra* note 70.

[83] ECONOMIST, *supra* note 60 (quoting Damisch).

[84] Fiechter, *supra* note 51, at 56. *See also* *Who's the Criminal? The Agony and the Ecstasy of Offshore Whistleblowing*, ECONOMIST, Feb. 14, 2013, http://www.economist.com/news/special-report/21571558-agony-and-ecstasy-offshore-whistleblowing-whos-criminal.

[85] ZUCMAN, *supra* note 51, at 83–92 (contrasting Switzerland with Luxembourg). I contrast MDSJs with failed jurisdictions along these lines below. *See infra* Chapter 10.B.

would create a "huge rift" in Swiss domestic politics. "Some bankers, as well as many academics and centrist and left-leaning politicians, think the country should bow to the inevitable and abandon strict secrecy." According to a Reuters report, such "pragmatists include big banks like UBS AG and Credit Suisse Group AG, which argue that to survive they have no choice but to surrender more information about their customers." At the same time, however, "a conservative old-guard, including politicians from the powerful right-wing Swiss People's Party and the heads of smaller private banks, sees such a surrender as a betrayal not just of clients but of core Swiss values."[86] Consequently, it appears that substantial cultural and social hurdles must be cleared for the Swiss to assess objectively, and market effectively, their other strengths as a cross-border financial center.

---

[86] Emma Thomasson, *Special Report: The Battle for the Swiss Soul,* REUTERS, Apr. 18, 2013, http://www.re-uters.com/article/2013/04/18/us-swiss-banks-specialreport-idUSBRE93H07620130418. The big banks' pragmatism partly reflects the fact that "they are far more diversified and less dependent on secrecy than small private banks." *Id.* The right-wing reluctance to abandon bank secrecy, meanwhile, partly reflects deep suspicion regarding centralized governmental power; as recently as 2009, the head of the Swiss Private Bankers Association "told Der Spiegel magazine that tax evasion by Germans was a 'legitimate defense by citizens' against a 'disastrous social welfare state.'" *Id.* (quoting Konrad Hummler).

# 9 Delaware

SCHOLARS AND PRACTITIONERS of U.S. corporate law are not accustomed to thinking about the state of Delaware amidst jurisdictions such as Bermuda, Dubai, Singapore, Hong Kong, and Switzerland. On close inspection, however, Delaware exhibits substantial commonalities with these jurisdictions in its historical, cultural, and geographic circumstances, as well as its economic development strategies, embodying the MDSJ concept every bit as well as the others. This degree of commonality among ostensibly disparate jurisdictions reinforces the argument that MDSJs can be coherently described as a "type" of jurisdiction prominent in cross-border finance.

## A. Mediating Financial and Political Power

Like the foregoing jurisdictions, Delaware is small and poorly endowed in natural resources. Among the smallest U.S. states in terms of both land area (with just 1,982 square miles, or 5,133 square kilometers) and population (with an estimated 935,614 inhabitants in 2014),[1] Delaware can "claim to be the smallest state when [both]

---

[1] *See* DELAWARE ECONOMIC DEVELOPMENT OFFICE, DELAWARE QUICK LOOK 2, 6 (Sept. 2015).

factors ... are combined."[2] Although agriculture was important to Delaware's economy in the nineteenth and early twentieth centuries, followed by manufacturing (notably chemicals) in the mid-twentieth century, since that time Delaware's economy has decidedly shifted toward services—particularly incorporation and related services.[3] Indeed, as of 2015, a "quarter of Delawareans work in finance or business services, a higher proportion than in any other state."[4] As Figure 9.1 reflects, Delaware today is extraordinarily reliant on incorporation and related fees, which "reached a record high of $867.2 million dollars in fiscal year (FY) 2012 and accounted for 26 percent of the State's general fund."[5] Delaware would establish a new record in FY 2013 of $883.4 million, representing 24 percent of the general fund,[6] and yet another record in FY 2014 of $927.8 million, representing 26 percent of the general fund.[7] Abandoned property held by Delaware-incorporated businesses brings additional revenue, while related professional service industries further contribute to Delaware's economy.[8] Strikingly, a total of "32.3 percent of all 2007 revenue of Delaware's state government came from businesses that for the most part were not doing business in Delaware."[9]

Although a sub-sovereign entity (like Bermuda, Dubai, and Hong Kong), Delaware in fact possesses—and relies upon—a relatively high degree of legislative autonomy in its area of specialization. As discussed above, the U.S. Constitution grants Congress power to "regulate Commerce with foreign Nations, and among the several States,"[10] but Delaware has retained substantial corporate lawmaking authority under the "internal affairs doctrine"—a long-standing choice-of-law rule under which the law of the jurisdiction of incorporation governs the internal

---

[2] WILLIAM W. BOYER & EDWARD C. RATLEDGE, DELAWARE POLITICS AND GOVERNMENT 1 (2009). *See also Population of USA States,* WORLDATLAS.COM, http://www.worldatlas.com/aatlas/populations/usapoptable.htm (last visited Apr. 2016) (providing state populations and land areas).

[3] *See* BOYER & RATLEDGE, *supra* note 2, at 9–13.

[4] *The First State Comes Last,* ECONOMIST, Apr. 4, 2015, at 29.

[5] JEFFREY W. BULLOCK, DELAWARE SECRETARY OF STATE, DELAWARE DIVISION OF CORPORATIONS 2012 ANNUAL REPORT 2 (2013) [hereinafter DIVISION OF CORPORATIONS 2012 ANNUAL REPORT]. *See also* JEFFREY W. BULLOCK, DELAWARE SECRETARY OF STATE, DELAWARE DIVISION OF CORPORATIONS 2011 ANNUAL REPORT 2 (2012) [hereinafter DIVISION OF CORPORATIONS 2011 ANNUAL REPORT]; *Not a Palm Tree in Sight: Some Onshore Jurisdictions Can Be Laxer than the Offshore Sort,* ECONOMIST, Feb. 14, 2013, http://www.economist.com/news/special-report/21571554-some-onshore-jurisdictions-can-be-laxer-offshore-sort-not-palm-tree-sight.

[6] JEFFREY W. BULLOCK, DELAWARE SECRETARY OF STATE, DELAWARE DIVISION OF CORPORATIONS 2013 ANNUAL REPORT 2 (2014) [hereinafter DIVISION OF CORPORATIONS 2013 ANNUAL REPORT].

[7] JEFFREY W. BULLOCK, DELAWARE SECRETARY OF STATE, DELAWARE DIVISION OF CORPORATIONS 2014 ANNUAL REPORT 2 (2015) [hereinafter DIVISION OF CORPORATIONS 2014 ANNUAL REPORT].

[8] BOYER & RATLEDGE, *supra* note 2, at 20, 112.

[9] *Id.* at 138.

[10] U.S. CONST. art. I, § 8, cl. 3. *See also supra* Chapter 3.A.

| Year | General Fund Revenue Collections | Percentage of Delaware General Fund |
| --- | --- | --- |
| 2009 | $767 million | 25% |
| 2010 | $854 million | 26% |
| 2011 | $859 million | 24% |
| 2012 | $867 million | 26% |
| 2013 | $883 million | 24% |
| 2014 | $928 million | 26% |

FIGURE 9.1 Delaware Division of Corporations General Fund Contributions, 2009–2014.*

* *See* JEFFREY W. BULLOCK, DELAWARE SECRETARY OF STATE, DELAWARE DIVISION OF CORPORATIONS 2009 ANNUAL REPORT 2 (2010), 2010 ANNUAL REPORT 2 (2011), 2011 ANNUAL REPORT 2 (2012), 2012 ANNUAL REPORT 2 (2013), 2013 ANNUAL REPORT 2 (2014), 2014 ANNUAL REPORT 2 (2015).

affairs of a corporation (subject to the omnipresent possibility of congressional interference).[11]

Although located within the contiguous 48 states, Delaware further resembles the other jurisdictions studied here in its cultural and geographic proximity to major markets and state economies within the United States. As William Boyer and Edward Ratledge (a political scientist and an economist, respectively) observe in their in-depth study of the state, the "location of Delaware on a peninsula just south of Philadelphia in the midst of the Boston-Washington megalopolis is central to the state's development." Being "midway between Washington, the center of the nation's political power, and New York City, the center of the nation's financial muscle," Delaware is perfectly positioned to "play[] a role on both of these stages."[12] A marketing piece by the Delaware Economic Development Office touts that "Delaware's strategic location in the mid-Atlantic region offers quick access to potential markets, including Boston, New York City, Philadelphia and Washington, D.C." Indeed, the piece adds, "both New York and Washington, DC, [are] just an hour and a half away."[13]

In a manner strongly reminiscent of Bermuda, Dubai, Singapore, Hong Kong, and Switzerland, Delaware's government works in close collaboration with professional communities to ensure that Delaware law remains cutting edge and that the marketplace knows it. Delaware's corporate lawmaking reflects "a unique partnership of the legal profession and state government," the former proposing draft

---

[11] *See infra* Chapter 9.B. *See also* ERIN A. O'HARA & LARRY E. RIBSTEIN, THE LAW MARKET 10, 119 (2009) (observing that the internal affairs doctrine applies to unincorporated business entities as well).

[12] BOYER & RATLEDGE, *supra* note 2, at 1.

[13] DELAWARE ECONOMIC DEVELOPMENT OFFICE, *supra* note 1, at 1–2.

legislation to the latter via the state's bar association.[14] Such close public-private collaboration partly reflects Delaware's small size, permitting "most business and government actors [to] know each other personally." This facilitates coordinated action across various constituencies and a high degree of political consensus.[15] Delaware's collaborative mode of corporate law production is further enhanced by the comprehensible reliance of a part-time legislature on private expertise,[16] as well as the fact that judges themselves are routinely drawn from the corporate bar.[17] As the aforementioned marketing piece suggests, "[b]usiness leaders will find easy access to elected officials from City Hall to Legislative Hall." The piece elaborates that "[g]overnment agencies work collaboratively to get businesses the resources they need without the usual bureaucratic red tape"[18]—phrasing reminiscent of Bermudian marketing efforts discussed above.[19] Indeed, government officials are heavily involved in marketing Delaware as a jurisdiction for incorporation; the Delaware Secretary of State's Division of Corporations and the judiciary alike actively promote Delaware's advantages around the world.[20] In 2013 this took the form of visits to Israel, Brazil, Singapore, and the Netherlands, as well as creation of a new website "highlighting the benefits of incorporating in Delaware to the international business and legal communities," including "helpful articles in ten languages (English, Arabic, Chinese, Dutch, French, German, Hebrew, Japanese, Portuguese, and Spanish)."[21]

In addition to the high degree of access that the foregoing mode of lawmaking offers, Delaware's consistently bipartisan politics—with relatively centrist parties considered "ideologically indistinguishable" in their commitment to business-friendly policies—itself appeals to corporate decision-makers.[22] Delaware's judiciary likewise reflects deliberate bipartisanship; since 1951, the state's constitution has permitted "no more than a bare majority . . . of the justices of the Supreme Court, the judges of the Superior Court, and the chancellor and vice-chancellors of the Chancery Court [to] be from the same major political party"—a structure suggesting that "Delaware has gone to extraordinary lengths to keep politics out of the judiciary."[23]

---

[14] BOYER & RATLEDGE, *supra* note 2, at 23.

[15] *See id.* at 26–27, 66, 147, 156.

[16] *See id.* at 147.

[17] *See id.* at 110.

[18] DELAWARE ECONOMIC DEVELOPMENT OFFICE, *supra* note 1, at 1.

[19] *See supra* Chapter 4.A.

[20] *See* DIVISION OF CORPORATIONS 2012 ANNUAL REPORT, *supra* note 5, at 3; DIVISION OF CORPORATIONS 2013 ANNUAL REPORT, *supra* note 6, at 3.

[21] DIVISION OF CORPORATIONS 2013 ANNUAL REPORT, *supra* note 6, at 3.

[22] *See* BOYER & RATLEDGE, *supra* note 2, at 59.

[23] *Id.* at 105–06.

## B. Business Entity Registration

To the degree that Delaware has been included in discussions of the role of small jurisdictions in cross-border finance, it has typically been assessed through the "tax haven" lens.[24] Setting aside for the moment whether this is a fair characterization, there would appear to be ample justification for discussing Delaware's attributes, strengths, and weaknesses through the same conceptual lens as the other jurisdictions studied here. Indeed, Delaware's endeavor to compete for incorporations starting in the late-nineteenth century appears to have inspired a similar mode of competition in tax policy among the cantons of Switzerland starting in the 1920s.[25]

Delaware's early efforts to break into the incorporation business strongly resonate with the MDSJ concept—a small jurisdiction with limited economic development options sought to compete for mobile financial business through cooperative public-private efforts to develop and market an attractive regulatory regime. Delaware's story actually starts further up the seaboard, however, in the nation's financial capital—New York. In the early 1890s James Dill, a New York lawyer, convinced New Jersey to pursue incorporations through adoption of a permissive corporate statute, and then himself created a company to market New Jersey's law and assist with the mechanics of incorporation. By the turn of the century "New Jersey was earning so much from corporation filing fees and franchise taxes that it was able to abolish all property taxes and still pay off its entire state debt."[26] This shift in corporate activity from New York to New Jersey was itself the model for Delaware, the next state down the Atlantic coast.

An 1899 Note in the *American Law Review* titled "Little Delaware Makes a Bid for the Organization of Trusts" characterizes late-nineteenth century Delaware as almost island-like—a "tiny territory consist[ing] of a few clay hills and sand bars nearly surrounded by water." The Note derisively suggests that "the little community of truck-farmers and clam-diggers have had their cupidity excited by the spectacle of their northern neighbor, New Jersey, becoming rich and bloated through the granting of franchises to trusts which are to do business everywhere except in New Jersey."[27] Observing that capacity to do so was firmly rooted in the "sovereign"

---

[24] *See, e.g.*, RONEN PALAN, RICHARD MURPHY & CHRISTIAN CHAVAGNEUX, TAX HAVENS: HOW GLOBALIZATION REALLY WORKS 1, 227, 244 (2010).

[25] *See id.* at 109–12; *Enduring Charms: A Brief History of Tax Havens*, ECONOMIST, Feb. 14, 2013, http://www.economist.com/news/special-report/21571550-brief-history-tax-havens-enduring-charms.

[26] *How Delaware Became No. 1*, N.Y. TIMES, May 9, 1976, at 112. *See also* Frederick Tung, *Before Competition: Origins of the Internal Affairs Doctrine*, 32 J. CORP. L. 33, 76–82 (2006).

[27] Note, *Little Delaware Makes a Bid for the Organization of Trusts*, 33 AM. L. REV. 418, 418 (1899).

equality of U.S. states and associated legislative power,[28] the Note explains that Delaware had "enact[ed] a general corporation and trust law which beats that of New Jersey" in various respects aggressively marketed in New York by an entity called "The Corporation Trust Company of Delaware," which had "gone into the business of organizing other corporations in Delaware."[29] Just as occurred in New Jersey, "Wilmington attorney Josiah A. Marvel, with the aid of a New York attorney and the financial editor of a New York newspaper, drafted and secured unanimous approval in 1899 for the predecessor of [Delaware's] present General Corporation Law," and Marvel then formed the aforementioned company to market Delaware as a jurisdiction for incorporation.[30]

A pamphlet circulated by Marvel's company described the advantages offered by Delaware, including lower costs and taxes than New Jersey and less in the way of required activity within the state of incorporation, clearly communicating that the endeavor was aimed primarily at nonresidents.[31] The pamphlet even suggested that Delaware offered more substantial privacy, explaining that "examination of the books by intermeddlers is much more difficult under the Delaware law than under the laws of any other State."[32]

For over a decade New Jersey retained its dominant position.[33] Delaware's efforts finally paid off, however, in 1913 when Woodrow Wilson, then New Jersey's governor, proposed a series of reforms, colloquially called the "Seven Sisters Acts," to constrain perceived abuses that had arisen under New Jersey's statute—a move that prompted companies to move along to Delaware.[34] As a 1976 *New York Times* article looking back on Delaware's rise would observe, "Delaware's tinyness . . . was now recognized as its greatest virtue"—because it effectively ensured that "corporate franchise taxes would always matter," a reality reflected by the Delaware legislature's long-standing responsiveness to the corporate bar.[35] Today, Josiah Marvel's company has grown into the Corporation Service Company, a prominent provider of a range of corporate services in Delaware, including forming corporations and other

---

[28] *Id.* at 419.

[29] *Id. See also* William T. Quillen & Michael Hanrahan, *A Short History of the Delaware Court of Chancery— 1792–1992*, 18 DEL. J. CORP. L. 819, 835 (1993).

[30] N.Y. TIMES, *supra* note 26, at 112.

[31] *See* AM. L. REV., *supra* note 27, at 419–20, 423; N.Y. TIMES, *supra* note 26, at 112.

[32] AM. L. REV., *supra* note 27, at 423.

[33] *See* N.Y. TIMES, *supra* note 26, at 112.

[34] *Id. See also* Bruce G. Carruthers & Naomi R. Lamoreaux, *Regulatory Races: The Effects of Jurisdictional Competition on Regulatory Standards* 34 (2013), http://www.econ.ucla.edu/people/papers/Lamoreaux/ Lamoreaux484.pdf; O'HARA & RIBSTEIN, *supra* note 11, at 10, 110–13; PALAN ET AL., *supra* note 24, at 109–10.

[35] N.Y. TIMES, *supra* note 26, at 112.

business entities, maintaining good standing and keeping up with various required filings, and serving as the "registered agent" in Delaware for such companies.[36]

Delaware's dominance remains astonishing. Delaware is the jurisdiction of incorporation for "more than half of all U.S. publicly traded companies and 65 percent of [the] Fortune 500,"[37] notwithstanding the fact that as of 2006 just two Fortune 500 companies had headquarters in Delaware.[38] Delaware's trend lines, meanwhile, remain very positive. In 2011 they reported "strong 7 percent average growth over the last decade in the number of business entities in Delaware,"[39] with 8.9 percent growth in entity formation in 2012—bringing Delaware to the "significant milestone [of] one million active legal entities domiciled in the state."[40] By 2013 the total would exceed 1,052,000,[41] and by 2014 it would exceed 1,114,000.[42] This means that Delaware's business entity population exceeds its human population, estimated in 2014 to stand at 935,614.[43] It is also noteworthy that, in 2013, "83 percent of all new U.S. Initial Public Offerings (IPOs) were incorporated in Delaware,"[44] and that in 2014 the figure would reach "almost 89 percent."[45] In light of the foregoing, it is unsurprising that commentators continue to note Delaware's unique reliance on corporate franchise taxes.[46] (Figure 9.2 below provides data reflecting new business entity formations in Delaware from 2006 to 2014.)

Erin O'Hara and Larry Ribstein have characterized "the market for corporate law within the United States" as "the most pervasive example of a law market,"[47] but Delaware's dominance is widely considered unassailable. Under the "internal affairs

---

[36] *See* Corporation Service Company, *Our History*, https://www.cscglobal.com/careers/who_we_are-history.html (last visited Apr. 2016); Corporation Service Company, *About Us*, https://www.cscglobal.com/global/web/csc/who-we-are.html (last visited Apr. 2016). *See also* Leslie Wayne, *How Delaware Thrives as a Corporate Tax Haven*, N.Y. TIMES, June 30, 2012, http://www.nytimes.com/2012/07/01/business/how-delaware-thrives-as-a-corporate-tax-haven.html?pagewanted=all&_r=0 (reporting that Corporation Service Company "is the second-largest agent in the state").

[37] DIVISION OF CORPORATIONS 2013 ANNUAL REPORT, *supra* note 6, at 2. *See also* State of Delaware, Division of Corporations, *Why Incorporate in Delaware?*, http://corp.delaware.gov/ (last visited Apr. 2016); DIVISION OF CORPORATIONS 2012 ANNUAL REPORT, *supra* note 5, at 1.

[38] *See* KENT GREENFIELD, THE FAILURE OF CORPORATE LAW: FUNDAMENTAL FLAWS AND PROGRESSIVE POSSIBILITIES 108 (2006).

[39] DIVISION OF CORPORATIONS 2011 ANNUAL REPORT, *supra* note 5, at 1.

[40] DIVISION OF CORPORATIONS 2012 ANNUAL REPORT, *supra* note 5, at 1.

[41] DIVISION OF CORPORATIONS 2013 ANNUAL REPORT, *supra* note 6, at 2.

[42] DIVISION OF CORPORATIONS 2014 ANNUAL REPORT, *supra* note 7, at 1.

[43] DELAWARE ECONOMIC DEVELOPMENT OFFICE, *supra* note 1, at 6.

[44] DIVISION OF CORPORATIONS 2013 ANNUAL REPORT, *supra* note 6, at 2.

[45] DIVISION OF CORPORATIONS 2014 ANNUAL REPORT, *supra* note 7, at 1.

[46] *See, e.g.,* LEWIS S. BLACK, JR., WHY CORPORATIONS CHOOSE DELAWARE 1 (2007); FRANK H. EASTERBROOK & DANIEL R. FISCHEL, THE ECONOMIC STRUCTURE OF CORPORATE LAW 213 (1991); O'HARA & RIBSTEIN, *supra* note 11, at 111.

[47] O'HARA & RIBSTEIN, *supra* note 11, at 10.

doctrine," the law of the jurisdiction of organization generally governs a business entity's internal affairs[48]—a conflicts rule unique to the corporate context[49] that gives rise to the potential for a competition for corporate charters. Today, however, it is widely understood that no other state meaningfully competes with Delaware to attract incorporations by companies headquartered outside the given state's borders; at most, other states compete solely to keep companies headquartered within their own borders incorporated at home.[50] Accordingly, the only true competitive threat to Delaware would appear to be Congress, which has occasionally flexed its muscle in the field of corporate law (via the commerce clause)—though only sporadically, and typically in the aftermath of crises capturing national media attention.[51]

Although the early story recounted above sounds very much like a regulatory race to the bottom, Delaware's regulators, judges, and practicing bar alike rightly emphasize various institutional features contributing to the state's dominant position today. As a threshold matter, one must not overlook the (largely serendipitous) survival of distinct equity jurisdiction in Delaware, which has lent itself to the elaboration of a complex and nuanced case law on the fiduciary duties of care and loyalty owed by managers to the corporation and the shareholders.[52] As William Quillen and Michael Hanrahan observe, "Delaware's small size enabled equity to be efficiently administered in a single, centralized chancery court, unlike large states where it was more practical to administer equity in county courts."[53] Justice Randy Holland further explains (in a 2009 law review article) that this preserves today

---

[48] See RESTATEMENT (SECOND) OF CONFLICT OF LAWS §§ 302, 304 (1971); CTS Corp. v. Dynamics Corp. of America, 481 U.S. 69, 89 (1987). See also O'HARA & RIBSTEIN, supra note 11, at 108, 119.

[49] See GREENFIELD, supra note 38, at 110. On the emergence of the internal affairs doctrine in the nineteenth century, see generally Tung, supra note 26.

[50] See Lucian Arye Bebchuk & Assaf Hamdani, Vigorous Race or Leisurely Walk: Reconsidering the Competition over Corporate Charters, 112 YALE L.J. 553, 578 (2002); Christopher M. Bruner, Managing Corporate Federalism: The Least-Bad Approach to the Shareholder Bylaw Debate, 36 DEL. J. CORP. L. 1, 27–28 (2011); Carruthers & Lamoreaux, supra note 34, at 39; Robert Daines, The Incorporation Choice of IPO Firms, 77 N.Y.U. L. REV. 1559, 1570–74 (2002); Marcel Kahan & Ehud Kamar, The Myth of State Competition in Corporate Law, 55 STAN. L. REV. 679, 687 (2002); Roberta Romano, The States as a Laboratory: Legal Innovation and State Competition for Corporate Charters, 23 YALE J. REG. 209, 214 (2006).

[51] See O'HARA & RIBSTEIN, supra note 11, at 115–16; Bruner, supra note 50, at 26–28; Mark J. Roe, Delaware's Competition, 117 HARV. L. REV. 588, 596–601 (2003); Mark J. Roe, Delaware and Washington as Corporate Lawmakers, 34 DEL. J. CORP. L. 1, 6–11 (2009); Leo E. Strine, Jr., Breaking the Corporate Governance Logjam in Washington: Some Constructive Thoughts on a Responsible Path Forward, 63 BUS. LAW. 1079, 1084 (2008).

[52] See generally Quillen & Hanrahan, supra note 29. Quillen and Hanrahan attribute the early survival of equity jurisdiction in Delaware to the fact that "equity in Delaware was based and administered in a manner that eliminated the reasons for the ideological and political opposition to chancery courts that developed in other colonies"—notably the fact that equity in Delaware "was founded on statute, not the royal prerogative." This meant that "courts of equity in Delaware were not viewed as instruments of the Crown." Id. at 826.

[53] Id. at 832.

the important substantive advantage of addressing complex corporate law disputes before a Chancellor and Vice-Chancellors who "sit without a jury and issue well-reasoned decisions at the conclusion of each judicial proceeding"—an institutional feature facilitating the development of "precedents that provide the predictability needed for businesses to act with confidence."[54] This is reinforced by the fact that the parties have "an absolute right of [direct] appeal" to the Delaware Supreme Court,[55] facilitating authoritative development and clarification of the law. As Lewis Black sums it up, the "history and tradition of the Court of Chancery and the human capital of its excellent judges, cannot be magically transplanted to some other jurisdiction. The Court of Chancery is an institution unique to Delaware."[56]

The statute itself, meanwhile, remains a decidedly cooperative public-private undertaking. Black describes the Delaware General Corporation Law (DGCL) as "the great beneficiary of an unwritten compact between the bar and the state legislature," according to which "the legislature will call upon the expertise of the Corporation Law Section of the Delaware Bar Association to recommend, review and draft almost all amendments to the statute." This "understanding" is facilitated "by the fact that Delaware is such a small state" where "the people involved interact regularly."[57] The aim has been to maintain "an enabling statute" permitting "the maximum flexibility in ordering [corporate] affairs,"[58] often identified as a strength of Delaware along with its expert judiciary, responsive legislature, and service-oriented Division of Corporations.[59] To the latter point, although the standard filing fee to form a corporation or a limited liability company (LLC) stands at about $90, those willing to pay an extra $1,000 priority fee can have the formation process completed within one hour.[60]

As to whether Delaware adds substantial value, or rather pursues a regulatory race to the bottom, the foregoing capsule history suggests that—like the other jurisdictions studied here—Delaware exhibits legitimate competitive advantages. Setting

---

[54] Randy J. Holland, *Delaware's Business Courts: Litigation Leadership,* 34 J. CORP. L. 771, 773, 778 (2009). *See also* BLACK, *supra* note 46, at 5, 8.

[55] Holland, *supra* note 54, at 775–76.

[56] BLACK, *supra* note 46, at 7.

[57] *Id.* at 4. *See also* O'HARA & RIBSTEIN, *supra* note 11, at 112.

[58] BLACK, *supra* note 46, at 2.

[59] *See, e.g., id.* at 1; State of Delaware, Division of Corporations, *supra* note 37. The Division of Corporations adds that "Delaware's corporate and legal services community has unparalleled expertise . . . and receives strong, bipartisan support" from the government. DIVISION OF CORPORATIONS 2013 ANNUAL REPORT, *supra* note 6, at 1.

[60] *See* State of Delaware, Division of Corporations, *Expedited Services,* http://corp.delaware.gov/expserv. shtml (last visited Apr. 2016); State of Delaware, Division of Corporations, *Fee Schedule,* https://corp. delaware.gov/Julyfee.pdf (rev. July 1, 2014).

aside the hotly contested issue of the democratic legitimacy of a single (small) state writing de facto national corporate law,[61] however, it is critical to observe that Delaware's highly developed corporate case law and impressive set of institutional characteristics appear less relevant when one looks beyond large public companies that anticipate recurrent litigation in Delaware's courts.[62] When the focus turns to smaller corporations and LLCs, Delaware's purported advantages take on a different cast.

Consider, for example, the benefits of organizing a business entity in Delaware as summarized by "SFM Professional"—a Geneva-based "specialist corporate services provider offering dedicated account management to the professional intermediary market."[63] Their description of Delaware's offerings focuses particularly on the LLC, which SFM describes as offering "the possibility to have a US company with . . . similar advantages of an International Business Company (traditionally called 'offshore company')."[64] With respect to Delaware's "main characteristics" as a jurisdiction, SFM observes that (among other things) Delaware imposes no accounting or reporting requirements, taxes, or "paid up capital requirement," and further notes that there is "no public register of company officers." They add that Delaware maintains "[m]odern offshore legislation" and "an efficient Registry," while offering "a high level of anonymity and privacy."[65]

The Delaware Division of Corporations itself, although "barring registered incorporation agents listed on its website from marketing or promoting shell companies,"[66] nevertheless states at its website that "Delaware is a leading domicile for U.S. and international business entities," and directs those looking to establish such

---

[61] *Compare* William L. Cary, *Federalism and Corporate Law: Reflections upon Delaware*, 83 YALE L.J. 663 (1974) *with* Ralph K. Winter, Jr., *State Law, Shareholder Protection, and the Theory of the Corporation*, 6 J. LEGAL STUD. 251 (1977). *See also* Bruner, *supra* note 50, at 43–45; EASTERBROOK & FISCHEL, *supra* note 46, at 213–15; GREENFIELD, *supra* note 38, at 107–09.

[62] Whereas public companies are attracted to Delaware in part for the "extensive body of corporate case law" developed by "a talented bench and bar that specialize in corporate transactions," closely held companies "usually incorporate in the state in which they do most of their business"—in part "to avoid paying a separate franchise tax to a jurisdiction like Delaware in which the corporation does little or no business." ROBERT A. RAGAZZO & FRANCES S. FENDLER, CLOSELY HELD BUSINESS ORGANIZATIONS: CASES, MATERIALS, AND PROBLEMS 295–96 (2d ed. 2012).

[63] SFM Professional, *Who We Are*, http://sfmprofessional.com/who-we-are.html (last visited Apr. 2016).

[64] SFM Professional, *Delaware*, http://sfmprofessional.com/jurisdictions/delaware.html (last visited Apr. 2016). Other jurisdictions highlighted include Seychelles, Ras Al-Khaimah, Panama, Singapore, Cyprus, Belize, Gibraltar, Hong Kong, Mauritius, the Bahamas, Anguilla, the British Virgin Islands, the United Kingdom, Switzerland, and the Cayman Islands. *See id.*

[65] *Id. See also* TAX JUSTICE NETWORK, NARRATIVE REPORT ON USA 6–9 (2015).

[66] Veronika Oleksyn, *Shell, Shelf, and Other Jargon*, WASH. DIPLOMAT, Feb. 29, 2012, http://www.washdiplomat.com/index.php?option=com_content&view=article&id=8250:tax-haven-next-door-delaware-exposes-corporate-secrecy-in-elections&catid=1484&Itemid=428.

entities to pre-prepared sample forms[67]—one-page forms requiring no information about a corporation's shareholders or an LLC's members.[68] These forms straightforwardly reflect the little information required by the DGCL and the Delaware Limited Liability Company Act, neither of which requires identification of equity owners.[69]

Statistics reported by the Secretary of State confirm that Delaware has been enormously successful in the competition for organization of unincorporated entities, and that this category of business looms increasingly large for Delaware. According to the Division of Corporations' 2012 Annual Report, for example, strong growth in entity formation was largely attributable to LLCs. A total of 145,182 new entities were formed in Delaware in 2012, up 8.9 percent in total, but this reflects just "2.9 percent growth in corporation formation and nearly 10.8 percent growth in [LLC] formation."[70] Strikingly, Delaware has more than twice as many LLCs as corporations. As of August 9, 2013, 647,592 domestic LLCs were registered in Delaware, compared with 267,456 domestic corporations.[71] Figure 9.2 provides data summarizing new business entity formations from 2006 to 2014, reflecting at once the substantial growth of this business for Delaware, as well as their degree of reliance on LLC formations.

In light of the foregoing, it is unsurprising that Delaware—like Bermuda, Dubai, Singapore, Hong Kong, and Switzerland—has faced accusations that it functions as a "tax haven." A 2012 article in *The New York Times*, provocatively titled "How Delaware Thrives as a Corporate Tax Haven," reported that in addition to large, recognizable businesses, those employing Delaware entities have included Stanko Subotic, "a Serbian businessman and convicted smuggler"; Viktor Bout, "the Russian arms dealer known as 'the merchant of death'"; and Timothy Durham, "known as 'the Midwest Madoff.'"[72] So-called shell corporations being an easy way to launder money,[73] concerns have grown regarding the ease with which anyone can

---

[67] State of Delaware, Division of Corporations, *How to Form a New Business Entity*, http://corp.delaware.gov/howtoform.shtml (last visited Apr. 2016).

[68] *See* State of Delaware, Division of Corporations, Certificate of Incorporation: Stock Corporation (Form), http://corp.delaware.gov/incstk09.pdf (rev. July 2004); State of Delaware, Division of Corporations, Certificate of Formation: Limited Liability Company (Form), http://corp.delaware.gov/llcform09.pdf (rev. July 2004).

[69] *See* DEL. CODE ANN. tit. 8, § 102(a) (2016); DEL. CODE ANN. tit. 6, § 18-201(a) (2016).

[70] DIVISION OF CORPORATIONS 2012 ANNUAL REPORT, *supra* note 5, at 1. *See also* ECONOMIST, *supra* note 4, at 29.

[71] E-mail from John A. Celatka, ERP Systems Specialist, State of Delaware, Division of Corporations, to author (Aug. 14, 2013, 1:14 PM EST) (on file with author). Additionally, there were 8,045 foreign corporations; 3,105 foreign LLCs; 77,173 domestic limited partnerships; 230 foreign limited partnerships; 431 limited liability partnerships; and 23,172 statutory trusts. *Id.*

[72] Wayne, *supra* note 36. *See also* ECONOMIST, *supra* note 5.

[73] *See* Wayne, *supra* note 36.

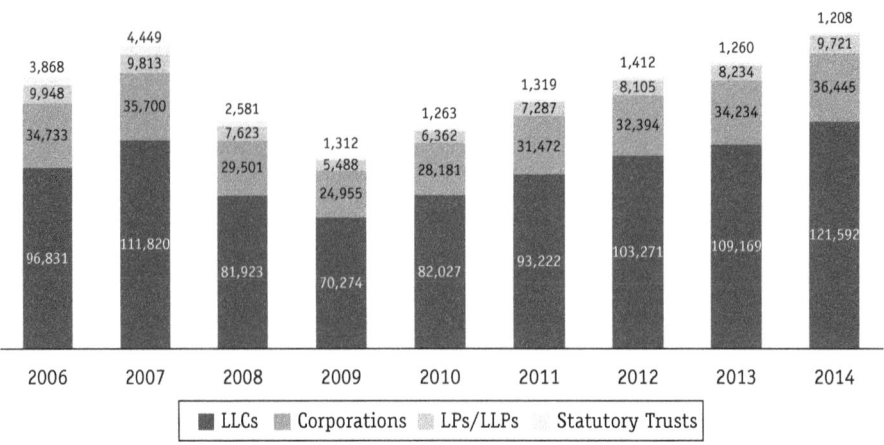

FIGURE 9.2  New Business Entity Formations in Delaware, 2006–2014.*

* *See* JEFFREY W. BULLOCK, DELAWARE SECRETARY OF STATE, DELAWARE DIVISION OF CORPORATIONS 2008 ANNUAL REPORT 1 (2009), 2009 ANNUAL REPORT 1 (2010), 2010 ANNUAL REPORT 1 (2011), 2011 ANNUAL REPORT 1 (2012), 2012 ANNUAL REPORT 2 (2013), 2013 ANNUAL REPORT 2 (2014), 2014 ANNUAL REPORT 2 (2015) (providing data on new formations of limited liability companies, corporations, limited partnerships/limited liability partnerships, and statutory trusts).

set up a Delaware business entity, with no information regarding equity ownership required. According to David Finzer of Capital Conservator, a registration agent for non-U.S. citizens, "Delaware is the state that requires the least amount of information. . . . Basically, it requires none. Delaware has the most secret companies in the world and the easiest to form."[74] Likewise, Richard Murphy of the Tax Justice Network brands Delaware "the biggest single source of anonymous corporations in the world,"[75] a perception leading Delaware to be viewed "as an onshore alternative with regulations more lax than such well-known offshore tax havens as the Isle of Man, Jersey and the Caymans, which require greater disclosure."[76] Indeed, in 2009 the Tax Justice Network branded Delaware "the most secretive financial jurisdiction

---

[74]  *Id.* (quoting Finzer).

[75]  *Id.* (quoting Murphy). *See also* RICHARD HAY ET AL., TOWARDS A LEVEL PLAYING FIELD: REGULATING CORPORATE VEHICLES IN CROSS-BORDER TRANSACTIONS 21 (2002) (review commissioned by the International Trade and Investment Organisation and the Society of Trust and Estate Practitioners, and conducted by Stikeman Elliott) ("The single member Delaware LLC . . . is ubiquitous in the 'offshore' world.").

[76]  Wayne, *supra* note 36. *See also* HAY ET AL., *supra* note 75, at 19–24, 37–39; TAX JUSTICE NETWORK, *supra* note 65, at 6–9; Sheldon D. Pollack, *Delaware: Tax Haven or Scapegoat?*, 70 ST. TAX NOTES 53, 54–55 (2013) (arguing that Delaware does not constitute a tax haven internationally, but acknowledging that "Delaware provides some greater privacy as to the identity of the owners of privately held corporations than do most states"). The British Virgin Islands represent Delaware's principal international competitor. *See* Andrew P. Morriss & Clifford C. Henson, *Regulatory Effectiveness in Onshore & Offshore Financial Centers* 23 (Univ. of Ala. Sch. of Law Working Paper, 2012), http://ssrn.com/abstract=2016310.

in the world."[77] According to *The Economist*, "[i]nvestigators joke that Delaware stands for 'Dollars and Euros Laundered And Washed At Reasonable Expense.' "[78] Although it is sometimes claimed that information on equity ownership can and should be gathered by banks, this approach preserves an easy end run—criminals can simply open "bank accounts for their U.S.-based shell companies in offshore jurisdictions with less rigorous customer identification requirements than in the United States."[79] Meanwhile other U.S. states have complained of the "Delaware loophole," through which companies have reduced their taxes elsewhere "by shifting royalties and similar revenues to holding companies in Delaware, where they are not taxed"—a practice estimated to have reduced tax payments to other states by $9.5 billion over a 10-year period.[80]

On the whole—just like Bermuda, Dubai, Singapore, Hong Kong, and Switzerland—Delaware's record is mixed; there is a strong case to be made that Delaware adds considerable value through the development of substantive corporate law and its handling of complex disputes involving public companies, yet other aspects of Delaware's efforts to attract cross-border organization of business entities and related financial activity give rise to concerns that appear quite well founded. Hence, although the trend lines remain positive, it is hardly surprising that Delaware has faced increasing pressure to respond to the perceived abuses described above—dynamics closely resembling those observed in each of the other jurisdictions studied here.

---

[77] *See* Veronika Oleksyn, *Tax Haven Next Door: Delaware Exposes Corporate Secrecy*, WASH. DIPLOMAT, Feb. 29, 2012, http://www.washdiplomat.com/index.php?option=com_content&view=article&id=8250: tax-haven-next-door-delaware-exposes-corporate-secrecy-in-elections&catid=1484&Itemid=428.

[78] ECONOMIST, *supra* note 5.

[79] *See* Oleksyn, *supra* note 77.

[80] Wayne, *supra* note 36. *See also* Pollack, *supra* note 76, at 54.

# III MDSJs and Other Financial Centers

# 10 Failed Small Jurisdictions and Successful Large Jurisdictions

## A. Revisiting the Ideal Type

Bermuda, Dubai, Singapore, Hong Kong, Switzerland, and Delaware all adhere closely to the MDSJ paradigm described in Chapter 3. In each case, a small jurisdiction with legislative autonomy and favorable geographic and cultural proximity to major economies has sought to establish a competitive niche in cross-border finance by investing heavily in human capital, professional networks, and related institutional structures; drawing together public and private expertise to create innovative regulatory structures at once conveying flexibility and credibility; and actively minimizing the political salience of cross-border finance, both domestically and diplomatically. In each case, these competitive attributes and development strategies appear to have loomed large in their respective successes. As Chapter 3 emphasized, however, limiting the analysis exclusively to jurisdictions that are both "small" and "market-dominant" in the pertinent respects would amount to selection upon the dependent variable, weakening the argument that adherence to the MDSJ paradigm contributed directly to their successes.

Accordingly, in this chapter I return to the five-part MDSJ "ideal type" and apply that metric to two sets of jurisdictions varying from those examined above in important respects. I first apply the MDSJ benchmark to small jurisdictions that have endeavored to create vibrant financial centers yet failed, focusing on two vivid examples—the South Pacific island of Nauru, and the former Caribbean island group of the Netherlands Antilles. Although these two examples hardly provide a robust test of my causal hypotheses, they nevertheless contrast in telling ways with the jurisdictions studied in Part II, strongly suggesting that the various elements of the MDSJ ideal type in fact foster success—by illustrating how deviations from them have factored in these other jurisdictions' failures.

I then apply the MDSJ benchmark to large jurisdictions that have succeeded in order to illuminate further the boundaries of my explanatory domain—in particular, by examining the degree to which the competitive attributes and strategies that I associate with MDSJs are in fact peculiar to such jurisdictions. Here I turn to the world's two most significant capital markets—"Wall Street" in New York and "the City" (sometimes referred to as "the Square Mile") in London. As I discuss below, these major global financial centers exhibit certain traits akin to the MDSJs studied in Part II—notably their geographic and cultural concentration—while differing starkly in other respects—notably their locations, historically positioning them as gateways to major domestic economies, their degrees of regulatory autonomy, and their greater breadth of financial services offerings, underwritten by the greater credibility that each derives from the support of a large sovereign. This latter category of comparisons also helps to illuminate further the types of specialized roles that MDSJs, in particular, play in cross-border finance relative to the world's largest and most diversified financial centers.

## B. Failed Small Jurisdictions

The MDSJ features comprising the ideal type presented in Chapter 3 reflect various historical, cultural, and geographic circumstances in which the given jurisdiction might find itself, as well as various forms of development strategies that successful jurisdictions have pursued in response to those circumstances. Broadly speaking, those smaller jurisdictions that have endeavored to develop vibrant cross-border financial centers yet have failed have tended to face circumstances and challenges similar to those faced by the MDSJs investigated in Part II, but have responded in very different ways. In this section I turn to two such jurisdictions—the South Pacific island of Nauru, and the former Caribbean island group of the Netherlands Antilles—and find that their failures largely reflect excessive reliance on secrecy and tax competition, without the ballast of higher value-added services or truly innovative regulatory solutions to complex problems. For the reader's convenience, Figure 10.1 summarizes significant deviations from the MDSJ ideal type discussed below.

| Feature | Nauru | Netherlands Antilles |
|---|---|---|
| *Small population and land area, limited natural resources?* | *yes* | *yes* |
| *Legislative autonomy?* | *yes* | *yes* |
| *Cultural proximity, favorable geography vis-à-vis major powers?* | *no*<br>• extremely remote Pacific island<br>• limited cultural/commercial ties | *no*<br>• required Dutch language filings<br>• competitors more familiar to U.S. |
| *Investment in human capital, professional networks, institutions?* | *no*<br>• shell banks existing solely on paper<br>• heavy reliance on selling sovereignty | *no*<br>• "Antilles sandwich"<br>• heavy reliance on U.S. tax treaty |
| *Balancing collaboration with, and oversight of, financial community?* | *no*<br>• heavy reliance on secrecy<br>• no functional financial regulator | *no*<br>• unfamiliar Dutch legal system<br>• did not invest in financial regulator |

FIGURE 10.1  Nauru and the Netherlands Antilles: Deviations from the Ideal Type.

Nauru provides a fascinating and illuminating example. In the early twentieth century the island fell under the control of a German-British consortium there to mine the island's substantial phosphate deposits. During World War I Nauru was occupied by Australia, later became a mandate of the League of Nations, and following Japanese occupation during World War II became a trust territory of the United Nations. Ultimately they gained their independence in 1968, and in 1999 they joined the United Nations "as the world's smallest independent republic." With a total land area of 21 square kilometers (just one-tenth the size of Washington, DC), the island had a population of 9,540 people as of July 2015.[1]

Occupying "one of the three great phosphate rock islands in the Pacific Ocean,"[2] the Nauruan people—upon achieving independence—lived quite well for a time. Indeed, while the phosphate lasted they were "among the richest people on earth," living almost exclusively on phosphate sales with "no taxes of any kind."[3] However,

---

[1]  *See* CENTRAL INTELLIGENCE AGENCY, THE WORLD FACTBOOK: NAURU, https://www.cia.gov/library/publications/the-world-factbook/geos/nr.html (last updated Apr. 26, 2016).

[2]  The other phosphate rock islands in the Pacific are Banaba (Kiribati) and Makatea (French Polynesia). *See id.*

[3]  *Paradise Well and Truly Lost,* ECONOMIST, Dec. 20, 2001, http://www.economist.com/node/884045. *See also* William Mellor, *Corruption, Poor Investing Have Bankrupted Nauru,* HONOLULU STAR-BULL. BUS., June 2, 2004, http://archives.starbulletin.com/2004/06/02/business/story4.html.

"intensive phosphate mining beginning in 1906 . . . left the central 90 percent of Nauru a wasteland and threatens limited remaining land resources,"[4] leaving Nauru acutely bereft of natural resources. As J.C. Sharman describes the island today, "all but a 200 m strip around its coastline . . . is an abandoned phosphate mine."[5] The financial difficulties that resulted from dwindling phosphate sales were compounded by poor investment of reserves, including "a London musical about Leonardo da Vinci that closed after five weeks."[6] Today Nauru is heavily reliant on imports and aid from Australia, and "rehabilitation of mined land and the replacement of income from phosphates are serious long-term problems."[7]

Nauru's motivations for turning to cross-border finance were, in light of the foregoing, broadly similar to what we have seen elsewhere—if considerably more urgent. Their strategies to attract cross-border financial business, however, have differed starkly. As Sharman explains, "[f]rom the late 1990s Nauru became a byword for the nexus between offshore finance, criminal money, and a complete lack of regulation," with "400 offshore banks housed in a tiny shed, and the $70 billion of Russian mafia money the Russian Central Bank . . . claimed had been laundered through the country."[8] Even though the hundreds of banks organized in Nauru "had no physical existence, consisting of just a license and a number, they could be used to link into the international electronic banking network."[9]

According to the U.S. Treasury Department's Financial Crimes Enforcement Network (FinCEN) in a July 2000 advisory, there were "serious questions whether the [Nauru Agency Corporation] is either in a position or possesses the authority properly to supervise any aspect of the offshore sector."[10] Put differently, FinCEN apparently could not definitively confirm whether Nauru had a functioning financial regulator of any sort. Nauru refused to comply with anti-money-laundering initiatives in the early 2000s, presumably reflecting their degree of reliance on the licensing of unsupervised offshore banks, and ultimately they were "cut off from all international

[4] CENTRAL INTELLIGENCE AGENCY, *supra* note 1. *See also* ECONOMIST, *supra* note 3.

[5] J.C. Sharman, *South Pacific Tax Havens: From Leaders in the Race to the Bottom to Laggards in the Race to the Top?*, 29 ACCT. F. 311, 312 (2005).

[6] Mellor, *supra* note 3.

[7] CENTRAL INTELLIGENCE AGENCY, *supra* note 1. *See also* Mellor, *supra* note 3; J.C. Sharman, *Canaries in the Coal Mine: Tax Havens, the Decline of the West and the Rise of the Rest*, 17 NEW POL. ECON. 493, 508 (2012); Kalinga Seneviratne, *Pressure on Pacific to Stop Money-Laundering*, ASIA TIMES ONLINE, June 29, 2000, http://www.atimes.com/oceania/BF29Aho1.html.

[8] Sharman, *supra* note 7, at 508. *See also* ECONOMIST, *supra* note 3; Mellor, *supra* note 3.

[9] J.C. SHARMAN, THE MONEY LAUNDRY: REGULATING CRIMINAL FINANCE IN THE GLOBAL ECONOMY 114 (2011).

[10] United States Department of the Treasury Financial Crimes Enforcement Network, FinCEN Advisory: Transactions Involving Nauru 2 (July 2000).

banking networks."[11] The residual financial system, if one could call it that, consisted of "one supermarket and the remaining shell of the government." The government continued to "provide some salaries and pensions in cash . . . thanks to residual income from tuna licensing rights and foreign aid from Australia and Taiwan," which funds were largely spent at the island's single supermarket. The supermarket, then, lent the cash to the government to cover fiscal deficits, ultimately settled by transfers from the government's Australian account to the supermarket's Australian account.[12]

In contrast with the MDSJs studied in Part II, Nauru relied almost exclusively on secrecy, permitting abusive practices such as money laundering to metastasize in a legal environment virtually bereft of substantive regulation. In seeking to understand this failure, however, it is important to recognize that Nauru and other South Pacific island jurisdictions face challenges in the development of real, value-added financial services that MDSJs generally do not. As Sharman has observed, more favorably situated jurisdictions experienced influxes of "employees and operations [of foreign firms] to the islands in order to beat the accusation of having 'no substantial economic activity'" that had been leveled by U.S. and other tax authorities. Over time, "successively greater layers of substance were added to the fiction of island-based companies"—a process prompting Bermuda and the Cayman Islands, for example, to become "world leaders in some aspects of the insurance and hedge fund industries." By contrast, South Pacific island jurisdictions such as Nauru "face the challenges of small size and remoteness to an extreme degree," rendering the development of value-added financial services in this manner far less likely to occur.[13] As *The Economist* described their circumstances, Nauru's "remoteness in the middle of the Pacific is impossible to exaggerate."[14] Accordingly, argues Sharman, such jurisdictions turning to cross-border finance in the face of extreme economic development challenges have "increasingly taken the standard route of copying legislation from the current leaders in the field and then engaging in fierce competition for business that has often generated only the thinnest of margins."[15] Unable to develop and sustain top-shelf work, they settle for shady, "low-margin pure 'booking center' activity whereby tax havens are providing a legal fiction for transactions and assets that are practically located onshore."[16] Today, although "[n]o reliable data exists for

---

[11] Sharman, *supra* note 7, at 509.

[12] SHARMAN, *supra* note 9, at 114–15. The virtual nonexistence of a Nauruan "financial system," Sharman argues, rendered pointless the subsequent Financial Action Task Force initiative to compel Nauru to adopt an expensive, state-of-the-art anti-money laundering regime. *See id.* at 115–17.

[13] *See* J.C. SHARMAN, HAVENS IN A STORM: THE STRUGGLE FOR GLOBAL TAX REGULATION 23 (2006).

[14] ECONOMIST, *supra* note 3.

[15] *See* SHARMAN, *supra* note 13, at 23.

[16] *Id.* at 119. *See also* Sharman, *supra* note 5, at 312.

determining Nauru's share of the global market for offshore financial services," the island "is widely regarded as a minnow."[17]

Other jurisdictions in the region have faced similar challenges and taken similar approaches, including the Cook Islands, the Marshall Islands, Niue, Palau, Samoa, and Vanuatu.[18] In general, such jurisdictions have "not invested much in setting up an offshore sector," and cross-border finance correlatively has generated little in the way of GDP or employment. Typically they have gravitated toward fields with low entry barriers, "simply requiring that [they] pass a package of legislation that could easily be copied from tax havens elsewhere"—such as "international business companies," banking licenses, and trusts—with only very low human capital requirements. In an extreme case, "Niue contracted out its entire offshore industry to Panamanian law firm Mossack Fonseca"[19] (thereby rooting such activity in a larger jurisdiction that, following release of the Panama Papers, has itself been intensely scrutinized and roundly criticized for trading in financial secrecy and resisting multilateral transparency initiatives[20]). Without substantial investment in human capital, professional networks, and related institutional structures, these jurisdictions have not developed the "spin-off benefits" that such investment has generated for the MDSJs.[21]

For lack of viable options, such jurisdictions have literally "attempted to sell or rent out some of [their] sovereign rights to meet development goals."[22] As *The Economist* described their situation in 2001, Nauru was effectively a sovereign for

---

[17] Tax Justice Network, Report on Nauru 1 (2013).

[18] *See* Sharman, *supra* note 5, at 312; Seneviratne, *supra* note 7. Generally speaking, each of these jurisdictions is similarly small in land area and population, with limited natural resources. *See* Central Intelligence Agency, The World Factbook: Cook Islands, https://www.cia.gov/library/publications/the-world-factbook/geos/cw.html (last updated Apr. 26, 2016); Central Intelligence Agency, The World Factbook: Niue, https://www.cia.gov/library/publications/the-world-factbook/geos/ne.html (last updated Apr. 26, 2016); Central Intelligence Agency, The World Factbook: Vanuatu, https://www.cia.gov/library/publications/the-world-factbook/geos/nh.html (last updated Apr. 26, 2016); Central Intelligence Agency, The World Factbook: Marshall Islands, https://www.cia.gov/library/publications/the-world-factbook/geos/rm.html (last updated Apr. 26, 2016); Central Intelligence Agency, The World Factbook: Palau, https://www.cia.gov/library/publications/the-world-factbook/geos/ps.html (last updated Apr. 26, 2016); Central Intelligence Agency, The World Factbook: Samoa, https://www.cia.gov/library/publications/the-world-factbook/geos/ws.html (last updated Apr. 26, 2016).

[19] *See* Sharman, *supra* note 5, at 314.

[20] *See* Geoff Dyer, *Papers Reveal at Least 33 People and Companies on US Sanctions Blacklist,* Fin. Times, Apr. 7, 2016, at 3; *After the Panama Papers: Who Next?,* Economist, Apr. 16, 2016, at 60–61; *The Panama Papers: A Torrential Leak,* Economist, Apr. 9, 2016, at 59–61; Nicholas Shaxson, *Panama Is Only One Head of the Tax Haven Hydra,* Fin. Times, Apr. 6, 2016, at 9.

[21] *See* Sharman, *supra* note 5, at 313–15.

[22] *Id.* at 311. *See also* Mellor, *supra* note 3.

hire, engaging in various "desperate money-raising ventures," of which offshore banking was just one—the common thread being the sale of sovereignty untempered by meaningful regulation. Other endeavors included recognizing Taiwan in exchange for aid, selling citizenship, and even "hir[ing] itself out as a detention camp for would-be immigrants to Australia" in exchange for "eight months'-worth of free fuel, two new electrical generators, ten scholarships for Nauruan students at Australian universities and a promise to pay off the island's accumulated medical bills."[23]

The inherent instability and vulnerability of such desperate efforts toward economic development are readily apparent. Recall, for example, the St. Kitts and Nevis "citizenship-for-sale" program that, as noted above, may distort the picture of Hong Kong's dependence on Mainland business listings (to the extent that de facto Chinese businesses are owned and controlled by those who have renounced Chinese citizenship in favor of citizenship in St. Kitts and Nevis).[24] Taking its present form in response to economic crisis, this program—largely the product of an enterprising Swiss lawyer[25]—offers full citizenship and a passport "in exchange for a US$250,000 donation, or a US$400,000 property purchase which must be held for five years," with "no residency requirement."[26] Expanded capacity for visa-free travel is thought to be the principal attraction of such programs for wealthy buyers from China, Russia, and the Middle East, but these programs have inevitably raised concerns that they facilitate tax evasion and money laundering, and that they may be used by "criminals, or even terrorists," to evade security measures. Accordingly, when Canada announced in November 2014 that "it would no longer allow St. Kitts citizens to enter without a visa, due to concerns about 'identity management practices within its Citizenship by Investment program,'" St. Kitts and Nevis found itself scrambling to recall and reissue passports lacking information on an individual's place of birth and prior names[27]—a response exemplifying the inherent vulnerability of an economic development program largely predicated on selling ease of admission to other countries. Such strategies, born of desperation, reflect

---

[23] *See* ECONOMIST, *supra* note 3. On the use of such strategies by small jurisdictions more generally, see Naren Prasad, *Small but Smart: Small States in the Global System*, in THE DIPLOMACIES OF SMALL STATES: BETWEEN VULNERABILITY AND RESILIENCE 41, 43–44, 48, 53–59 (Andrew F. Cooper & Timothy M. Shaw eds., 2009).

[24] *See supra* Chapter 7.B.

[25] *See* Jason Clenfield, *This Swiss Lawyer Is Helping Governments Get Rich off Selling Passports*, BLOOMBERGMARKETS, Mar. 11, 2015, http://www.bloomberg.com/news/articles/2015-03-11/passport-king-christian-kalin-helps-nations-sell-citizenship.

[26] *See* Ian Young, *St Kitts and Nevis Recalls Passports over Security Concerns from Canada and US*, S. CHINA MORNING POST, Dec. 9, 2014, http://www.scmp.com/news/world/article/1659120/st-kitts-and-nevis-recalls-passports-over-security-concerns-canada-and-us.

[27] *See* Clenfield, *supra* note 25.

the instability and host of challenges that inhibit development of real, value-added cross-border financial services of the sort exhibited by the MDSJs studied in Part II.

The Netherlands Antilles provides another vivid example of failure to invest in real, value-added cross-border financial services capacity, which ultimately undercut the effort to develop a vibrant financial center of the sort achieved by the MDSJs. In the Netherlands Antilles, however, events transpired in a very different manner from that observed in Nauru and other South Pacific jurisdictions. Whereas Nauru's failure reflects heavy (perhaps even exclusive) reliance upon secrecy in a desperate attempt to profit through the sale of sovereignty, the Netherlands Antilles' failure reflects ill-considered reliance on an unstable treaty-based tax advantage.

In 1954, Sint Maarten, Curaçao, and other Dutch possessions in the Caribbean became the Netherlands Antilles—a part of the Kingdom of the Netherlands that endured for about 50 years before the citizens of Sint Maarten and Curaçao voted in referenda to become self-governing (ultimately taking effect in October 2010).[28] During its formal existence, however, the Netherlands Antilles broadly resembled the other jurisdictions studied in this book, being quite small in land area and population, with limited natural resources. Sint Maarten is just 34 square kilometers in land area (approximately one-fifth of Washington, DC's size) with a population of approximately 37,000 in 2014,[29] and Curaçao is 444 square kilometers (approximately twice Washington, DC's size) with a population of approximately 148,000 in July 2015.[30] Reflecting the lack of natural resources, the Spanish dubbed the area "islas inutiles, or 'useless islands,' and surrendered them without serious resistance to the Dutch in 1634."[31] Like the jurisdictions studied in Part II of this book, the Netherlands Antilles endeavored in the twentieth century to create a vibrant financial center[32]—yet unlike them, the Netherlands Antilles ultimately failed.

---

[28] Sint Maarten's referendum occurred in 2000, and Curaçao's occurred in 2005 and 2009. *See* CENTRAL INTELLIGENCE AGENCY, THE WORLD FACTBOOK: CURACAO, https://www.cia.gov/library/publications/the-world-factbook/geos/cc.html (last updated Apr. 26, 2016); CENTRAL INTELLIGENCE AGENCY, THE WORLD FACTBOOK: SINT MAARTEN, https://www.cia.gov/library/publications/the-world-factbook/geos/sk.html (last updated Apr. 27, 2016).

[29] *See* CENTRAL INTELLIGENCE AGENCY, THE WORLD FACTBOOK: SINT MAARTEN, *supra* note 28.

[30] *See* CENTRAL INTELLIGENCE AGENCY, THE WORLD FACTBOOK: CURACAO, *supra* note 28.

[31] Craig M. Boise & Andrew P. Morriss, *Change, Dependency, and Regime Plasticity in Offshore Financial Intermediation: The Saga of the Netherlands Antilles*, 45 TEX. INT'L L.J. 377, 384 (2009).

[32] The Netherlands Antilles' cross-border financial industry was principally based in Curaçao. *See* Sharman, *supra* note 7, at 505. Today, "the mainstays of this small island economy" are said to include tourism, petroleum refining, and "offshore finance," with almost 84 percent of GDP arising from services, yet per capita GDP remains low, at around $15,000—substantially below Sint Maarten, where the economy is largely based on tourism. *See* CENTRAL INTELLIGENCE AGENCY, THE WORLD FACTBOOK: CURACAO, *supra* note 28; CENTRAL INTELLIGENCE AGENCY, THE WORLD FACTBOOK: SINT MAARTEN, *supra* note 28.

The Netherlands Antilles' prominence in cross-border finance, while it lasted, rested on a narrow and unstable foundation—a peculiar tax advantage derivative not of the Netherlands Antilles' own law, but rather arising from their tax treaty with the United States. In their extensive case study, Craig Boise and Andrew Morriss explain that the Netherlands Antilles' advantage rested entirely on the so-called "Antilles sandwich"—a structure that "exploited the then-existing difference between high withholding tax rates that applied to interest payments made by U.S. borrowers to foreign persons, and the low rates of tax or outright tax exemption that applied to interest payments made by U.S. borrowers to residents of the Netherlands Antilles."[33] As a consequence, the treaty effectively permitted corporate borrowers in the United States to establish subsidiaries in the Netherlands Antilles, which could then "issue Eurobonds to foreign investors and on-lend the proceeds of the bond offering" back home. The U.S. corporate parents, then, would make interest payments to their Netherlands Antilles subsidiaries, which would ultimately pass along interest payments to the holders of the Eurobonds. "In this manner," Boise and Morriss explain, "U.S. corporate borrowers gained access to the Eurodollar market while the interest payments they made to foreign investors were subject only to residence taxation in their own countries, plus the minimal Antilles tax applicable to the interest-rate spread (profits) retained by the finance subsidiary."[34]

This treaty-based competitive advantage existed from 1955—when the U.S.-Netherlands tax treaty, including this exemption from withholding tax, was extended to the Netherlands Antilles (following shortly upon the jurisdiction's formal creation in 1954)—and while it lasted, it "sparked an economic boom."[35] Indeed, "Eurobond issues through the Antilles for a while represented nearly all US bond issues."[36] The latent vulnerability to unilateral revocation ultimately manifested itself in 1984, however, when the United States finally decided "to eliminate the withholding tax on interest payments made to foreign lenders, which rendered the interest withholding provision of the U.S.-Netherlands Antilles tax treaty unnecessary." Following this move, "the bulk of the Antilles financial intermediation sector was wiped out."[37] As their Finance Minister put it, the subsequent decision of the United States to cancel its tax treaty with the Netherlands Antilles constituted

---

[33] *See* Boise & Morriss, *supra* note 31, at 379–80. *See also* RONEN PALAN, RICHARD MURPHY & CHRISTIAN CHAVAGNEUX, TAX HAVENS: HOW GLOBALIZATION REALLY WORKS 144 (2010).

[34] *See* Boise & Morriss, *supra* note 31, at 409. *See also* Reuven S. Avi-Yonah, *Globalization, Tax Competition, and the Fiscal Crisis of the Welfare State*, 113 HARV. L. REV. 1573, 1580 (2000).

[35] *See* Boise & Morriss, *supra* note 31, at 409.

[36] TAX JUSTICE NETWORK, NARRATIVE REPORT ON CURAÇAO 2 (2015).

[37] *See* Boise & Morriss, *supra* note 31, at 380–82. *See also* Sharman, *supra* note 7, at 506; TAX JUSTICE NETWORK, *supra* note 36, at 2–3.

"a national disaster."[38] Today, Curaçao—"by far the dominant player among the former Netherlands Antilles' islands" in terms of cross-border financial activity—is regarded as "a tiny player."[39]

Although the Netherlands Antilles possessed certain strengths resembling those exhibited by the MDSJs, it ultimately failed to undertake the breadth and depth of strategic investments that have brought the MDSJs such extraordinary success. Curaçao had some historical experience with cross-border finance, having been a popular site for reincorporation of Dutch multinational corporations during World War II—indeed, Curaçao was "among the first of the offshore jurisdictions."[40] Furthermore, the Netherlands Antilles (once formed) was granted "virtually complete autonomy" in regulation, including "almost complete legal autonomy on fiscal matters"[41]—the critical resource of financial and regulatory innovation, as we have seen. Yet in the 1980s, by which time U.S. tax authorities had vocally objected that the tax treaty with the Netherlands Antilles represented a de facto "one-way treaty with the world" (via formation of legal entities there, a problem compounded by "bearer shares" concealing beneficial ownership[42]), authorities in the Netherlands Antilles failed to perceive and respond aggressively to their extreme vulnerability.

As Boise and Morriss observe, "to survive in the midst of change requires legislative agility"—yet the Netherlands Antilles lacked "flexibility and agility in responding to changes in the economic environment and in the legal regimes in both competing and onshore jurisdictions." In the 1980s they made limited attempts to extend the use of existing structures into captive insurance, but "unlike Bermuda and Cayman, [they] failed to create any specialized legal or regulatory structures for captive insurers and eventually lost momentum compared to those jurisdictions." Indeed, "it was nearly a decade after the cancellation of the U.S. tax treaty before Antilles passed any significant legislation to create exploitable legal differences that would resuscitate its offshore financial sector."[43] As Boise and Morriss sum it up, they "failed to adapt in time to the changes in U.S. attitudes and did not develop substitute financial intermediation and regulatory arbitrage products to replace the Antilles sandwich structures before its demise."[44]

Several weaknesses, it would seem, contributed to this puzzling inaction in the face of predictable decline. As a threshold matter, the Netherlands Antilles lacked

---

[38] See Boise & Morriss, supra note 31, at 424–26. See also PALAN ET AL., supra note 33, at 144.

[39] TAX JUSTICE NETWORK, supra note 36, at 1–2.

[40] See Boise & Morriss, supra note 31, at 393–95, 406. See also TAX JUSTICE NETWORK, supra note 36, at 1–2.

[41] See Boise & Morriss, supra note 31, at 398–99.

[42] See id. at 414–17.

[43] Id. at 432–37.

[44] Id. at 382.

the degree of regulatory autonomy possessed by British Overseas Territories and Crown Dependencies, and the Dutch government did not promote offshore finance as a means of economic development as the British government has.[45] At the same time, they "failed to expand and upgrade [their] financial regulatory bodies to build confidence in the onshore business and regulatory communities in [their] ability to control illegal activity, as occurred in other jurisdictions."[46]

These weaknesses were compounded by practical inability to perform the sorts of cultural and geographic bridging functions performed by the MDSJs studied in Part II. Although there is "some English common law influence" in Curaçao's legal system, it is fundamentally "based on Dutch civil law"[47]—a system unfamiliar to U.S. financiers and lawyers, which Boise and Morriss characterize as a "handicap." The example of Switzerland (discussed in Chapter 8) suggests that reliance on civil law does not, in itself, prevent the development of vibrant financial services. The Netherlands Antilles further hampered their own development, however, by requiring the filing of legal documents in Dutch—"a practice one attorney in a competing jurisdiction characterized as 'medieval' and which increased transactions costs for non-Dutch companies." Once the U.S. tax treaty was canceled, the Netherlands Antilles predictably found itself unable to compete with nearby jurisdictions that "offered familiar, common-law, English-language legal systems."[48]

Overall, the cases of Nauru and the Netherlands Antilles present jurisdictions that appear to have failed precisely because they lacked the full strengths, and failed to embrace the range of competitive strategies, described in the MDSJ ideal type set forth in Chapter 3. Although I have focused here on just a couple illustrative cases, it is important to observe that they are hardly unique. Barbados, for example, presents another vivid example of a treaty-based tax advantage enjoyed by a small jurisdiction similarly disappearing at the unilateral direction of the United States.[49] Others, meanwhile, have drawn comparisons similar to those drawn here, suggesting that among

---

[45]  *See id.* at 437, 447.

[46]  *Id.* at 414.

[47]  CENTRAL INTELLIGENCE AGENCY, THE WORLD FACTBOOK: CURACAO, *supra* note 28.

[48]  *See* Boise & Morriss, *supra* note 31, at 406, 414, 426.

[49]  *See* JOINT COMM. ON TAXATION, JCX-55-04, EXPLANATION OF PROPOSED PROTOCOL TO THE INCOME TAX TREATY BETWEEN THE UNITED STATES AND BARBADOS (2004). A small island jurisdiction in the Eastern Caribbean, see CENTRAL INTELLIGENCE AGENCY, THE WORLD FACTBOOK: BARBADOS, https://www.cia.gov/library/publications/the-world-factbook/geos/bb.html (last updated Apr. 26, 2016), Barbados for a time benefited from a provision in its U.S. tax treaty that permitted "a company that is legally resident in Barbados to claim the benefits of reduced U.S. withholding tax rates by virtue of being publicly traded, even in cases in which the company has no meaningful economic presence in Barbados and is subject to only nominal levels of taxation there." This prompted "corporate inversion" transactions by U.S. multinational companies that had the effect of "erod[ing] the U.S. tax base"—until the provision was replaced in 2004. *See* JOINT COMM. ON TAXATION, *supra*, at 2.

jurisdictions commonly regarded as successful "tax havens" today, those more dependent on narrower, secrecy-based advantages will likely face greater future vulnerabilities than those with more diversified financial services offerings and economies. Gabriel Zucman, for example, compares Switzerland, which "does not live off of financial opacity" and "would do very well if it completely disappeared," with Luxembourg, which has prospered "by commercializing its own sovereignty" in a manner resembling other "microstates," and now hosts a financial center that, Zucman charges, "literally lives off of the accounting manipulation of multinationals and the fraud of individuals"[50]—a business model clearly vulnerable to concerted European regulatory responses.

Overall, although both Nauru and the Netherlands Antilles are small and poorly endowed in natural resources, turning to cross-border finance for reasons broadly resonating with those encountered among the jurisdictions studied in Part II, and although both possess appreciable regulatory autonomy of the sort permitting financial and regulatory innovation, neither could pull it off in the end. Neither jurisdiction mustered substantial investment in human capital, professional networks, and related institutional structures; neither managed to diversify their offerings through creation of innovative regulatory regimes; neither developed the oversight capacities to cultivate trust with foreign market actors and regulators; and neither managed to perform bridging functions of the sort that have typified MDSJs. Consequently, abusive practices proliferated—and without real, value-added financial services to balance the ledger, their reputations for probity and propriety predictably deteriorated.

Accordingly, these would seem to be cases in which the "tax/secrecy haven" label is fairly and accurately deployed—and it is precisely their reliance on this approach that brought them to failure. Conversely, the contrast with the jurisdictions investigated in Part II suggests that adherence to the MDSJ paradigm actually did play a causal role in the extraordinary, and far more stable, successes achieved by Bermuda, Dubai, Singapore, Hong Kong, Switzerland, and Delaware.

## C. Successful Large Jurisdictions

By any coherent measure, New York and London fall at the opposite end of the spectrum from the likes of Nauru and the Netherlands Antilles, representing the two largest and most significant financial centers in the world.[51] (Their rankings by one

---

[50] *See* GABRIEL ZUCMAN, THE HIDDEN WEALTH OF NATIONS: THE SCOURGE OF TAX HAVENS 83–92 (Teresa Lavender Fagan trans., 2015).

[51] *See generally* MARK YEANDLE & NICK DANEV, THE GLOBAL FINANCIAL CENTRES INDEX 15 (2014) (index sponsored by the Qatar Financial Centre Authority and produced by the Z/Yen Group); Z/Yen Group Limited, *Global Financial Centres Index 19: Information Pack,* http://www.longfinance.net/

influential measure of financial center competitiveness are reflected in Figure 10.2 below.) Indeed, some have concluded that they represent the only "truly global financial centers,"[52] and insofar as they inhabit two of the world's largest domestic economies,[53] they do not fit the MDSJ paradigm that I have presented in this book. This section examines similarities and differences with the MDSJs studied in Part II to illuminate the degree to which the characteristics and strategies that I associate with the MDSJs are truly unique to that category. Broadly, these major global financial centers exhibit certain traits akin to the MDSJs—notably the geographic and cultural concentration of their financial centers—while differing starkly in other respects—notably their locations, historically positioning them as gateways to major domestic economies, their relative degrees of regulatory autonomy, and their greater breadth of financial services offerings, underwritten by the greater credibility that each derives from the support of a large sovereign. This latter category of comparisons also helps to illuminate further the types of specialized roles that MDSJs, in particular, play in cross-border finance relative to the world's largest and most diversified financial centers.

As we have seen, MDSJs (and would-be MDSJs) look to cross-border finance as a promising economic development strategy that remains available to them notwithstanding their small size and relative lack of natural resources. The dominant global centers in New York and London, by contrast, arose in very different ways.

New York's rise to global dominance, and the manner in which it has maintained that position, reveal the differences between global financial centers and the MDSJs most starkly—the most obvious distinction being that New York, embedded within the enormous national economy of the United States, "will inevitably have a very large number of domestic borrowers, lenders, and investors."[54] New York's

---

global-financial-centre-index-19/992-gfci-19.html (reporting that, in every iteration of the Global Financial Centres Index, London and New York have each ranked first or second, while Singapore and Hong Kong have each ranked third or fourth). *See also* DOUGLAS W. ARNER ET AL., ASSESSING HONG KONG AS AN INTERNATIONAL FINANCIAL CENTRE 19–21 (2014) (observing that Hong Kong, though generally regarded as third largest, in fact lags London and New York substantially in portfolio assets and in foreign exchange markets); TAN CHWEE HUAT & JOSEPH LIM YOUNG SAIN, SINGAPORE AND HONG KONG AS COMPETING FINANCIAL CENTRES 25–28 (2007); THECITYUK, KEY FACTS ABOUT THE UK AS AN INTERNATIONAL FINANCIAL CENTRE 6–7 (July 2015).

[52] *See* Ronen Palan, *International Financial Centers: The British-Empire, City-States and Commercially Oriented Politics,* 11 THEORETICAL INQUIRIES L. 149, 155 (2010).

[53] In terms of GDP, the United States had the largest economy in the world in 2014 with approximately $17.4 trillion, and the United Kingdom had the sixth largest economy with approximately $3.0 trillion. *See* World Bank, *GDP at Market Prices (Current US$),* http://data.worldbank.org/indicator/NY.GDP. MKTP.CD?order=wbapi_data_value_2013+wbapi_data_value+wbapi_data_value-last&sort=desc (last visited Apr. 2016).

[54] *See* SASKIA SASSEN, CITIES IN A WORLD ECONOMY 216 (4th ed. 2012). Tokyo was long considered by many to rate with New York and London as a global financial center, *see, e.g. id.,* but New York and London

| Jurisdiction | Rank |
|---|---|
| London | 1 |
| New York | 2 |
| Singapore | 3 |
| Hong Kong | 4 |
| Tokyo | 5 |
| Zurich | 6 |
| Washington DC | 7 |
| San Francisco | 8 |
| Boston | 9 |
| Toronto | 10 |
| Chicago | 11 |
| Seoul | 12 |
| Dubai | 13 |
| Luxembourg | 14 |
| Geneva | 15 |
| Shanghai | 16 |
| Sydney | 17 |
| Frankfurt | 18 |
| Shenzhen | 19 |
| Osaka | 20 |
| — | — |
| Beijing | 23 |
| — | — |
| Bermuda | 50 |

FIGURE 10.2 Global Financial Centres Index, 2016 Rankings.*
* *See* Z/Yen Group Limited, *Global Financial Centres Index 19: Information Pack,* http://www.longfinance.net/global-financial-centre-index-19/992-gfci-19.html (last visited Apr. 2016).

rise indeed began with commerce, driven by its geographic superiority as a port offering deep water at the mouth of a substantial river (the Hudson), an easily defensible island (Manhattan, "surrounded on three sides by water"), and a central location along the Eastern Seaboard (relative to other early ports).[55] New York's geographic superiority in turn led to the development of manufacturing capacities that

tend increasingly to be placed in a category unto themselves. *See, e.g.,* Palan, *supra* note 52, at 155. *See also* V. Le Leslé et al., *Why Complementarity Matters for Stability—Hong Kong SAR and Singapore as Asian Financial Centers* 6 (IMF Working Paper WP/14/119, 2014) ("Tokyo is no longer perceived as a truly global financial center, but rather as a more . . . domestic FC with a very large market.").

[55] *See* Edward L. Glaeser, *Urban Colossus: Why Is New York America's Largest City?,* FRBNY Econ. Pol'y Rev., Dec. 2005, at 9–12.

"transformed products from outside the United States into finished goods to be sold within the country"—the three prime examples being sugar refining, publishing, and garments. In each case, as "New York was a hub and products were dispersed throughout the country and the world after entry into that hub, it made perfect sense to perform the manufacturing in the city."[56] The transport hub and manufacturing industries were each reinforced, then, by New York's further role in the late nineteenth century as "the entryway for immigrants into the United States." As economist Edward Glaeser has observed, "[e]thnic neighborhoods made the transition to the New World easier, and New York as a city acquired over time a remarkable capacity to cater to immigrant needs." This was facilitated, he adds, by "the traditional New York industries, especially the garment trade, [which] were able to increase in scale to accommodate extra labor without a huge drop in wages."[57] By 1860 "New York was far and away the biggest and most important city in the United States," dominating shipping, immigration, and increasingly manufacturing as well, and as ships grew larger over the course of the nineteenth century, "a centralizing tendency" favored larger ports such as New York that "could accept their bigger cargoes."[58]

Like its manufacturing capacity, New York's role as a financial center ultimately traces back to its superiority as a port. Wall Street, Glaeser observes, "has its origins as an organization designed around sharing risk on sea voyages." And with respect to finance more generally, geography favored New York over other major U.S. cities as well. Although Philadelphia was "a close rival" in the early nineteenth century "as a center for trading stocks and bonds," New York ultimately prevailed due to its "greater connection to England," which "became increasingly important in the late nineteenth century as English capital financed American development"; the greater local demand for financing arising from its growing dominance in manufacturing; and ultimately the "great incentive to agglomerate in finance," reflecting "the returns to knowing the latest fact." As Glaeser explains, "this meant that once New York had a slight edge, the edge turned into a complete preponderance as the financial community came to the city to obtain access to the latest information."[59]

Until the 1920s New York's prominence was a function of its roles as principal port, manufacturing center, and provider of domestically oriented finance; New York was not an "international" financial center, as such, before that time. As Mira Wilkins explains, however, although the United States was "a debtor nation

---

[56] *Id.* at 7.
[57] *See id.* at 8–9, 18.
[58] *See id.* at 10, 13.
[59] *See id.* at 20–22.

in world accounts" before World War I, it did possess "certain distinguishing features that made it unlike contemporary debtors," setting the stage for a rise to global prominence—the sheer magnitude of the U.S. economy and industry, "drawing in more foreign capital than any other single country"; a tradition of domestic financing for industry, yet with some degree of reliance on foreign capital, notably to finance the railroads; a growing number of "multinational enterprises"; a growing number of investment bankers with "skills in intermediating domestic and foreign capital, into American public and private uses"; additional banks that, "while neither national nor international in terms of branches, none the less had become large, sophisticated money market institutions"; and, finally, the New York Stock Exchange—largely domestically oriented, though unique in magnitude among debtor nations.[60]

Following World War I, these latent strengths manifested themselves as the United States filled the economic and financial void created by the war's devastation of Europe. As the United Kingdom—which had previously been "the foremost creditor nation"—receded, the U.S. dollar grew increasingly dominant in international trade, and the United States became a significant creditor nation at a time when there were few other contenders for global economic dominance. "New York became a truly international financial hub, as never before in its history," poised to "transform its pre-war financial infrastructure to serve the needs of America's domestic economy and the world economy as well."[61]

Critically, 1920s New York developed "institutional structures ... to combine the inward investments with the far more substantial outward ones." This included bringing the growing number of domestic securities issuances to the expanding global market for U.S. securities, while at the same time handling the growing number of "dollar-denominated securities issued and traded in the United States to finance governments and corporations outside the United States"—the latter reflecting the increasing perception abroad that the United States was "where abundant capital seemed available."[62] At the same time, there was a growing market among foreign investors for foreign securities issuances in the United States, reflecting the

---

[60] See Mira Wilkins, *Cosmopolitan Finance in the 1920s: New York's Emergence as an International Financial Centre*, in THE STATE, THE FINANCIAL SYSTEM AND ECONOMIC MODERNIZATION 271, 271–72 (Richard Sylla, Richard Tilly & Gabriel Tortella eds., 1999) (emphasis removed). *See also* ARMAND VAN DORMAEL, THE POWER OF MONEY 11–12 (1997) (describing J.P. Morgan's personal role in bridging British and American finance in the late nineteenth century).

[61] See Wilkins, *supra* note 60, at 272–74. *See also* CATHERINE R. SCHENK, HONG KONG AS AN INTERNATIONAL FINANCIAL CENTRE: EMERGENCE AND DEVELOPMENT 1945–65, at 120 (2001); VAN DORMAEL, *supra* note 60, at 16–17; Glaeser, *supra* note 55, at 22.

[62] See Wilkins, *supra* note 60, at 275–77.

"higher coupon rate" often available in New York, relative to London (thought necessary to attract U.S. interest in unfamiliar foreign issuers); arbitrage opportunities; and the ability this offered to "evade turnover taxes and income taxes," as well as "restrictions imposed on foreign issues," at home[63]—an indication that New York's rise as an international financial center was at least partly aided by opportunities offered to avoid regulation imposed elsewhere.

Indeed, the foregoing steps in New York's financial development were typified by "the relative absence of American government participation." As Wilkins sums it up, "the story of cosmopolitan finance in the 1920s was one of virtually no regulation." New York rose to global prominence in the wake of World War I "not because of any action or lack of actions of the US government, but because the United States was where the capital and the capital markets were."[64] The crash of 1929 revealed "all kinds of market imperfections," to be sure, but in this period New York nevertheless did create "networks of information . . . and resource allocation" that now work in tandem with New Deal regulatory structures of the 1930s to undergird New York's global dominance in finance.[65] Today New York occupies the top echelon of global finance with London, followed by the dominant East Asian financial centers of Singapore and Hong Kong.[66] In the 2014 Z/Yen index of global financial centers, New York just edged out London for "the top spot" by "a shaky [and] statistically insignificant" margin,[67] but as of this writing London holds the top spot by a margin likewise considered "fairly insignificant."[68]

In certain respects there are clear commonalities between New York and other financial centers, including the MDSJs studied in Part II of this book. Notably, "Wall Street" reflects the same "great incentive to agglomerate in finance"[69] that one observes in all jurisdictions prominent in cross-border finance—including Bermuda, Dubai, Singapore, Hong Kong, Switzerland, and Delaware. Likewise, we have observed some degree of dependence on low regulatory burdens (or virtual lack thereof)

---

[63] *See id.* at 277–78.

[64] *See id.* at 280–82.

[65] *See id.* at 283–85.

[66] *See* YEANDLE & DANEV, *supra* note 51, at 2–6; Z/Yen Group Limited, *supra* note 51 (reporting that, in every iteration of the Global Financial Centres Index, London and New York have each ranked first or second, while Singapore and Hong Kong have each ranked third or fourth).

[67] YEANDLE & DANEV, *supra* note 51, at 1. *See also* John Glover, *New York Strips London of Mantle as World's Top Financial Center,* BLOOMBERG, Mar. 16, 2014, http://www.bloomberg.com/news/2014-03-15/new-york-steals-london-s-mantle-as-world-s-top-financial-center.html; James Pickford, *New York Ousts London as Top Financial Centre,* FIN. TIMES, Mar. 15, 2014, http://www.ft.com/cms/s/0/9a8fbf6a-ab89-11e3-aad9-00144feab7de.html.

[68] *See* Press Release, Z/Yen Group Limited, Global Financial Centers Index: London Remains on Top and Singapore Climbs to Third Place (Apr. 6, 2016); Z/Yen Group Limited, *supra* note 51.

[69] Glaeser, *supra* note 55, at 22.

in New York's rise to international prominence in the 1920s, just as we have observed in the early days of other financially prominent jurisdictions. Yet as the foregoing capsule history demonstrates, New York's emergence and persistence as a global financial center rest on a set of strengths—some serendipitous, some cultivated—that differ fundamentally from what we have observed elsewhere. Ultimately, New York became the "urban colossus"[70] of the twentieth and twenty-first centuries due to its strengths as an entry point to the economic colossus of those centuries—the United States itself.[71] Being located within the United States, and facing no substantial competition as a financial entry point to the world's largest economy,[72] New York encounters the financial world from a position of extraordinary—and fundamentally unique—innate strength. Accordingly, although the quality of New York-based law and regulation, and regard for New York's courts, may be consequential factors in attracting cross-border financial business,[73] New York's dominance as a global financial center is not fundamentally derivative of the perceived attractiveness of its regulatory environment to anything like the degree observed in jurisdictions such as Bermuda, Dubai, Singapore, Hong Kong, Switzerland, and Delaware.

The historical foundation for London's dominance in finance loosely resembled New York's, but has evolved since the 1960s in a manner that casts an interesting light on the development strategies of the MDSJs themselves. By the late sixteenth century London was already "the world's busiest maritime port" and "the major European entrepôt on the transatlantic and Asian trade routes," making it "the most important centre for trading cargoes and commodities."[74] During the seventeenth and eighteenth centuries, as Britain's naval power and empire expanded, London's prosperity grew accordingly, and by the nineteenth century the city surpassed Amsterdam as "the leading international financial centre."[75] Following

---

[70] *Id.* (thus referring to New York in his title).

[71] *See* Palan, *supra* note 52, at 158.

[72] *See* Glaeser, *supra* note 55, at 21 ("New York's move into finance and management is not really paralleled by any of the other older [U.S.] cities."). This contrasts starkly with Hong Kong—arguably analogous as an entry point to China—which faces real competition from other domestic financial centers that, given the current political troubles in Hong Kong, might well find governmental favor moving forward. *See supra* Chapter 7.B.

[73] *See, e.g.,* STEPHEN J. CHOI & A.C. PRITCHARD, SECURITIES REGULATION: CASES AND ANALYSIS 16 (3d ed. 2012) ("The NYSE is not only the largest securities market in the United States in terms of market value, it also provides a good degree of the regulation governing securities transactions."); Jo Braithwaite, *Law after Lehmans* 8–9 n.48 (London Sch. of Econ. Law, Society and Economy Working Papers 11/2014) (observing the dominance of English and New York law and courts in international financial transactions).

[74] RICHARD ROBERTS & DAVID KYNASTON, CITY STATE: A CONTEMPORARY HISTORY OF THE CITY OF LONDON AND HOW MONEY TRIUMPHED 183 (2002).

[75] *See id.* at 4. *See also* SCHENK, *supra* note 61, at 120; Catherine R. Schenk, *International Financial Centres, 1958–1971: Competitiveness and Complementarity, in* EUROPEAN BANKS AND THE AMERICAN

World War I, however, as described above, London's financial center was surpassed by New York's—a development mapping onto the decline of the British Empire and British manufacturing (discussed below), as well as the United States' rise as the world's leading creditor nation. Accordingly, over the course of the twentieth century London effectively lost the sort of internal economy that had previously supported its status as a global financial center, and that underwrote New York's rise.

Notwithstanding the foregoing, however, London today rivals New York as the other truly global financial center. As of 2014 the United Kingdom had a trade surplus of $95 billion in financial services, "more than the combined surpluses of the next three leading countries (US, Switzerland and Luxembourg)."[76] The United Kingdom "accounts for 41 percent of global foreign exchange trading," with "[t]wice as many US dollars . . . traded on the foreign exchange market in the UK than in the US."[77] Likewise the United Kingdom is the global leader in international bond trading "with an estimated 70 percent of secondary market turnover" and interest rate derivatives trading "with a 49 percent share in 2013,"[78] and is second (to the United States) in international bonds outstanding, hedge funds, and private equity funds.[79] The United Kingdom is also "the largest centre for cross-border banking with 17 percent of the outstanding value of international bank lending" as of September 2014, and is "one of the leading global centres for Islamic finance."[80] At the same time, the United Kingdom is a global leader in maritime services, legal services, and dispute resolution,[81] and hosts "the world's largest international insurance market," including Lloyd's.[82]

Today London is widely considered the world's most "global city" (with only New York coming close).[83] As Saskia Sassen describes it, "London, with its enormous presence of foreign firms from all over the world and its strong Eurodollar and foreign-exchange markets, is extremely international, whereas New York and Tokyo, with their vast national economies, will inevitably have a very large number of domestic borrowers, lenders, and investors."[84] According to the 2014 Z/Yen rankings by financial industry sectors, London ranked first in "government & regulatory"

---

CHALLENGE: COMPETITION AND COOPERATION IN INTERNATIONAL BANKING UNDER BRETTON WOODS 74, 78–79 (Stefano Battilossi & Youssef Cassis eds., 2002).

[76] THECITYUK, *supra* note 51, at 3, 6.

[77] *Id.* at 5, 11.

[78] *Id.* at 13, 15.

[79] *Id.* at 13–14.

[80] *Id.* at 10, 18. *See also* ROBERTS & KYNASTON, *supra* note 74, at 67–71.

[81] *See* THECITYUK, *supra* note 51, at 5, 16–18, 20–21.

[82] *See* ROBERTS & KYNASTON, *supra* note 74, at 74–75.

[83] *See id.* at 180–83.

[84] SASSEN, *supra* note 54, at 216.

and "professional services," second in "investment management" and "insurance," and third in "banking."[85]

Having gradually lost the sort of "vast national economy" to which Sassen refers, how did the United Kingdom—and, specifically, London—regain the global stature in finance that it lost in the wake of World War I? London's resurgence effectively dates to the early 1960s,[86] and to understand how it unfolded we must return in greater detail to a series of events treated only briefly in prior chapters of the book[87]—the Euromarkets, which in their modern manifestation trace their origins to London.

As the "governor of the imperial engine," London had long exhibited "a decisively outward-looking character"[88] reminiscent of other jurisdictions explored in this book, and in the 1960s London effectively created a new form of "offshore" market—a market for cheaper finance outside one's own jurisdiction.[89] The emergence of this market in London has been called "the major development" in finance "since the appearance of banknotes."[90] Financial activity in London began to pick up, to be sure, following World War II as international trade expanded,[91] but the real explosion followed the development of the so-called Eurodollar market in the 1960s, which allowed the City to build its revival upon steadily increasing holdings of U.S. dollars outside the United States.[92]

It is worth pausing here to clarify the terminology. In this context, "euro" refers not to the shared European currency, or even to the European continent—rather, it refers to dealings outside the jurisdiction of any given currency. The term "Euromarket" refers generally to "an international financial market (or rather a series of markets) specializing in nonresident finance."[93] The term "Eurodollar," then, refers to "a deposit denominated in United States dollars at any bank located outside the United States, including a foreign branch of a United States bank," and likewise the term "Eurobond" refers to bonds denominated in a particular currency but issued outside that country (say, dollar-denominated bonds issued in London).[94] It is from these forms of assets and transactions that London's modern financial center grew.

---

[85] *See* YEANDLE & DANEV, *supra* note 51, at 1–5, 31.

[86] *See* ROBERTS & KYNASTON, *supra* note 74, at 4.

[87] *See supra* Chapters 2.C, 6.A.

[88] TAX JUSTICE NETWORK, NARRATIVE REPORT ON UNITED KINGDOM 3 (2015).

[89] *See* ROBERTS & KYNASTON, *supra* note 74, at 63–64.

[90] VAN DORMAEL, *supra* note 60, at 141.

[91] *See* ROBERTS & KYNASTON, *supra* note 74, at 62–63.

[92] *See id.* at 88; VAN DORMAEL, *supra* note 60, at 93–94.

[93] Palan, *supra* note 52, at 152.

[94] VAN DORMAEL, *supra* note 60, at 90, 98–99.

Although a nascent and little-known Eurodollar market emerged between the 1920s and the 1950s to service dollar-denominated transactions for Communist governments,[95] the modern Eurodollar market grew from the effort of U.S. banks to end run "restrictive financial regulations"—starting in the late 1950s and accelerating through the 1960s and early 1970s.[96] During this period, the United States moved from a substantial trade surplus to a substantial trade deficit,[97] and enormous dollar surpluses accumulated outside the United States due to a variety of factors, including Cold War- and Vietnam-related military spending, growing "foreign direct investment by US corporations," and increased borrowing by foreigners in the United States—the result of "banking regulations such as Regulation Q [that] continued to keep American interest rates, particularly short-term rates, artificially lower than in other countries."[98]

The U.S. policy response to this outflow of dollars was to "attack it directly . . . by restricting the ability of the leading banks and other Wall Street institutions to mediate dollar outflows"—President Kennedy's 1963 Interest Equalization Tax representing one such effort.[99] As Catherine Schenk explains, however, the U.K. government took a very different approach to the challenge of "how to ensure convertibility at a fixed exchange rate while supporting persistent balance of payments deficits and encouraging the use of the national currency as a reserve currency." Whereas the United States sought "to constrain the flow of capital from the US economy to the rest of the world while not discouraging the use of dollar balances held abroad," the United Kingdom sought "to encourage the activities of London as an international financial centre," which "benefited the balance of payments by generating a persistent short-term capital inflow and invisible earnings."[100] The upshot of this combination of policy responses across the Atlantic was "an acceleration of foreign banking subsidiaries in London," where higher rates of interest were permitted. "From 1965 to 1971, 69 foreign banks opened branches in London, of which almost 40 percent were American banks."[101]

---

[95] *See id.* at 91–93.

[96] *See* Richard Sylla, *United States Banks and Europe: Strategy and Attitudes, in* EUROPEAN BANKS AND THE AMERICAN CHALLENGE, *supra* note 75, at 53, 56, 65–66.

[97] *See* VAN DORMAEL, *supra* note 60, at 71.

[98] *See* Sylla, *supra* note 96, at 63–64. *See also* VAN DORMAEL, *supra* note 60, at 80. As Sylla explains, U.S. corporations "were establishing production and distribution facilities in Europe to avoid having to pay Europe's common tariffs on imports." Sylla, *supra* note 96, at 62.

[99] *See* Sylla, *supra* note 96, at 64–65. *See also* PALAN ET AL., *supra* note 33, at 131–35.

[100] Schenk, *supra* note 75, at 90–92, 97. *See also* RAWI ABDELAL, CAPITAL RULES: THE CONSTRUCTION OF GLOBAL FINANCE 7–8 (2007); Palan, *supra* note 52, at 163–65.

[101] Schenk, *supra* note 75, at 85, 95.

As Armand Van Dormael summarizes it, the consequence was "the massive transfer of dollar lending in New York to Eurodollar lending in London, under the benevolent patronage of the Bank of England, outside the reach of any government supervision."[102] It is critical to observe that "the Bank of England tended to support the activities of the City of London"—in the first instance to bolster "the attractiveness of sterling," but increasingly "as a net earner for the balance of payments."[103] Indeed, Schenk concludes that "British authorities deliberately pursued policies that would attract customers for international finance to London," adding that in aid of this effort "there were no restrictions on the operation of overseas banks in London"[104]—a (non)regulatory inducement strongly resonating with criticisms directed toward small would-be financial centers today. Although "the precise policy and legal steps that gave rise to the Euromarket [are] somewhat vague," Ronen Palan notes that "the Bank of England's decision not to intervene in these sorts of transactions was interpreted in the context of the English common law to imply that the Bank regards certain types of financial transactions between nonresident parties undertaken in foreign currency as if they do not take place in the UK." Accordingly, the Euromarket flourished "due to a tacitly accepted understanding by which the Bank of England regarded certain types of financial transactions as if they were taking place elsewhere."[105]

As I have suggested above,[106] the global impacts of the foregoing developments were profound—indeed, it is not an overstatement to say that the advent of Eurodollars contributed directly to the demise of the Bretton Woods system of fixed exchange rates and the total internationalization of finance.[107] Under Bretton Woods, other currencies were fixed relative to the U.S. dollar and "the United States agreed in official transactions with other countries to exchange dollars for gold at the rate of $35 per ounce"—an arrangement reflecting the fact that "the US government possessed most of the world's monetary gold" when the system was established. As dollar surpluses outside the United States grew through the 1960s, however, the "commitment and the ability of the United States to maintain dollar-gold convertibility began to be doubted by foreign leaders."[108] By the early 1970s, as Richard Sylla explains, the Nixon

---

[102] VAN DORMAEL, *supra* note 60, at 95. *See also* TAX JUSTICE NETWORK, *supra* note 88, at 4.

[103] Schenk, *supra* note 75, at 79, 85. *See also* PALAN ET AL., *supra* note 33, at 131–35; TAX JUSTICE NETWORK, *supra* note 88, at 4.

[104] Schenk, *supra* note 75, at 88–89.

[105] Palan, *supra* note 52, at 160–61. *See also* PALAN ET AL., *supra* note 33, at 132; VAN DORMAEL, *supra* note 60, at 93–94, 96–97.

[106] *See supra* Chapters 2.C, 6.A.

[107] *See* ROBERTS & KYNASTON, *supra* note 74, at 113–14.

[108] *See* Sylla, *supra* note 96, at 63–64. *See also* VAN DORMAEL, *supra* note 60, at 72–73, 76–77.

administration had "realized the inconsistencies of US policies that flooded the world with dollars while committing the country to redeem them with a relatively fixed stock of gold," and ultimately "they abandoned the dollar-gold link in steps from 1971 to 1973," moving the world "from a fixed to a floating exchange-rate regime."[109] This shift to floating exchange rates forced multinational businesses to grapple with currency risks,[110] prompting U.S. banks serving them "to stay in London, which had become the centre of the Eurocurrency markets and now would become the centre of foreign-exchange speculation and hedging." As of the mid-1970s, foreign banks "controlled more than half the total assets (sterling and foreign currency) of the UK banking sector, and nearly half of all the foreign-bank assets were American."[111]

More broadly, these developments gave rise to the global financial marketplace that many smaller jurisdictions now inhabit, governed by what Citicorp's Walter Wriston described as the "information standard"—the notion that "bad monetary and fiscal policies anywhere in the world are reflected within minutes on the Reuters screens in the trading rooms of the world," prompting money to move "where it is wanted" and "where it's well treated." This new reality, Wriston argued, had the effect of constraining—and perhaps even redefining—sovereignty itself, by "exerting a discipline on the countries of the world."[112] The competitive (and, perhaps inevitably, deregulatory) forces unleashed led directly to the expansion of the Euromarkets beyond London—and particularly to smaller jurisdictions, which found the opportunities presented deeply attractive, for reasons explored in Part II of this book. As Palan suggests, the U.K. corporate tax left financial institutions open to other possibilities, and the fact that "the Euromarket was open only to non-residents [left] British banks and corporations paradoxically at a disadvantage" and looking for "residency in other British-dominated jurisdictions to allow them to participate in the Euromarket." Small jurisdictions—particularly those with ties to the United Kingdom—were enthusiastic hosts, and (as discussed above) the U.K. government recognized that fostering "offshore" finance in such jurisdictions could reduce their dependence on U.K. aid.[113]

Notwithstanding London's decidedly commercial origins, and the outgrowth of finance from the strength of the domestic economy in a manner closely resembling that observed in New York, postwar London's rise in cross-border finance more closely resembles the circumstances and strategies observed in the MDSJs discussed

[109] Sylla, *supra* note 96, at 67. *See also* VAN DORMAEL, *supra* note 60, at 80–83.

[110] *See* VAN DORMAEL, *supra* note 60, at 84–86.

[111] Sylla, *supra* note 96, at 66–67.

[112] *See* ROBERTS & KYNASTON, *supra* note 74, at 119 (quoting Wriston, emphasis removed). *See also* VAN DORMAEL, *supra* note 60, at 143–44, 152–53.

[113] *See* Palan, *supra* note 52, at 167–68.

in Part II of this book—a fascinating and illuminating transition. London's financial district—the "City"—is far more substantial relative to the size of the U.K. economy than New York is relative to the size of the U.S. economy,[114] and of course part of the broader historical context of the United Kingdom's postwar rise in cross-border finance has been the erosion of the commercial and manufacturing base[115] that had prompted and supported the City's initial rise to prominence in prior centuries. In this light, although it would be absurd to equate the circumstances of one of the world's largest economies with those of the much smaller and less populous jurisdictions studied in Part II, we can nevertheless draw a crude analogy.

With London we find a major urban center achieving financial dominance initially as a gateway to an enormous domestic economy turning increasingly toward cross-border services in a postcolonial era of industrial decline—an economic development strategy more closely approximating what we observe in the MDSJs. Indeed, as Richard Roberts and David Kynaston have observed, "no other country in the world is now so economically dependent on its financial services industry,"[116] and the economic significance of finance for the United Kingdom is readily detectable in its foreign policy, particularly toward Europe. For example, the euro was rejected by the United Kingdom principally because adopting it would "run diametrically counter to the City's uniquely *global* historical trajectory" and threaten "unfortunate regulatory implications, potentially eroding one of London's key competitive advantages—namely, a traditionally light but assured hand on the regulatory tiller,"[117] phrasing reminiscent of the balance between flexibility and oversight that the MDSJs have sought to strike. Thus it is unsurprising that Chancellor of the Exchequer Gordon Brown "deemed the City's contribution to be so significant that one of his famous 'five tests' in 1997 for the UK's readiness to join the euro was that it should not damage the City to do so."[118]

Over time the resemblance between London's strategy and that of the MDSJs has only become clearer. In addition to London's extraordinary investment in human capital, professional networks, and institutional structures,[119] the "City" in

---

[114] *See* Schenk, *supra* note 75, at 81.

[115] *Cf.* Robert Skidelsky, *Meeting Our Makers: Britain's Long Industrial Decline*, NEW STATESMAN, Jan. 24, 2013, http://www.newstatesman.com/culture/culture/2013/01/meeting-our-makers-britain%E2%80%99s-long-industrial-decline (reviewing NICHOLAS COMFORT, THE SLOW DEATH OF BRITISH INDUSTRY: A SIXTY-YEAR SUICIDE, 1952–2012 (2013)).

[116] ROBERTS & KYNASTON, *supra* note 74, at 192.

[117] *Id.* at 195.

[118] *Id.* at 79.

[119] *See* YEANDLE & DANEV, *supra* note 51, at 36 (ranking London first among major financial centers in "financial sector development" and second in "human capital," "business environment," "infrastructure," and "reputational and general factors").

particular resembles the MDSJs to a striking degree. Although metropolitan areas, as such, do not themselves possess the sort of legislative autonomy upon which the MDSJs rely,[120] in London's financial district we find a roughly analogous circumstance due to the Bank of England's proximity to and depth of connection with the "City." Caroline Bradley has observed the cultural homogeneity that underwrites the distinctly British form of "gentlemanly capitalism," referring to the tendency for public and private movers alike to know one another and share substantial class-based ties.[121] She explains that the "City of London was for a long time controlled through this common culture of the governing class, regulated through unwritten and informal rules rather than formally through legislation," adding that some "still talk about the Governor of the Bank of England controlling participants in the financial markets by raising his eyebrows." Indeed, Bradley rightly emphasizes that the Bank of England is itself "part of the City of London . . . in a way that other central banks and bank regulators are not"[122]—a geographic reality bringing the U.K. public and private financial sectors into close proximity in a manner more closely resembling the MDSJs than their counterparts in the United States, where the finance capital and the political capital inhabit different cities. In this light, London's financial center would appear to share a number of the core attributes identified in this book with smaller jurisdictions, including geographic proximity,[123] close public-private ties,[124] and a sort of regulatory autonomy in finance derivative of such close local connections with the relevant national regulator—which, in London's case, largely chose to stay out of the financial sector's way.

Additionally, London's unique degree of reliance on finance further reflects its capacity to perform cultural and geographic bridging functions of the sort observed in the MDSJs—indeed, the City has placed greater emphasis on hosting global financial activity than participating directly in that activity. Roberts and Kynaston vividly analogize the City to Wimbledon—each representing "a tournament hosted by Britain but dominated by foreign players"[125]—and there are various ways in which London can be described as performing the sorts of bridging functions that permit it to serve as

---

[120] *See supra* Chapter 2.B.iii.

[121] *See* Caroline Bradley, *Transatlantic Misunderstandings: Corporate Law and Societies,* 53 U. Miami L. Rev. 269, 307 (1999).

[122] *Id.* at 309.

[123] While London's financial district has expanded to Canary Wharf over recent decades, this move was prompted primarily by the need for new office facilities at a reasonable price. *See* Palan, *supra* note 52, at 159. *See also* Roberts & Kynaston, *supra* note 74, at 37–44.

[124] On this point it is worth noting the Financial Services Trade and Investment Board, created in 2013 to bring together various public and private actors "to identify trade and investment priorities and to support UK based firms in pursuing these vigorously across the globe." *See* TheCityUK, *supra* note 51, at 3.

[125] Roberts & Kynaston, *supra* note 74, at 105.

a global host for cross-border financial transactions. London has long bridged Europe and North America, facilitating transactions in both directions, and the English language and English law loom large as the predominant commercial and legal languages of such transactions.[126] "London has benefited from Britain's dominant position as a host for US multinationals," Schenk explains, "which generated demand for international financial services in London. Geographically and culturally, Britain was the main link between the USA and the rapidly growing European economies."[127]

In a sense, London illuminates the distinction between the gateway-type role of a major-economy financial center such as New York, on the one hand, and the bridging-type role of the MDSJs, on the other, by illustrating the changing historical and economic conditions under which a jurisdiction with the former strategy might gradually shift toward the latter. Indeed, in London's case, this shift appears to have been quite deliberate—or at least not unwelcome to the Bank of England of the late 1950s, which recognized that hosting "offshore" activity, as many now call it, could prove quite lucrative.

The suggestion that late-twentieth-century London sought to become "Hong Kong West"[128] is telling in this regard, although the more fitting comparison would be Singapore. In a foreword to Z/Yen's 2014 Global Financial Centres Index, Michael Mainelli implicitly analogized New York to Hong Kong, on the one hand, and London to Singapore, on the other, suggesting that "[w]ithout the large domestic economies behind New York and Hong Kong, London needs to act more like a Singaporean city state with a global economy."[129] Here Mainelli contrasts London's circumstances with the ballast that an enormous domestic economy would provide—though the New York-Hong Kong analogy, it must be acknowledged, is at best a loose one in light of the Mainland-related risks now faced by Hong Kong.[130] Although, in historical terms, it was Singapore that took its cues from London's playbook,[131] the more recent suggestion that London now pursues at a global level the sort of role that Singapore has established for itself in East Asia

---

[126] See id. at 182–85. See also THECITYUK, supra note 51, at 9.

[127] Schenk, supra note 75, at 80. More generally, London's MDSJ-type bridging capacities have also rendered the city appealing to the "superrich"—notably, London's security, pro-finance political orientation, capacity to facilitate substantial transactions at low cost, "comprehensive and (pretty much) honest legal system," cultural offerings, and ease of moving capital to and from historically related jurisdictions with similar appeal (including Hong Kong and Singapore) all render London attractive. See Paul Johnson, London and the Superrich, FORBES, June 18, 2014, http://www.forbes.com/sites/currentevents/2014/06/18/london-and-the-superrich/print/.

[128] See ROBERTS & KYNASTON, supra note 74, at 102.

[129] See YEANDLE & DANEV, supra note 51, at 1. The title of Roberts and Kynaston's book, City State, points in the same direction. See generally ROBERTS & KYNASTON, supra note 74.

[130] See supra Chapter 7.B.

[131] See supra Chapter 6.A.

is itself revealing, underscoring as it does London's transition from gateway to a domestic economy toward host of a global financial tournament.

It nevertheless remains the case that New York and London inhabit a distinct category in the magnitude and scope of financial services offered, and this points toward an important underlying distinction that helps illuminate the MDSJs' tendency to focus on particular fields of financial specialization. Simply put, the strength and resources of the sovereign can be expected, over time, to condition the magnitude and scope of financial services in a given jurisdiction—particularly in areas such as banking, straightforwardly giving rise to sovereign exposure.[132] This has been vividly illustrated in the United States and the United Kingdom themselves, where national governments were called upon to provide enormous bailout packages to failed financial institutions—which the enormous U.S. and U.K. balance sheets allowed their governments to provide.[133] The corollary for smaller jurisdictions observing such dynamics is that it behooves them to think hard, in advance, about what the sovereign could credibly backstop, and how. Although there are certainly smaller jurisdictions that have stably maintained substantial banking activities, this has predominantly reflected a combination of conservative regulation—notably, rigorous capital requirements—and unique circumstances—notably, capacity to generate and maintain "significant fiscal and foreign exchange buffers," as in Hong Kong and Singapore.[134] Smaller jurisdictions that failed sufficiently to replicate such strategies for managing the risks associated with substantial banking activities have, in the extreme, faced catastrophic consequences—as in Iceland, where the banking system ultimately collapsed[135]—or at least have found it necessary to rein in the banking system after the fact.

On this latter point, Switzerland provides an illuminating example. As discussed above, the Swiss banking system is quite large relative to the Swiss economy—indeed, in 2010 Swiss banking assets "were approximately 6.6 times gross domestic product (GDP), and total assets of each of Switzerland's two largest banks (Credit Suisse and UBS) were more than twice Swiss GDP."[136] Accordingly, having to bail

---

[132] *See* International Monetary Fund, *Cross-Cutting Themes in Economies with Large Banking Systems* 3, 23 (IMF report, 2010).

[133] For background, see Christopher M. Bruner, *Corporate Governance Reform in a Time of Crisis*, 36 J. Corp. L. 309, 311–17 (2011); Christopher M. Bruner, *Conceptions of Corporate Purpose in Post-Crisis Financial Firms*, 36 Seattle U. L. Rev. 527, 549–53 (2013).

[134] *See* International Monetary Fund, *supra* note 132, at 4, 8–10, 18–20. As the IMF observes, however, it remains telling that "the only two 'global' Asian banks," including HSBC, "were both headquartered in the (larger) UK jurisdiction." *Id.* at 23.

[135] *See id.* at 4, 8–9, 17.

[136] Daniel Bono et al., *The Swiss Response to the Basel III Framework and Other Regulatory Initiatives Aimed at Reinforcing Financial Sector Resilience*, Prac. L., Feb. 1, 2012, http://us.practicallaw.com/9-518-7639?q=&qp=&qo=&qe=.

out UBS in the wake of the crisis stung. As would eventually become apparent, risks and exposure had mounted due to "significant investment banking operations," and prudential supervision remained less robust than in Hong Kong and Singapore.[137] Consequently, the Swiss found themselves developing reforms "to clip the wings of too-big-to-fail banks and insulate the country's financial system" moving forward— principally by imposing stricter regulation that was aimed at directing UBS and Credit Suisse toward lower-risk forms of financial business.[138] The two big banks had already been subject to additional regulation exceeding international standards— the so-called "Swiss Finish"—but even stricter rules have been imposed since the crisis with the clear intent to direct these systemically significant institutions away from higher-risk investment banking activity, leading them "to focus more on less risky private banking."[139] By late 2010 these banks had already emphasized "their move towards lower risk, less capital-intensive businesses . . . shifting their focus to high-volume 'flow' trading on behalf of clients . . . and shutting down 'proprietary' trading activities using the banks' own money."[140] Stricter requirements were yet to come, however. In late 2015 Switzerland's Financial Market Supervisory Authority approved an increase in the total capital requirement for systemically significant banks (based on risk-weighted assets) from 19 percent to 28.6 percent, and amended "leverage rules" under which banks "will now need to hold 10 percent of their total exposures in going and gone concern capital—more than double the previous 4.56 percent." As one asset manager observed of these rules, "[w]hat this highlights is that big is not beautiful."[141]

Strikingly, the foregoing dynamics have even impacted the debate regarding whether a particularly finance-oriented sub-sovereign should pursue independence. Scotland's economy is heavily dependent on financial services, which in 2014 represented approximately 8 percent of Scottish GDP and employed approximately 12 percent of the workforce. Banking assets, meanwhile, "were 12.5 times larger than the country's [GDP]," exceeding pre-crisis Iceland (where banking assets were

---

[137] *See* International Monetary Fund, *supra* note 132, at 4, 6–9, 18.

[138] *See* Haig Simonian & Megan Murphy, *How Swiss Finish Was Factored In,* FIN. TIMES, Oct. 4, 2010, http://www.ft.com/intl/cms/s/o/cc6b9960-cfe0-11df-bb9e-00144feab49a.html.

[139] *See Swiss Banks Get Stricter Rules than Basel III,* SWI, Oct. 4, 2010, http://www.swissinfo.ch/eng/swiss-banks-get-stricter-rules-than-basel-iii/28464958. *See also* Bono et al., *supra* note 136.

[140] *See* Simonian & Murphy, *supra* note 138.

[141] Helene Durand, *Swiss Finish Takes New Meaning as Finma Raises Capital Bar Again,* REUTERS, Oct. 23, 2015, http://www.reuters.com/article/markets-credit-suisse-gp-idUSL8N12M4I520151023 (quoting Laurent Frings, co-head of EMEA credit research at Aberdeen Asset Management). *See also Bank Regulator Backs New "Too Big to Fail" Measure,* SWI, Sept. 25, 2015, http://www.swissinfo.ch/eng/business/leverage-ratio_bank-regulator-backs-new--too-big-to-fail--measure/41682270; Joshua Franklin, *Swiss Lawmakers Vote to Demand Their Biggest Banks Hold More Capital,* REUTERS, Sept. 24, 2015, http://www.reuters.com/article/swiss-banks-capital-idUSL5N11U1KO20150924.

9 times GDP).[142] Accordingly, the continuing viability of this volume of financial activity became a major issue in the run-up to the referendum on Scottish independence. Once Britain confirmed that it would not enter a currency union with an independent Scotland and that the Bank of England would no longer backstop Scottish banks,[143] the question became whether Scotland could muster sufficient reserves to replicate the alternative approach taken, for example, in Hong Kong—and the answer appeared to be no. As one study concluded, "[m]ost countries do not and perhaps cannot self-insure by accumulating ring-fenced assets in advance on the same scale of Hong Kong. Certainly an independent Scotland would be in a very different position."[144] Accordingly, it was hardly surprising when major banks—including the economically and symbolically important Royal Bank of Scotland—confirmed a week prior that if the referendum were to pass, they would re-domicile in England to retain Bank of England backing and the associated market credibility.[145]

Ultimately the Scottish referendum was defeated, prompting market analysts to heave a "sigh of relief"[146] and closing an episode further illustrating the substantial constraints that smaller independent jurisdictions face with respect to the magnitude and scope of financial services offered. In light of the foregoing, and in contrast with New York and London, it is quite comprehensible that the jurisdictions examined in Chapters 4–9 would generally focus on particular fields of financial specialization that tend not to place public money at risk to such a degree—and that those offering more substantial banking services would, like Singapore, Hong Kong, and Switzerland, tend to exhibit exceptional capacity to self-insure through "significant fiscal and foreign exchange buffers," while at the same time imposing relatively stern regulation aimed at containing riskier forms of banking activity.

Through the broad comparisons drawn in this chapter, we can perceive more clearly what is distinctive about the MDSJs studied in Part II. Some smaller jurisdictions may well have motivations to pursue cross-border financial business similar

---

[142] *See* Chad Bray & Jenny Anderson, *R.B.S. and Lloyds Bank Say They'll Move if Scotland Votes for Independence,* N.Y. Times, Sept. 11, 2014, http://dealbook.nytimes.com/2014/09/11/two-banks-say-theyll-move-if-scotland-votes-for-independence/?_r=1. *See also* Angus Armstrong & David McCarthy, *Scotland's Lender of Last Resort Options* 1, 17 (Nat'l Inst. of Econ. and Soc. Research Discussion Paper No. 434, 2014).

[143] *See* Bray & Anderson, *supra* note 142; Armstrong & McCarthy, *supra* note 142, at 1–2, 11–14; Sam Fleming, *Scotland Is Warned of Emergency Lending Perils in Crisis,* Fin. Times, Aug. 7, 2014, http://www.ft.com/intl/cms/s/2/336d17f2-1e4c-11e4-9513-00144feabdco.html.

[144] *See* Armstrong & McCarthy, *supra* note 142, at 14–18, 21–26. *See also* Fleming, *supra* note 143.

[145] *See* Bray & Anderson, *supra* note 142.

[146] *See* Delphine Strauss, *Scotland's No Vote: Analysts React,* Fin. Times, Sept. 19, 2014, http://www.ft.com/intl/cms/s/0/a19b544a-3fd1-11e4-936b-00144feabdco.html (quoting multiple analysts to this effect).

to those observed in the MDSJs, yet fail to achieve anything approaching that level of success for lack of cultural and geographic advantages, and/or failure to invest in real, value-added services. Accordingly, they may indeed function as little more than "tax/secrecy havens" in a literal sense, effectively offering nothing more than a sovereign for hire. The MDSJs, by contrast, have substantially invested in real, value-added services, and often benefit from cultural ties and geographic advantages exceeding those possessed by less successful jurisdictions. Meanwhile, successful larger jurisdictions—specifically, the two truly global financial centers in New York and London—arose organically from commercial and industrial activity rooted in their own domestic economies, and have historically benefited from their ability to act as gateways to those productive capacities. New York, as we have seen, very much still fits this paradigm, whereas London does to a lesser degree—though London's transition from a domestically rooted gateway role to an MDSJ-style bridging role itself emphasizes the distinction between these financial center paradigms. It remains the case, however, that New York and London alike can maintain financial services of extraordinary magnitude and scope due in large part to the capacity of their sovereigns to backstop the risks—a dynamic illuminating why the MDSJs, generally lacking such capacity, tend to focus on particular fields of financial specialization.

# 11 Conclusions

THE FOREGOING EXAMINATION of Bermuda, Dubai, Singapore, Hong Kong, Switzerland, and Delaware reveals striking commonalities in their cultural and geographic circumstances, competitive strengths, and development strategies—a suite of common characteristics strongly suggesting that these jurisdictions represent a coherent category not comfortably accommodated by extant theoretical lenses. The comparisons drawn in the last chapter—with smaller jurisdictions that tried to establish financial centers yet failed, and with successful financial centers located in larger jurisdictions—further suggest that the suite of characteristics that I associate with MDSJs in fact played a causal role in their rise to global dominance.

In each of these cases we find a small jurisdiction possessing legislative autonomy and favorable geographic and cultural proximity to major economies—but few other development opportunities—striving to establish a competitive niche in a globalizing financial world by investing heavily in human capital, professional networks, and related institutional structures; working collaboratively across public and private sectors to balance innovative regulatory structures attractive to increasingly mobile financial flows with stable and robust oversight of the financial professional community; and, at the same time, actively seeking to minimize the political and diplomatic salience of cross-border financial services. To date their efforts have been richly rewarded, each achieving global dominance in a distinct field of cross-border finance. However, the desirability and legitimacy of the "market-dominant small jurisdiction" in cross-border finance remain contested for comprehensible reasons.

The extraordinary successes of these jurisdictions continue to fuel debate regarding whether they reflect a "race to the top," culminating in efficient and presumptively desirable financial and regulatory structures, or a "race to the bottom," undercutting desirable regulation in other jurisdictions.[1] Often the debate is styled in "parasite" versus "symbiont" terms[2]—terminology gesturing toward the equivocal sorts of roles that these jurisdictions play in cross-border finance vis-à-vis larger economies, while further gesturing toward the equivocal nature of global capital mobility itself.[3]

The difficulty of characterizing the role and impact of MDSJs as singularly good or bad, beneficial or harmful, legitimate or illegitimate, reflects the fact that we can offer no singular account of capital mobility, from which their successes ultimately derive.[4] The "parasite" characterization most directly denotes living "at the expense of another,"[5] and as such this association tends to present the relationship of MDSJs to larger economies in binary terms, implicitly suggesting that the latter are uniquely productive and stand wholly apart from the sorts of activities for which the former are criticized. At the same time, however, the "parasite" image conveys a complex spatial relation, connoting as it does the idea of literally inhabiting a border region or frontier[6]—a characterization broadly resembling the position of jurisdictions

---

[1] *See* Anna Manasco Dionne & Jonathan R. Macey, *Offshore Finance and Onshore Markets: Racing to the Bottom, or Moving toward Efficient?*, *in* OFFSHORE FINANCIAL CENTERS AND REGULATORY COMPETITION 8, 17–18 (Andrew P. Morriss ed., 2010) (styling the debate in this manner).

[2] *See, e.g.*, RONEN PALAN, RICHARD MURPHY & CHRISTIAN CHAVAGNEUX, TAX HAVENS: HOW GLOBALIZATION REALLY WORKS 13, 154–58 (2010); Godfrey Baldacchino, *Managing the Hinterland Beyond: Two Ideal-Type Strategies of Economic Development for Small Island Territories*, 47 ASIA PAC. VIEWPOINT 45, 47 (2006); Andrew K. Rose & Mark M. Spiegel, *Offshore Financial Centers: Parasites or Symbionts?* 22 (NBER Working Paper No. 12044, 2006).

[3] On the rise, fall, and rise again of capital mobility over the last century, and the "contest over the character of globalization—ad hoc or managed—[that] continues today," see RAWI ABDELAL, CAPITAL RULES: THE CONSTRUCTION OF GLOBAL FINANCE (2007).

[4] *See supra* Chapter 2.C. *See also* Albert O. Hirschman, *Exit, Voice, and the State, in* ALBERT O. HIRSCHMAN, ESSAYS IN TRESPASSING: ECONOMICS TO POLITICS AND BEYOND 246, 257 (1981) (essay originally published in 1978) (observing that "various exits do occur . . . in response to the arbitrary and capricious actions of the sovereign," yet that "exit of capital often takes place in countries intending to introduce some taxation that would curb excessive privileges of the rich or some social reforms designed to distribute the fruits of economic growth more equitably," which "damages the capability of capitalism to reform itself"). For an argument that incentives to engage in tax competition derive from developed-country policies favoring capital mobility, see Adam H. Rosenzweig, *Why Are There Tax Havens?*, 52 WM. & MARY L. REV. 923 (2010).

[5] OXFORD ENGLISH DICTIONARY ONLINE, parasite, *n.*, 1.a. (3d ed. June 2005).

[6] *See* OXFORD ENGLISH DICTIONARY ONLINE, para-, *prefix*, Etymology (3d ed. June 2005). For an etymological discussion, see generally J. Hillis Miller, *The Critic as Host*, 3 CRITICAL INQUIRY 439, 440–43 (1977). For a discussion of broader ambivalence regarding "frontier or periphery" domains, see Aharon

that, in one way or another, mediate distinct markets and profit from movements of money to and from those markets.[7]

In this final chapter I offer brief reflections on this debate—including the binary "us"/"them" depiction often advanced by major economic powers—as well as the future of MDSJs and the territorial mode of financial regulation that underwrites their competitive strengths and development strategies. Although strong policy prescriptions remain premature, the descriptive account presented in this book minimally provides some basis for reframing the debate in more neutral terms and urging the major economies to adhere to their own standards regarding tax information exchange and financial transparency.

The tax haven literature, in particular, often suggests that smaller jurisdictions engaging in cross-border financial competition are effectively parasites feeding on larger-economy hosts such as the United States and the European Union—a characterization suggesting that the former jurisdictions provide little to no value-added themselves.[8] The descriptive account presented in this book suggests that there are good reasons to question this one-dimensional depiction.

To be sure, there is no question that these jurisdictions vigorously compete on the basis of taxation, and I readily acknowledge that substantial tax and related abuses occur in all such jurisdictions. It is important to bear in mind, however, that to the extent such abuses occur, they often respond directly to straightforward flaws embedded within the tax regimes of major markets themselves. For example, as a report jointly published by the U.S. PIRG Education Fund and Citizens for Tax Justice observes, "U.S. law does not even require that [foreign] subsidiaries have any physical presence . . . beyond a post office box," and likewise that U.S. corporations "can avoid paying taxes by booking profits to a tax haven because U.S. tax laws allow them to defer paying U.S. taxes on profits that they report are earned abroad until they 'repatriate' the money to the United States." Accordingly, these organizations rationally encourage U.S. policymakers to "reform the corporate tax code to end the incentives" that prompt such abuses[9]—which, of course, U.S. policymakers possess unilateral power to do. Likewise, Gabriel Zucman observes that multinationals' tax

---

Kellerman, *Transitions in the Meanings of Frontiers: From Settlement Advance to Regional Development,* J. GEOGRAPHY, Sept./Oct. 1997, at 230, 230–31.

[7] *Cf.* SASKIA SASSEN, CITIES IN A WORLD ECONOMY 92 (4th ed. 2012) (observing that global cities both inhabit and "disconnect from their region").

[8] *See, e.g.,* PALAN ET AL., *supra* note 2, at 13; Dhammika Dharmapala, *What Problems and Opportunities Are Created by Tax Havens?,* 24 OXFORD REV. ECON. POL'Y 661, 671 (2008) (observing this depiction).

[9] ROBERT S. MCINTYRE ET AL., OFFSHORE SHELL GAMES 2015: THE USE OF OFFSHORE TAX HAVENS BY FORTUNE 500 COMPANIES 4, 18–19 (2015) (U.S. PIRG Education Fund and Citizens for Tax Justice report).

avoidance techniques fall "within the letter of the law," and that the "fundamental problem is that the corporate tax is not adapted anymore to today's globalized world."[10] The major economic powers may well lack the political and diplomatic will to alter these incentive structures and pursue comprehensive solutions to outright tax evasion—perhaps, for example, a "global financial register" such as that proposed by Zucman[11]—but of course in that case, as Thomas Piketty cautions, "we should not complain when the problem gets bigger and bigger."[12]

At the same time, however, as we have already seen, the suggestion that jurisdictions such as Bermuda, Dubai, Singapore, Hong Kong, Switzerland, and Delaware add no substantive value whatever cannot withstand even moderate scrutiny—the jurisdictions studied here plainly offer more than their tax regimes. To state the matter counterfactually, it is implausible that Bermuda could have achieved its current level of dominance in insurance and risk management, that Dubai could have achieved its current level of dominance in Islamic finance, that Singapore could have achieved its current level of dominance in wealth management, that Hong Kong could have achieved its current level of dominance in equity markets, that Switzerland could have achieved its current level of dominance in cross-border banking, and/or that Delaware could have achieved its current level of dominance in business entity registration solely through tax policy and financial secrecy.[13] Although the lack of good data regarding smaller jurisdictions active in cross-border finance inevitably hampers the analysis—a factual void that, as such debates go, has been filled by a substantial dose of ideology[14]—there is certainly evidence indicating that such jurisdictions have promoted innovation in their areas of specialization later emulated by larger markets,[15] and otherwise enhanced market efficiency within such larger markets.[16]

---

[10] Gabriel Zucman, The Hidden Wealth of Nations: The Scourge of Tax Havens 102 (Teresa Lavender Fagan trans., 2015).

[11] See id. at 92–98.

[12] Id. at x.

[13] Cf. Dionne & Macey, supra note 1, at 16 ("Successful OFCs are now complete alternative markets.").

[14] See Palan et al., supra note 2, at 46–50, 170–71, 213. See also The Good, the Bad and the Ugland: Havens Serve Clean as Well as Dirty Money, Economist, Feb. 14, 2013, http://www.economist.com/news/special-report/21571551-havens-serve-clean-well-dirty-money-good-bad-and-ugland; J.C. Sharman, Havens in a Storm: The Struggle for Global Tax Regulation 36–37 (2006) (observing that there is "remarkably little expert consensus" among economists regarding whether tax competition is beneficial or harmful).

[15] See, e.g., Andrew P. Morriss, The Role of Offshore Financial Centers in Regulatory Competition, in Offshore Financial Centers and Regulatory Competition, supra note 1, at 107, 115, 136–38; Robert T. Danforth, Rethinking the Law of Creditors' Rights in Trusts, 53 Hastings L.J. 287 (2002); Economist, supra note 14.

[16] See, e.g., Rose & Spiegel, supra note 2, at 15–16, 21–22.

The diplomatic and legal pressures that have arisen since the 1990s have not fundamentally eroded the MDSJs' advantages.[17] Although the OECD, in particular (along with the IMF, the Financial Stability Board, the United States, the European Union, and others) has pushed hard for greater transparency and exchange of tax-relevant information, attacking the secrecy and opacity said to be the sine qua non for such jurisdictions,[18] the damage has been limited—both because

---

[17] *See Sunshine and Shadows: Offshore Financial Centres Will Always Be Controversial, But They Will Stay in Business*, ECONOMIST, Feb. 14, 2013, http://www.economist.com/news/special-report/21571559-offshore-financial-centres-will-always-be-controversial-they-will-stay. *See also* Leslie Wayne, *How Delaware Thrives as a Corporate Tax Haven*, N.Y. TIMES, June 30, 2012, http://www.nytimes.com/2012/07/01/business/how-delaware-thrives-as-a-corporate-tax-haven.html?pagewanted=all&_r=0.

[18] *See* ORGANISATION FOR ECONOMIC CO-OPERATION AND DEVELOPMENT, THE GLOBAL FORUM ON TRANSPARENCY AND EXCHANGE OF INFORMATION FOR TAX PURPOSES (Apr. 16, 2012); Organisation for Economic Co-operation and Development, *List of Unco-operative Tax Havens*, http://www.oecd.org/countries/monaco/listofunco-operativetaxhavens.htm (last visited Apr. 2016); Organisation for Economic Co-operation and Development, *Jurisdictions Committed to Improving Transparency and Establishing Effective Exchange of Information in Tax Matters*, http://www.oecd.org/countries/monaco/jurisdictionscommittedtoimprovingtransparencyandestablishingeffectiveexchangeofinformationintaxmatters.htm (last visited Apr. 2016). *See also* Reuven S. Avi-Yonah, *The OECD Harmful Tax Competition Report: A Retrospective after a Decade*, 34 BROOK. J. INT'L L. 783, 784–87 (2009); Craig M. Boise, *Regulating Tax Competition in Offshore Financial Centers, in* OFFSHORE FINANCIAL CENTERS AND REGULATORY COMPETITION, *supra* note 1, at 50, 54–57, 66–69, 72; Jean-Rodolphe W. Fiechter, *Exchange of Tax Information: The End of Banking Secrecy in Switzerland and Singapore?*, INT'L TAX J., Nov.–Dec. 2010, at 55, 57–58; Richard K. Gordon, *The International Monetary Fund and the Regulation of Offshore Centers, in* OFFSHORE FINANCIAL CENTERS AND REGULATORY COMPETITION, *supra* note 1, at 74, 75, 83–88, 94–95; International Monetary Fund, Monetary and Exchange Affairs Department, *Offshore Financial Centers*, at pt. III (IMF Background Paper, June 23, 2000), https://www.imf.org/external/np/mae/oshore/2000/eng/back.htm; Andrew P. Morriss & Lotta Moberg, *Cartelizing Taxes: Understanding the OECD's Campaign against "Harmful Tax Competition"* 36–37 (Oct. 27, 2011), http://ssrn.com/abstract=1950627; J.C. Sharman, *Canaries in the Coal Mine: Tax Havens, the Decline of the West and the Rise of the Rest*, 17 NEW POL. ECON. 493, 500–01 (2012). On the shift in the OECD's focus since the 1980s from "elimination of double taxation" to "protect[ing] member states from competitive pressures," see Morriss & Moberg, *supra*, at 11–45.

The Financial Stability Board (FSB), as the name implies, "promotes international financial stability . . . by coordinating national financial authorities and international standard-setting bodies." Financial Stability Board, *About the FSB*, http://www.fsb.org/about/ (last visited Apr. 2016). *See also* Financial Stability Board, *Members of the FSB*, http://www.fsb.org/about/organisation-and-governance/members-of-the-financial-stability-board/ (last visited Apr. 2016); Financial Stability Board, *FSB Members*, http://www.fsb.org/about/fsb-members/ (last visited Apr. 2016). It was created in 2009 by the G20 to build on the work of its predecessor, the Financial Stability Forum (FSF). *See* Financial Stability Board, *Our History*, http://www.fsb.org/about/history/ (last visited Apr. 2016). The FSF found in 2000 that "OFCs, to date, do not appear to have been a major causal factor in the creation of systemic financial problems," FINANCIAL STABILITY FORUM, REPORT OF THE WORKING GROUP ON OFFSHORE CENTRES 1 (2000), but in 2009 the G20 directed the newly created FSB to pursue tax havens "to protect public finances and international standards." GROUP OF TWENTY (G20), DECLARATION ON STRENGTHENING THE FINANCIAL SYSTEM—LONDON SUMMIT (Apr. 2, 2009), at 4. *See also* GROUP OF TWENTY (G20), CANNES SUMMIT FINAL DECLARATION—"BUILDING OUR COMMON FUTURE: RENEWED COLLECTIVE ACTION FOR THE BENEFIT OF ALL" (Nov. 4, 2011), at 7–8 ("We are committed to protect our public finances and the global financial system from the risks posed by tax havens and non cooperative jurisdictions.").

their substantial legitimate advantages remain unaffected,[19] and because procedures under tax information exchange agreements (TIEAs) generally remain difficult to employ as a practical matter. Although the OECD's model Agreement on Exchange of Information on Tax Matters expressly trumps domestic bank secrecy laws,[20] the information requested must be "foreseeably relevant" to domestic tax matters, and the requesting party must have exhausted "all means available in its own territory to obtain the information"[21]—requirements aimed at precluding "fishing expeditions."[22] These requirements have generally rendered TIEAs "cumbersome, time-consuming, and expensive" to use, leading observers to conclude that they have not fundamentally altered the cross-border financial landscape.[23]

At the same time, however, it is critical to acknowledge that the major markets themselves are not above engaging in the very abuses they justly condemn. We have already seen that London increasingly functions like any "offshore" jurisdiction, clearly proclaiming its aim to host the world's most internationalized financial system, and the United States itself now represents what the Tax Justice Network

---

[19] *See supra* Part II. *See also* SHARMAN, *supra* note 14, at 103.

[20] *See* Organisation for Economic Co-operation and Development, Agreement on Exchange of Information on Tax Matters, art. 5(4), cmt. 46.

[21] *See id.* arts. 1, 5(1), 5(5). *See also* Organisation for Economic-Co-operation and Development, Model Convention with Respect to Taxes on Income and on Capital, art. 26 (condensed version, 2014).

[22] Organisation for Economic Co-operation and Development, *supra* note 20, cmts. 3, 57.

[23] *See* PALAN ET AL., *supra* note 2, at 244. *See also* Beckett G. Cantley, *Steering Into the Storm: Amplification of Captive Insurance Company Compliance Issues in the Offshore Tax Crackdown,* 12 HOUS. BUS. & TAX L.J. 224, 248–49 (2012); Steven A. Dean, *Philosopher Kings and International Tax: A New Approach to Tax Havens, Tax Flight, and International Tax Cooperation,* 58 HASTINGS L.J. 911, 961–62 (2007); *Automatic Response: The Way to Make Exchange of Tax Information Work,* ECONOMIST, Feb. 14, 2013, http://www.economist.com/news/special-report/21571561-way-make-exchange-tax-information-work-automatic-response; Fiechter, *supra* note 18, at 58–62. For a list of tax information agreements, see Organisation for Economic Co-operation and Development, *Exchange of Information: Tax Information Exchange Agreements (TIEAs),* http://www.oecd.org/tax/exchange-of-tax-information/taxinformationexchangeagreement-stieas.htm (last visited Apr. 2016). *See also* Organisation for Economic Co-operation and Development, *Exchange of Tax Information Portal: Bermuda,* http://eoi-tax.org/jurisdictions/BM#agreements (last visited Apr. 2016); Organisation for Economic Co-operation and Development, *Exchange of Tax Information Portal: Hong Kong, China,* http://eoi-tax.org/jurisdictions/HK#agreements (last visited Apr. 2016); Organisation for Economic Co-operation and Development, *Exchange of Tax Information Portal: Singapore,* http://eoi-tax.org/jurisdictions/SG#agreements (last visited Apr. 2016); Organisation for Economic Co-operation and Development, *Exchange of Tax Information Portal: Switzerland,* http://eoi-tax.org/jurisdictions/CH#agreements (last visited Apr. 2016); Organisation for Economic Co-operation and Development, *Exchange of Tax Information Portal: United Arab Emirates,* http://eoi-tax.org/jurisdictions/AE#agreements (last visited Apr. 2016); Organisation for Economic Co-operation and Development, *Exchange of Tax Information Portal: United Kingdom,* http://eoi-tax.org/jurisdictions/GB#agreements (last visited Apr. 2016); Organisation for Economic Co-operation and Development, *Exchange of Tax Information Portal: United States,* http://eoi-tax.org/jurisdictions/US#agreements (last visited Apr. 2016).

describes as the world's single largest "offshore" financial services market.[24] Regardless of one's ideological posture, it appears inescapable that the pertinent competitive activities of jurisdictions such as Bermuda, Dubai, Singapore, Hong Kong, and Switzerland cannot be categorically distinguished from those of the U.S. state of Delaware—or the United States as a whole, for that matter. Indeed, Delaware has similarly found itself branded a "parasite state" vis-à-vis other U.S. states,[25] while at the same time prompting charges of U.S. hypocrisy from foreign jurisdictions themselves tired of being selectively branded "tax havens" and "OFCs." It has not been lost on jurisdictions targeted in this manner that the United States has substantially ratcheted up required information disclosures regarding foreign accounts, notably through the Foreign Account Tax Compliance Act (FATCA)—which imposes reporting obligations regarding offshore accounts and assets upon U.S. taxpayers and foreign financial institutions alike[26]—and demanded that other jurisdictions agree to elaborate information exchange initiatives, while the United States itself fails to deliver this level of transparency to others.[27] The advent of FATCA and the

---

[24] *See* TAX JUSTICE NETWORK, NARRATIVE REPORT ON USA 1 (2015); Jose Martínez, *How the U.S. Became a Top Secrecy Jurisdiction,* TAX JUST. BLOG (Nov. 3, 2015), http://www.taxjusticeblog.org/archive/2015/11/how_the_us_became_a_top_secrec.php.

[25] WILLIAM W. BOYER & EDWARD C. RATLEDGE, DELAWARE POLITICS AND GOVERNMENT 136–37 (2009).

[26] *See* Internal Revenue Service, *Foreign Account Tax Compliance Act,* https://www.irs.gov/Businesses/Corporations/Foreign-Account-Tax-Compliance-Act-FATCA (last updated July 15, 2015); 26 U.S.C.S. § 6038D (2016) ("Information with respect to foreign financial assets"). *See also* 31 U.S.C.S. § 5314 (2016) ("Records and reports on foreign financial agency transactions"); Internal Revenue Service, Form 8938, OMB No. 1545-2195 ("Statement of Specified Foreign Financial Assets"); Cantley, *supra* note 23, at 250–54; Internal Revenue Service, *Comparison of Form 8938 and FBAR Requirements,* http://www.irs.gov/Businesses/Comparison-of-Form-8938-and-FBAR-Requirements (last updated Mar. 25, 2016); Internal Revenue Service, *FATCA Information for Individuals,* http://www.irs.gov/Businesses/Corporations/FATCA-Information-for-Individuals (last updated Apr. 12, 2016); Internal Revenue Service, *Report of Foreign Bank and Financial Accounts (FBAR),* https://www.irs.gov/Businesses/Small-Businesses-&-Self-Employed/Report-of-Foreign-Bank-and-Financial-Accounts-FBAR (last updated Dec. 11, 2015).

On the practical difficulties created for middle-class Americans living abroad, prompting some to go so far as to renounce U.S. citizenship to escape the expense and paperwork burden, see Liam Pleven & Laura Saunders, *Expatriate Americans Break Up with Uncle Sam to Escape Tax Rules,* WALL ST. J., June 16, 2014, http://online.wsj.com/articles/more-expatriate-americans-break-up-with-uncle-sam-to-escape-tax-rules-1402972439; Laura Saunders, *Offshore Accounts: What to Do Now,* WALL ST. J., June 20, 2014, http://online.wsj.com/articles/offshore-accounts-what-to-do-now-1403303712; *Checking the IRS Overseas,* WALL ST. J., Mar. 30, 2015, http://www.wsj.com/articles/checking-the-irs-overseas-1427759818. Meanwhile, "some banks have chosen to kick out their [U.S.] clients rather than comply." *See* Sophia Yan, *A Record 3,415 Americans Ditch Their Passports,* CNN.COM, Feb. 17, 2015, http://money.cnn.com/2015/02/12/pf/americans-expat-citizenship-passports/. For an argument that the tax revenue gains have been overestimated and the compliance costs underestimated, see Andrew Morriss, *The End of Offshoring?,* ACCOUNTANCY, Sept. 2014, at 49, 51. *See also Checking the IRS Overseas,* WALL ST. J., *supra* (suggesting that the Obama Administration's estimate of "$870 million a year in additional tax revenue . . . is probably overstated given changes in behavior by Americans and their overseas employers").

[27] *See* SHARMAN, *supra* note 14, at 105–06.

negotiations spurred by it may, to be sure, promote greater global financial transparency in the long run[28]—and I am prepared to assume that this represents good policy, and a likely outcome.[29] In the meantime, however, U.S. efforts to reciprocate in the exchange of tax and financial information have been halting at best.[30] U.S. banking regulations now impose greater reporting requirements with respect to nonresident individual accounts, but as Tracy Kaye explains, these requirements do not apply to accounts opened by non-individual entities such as corporations and trusts, "even though FATCA requires foreign financial institutions to report on accounts held by an entity where more than ten percent is owned by a U.S. person."[31] While the Tax Justice Network's 2015 Financial Secrecy Index ranked Switzerland first, Hong Kong second, Singapore fourth, the UAE (Dubai) tenth, and Bermuda thirty-fourth, the United States ranked third—hardly a resounding endorsement of the American track record on financial transparency.[32] (See Figure 11.1 below for these rankings.)

As discussed above, Delaware itself has increasingly become a jurisdiction of choice for opaque shell companies, and finds itself increasingly characterized as a form of tax/secrecy haven.[33] As one Geneva private banker put it, "[s]ome of the countries that have been targeting our system have offshore centers that are far less transparent than Switzerland. . . . Just look at a place like Delaware."[34] Indeed, Swiss

---

[28] Commentators have particularly emphasized FATCA's improvements relative to the European Union's failed savings tax directive. *See* ZUCMAN, *supra* note 10, at 69–72. *See also id.* at 30–31 (suggesting that for the merely "moderately wealthy," bank secrecy is already effectively gone).

[29] *Cf. The Panama Papers: A Torrential Leak,* ECONOMIST, Apr. 9, 2016, at 59–61 (reporting the view that "the spate of whistle-blowing since the global financial crisis has helped cool interest in using shell companies," and quoting a wealth management professional's remark that "[w]e're now telling clients they have to assume anything they do offshore will become public, and they'll have to be able to justify it when it does").

[30] *See generally* Tracy A. Kaye, *Innovations in the War on Tax Evasion,* 2014 BYU L. REV. 363 (2014). *See also* TAX JUSTICE NETWORK, *supra* note 24, at 3–6; ZUCMAN, *supra* note 10, at 62–64.

[31] *See* Kaye, *supra* note 30, at 387–93. The upshot, Kaye explains, is that "the bank deposit reporting rules only apply to the nonbusiness interest on directly held bank deposits of certain nonresident individuals." *Id.* at 389. *See also* Gabriel Zucman, *Taxing across Borders: Tracking Personal Wealth and Corporate Profits,* 28 J. ECON. PERSP. 121, 142–45 (2014).

[32] *See* Tax Justice Network, *Financial Secrecy Index—2015 Results,* http://www.financialsecrecyindex.com/introduction/fsi-2015-results (last visited Apr. 2016).

[33] *See supra* Chapter 9.B; TAX JUSTICE NETWORK, *supra* note 24, at 6–9.

[34] Raphael Minder, *Pressure Mounts on Vaunted Secrecy of Switzerland's Banks,* N.Y. TIMES, May 23, 2013, http://www.nytimes.com/2013/05/24/business/global/swiss-banking-secrecy-under-pressure-from-europe.html?pagewanted=all (quoting Edouard Cuendet). *See also Tax Havens: The Missing $20 Trillion,* ECONOMIST, Feb. 14, 2013, http://www.economist.com/news/leaders/21571873-how-stop-companies-and-people-dodging-tax-delaware-well-grand-cayman-missing-20; RICHARD HAY ET AL., TOWARDS A LEVEL PLAYING FIELD: REGULATING CORPORATE VEHICLES IN CROSS-BORDER TRANSACTIONS 19–24, 37–39 (2002) (review commissioned by the International Trade and Investment Organisation and the Society of Trust and Estate Practitioners, and conducted by Stikeman Elliott); Sharman, *supra* note 18, at 501.

| Jurisdiction | Rank |
|---|---|
| Switzerland | 1 |
| Hong Kong | 2 |
| USA | 3 |
| Singapore | 4 |
| Cayman Islands | 5 |
| Luxembourg | 6 |
| Lebanon | 7 |
| Germany | 8 |
| Bahrain | 9 |
| UAE (Dubai) | 10 |
| — | — |
| United Kingdom | 15 |
| — | — |
| Bermuda | 34 |

FIGURE 11.1  Financial Secrecy Index, 2015 Rankings.*

* *See* Tax Justice Network, *Financial Secrecy Index—2015 Results,* http://www.financialsecrecyindex.com/introduction/fsi-2015-results (last visited Apr. 2016).

bankers "bristle that even as American authorities have focused on the Swiss, they have not shown the same zeal when it comes to opening up their own banks and states to scrutiny."[35] *The Economist* reports that "[i]ll-gotten gains often receive a warm welcome in large OECD countries, some of which offer more corporate secrecy than the leading tax havens"[36]—a reality fueling the growing perception that "the principal conduits for money laundering are the world's largest financial centers, London and New York."[37] As the Tax Justice Network has observed, tax haven designations established by international organizations "are frequently skewed by political expediency" to "exclude or downplay large, powerful nations and highlight small, weaker ones," yet "the offshore world . . . includes some of the world's biggest economies."[38] It is striking that, by the Tax Justice Network's reckoning, "the U.S.A. accounts for one fifth of the global market for offshore financial services"

---

[35]  Minder, *supra* note 34.

[36]  ECONOMIST, *supra* note 14. *See also* J.C. SHARMAN, THE MONEY LAUNDRY: REGULATING CRIMINAL FINANCE IN THE GLOBAL ECONOMY 86–90 (2011).

[37]  PALAN ET AL., *supra* note 2, at 207. *See also* SHARMAN, *supra* note 36, at 9, 163.

[38]  *See* Tax Justice Network, *FAQ: Tax Havens,* http://www.taxjustice.net/faq/ (last visited Apr. 2016).

and the United Kingdom accounts for 17 percent,[39] whereas Singapore, Hong Kong, and Switzerland each fall in the 3–5 percent range[40] and Bermuda and Dubai each account for well under 1 percent.[41]

To be sure, those in Congress leading the charge against "tax havens" and "OFCs" have at the same time advanced similar initiatives domestically. Former Michigan Senator Carl Levin, who as of 2013 had "been holding hearings and conducting investigations into the offshore world for nearly three decades,"[42] similarly "long complained that it takes more information to get a driver's license than to set up a corporation in America." Indeed, Levin took direct aim at domestic shell companies by advocating legislation forcing states to collect beneficial ownership information for companies they incorporate.[43] To date, however, such initiatives have foundered for predictable reasons—they contradict the interests of powerful private and public interests alike. "Most vocal is the National Association of Secretaries of State," *The New York Times* reports. "It is backed up by the Chamber of Commerce, the American Bar Association and the state of Delaware, which is the lone state to have hired a lobbyist to work on the matter."[44]

At the same time, the U.S. position regarding the desirability of tax information exchange is substantially undercut by the fact that the United States itself refuses to provide information to other countries regarding nonresident alien accounts. "Under U.S. tax laws, interest income on accounts held by non-resident aliens is not taxable"[45]—a policy dating to the Revenue Act of 1921 intended to "encourage foreign

---

[39] *See* TAX JUSTICE NETWORK, *supra* note 24, at 1; TAX JUSTICE NETWORK, NARRATIVE REPORT ON UNITED KINGDOM 1 (2015).

[40] *See* TAX JUSTICE NETWORK, NARRATIVE REPORT ON SINGAPORE 1 (2015); TAX JUSTICE NETWORK, NARRATIVE REPORT ON HONG KONG 1 (2015); TAX JUSTICE NETWORK, NARRATIVE REPORT ON SWITZERLAND 1 (2015).

[41] *See* TAX JUSTICE NETWORK, REPORT ON BERMUDA 1 (2015); TAX JUSTICE NETWORK, NARRATIVE REPORT ON DUBAI 1 (2015).

[42] Scott Higham, Michael Hudson & Marina Walker Guevara, *Piercing the Secrecy of Offshore Tax Havens*, WASH. POST, Apr. 6, 2013, https://www.washingtonpost.com/investigations/piercing-the-secrecy-of-offshore-tax-havens/2013/04/06/1551806c-7d50-11e2-a044-676856536b40_story.html. *See also* Cantley, *supra* note 23, at 242–43, 250–51. In general, the political left has more vigorously opposed offshore finance than the political right has—the former perceiving a drain on revenue available for social programs whereas the latter perceives a healthy discipline upon tax levels. *See, e.g.,* SHARMAN, *supra* note 14, at 61–62; Morriss & Moberg, *supra* note 18, at 30, 38–39, 41–43.

[43] Wayne, *supra* note 17; Kaye, *supra* note 30, at 389–90.

[44] Wayne, *supra* note 17. *See also* Veronika Oleksyn, *Tax Haven Next Door: Delaware Exposes Corporate Secrecy*, WASH. DIPLOMAT, Feb. 29, 2012, http://www.washdiplomat.com/index.php?option=com_content&view=article&id=8250:tax-haven-next-door-delaware-exposes-corporate-secrecy-in-elections&catid=1484&Itemid=428; TAX JUSTICE NETWORK, *supra* note 24, at 8–9.

[45] Scott A. Schumacher, *Magnifying Deterrence by Prosecuting Professionals* 44 (Univ. of Wash. Sch. of Law Legal Studies Research Paper No. 2013-17, 2013), http://ssrn.com/abstract=2243093.

persons to use U.S. banks and savings institutions."[46] Accordingly, "U.S. banks are . . . . not required, and do not, issue 1099 forms with respect to these accounts," effectively hampering U.S. reciprocation under TIEAs. The upshot, as Scott Schumacher explains, is that "the U.S. is one of the favorite places of foreigners to hide their money"[47]—a reality tending to undermine U.S. credibility and leadership on tax information transparency. As Schumacher concludes, "the U.S. and other developed countries cannot posture about the evils of bank secrecy and tax haven abuses, while tolerating similar practices within their own borders. . . . Hypocrisy does little to boost the integrity of the tax system."[48]

From a similar perspective, Daniel Hemel has argued that "at the heart of offshore tax evasion are the U.S. portfolio interest exception and the U.K. exemption of outbound dividends," which respectively allow foreign investors to "earn interest on U.S. bonds and dividends on U.K. stock without facing a withholding tax." These policies, Hemel observes, result in "much of the world's offshore wealth . . . passing through New York or London." This effectively means that "the United States and United Kingdom face a complicated set of incentives when it comes to cracking down on offshore tax evasion," in turn rendering it "difficult to distinguish the villains from the innocents."[49]

As of this writing, the credibility gap on these issues unfortunately continues to grow. Although the U.S. initiative embodied in FATCA successfully advanced efforts elsewhere—most notably prompting the "Common Reporting Standard (CRS), a transparency initiative overseen by the OECD . . . that is emerging as a standard for the exchange of data for tax purposes"—the United States has refused to sign on in light of the many bilateral agreements already entered.[50] However, U.S. reciprocation remains "patchy," in that "[i]t passes on names and interest earned, but not account balances; it does not look through the corporate structures that own many bank accounts to reveal the true 'beneficial' owner; and data are

---

[46] CHARLES H. GUSTAFSON ET AL., TAXATION OF INTERNATIONAL TRANSACTIONS: MATERIALS, TEXTS AND PROBLEMS 238 (4th ed. 2011). *See also* TAX JUSTICE NETWORK, *supra* note 24, at 1–4; Ernest R. Larkins, *Multinationals and Their Quest for the Good Tax Haven: Taxes Are but One, Albeit an Important, Consideration*, 25 INT'L LAW. 471, 483 (1991).

[47] Schumacher, *supra* note 45, at 44. *See also* TAX JUSTICE NETWORK, *supra* note 24, at 4–6; Kaye, *supra* note 30.

[48] Schumacher, *supra* note 45, at 51. *See also* SHARMAN, *supra* note 14, at 90–91.

[49] Daniel Hemel, *What's the Matter with Luxembourg?*, NEW RAMBLER, Jan. 13, 2016, http://newramblerreview.com/book-reviews/economics/what-s-the-matter-with-luxembourg (reviewing GABRIEL ZUCMAN, THE HIDDEN WEALTH OF NATIONS: THE SCOURGE OF TAX HAVENS (2015)).

[50] *The Biggest Loophole of All*, ECONOMIST, Feb. 20, 2016, at 51, 51. *See also* Organisation for Economic Co-operation and Development, *Common Reporting Standard (CRS)*, http://www.oecd.org/tax/automatic-exchange/common-reporting-standard/ (last visited Apr. 2016).

only shared with countries that meet a host of privacy and technical standards," which "excludes many non-European countries."[51] Accordingly, *The Economist* has observed that "America seems not to feel bound by the global rules being crafted as a result of its own war on tax-dodging," prompting "some to brand America a hypocrite." Indeed, reluctance to fully reciprocate is increasingly thought to reflect an aim of "giving America's financial centres an edge"—a perception reinforced by the fact that the United States "has picked up business as regulators have increased information-exchange and scrutiny of banks and trust companies in Europe and the Caribbean."[52]

Meanwhile, in contrast with the United Kingdom "which will soon have a public register of companies' beneficial owners," similar federal legislative efforts in the United States remain "stymied" by "business lobbyists and states with lots of registered firms, led by Delaware."[53] According to a *Bloomberg* report, as of January 2016, 97 jurisdictions had signed on to the OECD's CRS initiative, and "only a handful have declined: Bharain, Nauru, Vanuatu—and the United States."[54] As *Bloomberg* summarized the resulting situation, "[a]fter years of lambasting other countries for helping rich Americans hide their money offshore, the U.S. is emerging as a leading tax and secrecy haven for rich foreigners. By resisting new global disclosure standards, the U.S. is creating a hot new market, becoming the go-to place to stash foreign wealth."[55] More generally, the Tax Justice Network has expressed the view that "the United States has played a pioneering role in devising ways to defend itself against foreign tax havens, but has failed to address its own role in attracting illicit financial flows and supporting tax evasion."[56]

Such views are broadly consistent with prior claims to the effect that financial transparency and information exchange initiatives—compelling as the underlying policy rationales may be—reflect in practice an instrumental effort by larger jurisdictions to insulate their own financial centers from growing competition, rendering

---

[51] ECONOMIST, *supra* note 50, at 51.

[52] *Id. See also* Jesse Drucker, *The World's Favorite New Tax Haven Is the United States,* BLOOMBERGBUSINESS, Jan. 27, 2016, http://www.bloomberg.com/news/articles/2016-01-27/the-world-s-favorite-new-tax-haven-is-the-united-states. *Cf.* Hemel, *supra* note 49 ("The United States would be quite happy if U.S. citizens and residents pay U.S. tax on their worldwide investment income while foreign investors can escape home-country taxation on their U.S.-source interest and dividends. FATCA may allow the United States to arrive at this outcome unilaterally.").

[53] ECONOMIST, *supra* note 50, at 51.

[54] Drucker, *supra* note 52.

[55] *Id.*

[56] TAX JUSTICE NETWORK, NARRATIVE REPORT ON USA 1–2 (2013). *See also* JAMES S. HENRY, THE PRICE OF OFFSHORE REVISITED: NEW ESTIMATES FOR "MISSING" GLOBAL PRIVATE WEALTH, INCOME, INEQUALITY, AND LOST TAXES 43–45 (July 2012) (report for the Tax Justice Network).

the purported rationales (inhibiting money laundering and terrorism financing, ensuring financial stability, and so on) at least partially pretextual.[57] Indeed, it is striking that under the USA Patriot Act's "counter-money laundering" regime, assessment of whether a jurisdiction warrants "primary money laundering concern" expressly includes as a "potentially relevant" factor "the extent to which that jurisdiction is characterized as an offshore banking or secrecy haven by credible international organizations or multilateral expert groups"[58]—even though, again, the main money laundering centers are widely thought to be London and New York. Growing recognition of the foregoing realities may account for the dual nature of the public reaction to the Panama Papers—at once reflecting entirely predictable indignation at public leaders' resort to opaque "offshore" financial structures and continuing suspicion that such devices may hide all manner of wrongdoing, yet at the same time acknowledging legitimate benefits of cross-border finance[59] and recognizing that major markets themselves embody precisely the same trade-offs. As one commentator observed, "[f]irms in the United States play the same role as Mossack Fonseca, possibly on a larger scale, and they are doing so with the tacit blessing of our lax financial secrecy laws."[60]

At the same time, focusing solely on the United States in its totality as the relevant jurisdictional comparison with MDSJs such as Bermuda, Dubai, Singapore, Hong Kong, and Switzerland fuels the "parasite" indictment by emphasizing the contrast between the world's largest domestic economy and considerably smaller economies.

---

[57] *See, e.g.*, Rose-Marie Belle Antoine, *The Legitimacy of the Offshore Financial Sector: A Legal Perspective, in* OFFSHORE FINANCIAL CENTERS AND REGULATORY COMPETITION, *supra* note 1, at 30, 33–34; HAY ET AL., *supra* note 34, at 1–2, 10, 16, 42; Morriss & Moberg, *supra* note 18, at 29, 34–35; Emma Thomasson, *Special Report: The Battle for the Swiss Soul*, REUTERS, Apr. 18, 2013, http://www.reuters.com/article/2013/04/18/us-swiss-banks-specialreport-idUSBRE93H07620130418; Rolf H. Weber, *Swiss Banking Secrecy in Evolution*, 18 BANKING & FIN. L. REV. 317, 337–38 (2003); Dariusz Wójcik, *Where Governance Fails: Advanced Business Services and the Offshore World*, 37 HUM. GEOGRAPHY 330, 344 (2012).

[58] 31 U.S.C. § 5318A(c)(2)(A)(v) (2016) (codifying, as amended, USA Patriot Act of 2001 § 311(a)).

[59] *See, e.g.*, ECONOMIST, *supra* note 29; *The Lessons of the Panama Papers*, ECONOMIST, Apr. 9, 2016, at 14–16; Vanessa Houlder, *Tax Havens Seen as "Grease on Wheels" of Cross-Border Trade*, FIN. TIMES, Apr. 8, 2016, at 4. *See also* Max Ehrenfreund, *What the Panama Papers Don't Say about Global Finance Is Just as Troubling*, WASH. POST, Apr. 14, 2016, https://www.washingtonpost.com/news/wonk/wp/2016/04/14/what-the-panama-papers-dont-say-about-global-finance-is-just-as-troubling/ ("Banks' withdrawal from some markets in East Africa, the Middle East, Latin America and other regions has provoked an international debate about the costs and benefits of authorities' efforts to counter illicit finance.").

[60] Matthew Gardner, *Panama Papers and America's Problem*, CNN.COM, Apr. 5, 2016, http://www.cnn.com/2016/04/05/opinions/panama-papers-american-problem-opinion-gardner/. *See also* Brooke Harrington, *Panama Papers: The Real Scandal Is What's Legal*, ATLANTIC, Apr. 6, 2016, http://www.theatlantic.com/business/archive/2016/04/panama-papers-crimes/477156/ (observing the "offshore" dimensions of U.K. and U.S. financial centers); *Room for Debate: Cracking Shell Company Secrecy*, N.Y. TIMES, Apr. 7, 2016, http://www.nytimes.com/roomfordebate/2016/04/07/cracking-shell-company-secrecy (multiple commentators observing that U.S. legal structures permit substantially similar financial secrecy).

At a functional level, however, one in fact must disaggregate the United States—for the simple reason that mobile capital does so in evaluating its options. In many areas of cross-border financial services, the relevant comparison in fact involves individual U.S. states—for example, Bermuda versus Vermont for captive insurance, or the British Virgin Islands versus Delaware for business entity organization.[61] When the comparison is drawn in this alternative manner, the selective "parasite" characterization appears less tenable—not because there is no pertinent sense in which these outward-oriented jurisdictions feed off financial flows rooted in economic activity occurring elsewhere, but rather because similar charges can be leveled with substantial force against competitors within the United States. Whatever the strengths and weaknesses of these arguments, they cannot categorically differentiate foreign MDSJs from their U.S. competition.

The resilience of MDSJs—both those embedded within major economies and those located elsewhere—raises related, though distinct, questions about territorially defined regulatory authority, which has clearly been a critical driver of the many successes achieved by Bermuda, Dubai, Singapore, Hong Kong, Switzerland, and Delaware. What do the foregoing developments tell us about the future of territorial financial regulation? And how might the regulation of cross-border financial activity evolve in the future?

Although capital mobility is often said to undermine territorial sovereignty,[62] its impact is better described as double-edged. Capital mobility may often inhibit regulatory initiatives among the major economic powers, but mobile capital at the same time enhances—and in some cases depends upon—the value of territorial sovereignty for MDSJs. Although the globalization of finance may, to be sure, represent a capitalist desire to achieve de facto statelessness, as observers have claimed,[63] strictly speaking there is no such thing. The dynamics described in this book are themselves in fact an expression of territorial sovereignty and the legislative autonomy that comes with it.[64] It is the combination of immobile regulation with mobile capital that gives rise to cross-border financial regulatory competition. The consequence, critical to any coherent assessment of the matter, is that there are powerful

---

[61] See Andrew P. Morriss & Clifford C. Henson, *Regulatory Effectiveness in Onshore & Offshore Financial Centers* 23, 26–28 (Univ. of Ala. Sch. of Law Working Paper, 2012), http://ssrn.com/abstract=2016310; Tax Justice Network, *supra* note 24, at 8. Note that Vermont, like Delaware, is among the smallest U.S. states both in population and land area. *See Population of USA States*, WorldAtlas.com, http://www.worldatlas.com/aatlas/populations/usapoptable.htm (last visited Apr. 2016) (providing state populations and land areas).

[62] *See supra* Chapter 2.A.

[63] *See, e.g.*, William Brittain-Catlin, Offshore: The Dark Side of the Global Economy 22–24, 120–21 (2005). *See also* Palan et al., *supra* note 2, at 21, 87.

[64] *See supra* Chapter 3.A.

and well-endowed constituencies with strong incentives to maintain territorial financial regulation—and, accordingly, territorial sovereignty itself.[65]

This recognition casts the counter-initiatives of the United States and other major economies in a different light. In effect, attacks upon "tax havens" and "OFCs" amount to a twofold effort. First, the major economies seek to shore up their own sovereignty by consolidating their political power over cross-border finance.[66] Second, they seek to shore up their own financial centers by consolidating their market power over cross-border finance—hence a series of regulatory "double standards [that], far from being accidental, are the result of 'a policy of commercial hegemony' designed to keep tax havens in their place."[67] Such efforts could well bear fruit to the extent that a given MDSJ depends upon market access in the United States and other major economies.[68] The problem with reliance on this approach, however, is that these jurisdictions depend less upon access to historically dominant Western markets each day. As J.C. Sharman has observed, the "'push' of the threat of being cut off from OECD markets has coincided with a 'pull' from newly-rich customers in the developing world."[69]

As the MDSJ customer base diversifies and shifts eastward, the ability of major economies to exert leverage through threats of market access denial can be expected to attenuate.[70] As this occurs, calls for greater transparency in company registration and tax-relevant information will increasingly have to rest on moral suasion. Accordingly, should such initiatives remain priorities for policymakers in the United States and other major economic powers, they may have no alternative but to start by cleaning up their own backyards. In the meantime, however, we should harbor no illusions about why the jurisdictions described here as "market-dominant small jurisdictions" have so aggressively pursued cross-border financial services

---

[65] *See* BRITTAIN-CATLIN, *supra* note 63, at 114–15. *Cf. supra* notes 43–44 and accompanying text (describing similar incentives and dynamics within the United States).

[66] *See, e.g.*, PALAN ET AL., *supra* note 2, at 198–99, 241.

[67] *See Not a Palm Tree in Sight: Some Onshore Jurisdictions Can Be Laxer than the Offshore Sort*, ECONOMIST, Feb. 14, 2013, http://www.economist.com/news/special-report/21571554-some-onshore-jurisdictions-can-be-laxer-offshore-sort-not-palm-tree-sight. *See also* HAY ET AL., *supra* note 34, at 1, 24, 42; Sharman, *supra* note 18, at 494, 499.

[68] *See* Sharman, *supra* note 18, at 494–95.

[69] *Id.* at 495. *See also* ECONOMIST, *supra* note 17. *Cf.* Christopher M. Bruner, *States, Markets, and Gatekeepers: Public-Private Regulatory Regimes in an Era of Economic Globalization*, 30 MICH. J. INT'L L. 125, 174–76 (2008) (describing a broadly similar challenge facing U.S. efforts to maintain regulatory dominance over bond markets and the Internet).

[70] *See* SHARMAN, *supra* note 14, at 158; Sharman, *supra* note 18, at 505–06, 510–11. *See also* Z/Yen Group Limited, *Global Financial Centres Index 19: Information Pack,* http://www.longfinance.net/global-financial-centre-index-19/992-gfci-19.html (last visited Apr. 2016) (reporting that Singapore, Shanghai, Busan, and Hong Kong are among the top five financial centers globally that are considered most likely to become more significant).

opportunities, and why they have succeeded in achieving global dominance in their specialized fields.

Regulatory failings and associated abuses in such jurisdictions legitimately prompt close attention from observers around the world, but so should their very real and legitimate successes. Conversely, major market successes legitimately prompt extensive academic and journalistic study, but so should their own very real regulatory problems. Competition to thrive in the global financial services market is fierce, and some small jurisdictions that have profited predominantly through abusive practices will ultimately fail as global standards steadily improve. Others—including those examined here, in my view—will very likely continue to thrive due to substantial innate advantages and the desirability of their unique service-based capacities. Ultimately, the complexities of capital mobility and modern cross-border finance are such that no jurisdiction—large or small—can plausibly claim to remain untainted by the sorts of abuses that comprehensibly preoccupy consumers of contemporary academic literature, financial press, and political discourse. Sustained and even-handed focus on fundamental regulatory problems—whether manifesting themselves in small, potentially far-flung jurisdictions, or in the world's major economies—should be the order of the day.

MDSJs differ substantially in their particularities, but at a mid-level of abstraction they exhibit striking commonalities in their historical, cultural, and geographic circumstances, as well as their economic development strategies and fundamental sources of competitive advantage. This book can at most provide an introduction to this fascinating type of jurisdiction and, it is hoped, prompt more nuanced and contextualized analysis of their roles and significance in cross-border finance.

# Index

CPSIA information can be obtained
at www.ICGtesting.com
Printed in the USA
BVHW071112201118
533427BV00007B/26/P